# THE NEW HISTORY
# OF LITERATURE

# AMERICAN
# LITERATURE
# TO 1900

# THE NEW HISTORY OF LITERATURE

Volumes 3, 6, 9, and 10 will be published in 1987,
and volumes 5 and 7 in 1988.

# AMERICAN LITERATURE TO 1900

·

EDITED BY

## MARCUS CUNLIFFE

Peter Bedrick Books
New York

First American edition published in 1987 by
Peter Bedrick Books
125 East 23 Street
New York, NY 10010

Library of Congress Cataloging-in-Publication Data

American literature to 1900.
  (The New history of literature)
  Bibliography: p.
  Includes index.
    1.American literature—History and criticism.
I. Cunliffe, Marcus.    II. Series.
PS88.A44    1986      810′.9     86–10835
ISBN 0–87226–132–8

Printed in Great Britain

10 9 8 7 6 5 4 3 2 1

# CONTENTS

# INTRODUCTION

Around 1900, the terminal point of this volume, not many literary historians in Europe or the United States would have been prepared to argue that there was such a thing as *an* American literature, or that the literature so far produced in America was worth an extensive analysis. Able American authors were conceded to exist. But they tended to be treated as men of individual merit – contributors (as Matthew Arnold saw it) to 'one great literature – English literature'. Their Americanness, in such a context, was generally viewed as a matter of geography rather than of cultural psychology.

Today the picture looks very different. The achievements of American writers during the twentieth century have made their nation's literature known throughout the world. Interest in American imaginative expression has as a result reached back into pre-twentieth-century eras. Authors such as Melville and Emily Dickinson, little known or forgotten in their own day, have acquired imposing posthumous reputations.

Possibly, as a few essays in this volume hint, the tendency has gone too far. In other words, American scholars may now overvalue that which was once undervalued, exaggerating the self-consciously native or national aspects of colonial and nineteenth-century culture. That is a matter for debate. What is beyond question is that this literature, less maturely rich than the contemporaneous national cultures of western Europe, has its own varied and often surprising riches, and that they intrigue other people as well as Americans. Indeed a majority of the essays in this volume happen to be by scholars who are not American, though all have a first-hand acquaintance with the United States. (By the same token, the American contributors to the volume have all made extended stays in Europe.) Britain, France, Ireland and Italy are represented; and, such is the relatively new-found prestige of American literature, authors could have been selected from a dozen countries.

The idea beyond the volume was however not to offer a foreigner's viewpoint on the United States, but simply to gather a diversity of informed opinions. The authors are agreed in being fascinated by American literature. No other common element has been proposed. They divide the field between them, both in the sense that their essays cumulatively 'cover' it, and in their variety of concerns and assessments. In one or two instances the approach may seem iconoclastic, or to quarrel with judgments ventured elsewhere in the volume. This seemed entirely desirable to the editor: nothing is more dreary than a compilation of politely modulated approval.

The volume is designed to stand on its own. The same editor is however responsible for a companion volume of essays on American literature since 1900. Taken together, the two provide a quite comprehensive view of nearly four centuries of the English written word in the new world.

Postscript: These essays were written in the 1970s. They, and the attendant bibliographies, have been revised for the new edition of *American Literature to 1900*. More extensive revision and amplification has been applied to the companion volume in the series, *American Literature since 1900* (1987).

MC

# 1

## THE CONDITIONS OF AN AMERICAN LITERATURE

*Marcus Cunliffe*

### Nationalism and Culture

Before the United States became politically independent there was literature *in* America. Viewed in retrospect, this was already showing some signs of a special American tone, or series of regional tones, notably in the general awareness of the symbolic power of the idea of a pristine Adamic new world, and in the desire to record the particular quality of some particular place – the New England township, perhaps, or the river-plantation society of the South, or the life of the back-country farmer. But these beginnings were modest and embryonic. In the high-spirited journal of Sarah Kemble Knight, for instance, who travelled in adventurous discomfort from Boston to New York in 1704, there is a vividly fresh response to the scenes around her. But it is as much a traveller's as a native's response. The reality before her may be that of mysterious tree silhouettes in some eerie night-time corner of the woods: her imagination, perhaps for comfort, turns these shapes into the rooftops of a metropolis such as London, which in fact she has never seen. Her dreams, or fears, are not wholly engaged by the real elements of the American landscape. Divided, conjectural imaginings formed in the American mind long after political independence was secured. To define and develop a literature of America was, as several essays in this volume reveal, a protracted and perplexing task.

One continuing curiosity of the American search for a cultural identity is that the extreme alternative conceptions on which the search must be based were themselves European. The Mexican historian Edmundo O'Gorman, in *The Invention of America* (1961), denies that the New World was ever 'discovered' – and not merely because the aboriginal 'Indians' had 'discovered' it thousands of years before Columbus. His point is that the realization of the existence of the American hemisphere came as a profound shock to European cosmographers. They had already established that the world consisted of three continents, the God-ordained trinity of Europe, Asia and Africa. When it became clear that Columbus and other explorers had stumbled upon a fourth continent the whole map of human knowledge had to be redrawn, literally and metaphysically. Did the new continent resemble known regions, so that it could be accommodated within the familiar categories, or was it quite different? Were the natives of America a branch of some race already accounted for, or were they men apart? They were pagans: were they beyond redemption? Why had God waited so long to disclose America to the rest of mankind?

Two very different sets of answers were offered to these questions in the sixteenth, seventeenth and eighteenth centuries – above all in the speculative, would-be scientific temper of the eighteenth century. One reshaping of cosmology encouraged the view that the late discovery of America was a providential blessing. America enshrined a principle of boundlessness, of new starts and new hopes for the human race. Its aborigines were unspoiled – noble savages – and in those beneficent new world climes the white settler too might experience a rebirth into innocence, simplicity, brotherhood. Rightly perceived, primitivism restored man to his primal sweetness. The golden age, the pre-corrupt stage of human history, might miraculously have been brought within reach of latter-day sensibility.

On the whole, and with important qualifications, this optimistic explanation of the significance of America was – understandably enough – the one that commended itself to the inhabitants of the thirteen British colonies that became the United States. One of the most celebrated hymns to American wholesomeness and opportunity came in the *Letters from an American Farmer* (1782), by the Frenchman J. Hector St John de Crèvecoeur, who had established himself as a farmer in New York state during the 1760s. When the Revolution destroyed his hypothesized Eden, he still snatched at a further illusion. Driven out from his farm he could seek refuge among the wigwams of America's first citizens: the Indians, uncursed by civilized passions, would allow him to dwell in peace among them. And with the successful conclusion of the revolutionary war it was easy to insist, as generations of American authors did, that their country enshrined a special principle of decent Quakerish equality. Indeed, as the first successful revolutionaries of the new world, the citizens of the United States annexed to their nation the whole assembly of optimistic, earthly-paradise legends that had been associated with the entire American hemisphere. In part perhaps this was an accident of nomenclature. 'The United States of America' was a remarkably imprecise name for a new nation, lacking a geographical location. To the irritation of some of the other nations of the new world (including the United States of Mexico), the citizens of the USA became known all-inclusively as 'Americans'. Whatever the reason, then, the United States acquired a symbolic penumbra. It seemed in some eyes to stand for more than a mere nation; and this penumbra was ideologically enlarged through the Declaration of Independence (1776), the Constitution of 1787, and a quantity of subsequent manifestoes, political, nationalist and cultural.

There was however an opposite, pessimistic set of explanations as to the significance of the new world, most fully expounded by certain French *philosophes*, among them Buffon, De Pauw, and the Abbé Raynal. In sum, this view asserted that the new continent was not regeneratively but degeneratively primitive. Possibly through the humidity of the climate (the exact explanation differed), animal and human life in America were asserted to be backward and puny. There were no horses in America, until the coming of the Spanish *conquistadores*. No animals had been satisfactorily domesticated. The natives, it was said, were precocious but short-lived, deficient in sexual appetite and other human essentials. Raynal and a number of his contemporaries contended that this blight had transmitted itself to the white settlers and their livestock: they became smaller and less robust than was the case in the old world.

The degeneracy argument soon lost scientific sanction, in the face of abundant evidence to the contrary. Yet it survived in other forms: for example, as a conviction that there was something meagre, even tainted, in the American atmosphere. However much the Americans might boast of the rising glories of their land, they would always remain culturally stunted in relation to the mother-continent of Europe. America's literary products must necessarily be either derivative, even plagiaristic, or else uncouth, bizarre Caliban-cries. So here too the United States seemed to embody all the dark, pessimistic aspects that had also been associated with the whole hemisphere. The new nation came into a heritage of large extremes.

Each view, the clamantly optimistic and the bitterly pessimistic, figured within the American cultural scene, as writers debated the possibilities and the actualities of their situation. But the duality was

more commonly expressed in other ways. One impulse led the
Americans to repudiate their European heritage and to stress the
American environment. Such an emphasis seemed to them imperative if they were to express a genuine national consciousness. In
the late eighteenth century every people aware of its nationhood –
for instance, the Germans and the Russians – was busy exploring its
remote past, in order to recover the bardic origins of this sentiment.
The Americans likewise wished to define themselves culturally by
defining their roots. But the most ancient roots lay in Europe,
especially in Britain; and there was something not altogether convincing, in the contentions of Thomas Jefferson and other
American founding fathers, that they represented the true spirit of
Anglo-Saxon England, from which the English had departed. On
the other hand, Jefferson and other Americans had no easier job in
relating themselves to their hemispheric heritage in the shape of the
American Indians.

The Indian was potentially a powerful and beautiful symbol of
the new nation. He was an authentic inhabitant, proud, brave and
endowed with an often moving eloquence of understatement – as in
the famous speech of Logan (1774) cited in Jefferson's *Notes on the
State of Virginia*: 'There runs not a drop of my blood in the veins of
any living creature. This called on me for revenge. I have sought it:
I have killed many: I have fully glutted my vengeance. For my
country, I rejoice at the beams of peace. But do not harbor a
thought that mine is the joy of fear. Logan never felt fear. He will
not turn on his heel to save his life. Who is there to mourn for
Logan? Not one.' Cooper's Leatherstocking tales and Longfellow's
*Hiawatha* showed that for literary purposes the Indian could be as
significant an archetype as Beowulf or Tristan: a theme inter-
estingly explored, in the 1840s, by the Southern litterateur William
Gilmore Simms. Yet the potential could not be realized – at least
not until the twentieth century.[1] For the Indian was an enemy, or an
encumbrance, rather than an exemplar. He could be admired, but
only in defeat. He stood for an outmoded evolutionary stage: the
hunter must inevitably yield to the farmer in the march of white
progress. 'To live by tilling is *more humano*', wrote Hugh Henry
Brackenridge of Pennsylvania in 1782, 'by hunting is *more bestiarum*
[in the manner of the beasts]. I would as soon admit a right in the
buffalo to grant lands, as in Killbuck, the Big Cat, the Big Dog, or
any of the ragged wretches that are called chiefs and sachems.' In

[1] See Leslie Fiedler, *The Return of the Vanishing American* (New York, Stein and Day, 1969; London, Cape, 1969).

1855, in an admittedly severe review, a Boston newspaper reproached Longfellow for having perpetrated *Hiawatha*: 'We cannot but express a regret that our own pet national poet should not have selected as the theme of his muse something higher and better than the silly legends of the savage aborigines.' In short, nostalgia and supersession were the most that could be made of the quintessential American. The doom of the Indian was the price paid for progress. At that time it could not be seen as perhaps too big a price; and, in any case, it was a price not paid by the white American but by his sacrificed victim.

There were other available symbols of American nationalism – military heroes, statesmen and so on. George Washington, the commander-in-chief of the Revolution and subsequently the nation's first president, was a supremely satisfactory embodiment of American courage and integrity. In the half century after independence, there was fashioned an American ideology based on growth, movement, piety and republican democracy. Innumerable articles and editorials called for a culture appropriate to this creed, frequently picturing the culture of the old world as an insidious influence to be overthrown. 'The vital principle of an American national literature must be democracy,' declared the newly established *United States Magazine and Democratic Review* in 1837. 'Our mind is enslaved to the past and present literature of England.'

But the 'quest for nationality' remained difficult. It was all very well to extol the democratic purity of American life, and to decry the aristocratic and indelicate features of European literature. The traditional subjects of imaginative literature – love, war, chivalry, tragic grandeur, social entanglement – were deficient in the United States; and however much writers such as Nathaniel Hawthorne might take patriotic pride in the plainer texture of their native scene, they could not escape the feeling that their opportunities *as writers* were correspondingly reduced. They recognized yet chafed under a didactic obligation to speak well of America, to cast a clear vote for democracy, to be programmatic – in ways somewhat anticipatory of the later ideological imperatives of post-1917 Russia.

Even here, though, it was not possible to reach agreement as to what precisely was being attempted. A national literature was needed to help form a national character: that is, to provide Americans with first-hand descriptions of themselves, and with desirable modes of thought and feeling. But another aim was emulative: to prove to themselves and to Europeans that the new nation was 'civilized', and so capable of producing poets, novelists, scholars and artists who could match or even surpass those of the old world. The one endeavour, in itself rather hypothetical, emphasized a literature *of* America. The other, assuming that culture was universal and that America must ultimately be judged not according to its own rules but in the world-arena, postulated a level of *polite* culture: in other words, a literature *in* America that might or might not be specifically American in its outlook. The two needs co-existed, and competed, giving rise to a controversy that dragged on intermittently throughout the nineteenth century. The 'nationalists', including the Young America movement in the 1840s, could be accused of chauvinism. The 'universalists' could be accused of snobbishness and excessive deference to Europe.

The division between the two outlooks was rarely clear-cut. Longfellow, for example, was a 'universalist' to the extent that he owned a deep allegiance to the Europe of Dante, Shakespeare and Milton. But he also deliberately contributed, through *Hiawatha* and other poems, to the stock of native American themes. Walt Whitman, especially in his younger days, was almost blatantly a rooter for the USA; yet he came to believe

those convictions are now strongly temper'd. . . . I see that this world of the West. . . . fuses inseparably with the East, and with all, as time does – the ever new, yet old, old human race – 'the same subject continued', as the novels of our grandfathers had it for chapter heads.

Eventually such doubleness would be a source of strength, or at least of fruitful tension. But for much of the nineteenth century it engendered a nagging anxiety that could neither be ignored nor resolved. For every American author who travelled abroad, unless he promptly returned, there was the uneasy thought that he might somehow be betraying America, no matter how staunchly he upheld his native land in the presence of foreigners. The evolution of a national culture was an acutely if inevitably self-conscious affair. To go abroad in the cause of America's advancement was to risk setting America back: one meaning of 'national culture' cancelled out the other.

## The Conditions of Authorship

Another way of putting this is to say that America, while cherishing a belief in its progressive moral superiority to Europe, lagged behind culturally, and that this discrepancy placed particular strains upon the American ideology which – mingled as ideologies usually are with grosser considerations – insisted that knowledge should be accessible to all, and that claims to professional expertness were 'aristocratic'. These were in truth arguable propositions within the context of a would-be open democratic society. Thomas Jefferson, the economist Henry C. Carey, and Jacksonian radicals such as William Leggett were among those who at one time or another upheld the notion of a free trade in ideas. Why, they asked, should authors seek in effect to impede access to words and images in the common stock? If Eli Whitney's cotton-gin was not protected by patent, why should a play or a book be given such preference. Was not education a universal democratic right – a natural right, according to Horace Mann of Massachusetts? The case was contested by an increasing number of American authors – Washington Irving, W. C. Bryant, J. G. Whittier, R. W. Emerson, Mark Twain. Congress remained largely indifferent to their pleas, despite its general readiness to protect other forms of property. The grand conception of a spiritually and literally free flow of information was used to justify a profitable traffic in pirated European literature (again one is reminded of Soviet Russia, which in the twentieth century also refused to be bound by the publishing conventions of the rest of the world). In other words, the United States refused until 1891 to participate in an international copyright agreement. The traffic was two-way. Many an American book, including the prodigiously successful *Uncle Tom's Cabin* (1852) of Harriet Beecher Stowe, was pirated by unscrupulous British publishers, who paid no royalties to the hapless authors.[1] But since the greater volume of literature flowed westward out of Europe, the major effect was exerted upon rather than from the United States. British authors, notably Charles Dickens, protested vigorously at what they took to be sheer theft, and many of their American counterparts joined with them in urging a reform – to no avail. For Dickens and other Europeans the loss was merely financial: as American editorialists sanctimoniously reminded him, his reputation was nationwide in the United States thanks to the flood of instantaneous cheap reprints of his novels. But American authors suffered loss both in purse and in pride. With less grand reputations than their European contemporaries, they were in any case fighting to stake a claim to recognition. Since their books had to receive a royalty in

---

[1] 'There is an American lady living at Hartford, Connecticut, whom the United States has permitted to be robbed of $200,000. Her name is Harriet Beecher Stowe.' James Parton, 'International Copyright', *Atlantic Monthly*, October 1867.

the United States, they were at a fatal disadvantage in comparison with royaltyless publications. In the early 1840s, when conditions were aggravated by a severe financial depression, a Disraeli novel could be bought for half the price of one by James Fenimore Cooper; in a cheap edition, it was possible to buy a new Dickens novel for ten cents as against fifty cents for a new Cooper.

American authors were in other respects too made to feel the humiliation of dependence upon the old world, and of the neglect or parochialism of their countrymen. To establish their British copyright, and attempt to gain an income, they were under a strong inducement to secure prior publication of their works in London – as for example with Herman Melville's first books. This in turn reinforced the tendency of American readers to set their standards by those of the old world: to wait until European critics had pronounced an opinion on an American author before taking him seriously at home. And since prestige was determined by European criteria, there was an added pull upon the American writer to actually domicile himself in Europe, as Washington Irving and Cooper and Nathaniel Hawthorne did for long periods.

In Europe, among other things, they might enjoy the status of a profession, and the firm professionalism that was beginning to characterize the publishing industry. By 1820, when Irving was discovering the intoxication of popular success in London, American publishing appeared hopelessly ineffectual, in spite of the heroic efforts of one or two pioneers such as Mathew Carey of Philadelphia. No American publisher could command a nationwide market. Lacking in capital, the majority shared publication with other firms in several different cities. The result was a patchwork of spheres of influence, with a particular publisher and a particular city striving to establish a trading monopoly within a region. This corresponded to the hinterland of the city's whole economic pattern. William A. Charvat, the historian of American publishing, points out that up to 1850 these economic considerations gave New York and Philadelphia a bigger publishing region than Boston; before then, most of the work of New England authors was published outside New England. In Britain the mechanisms of publicity and reviewing were highly developed. Retail prices were firmly set and maintained; books were widely advertised and effectively distributed; book reviews, in comparison with the scene in America, generally appeared ample, mature and high-toned. In the United States, up to mid-century, books were wretchedly mishandled in these professional departments. The author himself was frequently forced to act as his own entrepreneur, assuming the financial and promotional activities that one would nowadays automatically take to be the province of the publisher. Such responsibility was all the more frustrating for writers like Edgar Allan Poe, Hawthorne and Melville, who could not lay their hands on the necessary cash. Reviewing, in Britain not invariably above suspicion, was in the United States either perfunctory or a matter of crude puffery. Operations were conducted by hacks of the calibre of Rufus Griswold (a middle-man remembered today only for the censorious deprecation with which he acted as Poe's literary executor). 'I puff your books, you know,' Griswold informed a publisher in 1843, 'without any regard to their quality.' Poe, like Whitman, was prompted to eulogize his own work. In the 1850s Thomas Bailey Aldrich, later a popular novelist, was a publisher's reader and junior literary man on the *New York Evening Mirror*. The Boston publisher James T. Fields used to send him inscribed copies of new books, and Aldrich assured him: 'I have access to every department of the "Mirror" and if I can be of service to you in any way, please command me heart and pen.'

In spite of their hindrances, some writers, female as well as male, made reasonable incomes. Few could survive though as men or women of letters – or perhaps wanted to pass themselves off as professionals, for a certain fastidious, anachronistic image of the writer as gentleman-amateur persisted in the United States a generation after vigorous professionals of the Dickens stamp had made their way to the top. Charvat has calculated that in the period 1800–70, between 60% and 75% of American male writers either held public office or tried to. This fact can, it is true, be interpreted in different ways. The practice of devising sinecures for writers was a well-known form of patronage in Europe; so one might argue that the American author was better treated than he liked to pretend. The most fortunate American beneficiary, James Kirk Paulding, had a snug berth in the Navy Department for a quarter of a century, during which time he managed to write no less than seventeen books and a quantity of other stuff. Hawthorne was a good Democrat, and received a good party man's reward in the shape of custom-house appointments in New England and (after writing a campaign biography for the successful presidential candidate Franklin Pierce) a consulate in Liverpool. A similar biography of Abraham Lincoln brought the young author William Dean Howells a delightful assignment as consul in Venice – an interlude that did much to fix his career as a cosmopolitan man of letters. Yet, certainly up to the Civil War, the common American interpretation of these rewards was pessimistic. They were taken as proof not of official munificence but of the beggarly status of what ought to have been a proud profession.

Around mid-century the situation began to improve. The population of the United States equalled and then began rapidly to exceed that of Britain. Improved communications were a double-edged weapon. At least one American author, the essayist N. P. Willis, believed that the advent of the steamship, in bringing the two shores of the Atlantic within a week of one another, was merely increasing Europe's cultural dominance over the new world. But internal ease of movement, especially through the spread of railroads, made it possible for enterprising native publishers to aim for the first time at a national audience. The achievement of Ticknor and Fields of Boston, founded in 1843, was an inspiration to rivals. At last an American firm was able to combine promotional flair with an excellent list of foreign and domestic authors, and to reap the benefits right across the continent. Another symptom of financial-cum-literary confidence was the immediate success of Boston's *Atlantic Monthly* (1857), which for a few years was *the* American magazine. Readers (Whitman among them) continued to subscribe to copies of the old British quarterlies and monthlies; and not all the other American monthly magazines established in the same decade had as easy a passage. Little by little, nevertheless, the whole apparatus of book-making and book-selling – printer, author, publisher, bookseller, reviewer – took shape.

The evolution coincided with a sudden burgeoning of native talent. Emerson, Thoreau, Hawthorne, Melville, Whitman now seem the major figures, though Longfellow, J. R. Lowell, Whittier, Oliver Wendell Holmes, and the historians Prescott, Motley and Parkman were more widely recognized at the time, in the years around 1850 that F. O. Matthiessen has celebrated as the 'American Renaissance'.

Perhaps something extraordinary was also happening during those years to English literature, at least in the field of the novel. If so, the world zeitgeist may be as important a factor as any peculiarly American circumstances. There is no doubt that British literati – Dickens, Disraeli, Thackeray, Bulwer-Lytton, Carlyle, Tennyson, Browning – still enjoyed prodigious reputations, as Rudyard Kipling, Robert Louis Stevenson and others were to do in the next generation. Throughout the century, the American theatre remained largely a reflection of British fashions in the drama – in themselves far from high; *Our American Cousin*, the play that President Lincoln was watching at the moment of his assassination in 1865, was an English farce. Nevertheless, after the 1850s no one could now assert that the world of American culture was merely derivative, or two-dimensional, as could legitimately if maliciously have been said of the first two or three decades of the century. Polite, middle-brow or popular, American literature was even making an impact across the Atlantic, as well as at home. Magazine after magazine – weeklies, monthlies, juvenile, religious, female – came into being and on the whole stayed in being. Apart from *Harper's* (1850) and the *Atlantic* (1857), poets, essayists, historians and novelists could gain a hearing and a livelihood in the New York *Galaxy* (1866), *Appleton's* (1869), *Scribner's* (1870) or *Century* (1881), or the Philadelphia *Lippincott's* (1868), which in the 1880s began to print entire novels or novelettes in each number. For good and for ill, certain books caught the public fancy – usually a transatlantic fancy also – to an extraordinary degree. They ranged from middle-brow moralism (Augusta Evans Wilson's *St Elmo*, 1866) to breezy comedy (Mark Twain's *Innocents Abroad*, 1869, and – with Charles Dudley Warner – *The Gilded Age*, 1873), from the touching domesticities of Louisa May Alcott (*Little Women*, 1868–9) to the more superficial parent–child imbroglios of John Habberton (*Helen's Babies*, 1876) and Frances Hodgson Burnett (*Little Lord Fauntleroy*, 1886), from the utopian reformism of Edward Bellamy (*Looking Backward*, 1888) to the simple yet arresting pieties of Charles M. Sheldon (*In His Steps*, 1897). Not the whole or the best of American literature, these at least indicated that authors and readers were finding contact in a considerable variety of ways. What they also indicated was the prominence, after about 1840, of women writers – columnists like Sara Payson Willis ('Fanny Fern'), editors such as Sarah Josepha Hale (*Godey's Lady's Book*), essayists (Margaret Fuller), poets (Lydia Sigourney), and above all novelists, in a profusion that made Nathaniel Hawthorne grumpily resentful of their commercial success.

## The South

Of all the figures mentioned in the previous pages only three – Jefferson, Poe, Mrs Wilson – were truly Southern, Poe by adoption since he was born in Boston of wandering parents; and the descent this sequence implies was dismally symptomatic of the fate of culture in the slave states.

At the time of the American Revolution the South, and Virginia in particular, appeared at least as rich in talent as any other section. Of the first five presidents, between 1789 and 1825, four were Virginians. Washington, Jefferson, James Madison, James Monroe: the so-called 'Virginia dynasty' ruled the nation, and could rest the claim on intellectual eminence as well as governmental sagacity. Jefferson, one of the most brilliant and inquisitive minds of his generation, secured his hold upon posterity as early as 1776, as the principal drafter of the Declaration of Independence. Madison, co-author of the *Federalist* papers of 1787–8, displayed a rare talent for political analysis. Monroe, less attractive and less profound, was still far from negligible. Their contemporaries might disagree with their opinions, or consider them poor administrators: none sought to argue that the South was an intellectual wasteland.

Up to 1860 Southern political leaders continued to make themselves felt in Washington. Three more – Andrew Jackson (1829–37) and James K. Polk (1845–9) of Tennessee, and the Virginia-born Zachary Taylor (1849–50) – were elected president. But after them no Southerner (with the doubtful exception of the Virginia-born Woodrow Wilson, elected from New Jersey) occupied the White House until the 'accidental' succession of Lyndon B. Johnson in the 1960s. By about 1830 the great days of Virginia were at an end. Some of the reasons were economic and geographical. The equally proud state of Massachusetts, in the North, was worried by a comparable threat of relative decline, as it lost population to the new Western territories and saw its abandoned farmsteads sink back into second-growth timber. The predominantly agricultural South suffered worse than Massachusetts in not developing new, industrial power; no Southern city was rich enough, or had a prosperous enough hinterland, to sustain the cultural life of a New York or Philadelphia or Boston.

The trouble was however more deeply seated. After 1830 the Southern mind became increasingly obsessed by one central issue, which infused all others – the issue of slavery. Slavery was the great anomaly of a professedly democratic society, the scourge upon the American conscience. But as debate grew fiercer and more uncompromising, the South devoted itself more and more intransigently and comphrensively to a defence of its 'peculiar institution' – and therefore also to an indictment of the 'free society' of the major culture. Not every Southern writer made slavery his principal theme. Poe's dream kingdoms were abstractly detached from time or place; the South Carolina novelist William Gilmore Simms often set his stories on the frontier or during the historic days when the great issue was not slavery but national independence. Yet until the end of the century and beyond no Southern writer could escape being influenced by the sentiment of Southernness – which in turn revolved around the place of the Negro in a brave new world. Southern professors weightily contended that there were innate racial differences between black and white – indeed, that the Negro might strictly speaking not even be of the human species. Ministers of the gospel found Biblical sanction for the practice of bondage. Political theorists, led by John C. Calhoun of South Carolina, insisted on the right of a minority (the South) to reject the will of the majority where its own needs were jeopardized. Other apologists such as the Virginia lawyer George Fitzhugh drew upon a selective reading of the new science of sociology to denounce the impersonality and fragmentation of life in the North (or in industrial Britain), and to recommend instead the stable, organic atmosphere of the Southern cotton-planter's domain.

The outcome, for the Southern mind, was a literature of grievance and daydream, with added overtones of nostalgia when defeat in the Civil War of 1861–5 ended the institution of slavery and destroyed all hopes of actual as distinct from emotional Southern secession from the Union. The 'Lost Cause', as postwar Southern novelists like Thomas Nelson Page conceived it, ministered to an unreal legend of a gracious, leisurely, gentlemanly civilization, crushed under the weight of Northern banks and factories. The legend was of course historically false. It evaded the problem of the evil inherent in slavery, and of the consequent degradation of the poor white, whose status depended upon emphasizing the difference between himself and the Negro. It assumed that while whites might write about black people, there could not be any serious presentation of life by black writers. It pretended that the Old South had never known commerce or emigration – despite the swift surge of settlement westward into Alabama, Mississippi and Texas. It was anachronistic, and deeply equivocal. The South distorted reality; its versions of ideality, as in the worst of Poe and Page, or in the highly sensitive poet Sidney Lanier, were oddly immature and insubstantial. For the democratic didacticisms of the North, the need to wave the banner of progressive democracy, the South substituted a far more disabling fantasy – an ideology of bygone chivalry.

Yet the clash between the two value-systems had its uses for the American mind. Northern democratic ideology inhibited the writer from voicing his misgivings as to the dangers of mere growth and movement, of commercial competition and the cash nexus (or 'the Almighty Dollar', as it came to be known). Such doubts tended to be expressed elliptically, in fantasy-novels such as Melville's *Mardi* and Cooper's *The Crater* and Twain's *Connecticut Yankee*, none of which sought to confront American reality. Even in flawed form, with all the blemishes of the Southern *parti pris*, it was therefore valuable that some debate should be stirred up on fundamental aspects of American capitalist-democracy. Some native counter-principle needed to be invoked. This is not to argue that, simply for dialectical purposes, it would have been necessary to invent Southern plantation slavery if it had never existed. The point is that the United States was socially and intellectually too unitary for its own good, or at any rate to nourish a rich imaginative life. So there was some genuine value in the diagram of alternatives established in the clash between Southern and Northern theories of the good life.

The extensions of this diagram have been surveyed in William R. Taylor, *Cavalier and Yankee: The Old South and the American National Character* (1961). He shows how through their literatures the slave and non slave states formulated a typology of American behaviour. At one extreme was the figure of the Yankee – quick, practical, resourceful and irreverent, yet also apt to be aggressive, unscrupulous and superficial. At the other extreme was the figure of the Cavalier – slow, traditional in outlook, lacking in adaptability, and yet embodying ancient virtues such as steadfastness, courtesy and dignity. The Yankee was future-oriented, the Cavalier devoted to the past. The Yankee was the hero, in general, of American nineteenth-century life, and so of its fiction. But he could not be felt to embody all the virtues desirable in a true American hero; nor was his way of life readily assimilable within the prevailing modes of Anglo-American literature. One senses the incompleteness, for instance, in the character Holgrave, the nominal hero of Hawthorne's *House of the Seven Gables* (1851) and in Hank, the brash protagonist of Twain's *Connecticut Yankee* (1889), each of whom has something glib and impervious in his very open-mindedness.

So for North and South alike, the realm of the Cavalier had a deep appeal. The Northern novelist, even if seeming to deplore the social inequalities of Southern life, could set his tale in the South without being accused of an un-American attachment to 'European' and 'aristocratic' styles. He could put into the mouth of a Southern character unpalatable or at any rate unconventional observations about American attitudes which would have seemed out of keeping as the opinions of a Northerner, and patronizing if voiced by a European. In nineteenth-century American fiction, with the partial and dazzling exception of Henry James, European characters are portrayed almost invariably as silly, ignorant or unsympathetic, or all three, when they refer directly to the United States. They are comic, as usually conceived by the author, in not knowing what they were talking about, and in not knowing that they do not know. Polonius, though tedious, at least gave good advice. These visiting Poloniuses, in American fiction, are bores who have nothing to offer. With Southern characters, however, there is a cutting edge. After the Civil War, with the added dignity that defeat may confer, they provide a wry counterpoint – the 'logic of Southern dissidence' in Henry Nash Smith's phrase – to the concerns of a nation vulgar in its victory over the Confederacy. This is a function of Basil Ransom in James's *The Bostonians* (1886), of Carrington in Henry Adams's *Democracy* (1880), and of the bleakly wise Ungar in Melville's long narrative poem *Clarel* (1876).

After the War there was too for the Southerners the covert satisfaction of believing that even if they had been wrong about slavery, they had been less hypocritical than the North. In Gilded Age America the free states were swift to reveal that whatever they said about the slave being their brother, they had no desire to welcome the freed Negro as a next-door neighbour. Northern readers showed themselves eagerly ready to accept the Southern version of either the romantic 'antebellum' plantation world – moonlight and magnolias – or of the new gallant South striving to restore its shattered society to a semblance of order. Again, however, such complex, inward responses could not furnish the South with a powerful literary impulse. The defeated Southerner could not for many years to come – perhaps not until the Agrarian movement of the 1920s – mount an acceptable direct critique of the official American value-system. Nor psychologically could he afford to explore the shortcomings of his own region. There was no financial reason to do so, certainly, when Northern readers warmed to idyllic fictional reconstructions of Cavalier-dom. There were strong-minded Southerners, such as George Washington Cable, who could not bear the situation. Cable, who had fought in the Confederate army, came North to live. But his public was more enthusiastic when he wrote picturesquely than when he endeavoured to tell the truth.

In short, the fate of the South in the nineteenth century, for the purposes of literature, was to provide a term in a dialectic rather than to exist abundantly in its own right: to *mean* rather than to *be*.

## The West

If the South was a static society, that of the American West symbolized movement. There were several successive Wests, as Henry Nash Smith explained in his study *Virgin Land* (1950). The geographical definition of the West kept on shifting with each wave of settlement; a characteristic vignette of nineteenth-century America showed in several panels the evolution of the same patch of ground from forest wilderness to pioneer clearing to prosperous farm, or from log cabin to college, courthouse and factory. Yesterday's wilderness was today's civilization. The West of 1800 became the Middle West of 1830.

There was a considerable shift, too, in the attitudes of the East to the West. Admiration for the frontier increased as the area of open land diminished. Frederick Jackson Turner's famous and influential essay, 'The Significance of the Frontier in American History' (1893), took as its initial, rather poignant text the announcement of the 1890 national census that there was no longer a frontier in the sense of a continuous belt of unsettled territory. The cowboy, that ideal representation of a man on his own under an infinite Western sky, did not emerge classically until 1902, with the publication of Owen Wister's *The Virginian*; and by 1902, though there were still cowboys in the West, the great days of the open-range 'cattle kingdom' were ended for ever. In the late eighteenth and early nineteenth centuries the pioneer Westerner was widely regarded in the East as a culturally deprived and brutalized person, a squalid misfit. 'The manners of the Indian natives are respectable,' wrote Crèvecoeur, 'compared with this European medley. Their wives and children live in sloth and inactivity; and having no proper pursuits you may judge what education the latter receive. Their tender minds have nothing else to contemplate but the example of their parents; like them, they grow up a mongrel breed, half civilized, half savage, except nature stamps on them some constitutional propensities.' As this final lukewarm phrase indicates, few were yet ready to believe that wild nature produced anything but wild men. 'Nature' was still conceived mainly as what man did to improve the wilderness. Crèvecoeur's hero, like Brackenridge's, was the yeoman farmer, living *more humano* not like a beast. Lyman Beecher, prominent New England clergyman and father of Harriet Beecher Stowe, thought of the West of *circa* 1830 as treacherous in its emptiness: it was empty of standards, guidelines, the means of salvation, and (he thought) stood in desperate need of a missionary crusade, launched from the East, to save its collective, unchurched soul. His still more prominent son, the Reverend Henry Ward Beecher, referred to the civilizing mission of westbound emigrants in a striking image of 1859: 'They drive schools along with them, as shepherds drive flocks. They have herds of churches, academies, lyceums; and their religious and educational institutions go lowing along the western plains as Jacob's herds lowed along the Syrian hills.'

The West was then a process, a spectacle, a vast theatre of events wherein was enacted man's capacity to 'conquer' nature. To a large extent it was a process of becoming like the East. In this way it supplied an internal analogue to the imaginative polarity between America and Europe. The Scottish observer James Bryce, in his *American Commonwealth* (1888), expressed the analogy as a series of ratios: as Europe was to Asia, as Britain was to continental Europe, as the United States was to Britain, so the American West was to the older-settled East – the former facing forward into the future, the latter glancing back over its shoulder, across the Atlantic.

For the West there was accordingly a cultural ambivalence similar to that of America as a whole *vis-à-vis* the old world. There was a passionate emulative eagerness to match the culture of the old seaboard states on their own terms. Regional scholar-boosters like Daniel Drake of Cincinnati expressed amazement at the progress already made in the new states, and the utmost optimism for the ultimate prospects. In truth, as Louis B. Wright showed in *Culture on the Moving Frontier* (1955), there was an astonishingly rapid spread of colleges, literary clubs, newspapers, and magazines like the Cincinnati and Louisville *Western Messenger* (1835–41), even if the magazines often proved over-optimistic in their belief that they could capture a local readership in the face of the established products of New York or London. Mrs Trollope saw dismayingly little evidence of culture in the Cincinnati of the 1820s: a more sympathetic observer might justly have been struck that there was so much, in a town whose site had been wilderness forty years earlier.

The other side of the coin was a feeling which grew with the decades, that the true symbolic meaning of the West was not its absorption of civilization but its atmosphere of adventurous openness. Romantic literature, powerfully exemplified in Cooper's Leatherstocking novels, encouraged the sentiment. 'Wilderness' gradually supplanted cultivated 'nature' as a cardinal principle of Americanism. The fact that it *was* the 'wild West', hitherto a reproach, became a boast, a positive quality, something that Europe did *not* have. Vernacular humour in the United States originated like every other cultural form in the East. Seba Smith, the creator of 'Major' Jack Downing, the irrepressible commentator on Jacksonian America, was a 'down-easter' from Maine. Sam Slick, another homely commentator of the era, spoke in a Connecticut dialect; his creator, T. C. Haliburton, was from Nova Scotia. The folk-humour of Hosea Bigelow referred to New England and was the invention of the Bostonian poet J. R. Lowell. G. W. Harris, the author of *Sut Lovingood's Yarns*, came from Pennsylvania. William T. Porter, whose magazine *The Spirit of the Times* (1831) provided a forum for a generation of 'Western' humour, was a Vermonter living in New York. The men who exploited the possibilities of Western and South-Western humour, including the largely 'ghosted' narratives of Tennessee's Davy Crockett, tended to be socially and politically a good deal more conservative than their creations: in American parlance they were Whigs rather than Democrats. Nevertheless the frontier West became recognized as the ideal *mise-en-scène* for native vernacular humour; and so little by little supplanted other regional variants. Lack of refinement could become a regional boast, a tall tale, a scene of ruffian hilarity and violence, as in such Sut Lovingood yarns as 'The Quilting Party', or in bits of Mark Twain. The 'feminized' East of sermons and sewing-circles thus found its literary antithesis in the scattered, half-formed communities of backwood, prairie and mountain country.

Apart from the joshing tales of South-Western humour, however, the first glamorously coherent literary West – a territory celebrated and in some respects invented by Artemus Ward, Bret Harte and Mark Twain – was California–Nevada. This domain had the exotic associations of former Spanish rule, the cachet of being the Far West (indeed, the farthest), the novelty of its feverish, mushroom mining camps, and the advantage of an ebullient new metropolis – San Francisco. All the complexity and ambivalence of the Western literary idea are epitomized in the career of Bret Harte, who like certain of the transitory settlements he wrote about hit a vein, knew a decade of glittering renown, and subsided into obscurity. Harte, who had arrived in California as a youth in 1854, was no rugged Westerner, but a sophisticate in outlook, the author (in *Condensed Novels*) of a set of witty salon-parodies of Dickens, Victor Hugo and other literary celebrities. His early attempts to treat California as a literary theme concerned the romantic Spanish past. He was never a wholehearted admirer of the white men who poured into the mining-frontier; he knew them to be often squalid and vicious – murderers, lynchers, desperadoes. The stories that brought him fame in the late 1860s, such as 'The Luck of Roaring Camp', were in intention perhaps as much ironical and even shocking as they were picturesque. It was his audience – largely an Eastern audience – that told him he had struck ore with his swift little sketches, at once tender and tough, of Poker Flat, Sandy Bar and Fiddle Town – names which he himself had lately thought merely ugly.

Emulative pride made the San Franciscans launch a magazine, of which Harte was the founding editor, to answer Boston's *Atlantic Monthly*. In that year, 1869, the first transcontinental railroad was completed. It seemed appropriate to name the new magazine the *Overland Monthly*: 'overland' suggested the westward pioneering surge. It also seemed appropriate to choose the California grizzly bear as the magazine's emblem. According to Mark Twain's recollection, Harte – gazing at an artist's rendering of the emblem – felt that it was not quite satisfactory. He resolved his uneasiness by sketching in a section of railway track, under the feet of the bear. What he now had was a creature of the untamed wilderness, symbolic of the pride of the West, furnishing a contrast to the railway's symbolic link with the East. But the emblem was of course also a puzzle, and a problem both to Harte and the whole concept of a culture of the West. Did California as represented by the bear want the railway to come through or not? And if not, what chance had the bear of stopping a locomotive? Two years later Harte himself was drawn East, by parlour car, all the way to Boston where he was fêted by the *Atlantic Monthly* circle and persuaded (with unfortunate literary consequences for himself) to transfer his allegiances to the Atlantic seaboard. Also present at a luncheon given in Harte's honour in Boston, wistful-envious because as yet far less famous, was Mark Twain; and Twain too before long had left the West to live in New England.

Like the South, though less stultifyingly, the West too had an abstract function for nineteenth-century American literature. As with the South, the imaginative potential was hardly perceived by those who began to chronicle it. The Southern mood was avowedly once of yesteryear – of thwarted hopes and gallant but vain resistance. The Western mood was altogether more robust. But perhaps the greatest lesson of the westward movement was also of the transitory pathos of human endeavour. The West failed, betrayed itself, in the act of succeeding. Imaginatively, its supreme significance was caught by Twain at the end of *Huckleberry Finn* (1885), with Twain's boy-hero apparently running away from 'civilization' into the as-yet unsettled territories. Neither Twain nor his contemporary critics were able to grasp the entire import of that evasion. The intermingling of actuality and fantasy characteristic of both South and West was a legacy that could not be thoroughly savoured by the American imagination until the next, twentieth, century.

## Conclusions

One way of writing American literary history is to dwell upon the reiterated determination of writers to create a distinct native literature, and to analyse the stages by which they succeeded. Twentieth-century scholars, looking back upon the period up to 1900, tend to emphasize developments in the American novel, though with some attention to Thoreau's *Walden*, the essays of Ralph Waldo Emerson, and the poetry of Walt Whitman and perhaps of Emily Dickinson. The central books in their canon are Hawthorne's *Scarlet Letter*, Melville's *Moby-Dick* and Twain's *The Adventures of Huckleberry Finn*. Within the canon – in some cases much influenced by D. H. Lawrence's *Studies in Classic American Literature* (1924) – they find a principle of difference: 'the pure elixir, the American thing,' in the words of the American poet Stephen Vincent Benét.

Sometimes they see this as a hidden, even unconscious essence. For Charles S. Feidelson, Jr, it embraces a propensity for symbolic language. R. W. B. Lewis ponders the subtleties of the notion of *The American Adam*. Harry Levin investigates *The Power of Blackness* (a phrase applied by Melville to Hawthorne) in American fiction. Leslie Fiedler (*Love and Death in the American Novel*) is intrigued by what he considers a covert fascination with themes of incest, homosexuality, miscegenation and necrophilia. Richard Poirier (*A World Elsewhere*, 1966) discerns a fascination with metaphors of architecture: the American writer, he suggests, has in most complex ways thought of a work of fiction as a construction, a house. Sacvan Bercovitch is interested in the persistence of Puritanism. Richard Slotkin and Michael Rogin stress the Indian-hating, Manifest-Destiny brutishness of American expansionism. Others dwell upon the rhetoric of republicanism, with its pride in America's ideal of liberty and equality, and its disdain for an old world deemed to be a den of iniquity. Whatever the particular thesis, these explorations imply a sharp contrast with European literature. Richard Chase, for instance, sees the major novels of the United States as 'romances' – a term deliberately used by Hawthorne – in which the writer, unlike his British counterpart, is continually losing control of his avowed, societal theme and being carried off into conjecture, dream and myth.

Chase and his colleagues do not unanimously contend that the result was a great literature. Some regard American literature as largely made up of failures and oddities. They might even agree with the summary verdict of the Spanish–American philosopher George Santayana, for example, that New England Transcendentalism produced 'a harvest of leaves' – something peculiarly dry and fruitless. It is the *peculiarity* that interests them, and the diagram of difference between an inchoate but powerful native impulse and a polished but mediocre or inappropriate 'Eastern' or European mode.

Certain problems arise from this kind of interpretation. One is that the esteemed, 'serious' literature of nineteenth-century America corresponds only tangentially with the twentieth-century vision of the past. Where do Longfellow, Whittier, Lowell, Holmes, W. D. Howells and others, greatly admired in their day, fit into the scheme of things? There is a gap, in other words, between our conception of the American psyche of Whitman's day and that of Whitman's contemporaries, most of whom had never heard of him but *had* heard of an essayist like George W. Curtis, who wrote in 1852:

We have none of the charms that follow long history. We have only vast and unimproved extent, and the interest with which the possible grandeur of a mysterious future may invest it. One would be loath to exhort a European to visit America for other reasons than social and political observation, or buffalo hunting. . . . The *idea* of the great western rivers, and of lakes as shoreless to the eye as the sea, or of a magnificent monotony of grass or forest is as impressive and much less wearisome than the actual sight of them.

One way of dealing with the problem is to admit and to categorize the gulf between a Whitman and a Curtis as a fundamental duality – related to the set of dualities already sketched in the pages above. A twentieth-century critic, Philip Rahv, has expressed the division as between the 'paleface' and the 'redskin' style in American literature. He was anticipated earlier in the century by Santayana, for whom the 'paleface' line constituted the 'genteel tradition' – a debilitated, uneasy mode, dominant in the nineteenth-century culture yet never able to come to terms with the entire American world.[1] For Santayana as for Rahv, the 'redskin' version of American reality was itself deficient; Rahv noted that American writers of fiction had been unable to portray a single credible intellectual, though they could deal very well with simple or untutored characters. So one might visualize American culture as divided between two value-systems, set in rivalry against one another instead of in a complementary relationship, of elegance and roughness, experience and innocence, sophistication and spontaneity.

There is much historical truth in this duality – provided that we realize the doubleness might well exist inside individual Americans (Mark Twain, Francis Parkman, Hawthorne, Willa Cather?) unwilling to opt definitely for either redskin or paleface alternative. An important corrective need is to give a fair hearing to the paleface tradition: to realize, that is, how much it governed nineteenth-century American literature, and how solid within limits its accomplishments were. A later chapter attempts to supply some materials for a sympathetic assessment of 'college culture' in the United States of its formative era. This is not incompatible with an appreciation too of the abstractly 'American' tinges of the national literary outlook, even among the genteel practitioners. Though he appears to apologize for the circumstance, and to assume that only the future will bestow meaning upon the raw materials to hand, note that even G. W. Curtis acknowledges that there is an element of *idea* in these materials. His very deprecation is extremely instructive. And he was correct, though not exactly as he understood the situation, to believe that it would take time to flesh out the abstractions.

---

[1] 'One half of the American mind,' said Santayana in a famous lecture of 1911, had remained 'slightly becalmed; it has floated gently in the backwater, while, alongside, in invention and industry and social organisation, the other half of the mind was leaping down a sort of Niagara Rapids. This division may be found symbolised in American architecture: a neat reproduction of the colonial mansion – with some modern comforts introduced surreptitiously – stands beside the skyscraper. The American Will inhabits the skyscraper; the American Intellect inhabits the colonial mansion. The one is the sphere of the American man; the other, at least predominantly, of the American woman. The one is all aggressive enterprise; the other is all genteel tradition.'

See James Ballowe, ed., *George Santayana's America: Essays on Literature and Culture* (Urbana, Illinois, and London, 1967), 20. Santayana's essay was first published in his *Winds of Doctrine* (1913).

# 2

# LITERARY CULTURE IN COLONIAL AMERICA

## Larzer Ziff

In *The Present State of Virginia* (1724), Hugh Jones, minister of Jamestown, Virginia and Chaplain to the Virginia Assembly wrote:

If New England be called a receptacle of Dissenters, and an Amsterdam of religion, Pennsylvania, the nursery of Quakers, Maryland the retirement of Roman Catholics, North Carolina the refuge of runaways, and South Carolina the delight of buccaneers and pirates, Virginia may justly be esteemed the happy retreat of true Churchmen.

Beyond the author's obvious religious opinion in this passage two central aspects of colonial cultural life can be glimpsed. The colonies are diverse – there is no one America but a plural culture. The colonies do not generate their own identities but take them from the European forces that are exerted upon them: one is a 'receptacle', another a 'retirement', yet another a 'refuge', and still another a 'retreat'. The diction of 1724 gives continuing life to an idea older than the actual settlement of English America (begun in 1607 in Jamestown), the idea of a land not only distant but different from the daily world the Englishman knew, one where the un-permitted was permissible, the inaccessible, accessible.

America was a marked area in the English imagination before it was a well defined place on English maps. It was, for example, the fancied retreat of swashbucklers where, finally, they could find the riches that would make them lords in their homeland. So in *Eastward Ho!* (1605) John Marston's Captain Seagull said of the Virginia Indians:

Why, man, all their dripping pans and their chamber-pots are pure gold; and all the chains with which they chain up their streets are massy gold; and for rubies and diamonds, they go forth on holidays and gather 'hem by the seashore, to hang on their children's coats, and stick in their caps, as commonly as our children wear saffron-gilt brooches, and groats with holes in 'hem.

Moreover, the wilderness of America would permit licentiousness in the acquisition of riches just as the riches themselves would put the possessors above customary social restraints. Captain Seagull insists, 'You shall live freely there, without sargeants, or courtiers, or intelligencers.'

Or the imagination conjured up an America whose vacancy was the natural space provided by divine providence for the reception of religious purity when the corruptions of Europe would inevitably exile it. So George Herbert (1633):

> Religion stands on tip-toe in our land
> Readie to pass to the *American* strand. . . .
> When Italie of us shall have her will,
> And all her calendar of sinnes fulfill, . . .
> Then shall *Religion* to *America* flee.

These examples illustrate the fact that America was first explored by Englishmen at a time when impatience with the vestiges of feudal institutions was outspeeding the capability of society to adjust to the demands of those who found no acceptable role within it. It was a time of discontent with a hierarchical and ritualistic church when portable capital was beginning to feel the competitive force it could exert against property in land. The explorers arrived with expectations built on their desire to achieve goals thwarted by conditions in the homeland.

America was a ground on to which were projected Europeans' discontents with their own civilization. Whatever message the land itself – its native inhabitants, its fauna, its flora, the scarcely comprehensible reaches and variety of its coast, the density of its hardwood forests, the stretch of its mountain chains – whatever message this America had for its new occupants would have to wait or to work deeply while, more obviously, Europe imposed its experiments. As Robert Frost wrote:

> The land was ours before we were the land's.
> She was our land more than a hundred years
> Before we were her people. She was ours
> In Massachusetts, in Virginia
> But we were England's.

The earliest writings produced in and about English America – explorers' accounts, letters, diaries, treatises – display ideas, aspirations, and activities that were checked in the homeland running to find fulfilment on a continent unmarked by landlords' boundaries and untamed by civil institutions. They also show how, gradually and subtly, the land itself modified the imagination of the settlers so that there came about not just an English culture abroad but an American style of life.

Three theoretical starting points for American literature are therefore suggested. American literature began when the idea of America began to engage the English literary imagination. Or American literature began when the first explorers of America wrote first-hand accounts of their visits to the new shores. Or American literature began when residents of America began to reflect the cultural consequences of the new land in their writings. Conventionally, American literary history accepts the second principle and for most purposes this is a prudent decision. But in accepting this starting point we must realize that the distinction between early writers who treated America without having seen it and those who actually visited is biographical rather than literary. The latter group had been conditioned by views current in England. They set forth with expectations so strong that frequently even when the reality they encountered differed from the ideal they had anticipated, they continued to write as if they had encountered the ideal.

There was little conscious falsifying in such behaviour. Most human beings see only what they are prepared to see; their field of vision is defined before they look. So Michael Drayton, who remained at home, wrote in 'To the Virginia Voyage' (1606) of a pastoral retreat that would nurture poetry, and John Pory, who actually endured uncouthness, ignorance, and hardship in Virginia, nevertheless echoed him when he affirmed (in a letter to Sir Dudley Carleton, 30 September 1619), 'I am resolved wholly to minde my business here and nexte after my pen to have some good booke alwayes in store, being in solitude the best and choicest company. Besides among these christall rivers and odoriferous woods I doe escape much expense, envye, contempte, vanity, and vexation of minde.'

### Early Eye-witnesses

Drayton concluded his poem to the Virginia expedition:

> Thy voyages attend,
> Industrious Hakluyt,
>   Whose reading shall enflame
>   Men to seek fame,
> And much commend
> To after times thy wit.

The principal guides to would-be travellers and colonists were, indeed, the ship captains' and explorers' accounts set forth in three large folio volumes by Richard Hakluyt as *The Principal Navigations of the English Nation* (1598). They satisfied curiosity as to the new land and also created a national maritime epic at the moment when England was emerging as a great sea power. Their popularity led Samuel Purchas to carry on the enterprise after Hakluyt's death, notably in his *Hakluytus Posthumus or Purchas His Pilgrimes* (1625). The voyages of Bristol captains such as Bartholomew Gosnold and Martin Pring down-coast from the Newfoundland fishing banks were, by the presence of their reports in these pages, elevated from the level of commercial speculation to that of calls to action for the discontented and the adventurous of the English nation.

Among the earliest of explorations was the expedition to Virginia fitted out by Sir Walter Raleigh in 1585, but few succeeding reports from America surpassed in accuracy those provided by two of its members. John White then made drawings of the American Indian that are better than any produced for another hundred years, and Thomas Harriot, mathematician and astronomer, then compiled his *Briefe and True Report of the New Found Land of Virginia* (printed in Hakluyt). For a generation after Harriot's *Briefe Report* fact and fancy were to be mixed liberally in travellers' accounts, but here at the outset of exploration was an admirably precise survey of the fauna, flora, and aborigines of North America and a remarkably shrewd estimate of the commercial potential of the land. In a day when English expectations were still based on the amazing mineral riches discovered in the new world by the Spaniards, Harriot unobtrusively described what was to become Virginia's true gold mine, uppowoc – or, as the Spaniards generally called it, tobacco.

Among the most impressive of the writings from America that followed Harriot's were those that dealt with the voyage rather than with the landfall. They are exciting as high adventure. They also convey the profound emotional significance of the sea change wrought by the long, hazardous Atlantic crossing. After suffering storms and starvation and observing totally unexpected marine phenomena (whales, sea phosphorescence, strange birds) the imagination was unsettled and scarcely recomposed itself when America was finally reached. The sea change contributed greatly to the tendency to magnify the strange into the wondrous rather than attach it to reality.

Examples abound in the literature up to 1650. The most famous is probably that of William Strachey, *A True Reportory of the Wracke and Redemption of Sir Thomas Gates, Knight* (1610 and printed in *Hakluytus Posthumus*). In a letter obviously seen by the Shakespeare who wrote *The Tempest*, Strachey described the eerie lights that appeared in the rigging, storms that beggared the classics for phrases of description, and shores (the Bermudas as we now know) that alternately seemed the home of the devil and the isles of the blessed. After such experience what was reality?

For another example, we can move ahead to 1649 and Colonel Norwood's account of his dolorous journey to the new world:

The infinite number of rats that all the voyage had been our plague, we now were glad to make our prey to feed on; and as they were insnared and taken, a well grown rat was sold for sixteen shillings as a market rate. Nay, before the voyage did end (as I was credibly inform'd) a woman great with child offered twenty shillings for a rat, which the proprietor refusing, the woman died.

Norwood, seeking Virginia after the collapse of Charles's cause, anticipated a region of royalist repose. Even the starvation scenes he reports are, in part, second hand, for as a gentleman he saw little, even on the tiny ship, of the commoners who so suffered. At Christmas-time, Norwood's group, the ancestors of all who were subsequently to steam the Atlantic first-class, scraped the meal tub and to their meagre findings added Malaga sack, sea water, fruit, spice, and oil in order to make a pudding that would help them distinguish Christmas from the other dreary days. This, he admitted, 'raised some envy in the spectators; but allowing some privilege to the captain's mess, we met no obstruction, but did peaceably enjoy our Christmas pudding.'

So firm a sense of social distinction was bound to run into difficulties in a land where dissenters found room to live outside of established boundaries, and, thus emboldened, could resist any authority that did not come armed with more than official titles. Indeed, Norwood's friend Sir William Berkeley, Governor of Virginia, was faced with the open rebellion of the settlers on his frontier.

The immediate cause of the rebellion was Berkeley's Indian policy. The settlers were eager for a decisive military conquest of the natives in spite of the governor's treaties with the Indians. They no longer saw a king, councillors, and a nation when they looked upon a chief, his sachems, and his tribe. Norwood commenting on the paint on the face of an Indian 'princess' admitted that it was unpleasant but could then say, 'I had reason to imagine the royal family were only to use this ornament exclusive of all others . . . and this conceit made it turn again, and appear lovely, as all things should do that are honour'd with the royal stamp.' The rebellion against Berkeley indicated that American reality was already countering such European fantasy with a democracy bred of land hunger, violence, and a practical estimate of civilized versus savage fire power.

The books of Captain John Smith stand out among the hundreds of accounts of America produced in the first fifty years of the seventeenth century. They capture monumentally the details and themes that are otherwise to be located in myriad journals, letters, and reports. Of the Captain himself before he entered the service of the Virginia Company we know little except for what he tells us and the veracity of his account has frequently been challenged. Smith's version is that in 1596, at the age of sixteen, he ran away from home to become a soldier of fortune in the Low Countries; that he served with the Austrians against the Turks in Transylvania, where he was captured and presented as a gift to the Turkish Pasha's wife in Constantinople; that she, in turn, sent him as a slave into her brother's domain east of the Black Sea; and that he escaped and underwent many exciting adventures before returning to England about 1604. Once returned, he plunged into the plans of the Virginia Company and sailed with the group that arrived at Jamestown in 1607. Though the sealed orders that were opened at arrival in America appointed Smith to the governing council, his peers' suspicion that he was mutinous debarred him from office at first. This suspicion seemed based upon Smith's propensity for independent action, a fortunate trait so far as the majority of his fellows was concerned since it was largely through his energetic exertions among the Indians while others on the council were rapt in dismay at the imminence of starvation that Smith preserved the lives of most with him. The effectiveness of his leadership gained him the presidency of the council over the protest of most of its members, but, injured in a gunpowder explosion in 1609, Smith was forced to return to England to tend to his injuries.

Back in England, as much to defend himself from the accusations of his enemies in the Company as to promote their venture, he produced his first writings on Virginia, descriptions that were to serve as the basis for his major work on the subject, *The General Historie of Virginia* (1624). The Captain was unable, however, to return to the new world until 1614 when the Virginia Company of Plymouth gave him direction of a voyage to explore New England,

so named by him on that trip. But the Company would not back
him any further than that exploration itself, a principal result of
which was his *Description of New-England* (1616), and though he
actively sought a position of leadership in subsequent settlements
he had to resign himself to remaining in London and affecting the
course of colonialism through his writings. The Pilgrims who
settled Plymouth in New England in 1620 were said to have
refused his services on the ground that his book cost less.

Smith's *Historie of Virginia* and *Description of New-England* provided the best available account of the history and topography of
those regions. His relatively accurate maps proved themselves in
use, and though his descriptions of the natives and the natural
resources are, at times, fanciful, they nevertheless contain a self-
evident core of reliability based on direct and shrewd observation.
The books, moreover, have literary importance because Smith, far
better than any of the other explorers, captured in his pages the
imperial vision that, intangible as it was, impelled early American
colonization. Though the founding of specific settlements must be
explained in terms of who actually settled with what financial
backing for what announced purposes, such detailed social
analyses are always in danger of losing the important general in
the particular. Smith, however, while rich in detail, also reflects
the headiness of his times in the assumptions he makes about the
audience of his work and in his rhetorical shaping of his materials
to the interests of that assumed audience. His eye for romantic
detail reinforces the literary strength of his work, as, for instance,
when he tells of his rescue from execution through the intercession of Pocahontas and thereby makes the first major contribution to American popular history.

'Who can desire more content,' Smith asked of the Englishman
of 1616, 'that hath small meanes; or but only his merits to advance
his fortune, than to tread, and plant that ground he hath pur-
chased by the hazard of his life?' If you have nothing else in life
you have your life, and America is the arena where that alone is a
sufficient stake with which to win riches and contentment. If you
are magnanimous, you can concentrate on the benefits to be
bestowed on posterity by opening this new land to them; if
religious, on the conversion of the savages; if a man of honour, on
the gaining of an attendant kingdom for your native land. Smith's
appeal is not broadcast on the winds, but addressed to a
population in England whom he knew to be restive:

Then, who would live at home idly (or thinke in himselfe any worth to live) only to eate, drink, and sleepe, and so die? Or by consuming that carelessly, his friends got worthily? Or by using that miserably, that maintained vertue honestly? Or, for being descended nobly, pine with the vaine vaunt of great kindred, in penurie? Or (to maintaine a silly shewe of bravery) toyle out thy heart, soule, and time, basely by shifts, tricks, cards, and dice? Or by relating newes of others actions, sharke here and there for a dinner, or supper; deceive thy friends, by faire promises, and dissimulation, in borrowing where thou never intendest to pay; offend the lawes, surfeit with excesse, burden thy Country, abuse thy selfe, despaire in want, and then couzen thy kindred, yea even thine owne brother, and wish thy parents death (I will not say damnation) to have their estates? though thou seest what honours, and rewards, the world yet hath for them will seeke them and worthily deserve them.

To such as recognized themselves in Smith's call to action America was pictured in the colours of abundance. He did not offer the gold of the Spaniards lying ready to hand, but, more relevantly to the Protestants of England, a place where one would tire himself in planting vines, fruits, and herbs, and sate his mind in contriving grounds that would please him. Then, when fatigued, the settler could take to his boat to recreate himself with angling, only to find that again he was profiting: 'And is it not pretty sport, to pull up two pence, six pence, and twelve pence, as fast as you can hale and veare a line?' Riches gained in such a fashion are more desirable than diamonds that lie about loose because they involve mental and spiritual fulfilment in the getting. More than wealth awaits one in America. Happiness is there, but it is to be won through settlement and domestication and will elude the mere marauder.

English America was to be a new English home while French America was but a fur-trading station and Spanish America a mine to be worked until the next boat left for home. In picturing America for the new life it made possible rather than as a land to be used and abandoned, Smith called the continent to the attention of communities of discontented sectaries as well as companies of adventurers.

Well into the seventeenth century the reasons Smith offered for colonization still set the tone, especially in the Southern colonies. Those who were actually settled there saw little reason for modifying the prospects of upward mobility held out by the Captain. In 1656, for example, John Hammond having surveyed the conditions in Virginia was still insisting that those who abused the plantation were 'black-mouthed babblers' who attacked not only the colony but God's providence in adding so flourishing a branch to England.

In his *Leah and Rachel* (Virginia and Maryland were the modern counterparts of these two fruitful sisters) Hammond echoed Smith in contrasting the honourable undertaking of inhabiting America with the 'desperate and miserable courses' open to those who remained in England.

Seventy years after Hammond, as we have seen, writings from America such as that of Hugh Jones continued to stress colonial life as an alternative to desperate courses at home. They continued to depend for their effect on the existence in England of a large number of people who had been left masterless by the break-up of feudal institutions. America has space and opportunity enough for them to act out their seemingly anarchic impulses so that they create rather than destroy, add to wealth rather than maintain a parasitic relationship to existing wealth, found families rather than await the death of parents, take leadership in a new political order rather than harry the existing order, institutionalize radical religious insights rather than smash established religion. What would make one American settlement more successful than another, therefore, was not necessarily the relative superiority of its physical situation and its natural resources. Cultural success would come, rather, to the colony that could take power from the impulses that were in rebellion at the situation in England and yet impose a form of social control over them; that could formalize a new set of habits out of discontent with the old. Such success came to Puritan New England, the colonial society that has exerted the greatest influence on the subsequent development of American culture.

## Puritan Writings

Faced with Stuart opposition as they had been faced with Tudor opposition, the leaders of the Puritan movement continued to maintain that they wished to accomplish the reform of the Church of England from within that institution. With the bishops, they regarded separation from the Church as schismatical and therefore heretical and punishable by imprisonment or death.

The single strongest Puritan state in New England, Massachusetts Bay, was built by such Puritans, men who were nonconforming but also nonseparating. In 1628 a small company under the leadership of John Endicott began a town at the present Salem, Massachusetts and two years later John Winthrop's company arrived and Boston, Massachusetts was founded. From 1630 to 1640 (when Puritan prospects in England took an upward turn) Massachusetts received a steady flow of immigrants – in 1630 alone thirteen ships brought over one thousand settlers.

The populous, self-assured colony of Massachusetts almost immediately overshadowed the tiny settlement of Plymouth, founded in 1620 by a band of Separatists. In 1684 this overshadowing was formalized by Plymouth's being incorporated into Massachusetts, and, for broad purposes, there is no need to do more than note that a Separatist Puritan tradition grew up side by side with an unseparating nonconformist tradition in Massachusetts. Church historians justly make much of the distinction that forms but a minor ramification for literary historians.

From the outset the American Puritans produced a confident flood of writings. One important aspect of their quarrel with the established church was their insistence upon the substitution of spontaneous worship for ritual, and widespread preaching for the minister's 'reading on a book' or simply omitting the sermon. At the core of Puritan belief was the conviction that the saved were saved by the direct operation of the Holy Spirit that not only came to the faithful, but, in effect, made them the faithful by providing them with the grace without which they could not have faith. The usual vehicle for the Holy Spirit in this operation was the spoken word of the minister.

The aesthetic that underlay this view of the sermon maintained that words were valueless in themselves, that they had, indeed, become idols in the fashionable sermons preached in the established church by such as Launcelot Andrewes, who carefully sustained their metaphors and built elegant verbal constructs in illustration of the Bible. Rather, there was the Word, and this was most accessible when the minister abandoned a concern for elegancies of style and preached his message plainly.

Such a view, however, did not in the first hundred years of Puritanism condone illiterate enthusiasm in the pulpit. On the contrary, the Puritans held that in order to be a fitting receptacle for the Word the minister must prepare himself through intensive study in the tongues of the Bible, in biblical commentary, in theology, and in sacred and humane history. The Puritan clergy were prodigies of learning, scarcely equalled in the history of the Protestant church, and within six years of their first mud and wattle huts in the New England wilderness, the settlers founded Harvard College, 'dreading', as they announce, 'to leave an illiterate Ministry to the Churches when our present Ministers shall lie in the Dust'.

This high respect for learning extended to the community at

large since the ecclesiastical polity of the Puritan church was based on the substitution of a universally accessible Bible for traditional ceremonies and rote prayers. Literacy was the key to success, and the Puritans established in Massachusetts the first widespread common schools in the history of the English-speaking peoples. Respect for general education was reinforced by the community's realization that in the absence of a titled ruling class, a ceremonial church, a landed gentry, even a town which had been lived in by generations who had worn habits in society as well as ruts in the road, in short, in the absence of familiar institutions chaos would prevail if new controls were not developed. The principal control was education.

Accompanying the emphasis on education was a widespread confidence among the early Puritans that the future was theirs. Perched on a rocky coast between an inhospitable forest and the fitful Atlantic, they saw themselves as the vanguard of an army that was to make history by providing a model of church and state that would eventually be followed throughout the world. They assaulted the future with incredible vigour. Large families and quick re-marriage after the death of a spouse (even for those in their sixties) were accepted manners. The only legal pattern of settlement was the township; if a man had to travel an undue distance from the town to his farm he still would not be permitted to reside on his farm until he had joined a group who would go with him into the country and there found another town, another church, and, in time, another school. The New Englanders moved in groups, leaving well-marked roads behind them. And few groups considered themselves established until they had acquired a preacher and a schoolmaster (frequently, of course, one and the same man in the early settlements). Each of these preachers was university trained so that New England had, in the seventeenth century, the highest proportion of university graduates in England or her possessions.

No small feature of this assault on the future was the written word that would describe, justify, glorify, and propagandize the New England way. This cultural climate explains the tremendous volume of writings fathered by a remote colony. By 1639 a printing press was working in Boston, but before and long after that date New Englanders were also sending manuscripts to London, there to be seen through the press by English friends. The first edition was almost always the Massachusetts author's proof sheet.

The main categories of New England writing are (1) directly or indirectly religious, which includes sermons, polemics, and ecclesiastical and civil political theories: (2) journals, diaries, letters, and histories; and (3) poetry. In addition there were a number of prose excursions on a variety of topics: science, education, the Indian languages, music, etc., but none of the monuments of the literature are excluded when one considers it under these three broad categories.

Since the Puritans distrusted elegance of style in the sermons, distrusted, as they put it, those who preferred Plato over Paul, the Muses over Moses, this genre, the most popular form of literature in seventeenth-century New England, today possesses little immediate interest. The forbidding appearance that Puritan sermons today have, however, should not mask the fact that for their original hearers and readers they not only provided religious edification, consolation, and caution, but constituted a central aesthetic experience. Cut off by choice from the theatre, painting, and much of *belles lettres*, the American Puritans were nevertheless men of sophisticated intelligence. Their apparently quenchless thirst for sermons, which led not only to morning and afternoon sermons on Sundays but to theological lectures on weekdays, unquestionably arose from the aesthetic pleasure these sermons provided as well as from religious zeal.

Indeed, so great was the appetite for sermons that the magistrates, pious as they themselves were, had to limit legally the amount of preaching for fear that material interests, essential to the infant colony, would be insufficiently attended. Scarcely a diary has come down from seventeenth-century New England that does not devote a major portion of its pages to commentary on the sermons heard that week; school children were disciplined to take mental or written notes so that they could on a Monday reproduce the main headings if not the entire content of the sermons they had heard.

If the modern reader can no longer take aesthetic pleasure from the sermons, he can, nevertheless, appreciate their contemporary appeal. Though plain in style, they are replete with learning so that they keep constantly in the ear as well as the minds of their auditors a sense of continuity with what, for them, was the best that had been thought and said in the past. In the sermon the preacher was developing one or another passage of the Bible to auditors who had a good reading acquaintanceship with that book and a thorough atmospheric familiarity with it through their laws, the conversation of their neighbours, the very metaphors of daily dialogue. The sermon was, therefore, not only a source of intellectual edification or spiritual admonition: it was also a constant reiteration and amplification of the mythology through which the community made sense of and drew strength from what was otherwise a most adverse reality – daily living in a primitive town on the edge of a forest.

The format of the sermon was designed to assist those who would either take it in short hand or attempt to commit its main themes to memory, who would, in effect, treat it as a work of literature that could be consulted at leisure. After the drawing out of the doctrine from the text of the sermon, the exposition of that doctrine was given in a numbered series of reasons and followed by a numbered series of 'Uses', that is, more or less practical applications.

Of the hundreds of sermons that survive from seventeenth-century Massachusetts those that attract the greatest attention today, of course, are those composed by certain celebrated figures or delivered in exceptional circumstances. The original settlers of Massachusetts regarded John Cotton (1585–1652), who had come from St Botolph's in Boston, Lincs, to the Boston church in 1633, as their foremost minister and his sermons should perhaps be sampled first by any reader attempting to gain some sense of the *genre*, though those by the man frequently regarded as his equal, Thomas Hooker (1586–1647), make handsomer use of common English diction.

Perhaps the most readable of the early sermons are those of Thomas Shepard (1605–49). An influential person as minister of Cambridge, where Harvard College was located, Shepard went farther than most of his contemporaries in attempting through imagery to make the sermon an emotional experience. In the main, the seventeenth-century Puritan sermon was designed to operate by degrees upon the consciousness of its auditor, as the words the preacher had spoken remained with him and opened the way for The Word. But Shepard attempted to locate an emotional experience in the sermon itself so that the auditor underwent a reaction while listening to the sermon akin to the responses a poet seeks to induce in his audience.

Not until the eighteenth century did a style of preaching become popular in America that strove for a strong psychological reaction at the very time of the sermon's being preached. Such a direct working on affections – remembered most commonly in its vulgarest form, as 'hell-fire preaching' – was at a far remove from the studied expositions of Cotton and Hooker, or even Shepard. But when Jonathan Edwards (1703–58), the greatest of native American theologians, turned to the original Puritan ministers for inspiration and guidance in his revival of Calvinistic thought and zealous, religious fervour, the man whose writings counted most for him was the man who first glimpsed the emotive power of the sermon, Thomas Shepard. Reread today, Shepard's *The Sincere Convert* (1640) or *The Sound Beleever* (1649) do make an appeal in a more moving manner than the works of his greater contemporaries, though, one must admit, this means also that they become exhibits in the pre-history of literary sentimentalism.

Like the sermons, the significant items in the vast amount of polemical theory on church and state produced by the American Puritans retain a vigorous life today principally because of their historical resonance. In narrower literary terms, they do not differ appreciably from those now consigned to the realm of the annalist. Taken collectively, these weapons in the wars between Congregationalist and Presbyterian, orthodox nonconformist and radical, theocrat and democrat, are impressive in the moral stamina and intellectual control over anarchic impulse that they reveal. Early during the Puritan intellectual revolution (1594), Richard Hooker on behalf of the established church had urged the iconoclastic opposition 'not to exact at our hands for every action the knowledge of some place of Scripture out of which we stand bound to deduce it ... but rather as the truth is, so acknowledge, that it sufficeth if such actions be framed according to the Law of Reason; the general axioms, rules, and principles of which Law, being so frequent in Holy Scripture, there is not let but in that regard, even out of Scripture such duties may be deduced by some kind of consequence'. His opponents denied Hooker the flexibility of what he called the Law of Reason, and in forcing relatively literal scriptural support for all church practices maintained a strong position from which established institutions and procedures could be attacked. That Law of Reason, they saw, led to the acceptance of conventions, customs, and traditions as unquestionable.

Now in established positions of power in New England and in debate with Presbyterian brethren coming to power in England, the American Puritans had to develop a defensive position, one that would stabilize the system they were establishing so that neither radicals nor Presbyterians could shake it. In the face of the radicals, they had to develop a rationale based on a more sensitive social sense than literal scripturalism; in the face of the Presbyterians they had to justify an organization, Congregationalism, that seemed self-destructive in its lack of external hierarchical controls.

In the writings devoted to this prodigious task the American Puritans developed distinctive views of their relation to history and to their fellow men, views that were to shape the development of a peculiarly American outlook. In the former matter, they attached themselves strongly to a mythical history of pure Christianity which for several centuries had been manifested mainly by fugitive groups such as the Waldensians. Modern history was viewed as a time of corruption, so that even while they justified the historicity of their church the American Puritans separated themselves from recorded history and, in effect, asserted that the past was dead. This, as will be seen, had profound effects beyond religion. And in the face of the Presbyterians, they developed a system of independent congregations; while these appeared to lack the connecting machinery that would ensure uniformity, they actually exerted control and checked anarchy and schism through a pervasive acceptance of the idea of man's sinfulness and of the need for the congregation to be made up of and controlled by those who had had the salvation experience. The Puritans were, in short, pioneering a form of social control through psychological acquiescence rather than through external restraint. It is useful to note that when Hooker's Law of Reason re-emerged triumphantly in the pages of John Locke it did so after the intervening stage of Puritanism so that reason became related to the individual's view of reality rather than to his acceptance of tradition. Locke, understandably, was one of the intellectual heroes of the American Revolution.

Of the many works in which one can see the outlook just described taking form several can be cited as major steps: *Church-government and Church-covenant Discussed* (1643) by Richard Mather; *The Keyes of the Kingdom of Heaven* (1644) by John Cotton, and *A Survey of the Summe of Church-Discipline* (1649) by Thomas Hooker.

Though the conservative (Anglican and Presbyterian) opposition to which such works were addressed was British, the radical opposition was American. Of the writing that attacked the social control exerted by the Puritan orthodoxy and insisted upon the extension of freedom of conscience to such as Baptists and Quakers, none equals in eloquence or consequence that of Roger Williams (c 1603–83).

From his first arrival in New England, at the age of twenty-seven, Williams was from the orthodox point of view a troublemaker. Believing in the total social consequences of eternal predestination, Williams argued that it was mindless and godless to coerce in matters of religion in this world, since neither compulsory attendance at an approved church nor banning of disapproved churches could affect God's eternal decree as to whether specific men were saved. He was therefore a passionate advocate of freedom of worship, not because there are many roads to heaven but because so strait and narrow is the path that coercion is fruitless.

Combined with his narrow and rigorous theological outlook (which led to bitter debates with Quakers such as George Fox even as it led him to advocating their right to settle and worship in New England) Williams possessed a temperament that was singularly open to the plight of the wronged in his world, red men as well as white. His consciousness of the terrible mystery of salvation freed him to do battle on behalf of persecuted groups whose souls were in sufficient jeopardy without adding to their immortal burden the mortal weight of persecution by their fellow men.

Banished from Massachusetts in 1635, Roger Williams went through the woods to Narragansett Bay where the Indians who liked him facilitated his settling. There, in time, he founded Rhode Island, chartered by Cromwell's parliament, the first American colony to permit absolute freedom of worship. His most celebrated work is *The Bloody Tenet of Persecution, Discussed* (1644), but though this reveals the whole of his courageous mind in a classic statement on behalf of freedom of worship, it does not reveal the whole of his compassionate person. For this one must go to his letters.

Puritan diaries, journals, and histories in the seventeenth century in the main reveal the simultaneous existence of two central features of the Puritan reality: the internalizing of social control through widespread acceptance of the relation between man and God in predestinarian terms as the crucial feature of life; and the continuity of contemporary experience with a mythological history of true religion and its discontinuity with the details of modern history. Very few diaries devote a significant portion of their content to social reality, but rather dwell on the soul-searching of the diarist. Events are generally recorded as 'evidence of God's disposition' rather than as noteworthy in themselves. Histories also tend to bypass the details of social reality; instead they emphasize those features that can most readily be analogized with the mythology of the tribulations of God's chosen people (most often the biblical Israelites, but also various 'pure' sects in the history of Christianity).

The texture of daily life and the combination of social and political interests, prominent aspects of diary and history in general, are, therefore, commonly missing from American Puritan writings in the seventeenth century. The spiritual focus of the diary and the mythological focus of the history seem quite clearly to be the preconditions for later American fiction, which, as many critics have noted, is most characteristically concerned with either psychological themes or themes of man's relation to the cosmos rather than with man's social existence (e.g. *The Scarlet Letter* by Hawthorne and *Moby-Dick* by Melville). Excellent representatives of these *genres* as they were most commonly practised are Thomas Shepard's *Autobiography* (in *Publications of the Colonial Society of Massachusetts*, XXVII, 1932) and Edward Johnson's history, *Wonder-Working Providence* (1653).

When the inevitable drift from the 'purity' of the founders began to gain momentum in the latter half of the seventeenth century, second and third generation orthodox believers sought to recall New Englanders to their mission. Accordingly, written history shifted from being a record of the ever-expanding triumph of a divine and essentially ahistorical band (as in Edward Johnson) to becoming a reminder of the integrity of the founding fathers. The lives of these fathers were held up as models of behaviour that dramatized and popularized the ideals of orthodoxy in a community in danger from secularization and democratization. The principal contribution to this kind of history was Cotton Mather's *Magnalia Christi Americana* (1702), a seven-part ecclesiastical history of New England which has as its core an immense collection of lives of the divines and governors of that region.

The chief exceptions to what has been said about histories are the journals of the two greatest political leaders, Governor William Bradford of Plymouth and Governor John Winthrop of Massachusetts. The same qualities that earned leadership for these men – including the remarkable combination of a far-sighted sense of mission with a shrewd attitude towards practical political necessities – inform their pages so that these works, *History of Plymouth Plantation 1620–1647* and *History of New England 1630–1649*, constitute the central telling of the migrations to the wilderness and the winning of the land. The greatest achievements of Puritan journalism, they are also the first important works of American history. Bradford's writing glows with a sense of rightness that is never self-righteous, a sense of destiny that is intensified rather than diluted by a profound humility. *Plymouth Plantation* is the first great literary treatment of a theme that was to become characteristic of American literature, that of the common man discovering his potential in direct confrontation with his own nature, the nature of savages, and the nature of a wilderness. It emerges from its context not just as a prime document of American Puritanism but as the first great work of American literature.

Since the Puritan distrust of *belles-lettres* is frequently related to a work ethic that lies at the powerful source of modern capitalism and is also interpreted as the consequence of a sourly negative view of culture, it is necessary to remember that the Puritans themselves offered as their explanation the second commandment: 'Thou shalt have no other gods before me.' This they thought included not just false gods but any objects that pretended to exist as ends in themselves. Works of art were, in this view, prime objects of idolatry and were therefore distrusted.

As has been seen, however, the general literacy and the specialized learning in classical tongues that were the usual preconditions for English poetry in the seventeenth century existed in abundance in New England and it is not, therefore, surprising that the amount of poetry produced was also abundant. The second commandment was not violated because almost all of these poems were produced for private edification, or, when public, aimed at didactic purposes, most often the commemoration of notable events, the exposition of theological doctrines, or the disarming of death through elegies. The popularity of the last-named kind of verse has lived on in American literature chiefly as a bottomless source of satire (e.g. Benjamin Franklin's 'Receipt to Make a New-England Funeral Elegy', 1722, or the lamented maiden poet in Mark Twain's *Huckleberry Finn*, 1884) but it now and then attained a primitive dignity, and, moreover, is significant as an indication of a theory of language that was to persist in the writings of Emerson, Thoreau, and others. The Puritan elegy dotes on pun and anagram. The discrepancy between these playful devices and the gravity of the subject is reconciled by an implicit belief in the thingness of names. When Adam named each beast after its kind, he was not arbitrary. The leopard was called a leopard because Adam saw its leopardness. So lurking in each man's name as pun or anagram was his essence, and funeral elegies risked and sometimes crossed over into ludicrousness in development of such concepts.

Scarcely a seventeenth-century Puritan minister existed who did not leave among his unpublished papers some poems written for his own edification; indeed, so widespread was the practice that there is good reason to believe that a worthy amount of early New England verse is yet to be uncovered. Not until 1939 were the poems of Edward Taylor (c 1644–1729), now regarded as America's best early poet, published; not until 1960 was a full edition available. Born in England, Taylor emigrated to Massachusetts as a lad, was graduated from Harvard in 1671, and went off to spend the rest of his life as pastor and physician of the frontier town of Westfield where he was notable for the extreme conservatism of his ecclesiastical views.

Principal among Taylor's poems are the nearly two hundred *Preparatory Meditations*, each based upon a text on which Taylor set his sermon on a Sunday on which he administered the sacrament. As a means of preparing himself for his task, Taylor wrote these poems, and their constant theme is the miracle of man's union with God. In a manner that can be related to Herbert and Crashaw, Taylor conveys his wonder that so base a creature as man through his knowledge of himself has the capacity to be elevated above all creatures and objects on the earth and in the heavens. Unlike the metaphysical poets, however, Taylor's imagery is mixed and his lines frequently rough, because the pattern his meditations follow is not that of metaphoric elaboration but of mystical contemplation – awakening, purgation, rapture, and union.

In addition to the *Preparatory Meditations*, Taylor wrote a number of miscellaneous poems more 'metaphysical' in their conceits, and a long epic-like poem, *God's Determination*, dealing with the spiritual combat waged between God and Satan on the battleground of man's soul.

The best-known book of American verse in the England of the seventeenth century was that of Anne Bradstreet (c 1612–72), *The Tenth Muse Lately Sprung Up in America* (1650). The daughter of the sometime governor of the colony, Thomas Dudley, Mrs Bradstreet was married to an important magistrate who himself became governor; as such she was the busy manager of a household. Without her knowledge, a brother-in-law took a copy of her poems to England and arranged for their publication, and she became an overnight sensation, as much for the fortuitous reasons that she was a woman and lived in wild America as for the solid reason that there was great worth in her verse.

The poems that were most celebrated in Mrs Bradstreet's day were long exercises in didactic philosophizing that reflect the influence, among others, of Quarles, Du Bartas, Sidney, and Raleigh. Today the preference is for her shorter verse which turns on domestic concerns and on her engagement with nature. Though she adhered to the relatively closed system of Puritan values, she admitted into her nature verse a sense of the immense attraction of the physical world, and though she moved from the compelling beauty of this setting to an affirmation of the superiority of timeless paradise, she did so neither automatically nor in dismissal of the haunting claims of the natural universe.

The most 'popular' American work in the field of poetry was *The Day of Doom* (1662) by the otherwise unpopular and ineffective preacher of Malden, Michael Wigglesworth (1631–1705). This long work in ballad meter dramatizes the day of judgment and in so doing provides a verse catechism in basic predestinarian doctrine. It is estimated that the work sold in the ratio of one for every twenty-two persons in New England, and one for every forty-five persons in the American colonies as a whole. Easily satirized today for notorious passages such as those in which Christ assigns to infants the easiest room in hell, *The Day of Doom* still impresses because of its sure dramatic sense and the unflinching manner in which Wigglesworth faced up to the harder problems of predestinarian doctrine and wrote his verses through them rather than around them.

By the close of the seventeenth century the New England economy was well into a decided shift from agriculture to commerce, and the world its seaport towns tied it to was not merely that of the other colonies and of England, but that of the Atlantic community – Caribbean and South Atlantic islands, Spain, and Continental ports. In the Middle Atlantic region the sleepy Dutch colony of New Netherlands with its new name, New York, had begun to awaken under English rule, and Pennsylvania and New Jersey were becoming major farming areas, partly as the result of Quaker immigration. At the same time, the Southern colonies were stabilizing around the discovery of staple crops that could be profitably raised in a plantation economy. In general, therefore, the America of the early eighteenth century expressed a diversity of busy cultures and its principal literature reflected this.

## A Diversity of Cultures

In the first half of the eighteenth century the accumulation of wealth in several American centres such as Boston and Philadelphia encouraged nascent writers to produce work that was more 'literary' than any earlier American pieces. At the same time, however, the colonial condition worked against the establishment of a native tradition or of a professional writing class. The great models were Milton, Addison, Swift, and Pope. Those who would be men of letters aspired to careers in London. Thus, though a considerable amount of *belles-lettres* has survived from the period, it today appears weak, imitative, and dull.

The exciting writings of the period are, in the main, those that were produced, with varying degrees of literary consciousness, out of a critical but understanding reaction to life in one or another American colony. They are principally journals of experience, eminently readable because of the shock of discovery they contain. For the first time, scenes, characters, and issues that were to become typical of a great deal of the best in American literature find their way on to the page.

In Virginia, the wealthy William Byrd (1674–1744), shining representative of the planter aristocracy, familiar with drawing rooms in London and on the plantations, owner of the largest library in the colonies, founder of the city of Richmond, and member of the Royal Society, kept a secret diary, first deciphered and published in this century, and wrote journals of two of his journeys in the Southern colonies. These form an unrivalled picture of class, commerce, and habit in Virginia. They compel the same interest as does a novel because in them Byrd combines the erudition of a leisured man and the conscious snobbery of a colonial aristocrat with the industrious acquisitiveness of a wealthy man in a land where money lies ready to be made and the shrewd hardiness of a pioneer, at ease in the wilds. Driven into a rude house by rain, Byrd can gossip with the owner about scandals in London high society; with equal assurance in his own mansion he can busy himself about a new process of refining ore or of curing diarrhoea.

It is a truism that the English Augustan reflected in the classic balance of his art and architecture a profound dread of social and natural disorder. In America, his peer William Byrd lived in the centre of a vast plantation which with its mansion, its gardens, its fields, its master, its skilled mechanics, its indentured servants, and its slaves resisted the natural and social anarchy which Byrd knew from experience were at its very borders. In his journeys into the wilderness, such as that described in *History of the Dividing Line* (written 1729), Byrd camped among the poor white settlers who lived in the fringe between white society and agriculture and red tribesmen and hunting. They raised few crops, allowed their pigs to roam unfenced, and took what nature most readily made available. In the shiftlessness and lack of servility of this class Byrd saw a potential for the immense wasting of natural resources and for social conflicts.

But the same frontier inhabitant in other writings of the period was already launched on the literary road that would carry him to mythological proportions. His failure to settle in one place was seen as the result of his passion for liberty. His failure to return to nature by farming what he took by gleaning was seen as the result of his bold mastery of his environment. He was the frontiersman, as fierce, hardy, and free as the Indians and the panthers from whom he learned, yet as morally sensitive and as aesthetically sensible as a maiden of seventeen because his character had been formed with only nature as its model. He would wrestle with and knife a bear, and that same day reverberate to the thrill of a sunset. Such a figure, for example, was the Daniel Boone whom the writer John Filson presented in his *Kentucke* (1784) – based in part on the real Daniel Boone and in part on a romantic doctrine of the sensibility.

Byrd's squatter and Filson's Boone were early representatives of a literary tradition that has since produced the river settlers in Mark Twain, the Deerslayer of James Fenimore Cooper, and the cowboys of the Hollywood movies. They are the two halves of the ambiguity of freedom associated with the American West: license to realize one's potential or license to overpower; opportunity to stand out from under the shadow of established social restrictions, or to ignore responsibility to one's fellow man.

In marked contrast to the writings of Byrd are those of John Woolman (1720–72) a meagrely educated New Jersey Quaker who at the age of twenty-six responded to the inner call and began the series of travels to preach to gatherings of Friends in America and in Great Britain that he incorporated into the classic document of the voyage of his inner spirit, his *Journal* (1774). In place of the class consciousness so pervasive in English writings of this period is the appealing democratic simplicity derived from Woolman's conviction of the equality of men in the eyes of God. At times, his earnest sincerity prompts a smile as he presents himself giving the whole of his serious mind even to those who did not solicit it; but the dominant impression his remarkable journal makes is of the sanity of coherent radical thought. As Woolman criticizes the institution of slavery or counsels young men who do not wish to kill and yet do not wish to be called cowards in a time of Indian wars, his absolute belief in the brotherhood of men and his healthy inability to see the relevance of class and social custom to basic moral issues free him to consider the problems of his society sanitively. He pioneered the style that became characteristic of a good deal of what is best in American radical writing, a manner singularly unattached to social experience as the term is commonly used but singularly trenchant because such attachment is replaced by a vision of the equality of men that sees connections to which others, trammelled by their social position, have been blinded.

The third great journal keeper of the period was the Puritan merchant and judge Samuel Sewall (1652–1730) whose massive *Diary* is the record of New England's spiritual movement from piety to morality, economic movement from agriculture to commerce, and social movement from cropped heads to wigs. A great deal of what has entered folklore as essentially Puritan – excessive neighbour-watching, brooding over moral minutiae, self-righteous protection of class privileges – was in solution in the first half-century of New England life but crystallized in Sewall's day. The reader of the *Diary* may there see Puritan becoming Yankee. But if in its pages penny saving and soul saving seem to intermix as inseparable elements of the New England character, there are also present the strengths of a continuing high regard for the life of the mind, an unshakable social conscience, and a spirit of political self-sufficiency. These were to make Boston the powder barrel of the American Revolution.

## Towards Revolution

The luxuries of Byrd's plantation in Virginia, the plainness of Woolman's gatherings in Pennsylvania, and the bourgeois sturdiness of Sewall's Massachusetts were not, of course, exclusive properties of each of these colonies. By the middle of the eighteenth century Quaker merchants in Philadelphia were moving towards opulence, a dissenting yeoman strain was entrenched in the Southern colonies, and Quaker radicalism was evident in New England. Still, the American colonies represented a variety of cultures. There were New Englanders, New Yorkers, Virginians, etc.; or there was a Yankee, a Quaker, a Southerner, etc. But was there an American?

In the colonial period this question received its fullest treatment in the pages of Michel-Guillaume Jean De Crèvecoeur (1735–1813) who signed himself J. Hector St John de Crèvecoeur. His *Letters From an American Farmer* (1782) presented a picture of life that captured the quality of daily reality in various sections of America. But beyond this significant achievement, Crèvecoeur, an immigrant from Normandy, possessed the genius for generalization that was characteristic of the great French social writers of the century, and he applied it to the question of whether the American colonies shared a new identity that was more important than their cultural dependence upon England. 'What is an American?' was the title of one of the *Letters*.

Crèvecoeur began by admitting that the basis of American society was material: '*Ubi panis ibi patria*'. But he moved from this principle to construct a set of cultural consequences quite the reverse of those usually attached to it. Conventionally, it was argued that if all an otherwise heterogeneous people had in common was the material motive then they could produce no meaningful culture since they would depend for order upon the institutions of the ruling country. Crèvecoeur, however, argued that the conditions of natural amplitude and social mobility in America – conditions that attracted the economically and politically discontented from Europe – also formed the bases of a new culture. In Europe life was constrained by inherited class distinctions, limited land, and traditional patterns of behaviour, almost all of which were artificial in their relationship to the real nature of man. In America, freed from such constraints, men were in the process of constructing a new culture, one that was, ideally, the culture that every man in Europe would have if he were not encumbered by inherited institutions. Theatres, concert halls, a professional writing class, and such, Crèvecoeur regarded as products of the same social organization that produced the pauperized masses in the cities, the brutalized labourers on other people's fields in the country, and the wars between nations. The American would produce only the culture he needed, and if this came to no more than a rude song sung at sunset in the dooryard after a day in his own fields, then that was culture enough since it had a genuine and direct relationship to those who produced it.

*Letters From an American Farmer* is the first major statement of the promise of America not just as a natural treasure house but as a social and cultural model of man recovering his identity. This theme was to resound in the history of American letters: in Emerson's call to writers in 'The American Scholar'; in Whitman's *Leaves of Grass*; in the renascence of literature during the second two decades of the twentieth century. Most closely in time to Crèvecoeur it was advanced by Philip Freneau (1752–1832), a poet who came of age in the 1770s when his literary talents were pressed into the service of the war with England. He wrote patriotic poems remarkable for the viciousness of their anti-British sentiment. After the war, Freneau spent a long life in political journalism, most of it

on behalf of the Jeffersonian party, and to his political verse he
added a worthy body of lyric poems on American natural scenes.
Some of these, such as 'The Indian Burying Ground', are
significant contributions to the development of romantic verse in
England as well as in America. Jeffersonian that he was, Freneau
was committed to the decentralization of power in America, which
meant, in effect, that when faced with the question of whether the
new nation should risk anarchy through maintaining a loose central
system, or loss of some freedoms through stabilizing itself with a
strong central government, he chose the former. This meant, in
turn, that he willingly relinquished a high culture based on solid
social institutions in favour of a spontaneous popular culture.

Ironically, however, the closer the colonies drew to actual separation from Great Britain and the more vehement the rhetoric that
asserted an American political identity became, the more British
was the tone and structure of what was said. Before the issue came
to arms the arguments were constitutional and the arguers were, in
the main, lawyers, men who by definition were trained in the
English tradition. They knew their Locke. They knew their canon
and their common law. These were the armouries to which they
went for their weapons.

The major American writings of the eighteenth century, because
of their immense consequences, are, quite obviously, the political
writings. James Otis, John Adams, John Dickinson, Thomas
Jefferson, James Madison – the list can be greatly expanded – were
men of consequence because they were men of literary talent. The
words of an Otis speech or of Jefferson's *Declaration of Independence*
possess a force commensurate with their cause and lend elegance to
it. This great flow of political writing reveals a supreme consciousness of the importance of the historical moment unmarred by
self-consciousness or pomposity. Adams or Jefferson stated his case
as if the whole of mankind and of posterity were listening.

The crucial catalyst in the argument with England was supplied
by an Englishman who became an instant American, Thomas Paine
(1737–1809). After a restless youthful career as social underdog
and agitator in England, Paine arrived in Philadelphia in 1774,
within months of the outbreak of armed conflict. Even after the first
shots were fired (in April 1775), militia companies were gathered
and military supplies were voted by men who regarded their actions
as part of a demand for rights within the British system. No
significant voice had been raised for independence: troops pledged
loyalty to the crown even as they marched off to confront redcoats;

politicians supported the war effort while sincerely deploring any goal other than the establishment of American liberty under King George.

This situation was changed overnight by Paine's pamphlet *Common Sense* (1776). That it spread like a brushfire through the colonies and converted thousands, including most of the influential leaders such as George Washington, to viewing their war as one for independence indicates that the sentiment lay close to the surface ready to spring forth at the right touch. That Paine's was the right touch indicates that *Common Sense* is a remarkable source for ascertaining the cultural reality of revolutionary America.

*Common Sense* reveals that a people who had emigrated from Europe were not only ready to have done with Europe but also that in their common thoughts and feelings they were already divorced from modern history. They no longer believed that the past determined the present. Rather, the Americans saw themselves as coterminous with a fabulous history that included sturdy freemen in a state of nature and stout yeomen bringing their rulers to acknowledge a charter of liberties.

As a corollary the American populace evinces a confidence in the manipulation of immediate facts and a distrust of theorizing. *Common Sense* is not just the title of the pamphlet, it is the pen name of the pamphleteer and the very tone of his utterance: 'In the following pages I offer nothing more than simple facts, plain arguments, and common sense; and have no other preliminaries to settle with the reader than that he will divest himself of prejudice and prepossession, and suffer his reason and his feelings to determine for themselves.' Paine constantly associates exigency and the facts with what is natural, and tradition and theory with what is unnatural. He must, for example, show that the ties to Great Britain which appear natural in the sense that a child is naturally tied in feeling to the parent are really the outcome of the violation of natural order. Hence his characterization of the origins of the English crown as 'A French bastard landing with an armed banditti and establishing himself king of England against the consent of the natives.'

The political prospect for a culture committed to the present and to pragmatism was heady. But the literary prospect was clouded. The line between the natural and the brutish is a fine one, as is that between reliance on common sense and outright anti-intellectualism. From Cooper through Hawthorne, Melville, and James to Faulkner and Hemingway these tensions were to be revealed.

*Franklin and Edwards*

The completest man of letters, the completest man, of America's eighteenth century was Benjamin Franklin (1706–90). Born into Cotton Mather's congregation in Boston, and chiefly self-educated, at the age of seventeen while an apprentice in his brother's printing shop he wrote imitations of the *Spectator* adapted to the local scene that were the best of many such efforts of his time. In 1723 he ran off from his apprenticeship to Philadelphia and there began a rise from rags to riches, centred on the printing business, that makes his *Autobiography* (first complete publication, 1818) the classic telling of this persistent American tale.

Franklin was an internationally eminent inventor and scientific experimenter, a brilliantly skilful politician and social organizer, and an innovative philanthropist. He contributed to the understanding of electricity and constructed musical instruments, served as adviser on all political moves of the new nation, as representative of the colonies to England and of the nation to France, and founded hospitals, universities, and street-cleaning departments. And throughout a brilliantly busy career, Franklin wrote: satires on American life and on Anglo-American relations; political, economic, and social treatises; bagatelles; the most engaging set of aphorisms in the American language; clear and persuasive speeches and letters; and his autobiography.

When young Ben Franklin ran off to Philadelphia he dramatized the relationship between Puritan thought and the enlightenment. He carried with him the Puritan habits of outward industriousness and inward stock-taking, but for him the fundamental distinction between piety and morality was no longer meaningful. The Puritans held that the possession of grace saved, and that one who was in such possession, the pious man, was therefore a good man. All who were pious would presumably be useful citizens, but the reverse was not true since there were many hypocrites and the crucial factor was piety. But for Franklin a condition that did not manifest itself outwardly was useless for the main business of the world, the well-being of mankind. What mattered were actions and their consequences, not inner causes. Morality was all the piety needed.

As a result Franklin was immersed in activity – business, good works, politics, and experimentation. His inherited habit of taking an inventory was not turned toward searching the soul for signs of grace but toward examining his daily behaviour for means of improvement. He believed that a calculus of conduct could be constructed. His inherited habit of industriousness led him to an early success in business, but not without his adding to industriousness the appearance of industriousness. Working hard, he realized, was one key to success, but the other was having a reputation as a hard worker and he took care that his neighbours should see him up early in the morning toiling away in his shirt sleeves.

Franklin brought his exceptional gifts for total operation to his writings. They are unmatched in canniness and persuasiveness. There is no one Benjamin Franklin, author, but a variety of voices, each ideally suited to the argument in hand. He is the King of Prussia for the purposes of political satire; Polly Baker, a promiscuous Connecticut wench, for social satire; Publius, a prudent citizen, for a municipal proposal; Father Abraham, an unread but common-sensical countryman, for aphorisms of daily living. Even the author of the *Autobiography* is a *persona*, a fatherly old man who matches the advisory intent of the work rather than the considerably more robust Benjamin Franklin. Starting always from actual conditions, Franklin is an author of entire efficiency, moving to a rearrangement of the given that will result in the benefit, instruction, or amusement of his readers. Conscious of the chasm slowly opening between the British and the American use of English he was master also of the appropriate diction for the occasion.

Jonathan Edwards (1703–58) was Franklin's contemporary. The son of a minister in rural Connecticut, he early underwent the series of spiritual crises analysed in his remarkable *Personal Narrative* (written c 1740). Man's relation to God was the central fact of life for Edwards throughout his life. He entered Yale College before he was thirteen and after graduation continued his theological studies, tutored, was ordained minister, and finally, in 1726, became assistant to his grandfather, Solomon Stoddard, preacher of Northampton, Massachusetts and the great champion of liberal theology in New England.

In his youth Edwards had been drawn to science and had produced precocious papers on zoological observations; had studied Newton; had mastered Locke's psychology; and had written astute notes on the mind in the vein of Berkeley. He was, in short, a deeply pious son of the Puritans who, nevertheless, possessed an 'enlightened' grasp of modern scientific theories.

At Northampton Edwards eventually succeeded his grandfather and in an astonishing renovation of Puritan ideals he returned that church to a much more rigorous theological and ecclesiastical position than it had had under his permissive predecessor. Edwards was a central figure in the revivalism that swept the back counties of America. When the liberal clergy of the cities urbanely refuted what they considered to be primitive enthusiasm, they were countered not by a backwoods Bible thumper but by a man who had rethought metaphysics, psychology, ethics, and history with a full knowledge of modern theories. Calvinism, in rapid decline by the second decade of the century, seemingly archaic and notably vulnerable to the discoveries of science and the advance of rationalism, re-emerged as a force in American life because it received a rejuvenation from the greatest American 'pure' thinker of his century, Jonathan Edwards.

In his *Treatise Concerning Religious Affections* (1746) Edwards restored emotion to religion not as the property of fanatics but of all men moved by God; in his *Divine and Supernatural Light* (1734) he wrote powerfully of the absolute existence of grace; in *Freedom of Will* (1754), perhaps his finest work, he demonstrated the compatibility of modern psychology and predestinarian theory; and in his *Nature of True Virtue* (1765) he closed whatever gap might have been left in his system of ethics because of his insistence on the pre-eminence of piety. These are but some of the high points of a distinguished list of treatises, sermons, and narratives. Yet gigantic as were his intellect and his influence, personally Edwards seemed a failure. The Northampton congregation, uncomfortable with his almost glacial severity, took an unprecedented step and humiliated him with a dismissal. The only employment he could find was as missionary to a rundown settlement of 'Christian' Indians, and most of his last years (1750–8) were spent in the rude frontier town of Stockbridge where he alternated work on monumental treatises such as *Freedom of Will* with simple preachments to a group of broken men.

Franklin's emphasis on social reality and Edward's emphasis on psychology, Franklin's pragmatism and Edwards's idealism, Franklin's political pursuits and Edwards's cosmological pursuits, Franklin's practical morality and Edwards's divine piety, Franklin's universal popularity and Edwards's severe isolation, these contrast strongly even as the similarities fascinate: a common descent from Puritanism, a common recognition of modern rationalism, a common interest in science, a common passion for work. The two men summarize the courses of the life of the mind in their time and they epitomize the potential of the cultural patterns that had crystallized in America on the eve of the Revolution. Franklin's style was to be that of American life at its healthiest, confident in the ability of hard work, common sense, and common decency to overcome the resistances of the world. Edwards's style was to typify most of American literature at its best, isolated from the details of social reality and consumed with a concern for the working of the psyche and the relation of the individual to the cosmos. And like Edwards, a startling proportion of American writers were to receive one or another form of dismissal from their immediate society.

The America of promise elaborated by English writers and promoted by early explorers had in two hundred years cohered into a group of separate regions which, nevertheless, shared perceptions and feelings distinct from those produced by daily life in England. During that period no homogeneous body of American literature developed. But much good writing was done; and it was at its best when it caught the quality of life engendered by new conditions. This new way of reacting to experience was the harrowed soil from which a literature was to grow once the new nation had a consciously literary class. When great American literature began appearing in the nineteenth century, it came from the pens of men whose strengths and limitations had been determined by the landscape of which Captain John Smith wrote, the social habits with which Benjamin Franklin dealt, and the kind of God with whom Jonathan Edwards wrestled in love.

# 3

# THE GOD THAT NEGLECTED TO COME: AMERICAN LITERATURE 1780–1820

## Martin Green

Our title refers to Professor Godbole's song in E. M. Forster's *Passage to India*. The singer has invited the god Shri Krishna to come to him, calling come, come, come, come, but the god refuses to come. 'But he comes in some other song, I hope?' said Mrs Moore gently. 'Oh no, he refuses to come.' And later Forster associates the false dawn seen and then not seen on the way to Marabar with the coming and then not coming of a god to inhabit the drab countryside. The earth of India calls for a god to come to it, to give it meaning and splendour, but the god 'neglects to come'.

Many American critics at the beginning of our period were calling 'come, come, come, come', to the god of literature. But anyone who reads what got written is bound to find it as disappointing as they did themselves. In every genre, for forty years (and think what those forty years produced in England, and in Germany) the harvest was very thin. And this phrasing ('disappointment' and 'thin harvest') comes to mind because expectations were high for something better, and with reason. We now, it seems to me, must share that disappointment, when we think of what eighteenth-century colonial writers had achieved, Franklin, Jefferson, Edwards, and of the enormous potency of the ideas of revolution, of nationhood, of independence, of nature, of reason, all of which *belonged* to Americans in this period. The generation of them who lived between 1750 and 1830 – it happens to be one clearly grouped by dates – included several who had set their hearts on being great American writers. We shall note how many of the men we mention planned, when they did not write, epic or prophetic poems on American subjects.

Hugh Henry Brackenridge wrote one, at the beginning of his life, and when he later observed that he had never 'been a writer', for lack of the right city, his case became a paradigm of many others.

Nature intended me for a writer [he said in his novel *Modern Chivalry*], and it has always been my ambition. How often have I sighed for the garrets of London; when I have read histories, manners, and anecdotes of Otway, Dryden, and others, who have lived in the upper stories of buildings, writing paragraphs, or essays in prose and verse, I have lamented my hard fate that I was not one of these.[1]

*Why* did American cities so fail their writers in this period?

Most people, both now and in the past, agree that these writers are disappointing. There has never been a school of taste that discovered prime virtues in Brackenridge, Freneau, Brown, the Hartford Wits, etc. And certainly in their own time there was a very acute disappointment among Americans, an acute feeling of failure, disguised sometimes as defensiveness. As late as 1889, Henry Adams's discussion of the problem in 'American Ideals', Chapter 6 of his *History of the United States*, is curiously defensive about America's artistic poverty in this period. His rationalization is that Americans were '*living* in a world of dream, and *acting* a drama more instinct with poetry than . . .' They didn't need literature as Europeans did. '. . . The unconscious poet breathed an atmosphere which the self-conscious poet could not penetrate.' This strikes me as pretty unconvincing, and it is interesting to see so sophisticated a man so agitated. The problem was still alive for him.

The subject was, in earlier days, a favourite theme for the annual orations to Phi Beta Kappa societies. The most famous of these was Emerson's 'The American Scholar' (1837) which ended – or has been credited with ending – the impotence it analysed; but there were many before.

Charles Jared Ingersoll gave some details of America's humiliating dependence on England, in his well-documented address to the American Philosophical Society for 1823, 'A Discourse Concerning the Influence of America on the Mind'. He pointed out, as evidence of continued intellectual dependence on Britain, that 200,000 copies of the Waverley novels had poured from American presses in the preceding nine years, and the *Edinburgh Quarterly* and *Quarterly Review* were reprinted in America, and sold 4,000 copies each. (More modern figures say 500,000 copies of the Scott novels by then – and thirty-five towns were to be named Waverley.) It is worth noting that both the historical novel and the quarterly review were new ideas, new cultural formulas, not

---

[1] Brackenridge finally offered his *name* to Sir Walter Scott for a character in a Waverley novel. By then that seemed to him, I presume, the best chance he had left to inscribe himself on the honour roll of literature.

continuations of something established; and even more worth noting – because America's relation to England was in some ways like Scotland's – that they were the products of Edinburgh, not of London.

George Tucker's essay 'On American Literature', which appeared in the Philadelphia *Port-Folio* in 1813, compared America with Scotland and Ireland. Ireland, apparently so unfavourable an environment for intellectual life, according to the contemporary theory, had given Goldsmith, Berkeley, Sheridan, Moore, Swift, Burke, and Curran to English literature. Scotland had given Smollett, Thomson, Boswell, Burns, Mackenzie, Hume, Smith. English literature in the late eighteenth century was largely the work of people in some degree provincial. (The two significant novelists writing in English, when the *North American Review* began, in 1815, seemed to it to be Scott and Maria Edgeworth, a Scotsman and an Irishwoman. And they were so partly because they were so well placed for using local colour and legendary history.) Why then, Tucker asked, was America not achieving more? Great Britain, he said, had eighteen million people and produced 500–1,000 new books a year. The USA had six million people and produced twenty. His answer was that there were fewer college students in America, even proportionately, and they spent fewer years at their studies; and there was no profession of authorship in American life, like that which Samuel Johnson exemplified in London. But these were answers which could not satisfy.

There were of course those who felt that the debate itself was a mistake; that American writers should concentrate on being writers rather than American, or that literature in a democracy was bound to wither. These tended to be disaffected minds, sardonic or embittered, New England Federalists uneasy with the new America, like Joseph Dennie or Fisher Ames.[1] But they were not necessarily the least acute. Fisher Ames's essay, 'The Mire of Democracy' (1805), seems to me to show some impressive insights into what exciting literature-and-ideas are like, and to make some bold, quasi-Nietzschean contrasts between the culture of ancient Greece and that of his own America.

But the representative voices were rather those of the Channing brothers of Boston, each of whom had something to say on this subject; William Ellery, the Unitarian leader, Edward Tyrrell, the Professor of Rhetoric at Harvard, and even Walter, the physician.

---

[1] Both men are identified later in the chapter.

They all still hailed the coming of a great American literature, while admitting the poverty of what had so far been achieved. The third brother, in the *North American Review* in 1815, made a moral analysis of the problem, reproaching his countrymen for having lacked literary enterprise and intellectual courage. The only American literature so far, he observes, is that of the Indians. What white Americans have written has lacked national idiosyncrasy, and so it has none of what dazzles us in recent German literature. (This shrewd thrust was as painful for Americans as the comparison with Scotland, for the Germans too seemed to have started from scratch in the eighteenth century, literarily speaking. We must keep Scotland and Germany on our right hand and our left hand, as we examine America, to throw light on our problem.) In an article the next year in the same magazine, Edward Tyrrell Channing made similar points, exalting the sanctity of original genius, deploring the tyranny of the classics, using 'Augustan' to label a period of literature inferior to 'Elizabethan'. Bold, wild, free originality – who out of the nations of the world should produce that but democratic America? Where but in America was Nature bold and wild and free – Niagara, the Mississippi, the prairies, the mountains – why then such dull and feeble poetry? Again the analysis was moral, the solution an exhortation. While William Ellery Channing, in the *Christian Examiner* for January 1830, wrote in 'Remarks on National Literature' that the real product of a country is *men*. No one has yet tried to produce a superior race of *men*. This is America's destiny. And the most powerful means to that end is literature. Modern conditions of life, which stress privacy, favour literature, where the conditions of ancient life favoured politics. The new American literature we are waiting for will derive from this religious impulse. But that was 1830, and they were still waiting for it.

To help make sense of our problem, I want to divide the writers up according to the cities they belonged to, Boston, Philadelphia, New York, Hartford, rather than any other way. In those days, because distances were more absolute and active facts than they are now, people did belong more to the cities they lived in. In the case of writers, the nexus, the placenta, was primarily the magazine in which they published, and the literary club which contributed to and financially supported and generally encouraged that magazine. The clubs were social as well as intellectual organizations, members eating and drinking together; and newspapers, magazines, book-publishing and book-selling were all closely interconnected – anyone having a hand in one almost inevitably had a hand in the others; and it was by living in this complex of activities and personalities that a writer got his sense of what was likely to please discriminating readers, of how well he had done with his last effort, of who was worth imitating, of who deserved ridicule, and so on. This literary complex was of course somewhat different in each city, according to the personality of the city it belonged to. That is why it makes sense to call, say, Dennie a Philadelphia writer.

True, for a certain sort of writer, city life counts for so little that this way of conceptualizing his case would be too strained to be useful; for instance, the Romantic solitaries, Wordsworth and Emerson. But for the writers we have to deal with, it seems a useful tool. One immediate reward we get from the investment is the much sharper contrast between the four American cities and Edinburgh, instead of Scotland, and Weimar, instead of Germany. To belong to these two cities counted for a great deal in the best work of Scott and the *Edinburgh Review*, of Goethe and Schiller and Herder.[1] That is why it seems useful to ask, about the American writers, what city did each belong to, and how did it help him or harm him to belong to it. I hope to find, by asking that question, an answer to the main problem of the period.

But this is a history as well as an argument, and the word 'period' has its usual tendentiousness. It implies that the books written between the given dates have more in common than chronology, that they differ in some intrinsic way from books written before or after. But there are books and authors who are in the period only chronologically, and yet some account must be taken of them. The largest example in our case is the *Federalist*, papers written pseudonymously by Alexander Hamilton, James Madison, and John Jay in 1787–8 to promote the cause of the proposed Federal Constitution, the cause of a strong central authority over the individual states, and, as it turned out, the cause of manufactures, a National Bank, and a capitalist civilization. The debate on such issues continued, outside the *Federalist* Papers, until 1810, with contributions by Jefferson, John Adams, James Madison, Albert Gallatin, and John Taylor. These are important documents in the political history of the country, but in literary terms they are best regarded as the last flowering of the great political debate which had issued in so many pamphlets before and during the War of Independence. (Of 9,000 titles published by American presses between 1763 and 1783, 2,000

---

[1] I have chosen not to discuss London, because that had so many irrelevant advantages over the American cities, in size and in tradition. Moreover, it is not clear to me what character one could attribute to 'London literature' in our period.

were political pamphlets.) This debate was one of the most impressive manifestations of a 'high quality of life' in America, and, to
reduce it to literary terms, the exactness of language in the
pamphlets, the strenuousness of argument, and the unification of
thought and feeling, the passionate imagination, is worthy of study.
It is, by the contrast it provides, another reason why the literature
that followed, the literature of our period, is so disappointing. But
clearly, insofar as our period has a literary character, it is *not* that of
political pamphleteering, and in fact the *Federalist* Papers differ
from the earlier work in being drier, more formal, more purely of
political interest, less of literary-imaginative interest. The imaginative temperament of the age was Romantic, and the literary-
creative options it offered were scarcely compatible with the liberal-
rational mind behind those pamphlets. It is worth noting, by the
way, the lack of pamphlets setting forth rival versions of the United
States' aesthetic, in painting or literature or music. The equivalent
for that, when they finally came, were pretty ponderous essays in
quarterly magazines, very unlike Tom Paine's *Common Sense* or
*Crisis*. Had there been an aesthetic debate with anything like the fire
and pace of the political, the literary history of the period might
have been very different.

The *Federalist*, seen from a historical point of view, is a conservative answer to those radical pamphlets of twelve years before,
of which the most famous were *Common Sense* (1776) and *The Crisis*
(1776–83). These clearly belong to the early period even
chronologically, but *The Rights of Man* (1791–2) falls into the same
class as the *Federalist*, and Paine himself lived on until 1809, even
though – and this fact has a more than accidental parallelism with
the facts of literary history we are dealing with – he ceased long
before that to be a notable figure in America. Having gone back to
England in 1787, taken part in the French Revolution, and been
imprisoned by the Jacobins for a year, he returned to America in
1802 to find the Revolution, as he saw it, betrayed. He now disapproved the Federal Constitution (which he had praised in *The
Rights of Man*), he despised Washington, and he was in turn disapproved and despised by America, as an atheist and a drunkard.
Hooted by a mob in Trenton, New Jersey, literally refused the right
to vote at New Rochelle, he sank into extremest misery, both of
inward and outward life, and died alone, rejected, in 1809.

His silent but spectral presence, both before and after his death,
is an important fact about our period. How one feels about Paine –
*whether* one feels much about Paine – determines one's sensibility.

He was a true revolutionary hero. If words ever led to deeds, his did. If deeds ever changed the course of history, those he inspired did. And his own personal deeds were those of a hero; actually *losing* money on the best-selling *Common Sense* because he had given the copyright to Congress; taking the place in a Paris prison of an unknown Englishman whom he thought innocent. He is all the more powerful and poignant a hero for having also the weaknesses and vices of an adventurer of ideas; the impatience of all dialogue, the incapacity for close human relations, the brandy drunkenness, the personal squalor. This is not the place to analyse Paine's style or his thinking. I can only assert my own opinion, that if one believes in man's capacity to take a conscious stride forward, deliberately to abandon old habits, because he thinks them bad, and before he has acquired new ones, if, that is, one believes in revolution, then Paine is one's hero; and that, therefore, whatever one believes in, he is as significant a figure as Edmund Burke. For those who study American literature, he signifies the road not taken.

Alongside Paine stand Franklin and Jefferson. Franklin clearly belongs to the earlier period, but Jefferson lived on till 1826, and many of his letters and speeches during our period are of the highest quality and interest. But – and this is a striking fact about Jefferson – he remained as much an eighteenth-century man as Washington and Adams. This is striking because, being a man of so much more liberality of mind than either of them, he might be expected to be less easily outdated. One might object that all eighteenth-century radicals were outdated; that the great fact of the period was that its logic of history marched up to and through the American Revolution and up to and into the French Revolution – and at that point was refuted, became confused, broke down. There had to be a new, nineteenth-century logic, with its own radicalism and conservatism, before history made sense again. But in Paine's case, while that may be true for nineteenth-century readers, the twentieth century finds him not outdated. But Jefferson, who remains the most attractive figure in all American history, was a liberal rather than a radical hero. That very liberality of mind, that extraordinary range of interests and talents, that beautiful temperateness and health of temperament, prevented his making – in terms of a whole life – Paine's sort of unequivocal assertion. Not that Jefferson equivocates, but he balances, he combines. Jefferson's America, as much as Paine's, remained unrealized, remained an option not taken up, but standing where we do now, in the 1980s, we feel it as a less troubling challenge. The pressure on our minds now comes from people more like Paine. To them Jefferson's America is too much 'the best of both worlds', and until someone can give life again, either political or literary, to the liberal idea, Jefferson will stand a little to one side of the centre of our imaginations.

The literary forms in which earlier America had achieved distinction were, apart from the political pamphlets, the sermon and the description. Of this last there is one example within our time limits which demands some notice, Crèvecoeur's *Letters from an American Farmer* (1782). It had a considerable effect in its time, arousing excitement in, for instance, Byron, Southey, Coleridge, and Campbell; later it intrigued D. H. Lawrence, and indeed it is stimulating today. But this is the merit of the genre rather than the writer – his best quality is his naïveté, which in any other form might prevent our reading him. The material America offered its writers found its best expression in the description. Passages from William Bartram's *Travels* (1791), another contemporary example, can be traced as sources for Coleridge's 'Kubla Khan' and 'The Ancient Mariner', for Wordsworth's 'Ruth' and *The Prelude*, for Campbell's 'Gertrude of Wyoming' and Chateaubriand's *Les Natchez*. America has been an idea of extraordinary mythic power in the mind of the Western world, combining luxuriance of natural beauty with political and cultural idealism.

Crèvecoeur (1735–1813) finished his schooling in England, went to North America in 1755, and was very completely a son of the Enlightenment. The English edition of his book is dedicated to the Abbé Raynal, the French to Lafayette, and the very idea of the American farmer was a favourite philosophes' cultural image. In almost every detail he invokes the patronage of fashionable ideas. And though he manages his structural form very clumsily (he pretends to be a simple unlettered tiller of the soil, writing to a sophisticated British 'college man') he does manage to describe, for instance, the fight between the bees and the kingbird in Letter 2 in such a way that a great many of the ideas within 'America' are given a concrete, mythic, form. He is very attracted to bees and bees' nests, wasps' nests, even hornets' nests; they are models of industry, cleanliness, order, constructiveness; but at the same time he responds to the bright, sharp, destructive vitality of the kingbird. And even in his expository statements, his naïveté makes him interesting, the complacently flat-footed way he comes out with what most people merely imply. 'A pleasing uniformity of decent competence appears throughout our habitations. . . . Lawyer or merchant are the fairest titles our towns afford; that of a farmer is the only appellation of the rural inhabitants of our country. . . . we are the most perfect society now existing in the world.'

Crèvecoeur is, I think, a real myth-maker; as opposed, that is, to the fake myth-makers like Washington Irving. His is *the* Western – and therefore the American – myth, the WASP myth of creating civilization personally from scratch, reconstituting order and cleanliness and industry and productivity. Crèvecoeur's description of Nantucket, the Quaker Paradise, where men, even standing chatting in the marketplace, keep busy carving a piece of wood, is a minor classic in this line.

But *Letters from an American Farmer* belongs to an earlier period than ours, in all but date. In our period the description, the sermon, and the political pamphlet were yielding to the novel, the short story, the play, the lyric, the epic, the essay, the satire. America was now an independent nation, and it was time to write an independent national literature, to attempt the great literary forms.

The first writers we must consider are a group clearly associated with a particular city by their traditional label, the Hartford Wits, or the Connecticut Wits. These men all knew each other at Yale in the 1770s, and afterwards either lived in or visited each other at Hartford, in the 1780s. But the label of the city and the state draws attention to more than geographical or social propinquity. It announces an important ideological community and an agreement about literary standards, aims, and models, to the point of literal cooperation. Ideologically, Connecticut stood for the most conservative of all interpretations of Americanism, the most continuity with the pre-Revolutionary past compatible with uncompromising support of the Revolution. It was known as the 'land of steady habits', and it saw even Massachusetts as dangerously volatile, prone to anarchy and infidelism and worldliness. Steady habits meant primarily moral and social traditionalism, but it also involved economic principles, like a hatred of paper money and inflation and unpaid debts; political policy, like a firm hand to put down such 'democratic' uprisings as Shays's Rebellion in Massachusetts in 1786; and a religious policy of return to Jonathan Edwards's Congregationalism. They belonged especially by virtue of their religion, to America's oldest élite, the New England Calvinist saints. Timothy Dwight, the political spokesman of the group, himself a clergyman, dated the decay of Connecticut back to the decade before the Revolution, when British officers were the prime agents of moral and intellectual sophistication. The Revolution removed that danger, but men like Paine and Jefferson, with their 'French' ideas, were revealed as a yet greater threat. One of the Wits themselves, Joel Barlow, became a renegade, going over to what was thought to be, quite literally, the devil's party. 'Connecticut' was then a powerfully political ideology, and the Connecticut Wits were prominent among the men who kept their state steady. Timothy Dwight, above all, dominated the Federalist party there, and it was not until the year after his death, 1818, that that party ceased to dominate Connecticut. But he had ceased being a poet before 1800, and we are concerned with the years when he still was one. For twenty-five years the Hartford Wits wanted to be great poets as well as wanting to promote a certain politics, and the two concerns affected each other.

Hartford was not a large or important city, even by American standards, and as soon as Yale was measured up against European universities, it looked a small affair. Hartford only became incorporated as a city in 1784, and had no regular theatre until 1794. Its population at the beginning of our period was about 5,500 people. New Haven had only 4,000 people in 1795, and no hard pavements or street lighting. Whereas Philadelphia was the second English-speaking city in the world, with a population of 70,000 in 1800, and New York then had 60,000, Boston 25,000, Charleston 18,000, and Baltimore 13,000. But Weimar, with *its* neighbouring university town of Jena, was about the same size as Hartford, and in Weimar a group of poets with a 'reactionary' political position were creating a great new literature. Like Goethe, the Hartford Wits were determined to guide the national literature against the current of the times, and into the paths they approved. They belonged to the oldest American élite, and they had the confidence too of what they thought were new ideas, literary as well as political.

Intellectually, their training at Yale had centred around Locke's *Essay Concerning Human Understanding* and Jonathan Edwards's *Inquiry into the Freedom of the Will*, but in ethics and aesthetics the urbane spirit of Edinburgh had influence. They did not read Hume, but they read the moderates' answers to him, like James Beattie's 1770, *Essay on the Nature and Immutability of Truth*, and Lord Kames's *Elements of Criticism* of 1762. Kames believed in an innate taste, common to all men, in all times and places – an aesthetic version of the common sense of which Scottish philosophy made so much – and in a critical method that began with 'facts' and made 'experiments', rather than with principles. Yale, like Edinburgh, believed in seeing 'things as they are', which meant seeing them in

*all their* relationships, and in acting with the concurrence of the
majority in anything important. And this steady ethics allowed a
greater function to aesthetic education – for the refining of human
nature – than extremer doctrine might have. So that we find the
Wits writing Masters' Dissertations asserting the value of literature.
Trumbull's 'Essay on the Uses and Advantages of the Fine Arts'
advocated the study of literature (for its moral advantages) and even
pleaded for an abandonment of the neoclassic Rules. (In those days
vernacular literature was not ordinarily a subject for university
study. Mathematics, theology, and the classical languages were the
'solid learning' which Yale offered.) Dwight's 'Dissertation on the
History, Eloquence, and Poetry of the Bible' credited its authors
with literary genius, and defended them against the charges of
breaking the Rules. These are the marks of a strong faith in
literature, and the Wits also set out to write great American
literature themselves.

Ignoring such minor figures as David Humphreys and Lemuel
Hopkins, three are worth our describing. John Trumbull
(1750–1831) was very precocious as a boy, passed his entrance
exams to Yale at the age of seven, and was allowed to enter at
thirteen. After graduating, he spent a year away, and returned as a
tutor, 1772–3. During these years he wrote 'The Progress of
Dulness', a heroic couplet satire about fops and coquettes, much in
the manner of Pope and Gay, and much praised at the time. He
became a lawyer, serving for a time in John Adams's law office in
Boston, and then moved back to Connecticut, where he eventually
became Judge of the Superior Court. He was active in state politics,
was State Attorney for a time, but avoided serving in the Continental Congress. He wrote, on different occasions, some sharp
personal satire, but always retreated before the protests this
aroused. His whole career evokes the image of precocity, of a quick
mind, skilful in mimicry, that finds itself armed by education with
sharper weapons than it knows what to do with, and which therefore
avoids the confrontations in which they might be used. He had
practically given up his literary career by the time he was thirty-two,
and had stopped working hard at it by the time he was twenty-three.
And this precocity was rather emblematic of the Wits, different as
the others were from Trumbull in personal temperament. They
were all the late-born children of a culture about to decline, the
carefully nurtured and acclaimed prodigies of a tradition still determined to preserve what it had but not really eager to expand; on
the defensive against the new ideas of the time. Quakerism, Uni-

tarianism, Methodism, Episcopalianism, were all expanding while Connecticut Congregationalism was contracting. And in literature Trumbull rejected Wordsworth and Coleridge and Byron and Moore, even Crabbe and Southey.

Trumbull's most famous poem was 'M'Fingal', the first canto of which appeared in 1775. It describes the conflict between loyalist and patriot at the outbreak of the Revolution, in Hudibrastic verse, and though the name is a reference to Macpherson's supposed translation of a Scottish epic by 'Ossian', the actual figure of M'Fingal, the overweening loyalist, is closely related to Hudibras, another 'great' man with a rusty sword, a quarrelsome disposition, and a love of tropes. There were three editions of this during the war, and in 1782 Trumbull recast the poem and added two more cantos, and the whole thing was reprinted thirty times between 1782 and 1840. However, though it began as in some sense satire, it quickly became parody, and Honorius, M'Fingal's patriot opponent, is just as bombastic as he. And, ironically, after the war M'Fingal's rhetoric was often seriously cited in support of conservative policies – in the debate over the Federal Constitution, for instance – while Honorius was quoted in Fourth of July orations. Trumbull's mockery was too delicate, his criticalness and detachment of mind were drowned out by the loud political themes he tried to make use of. The whole story is an ironic comment on the ways literature and politics can mis-match, and on the Wits' unavailing attempts to marry the two.

The second Wit, more assertive, dogmatic, and powerful, was Timothy Dwight, Jonathan Edwards' grandson, known as 'Pope' Dwight. He too entered Yale at the age of thirteen, having already done the work of the first two years, and he too bears some of the marks of precocity, or at least of a certain thinness of experience. It is typical of him that *his* first book, published in 1785, was a biblical epic, 'The Conquest of Canaan', ten thousand lines of heroic couplets; presenting, as Leon Howard says, eighteenth-century Americans with Hebrew names, who talk like Milton's angels and fight like Homer's Greeks. There is a great deal of high discourse and noble gesture in it, and – someone has counted – forty terrible storms. Trumbull said one needed a lightning rod to read it. Dwight was certainly talented – as indeed was Trumbull – and that is most evident in the passages of description. But there is nothing in the poem that is his own. He was showing he could do what real poets, in England, had done.

His next poem, 'The Triumph of Infidelity' (1788) was dedicated ironically to Voltaire, and attacks atheism, rationalism, horseracing, drinking, Sunday amusements, etc. It is a satirical narrative, with footnotes signed Scriblerus, much parody of other poets, and harsh moral lectures on living persons. The 'hero' is Satan, and his victim-ally is Charles Chauncy, a liberal theologian in Boston. Satan's greatest enemy is Jonathan Edwards, 'that moral Newton and that second Paul'.

Dwight was headmaster of Greenfield Academy from 1783 to 1795, and in 1794 he published 'Greenfield Hill', a long but pleasant account of the countryside, of local history, of Connecticut institutions, etc. In Part 1 he imitates Thomson, in Part 2 Goldsmith ('The Flourishing Village' to contrast with 'The Deserted Village'), in Part 4 Beattie, and so on. Like Trumbull's, his love of literature never included a taste for lively *new* writing.

He became president of Yale in 1795, and remained so till his death, and was a great success, admired and loved by his students. Of his voluminous other writings we need mention only *Travels in New England*, published in 1821–2. This too has a good deal of charm, as he defends America against the sneers of British travellers, attacks the British quarterlies, expounds the virtues of owning property and steady habits, disapproves of frontiersmen. But we are a long way from the great poetry he set out to write.

The last of the three, Joel Barlow, is the most unlike Dwight, in opinions and in temperament. Dwight was always a father (he had looked after ten younger brothers and sisters during his teens) and Barlow always in some ways a son. This led to his being the most interesting case of the three, though not the most talented. For, leaving Connecticut in 1788, at the age of thirty-four he met with new figures of authority, in fact with Jefferson and Paine, and changed his opinions radically. The change did not help his poetry, however.

He studied at Yale from 1774 to 1778, and he had settled on the subject of *his* epic poem by 1779. He worked on it while he was an usher in Dwight's Academy and as a chaplain in the revolutionary army. The poem, called 'The Vision of Columbus', came out in 1787, dedicated to Louis XVI. It is a description of America's geography, and history, and future, told in the form of a vision. He took the history and geography directly from *The History of America*, by William Robertson of Edinburgh. Barlow's friends had helped and encouraged him in many ways. He was personally popular, and his undergraduate poetry had been highly thought of. For instance, David Humphreys helped him get subscriptions for copies from former army officers, and Barlow grossed 1500 guineas from the publication, with another edition issued five months later. Louis XVI took 25 copies, Washington 20, Lafayette 10, Franklin 6; there were twelve generals, and fifty-two captains, plus Hamilton, Paine, and Aaron Burr, on the list.

Barlow then became an agent selling Ohio land for the Ohio Company, and later for the Scioto Company, a shadier organization. (This story, a fascinating example of American speculation, can be read in J. L. Woodress's biography of Barlow.) On the latter's behalf he went to France, survived the collapse of the company, and stayed to take part in English and French radical politics. In London, through Paine's introductions, he moved in the circle of Blake, Godwin, Mary Wollstonecraft, and the Society for Constitutional Information. This was a logical enough development of *certain* tenets in the early creed of the Wits; the Rights of Man was a slogan of theirs in their War of Independence writings; but as applied by Paine and the Jacobins, it was anathema to them. Barlow had to sever all connections with his former allies in order to unite with his new ones. Like Paine and Mary Wollstonecraft, he composed an answer to Burke, called *Advice to the Privileged Orders of Europe* (1792), and a satiric poem, 'The Conspiracy of Kings', which together got him into trouble in England. In Paris, he was made a citizen of the Republic, and arranged to have *The Rights of Man* published when Paine was put into prison.

After a varied and successful career – he made a fortune by importing American and Scandinavian goods into France, and was a skilful consul in Algiers – in 1805 he returned to America. Like Paine he was out of sympathy with the country he found, and most of his former friends were alienated from him. He left New England to live in Washington, DC, to be near Jefferson. Jefferson and Robert Fulton, the inventor of the steamboat, were his main companions. (It is interesting to note how completely a certain life-style identified all these philosophe-radicals. Jefferson, Barlow, Fulton, Paine, and Franklin, all were inventors, all amateur scientists and gadget-makers, whose houses were full of ingenious devices.) Barlow revised 'The Vision of Columbus' and reissued it as 'The Columbiad' in 1807, in a version everyone agrees is worse, the diction artificially elevated and pedantic. He revised the most speculative book, the eighth, in the light of modern science, using the geology of James Hutton, the Edinburgh scientist. It was sumptuously printed and illustrated, but was on the whole derisively reviewed in America; and Barlow's deistic opinions caused him to be accused of atheism.

As has been seen, the form most practised by these writers was the epic poem, and it may well cause surprise that they should be known as the Hartford Wits. The label refers most directly to a brief episode in their lives, in the 1780s, when they were involved in political controversies over the sales of public lands and over the growth of the public debt and the debtor class; and when they expressed this concern by writing, collaboratively, a poem called 'The Anarchiad: A Poem on the Restoration of Chaos and Substantial Night'. This was published serially in the New Haven *Gazette*, and was more exactly a series of papers *about*, including extracts *from*, an alleged ancient prophetic manuscript in twenty-four books. This, like 'The Triumph of Infidelity', had footnotes signed Scriblerus, and like that poem ended with the defeat of Anarch/Satan, who, together with Daniel Shays, the rebel, is shown threatening Massachusetts. Barlow of course contributed to this poem, though it happened immediately before his departure for Europe and opposite opinions. The poem had little effect politically, and cannot be said to have much success literarily.

And why, with such high ambitions and energies, and with favourable circumstances, of mutual encouragement and external applause,[1] was so little achieved? The short term answer obviously involves their imitativeness. They were unable to achieve the degree of originality appropriate to their talents. But why had they to be so imitative? The case of Pope and Swift, or of Goethe, shows that conservative politics need not produce dreary writing. Their work does not suggest that they could have been poets of the first rank, but it does suggest that they could have written better than they did.

The next group of writers belong to Philadelphia, and though they are much less of a group, belong to each other and to their city in much more tenuous and tortuous ways, yet Philadelphia was so complex and powerful a phenomenon, so much more of a city than Hartford, that once we grasp all the different things it stood for, we can almost talk of Philadelphia Wits. But it stood for mutually opposed ideas in politics, and its writers, when they espoused those ideas, found themselves opposing each other instead of joining forces, as Trumbull and Dwight did. Sometimes they espoused more than one of those ideas, and made their own minds an ideological battlefield, like the city. It was America's city of painters (Benjamin West, Thomas Sully, Charles Willson Peale and his sons); it was the city of theatres (at one time about twenty theatres

---

[1] The first anthology of American poetry, *The Columbian Muse*, published in New York in 1794, gave over half its pages to the Connecticut group.

operated there); it was the city of science (Franklin's Philosophical Society, founded in 1743, and men like David Rittenhouse and Benjamin Rush); above all, perhaps, it was an international city. The most important linguistic minorities were the Germans, and the French, of whom there were 10,000 in Philadelphia at the beginning of our period, refugees from France or from Santo Domingo. German contributions to Philadelphia culture can be seen in names like David Rittenhouse and Caspar Wistar, professor of chemistry at the College, later to become the University of Pennsylvania. French contributions can be seen in names like John James Audubon, the naturalist, and Charles Lucien Bonaparte, who wrote several volumes of a fine *American Ornithology*; while Englishmen like Thomas Nuttall, the botanist, worked there; and of course Paine and the cantankerous journalist William Cobbett and Joseph Priestley the chemist left England to settle there. But perhaps most significant, in their immediate effects on the climate of ideas, were the Irish and Scottish immigrants. In the world of publishing, for instance, Mathew Carey, an Irishman, ran the most successful American magazine (1787–92), and became America's leading book-publisher, while William Duane edited *The Aurora*, a radical newspaper Freneau wrote for, and George Bryan was one of the political leaders of the old radicalism defeated by the Federal Constitution. The Irish were mostly radical. The Scottish influence was more evident in the world of learning and education. After Franklin, the two most powerful men of learning before the Revolution probably were the Scottish-born Provost William Smith of the Philadelphia College and Dr John Witherspoon of the College of New Jersey (Princeton). In science there was Alexander Wilson, another ornithologist; and the Medical School was founded in 1765 by a group of young doctors, all of whom had got their M.D.s in Edinburgh; Benjamin Rush wanted to make Philadelphia into another Edinburgh, and there were resemblances between the two cities. The leading printers, after Franklin and Bradford, were the Scotsmen Robert Bell, Andrew Steuart, and Robert Aitken, and what they published were (as everywhere in the English-speaking world) Scottish books: Robertson's *History of America* and *History of Charles V*, Ferguson's *Essay on the History of Civil Society*, Kames, Beattie, etc.

Philadelphia was, then, at the beginning of this period, a metropolis, the intellectual capital of the country, and the home of the extremest opinions on *both* sides of the crucial political question. Indeed it served as the national capital from 1790 to 1800. It was also the putative Jerusalem of the Enlightenment. (Voltaire said Penn had brought the golden age down to earth, and there was a tradition of such enthusiasm. Raynal, in his *Histoire des Deux Indes*, contrasted holy Pennsylvania with wicked Spanish colonialism in South America.) It was from French émigrés there that Charles Brockden Brown learned French, and was able to proceed to read through the volumes of that monument of liberal lore, the *Encyclopédie*.

There are four Philadelphia authors worth discussing: Joseph Dennie, Philip Freneau, Hugh Henry Brackenridge, and Charles Brockden Brown – that is, one Tory, one radical, and two with mixed elements. Of the four, Brackenridge (1748–1816) is least obviously a Philadelphian. He was actually born in Scotland, had a frontier upbringing in western Pennsylvania, went to college at Princeton in New Jersey (where Freneau and James Madison were classmates), and spent his later years some distance away from Philadelphia. But, for the Pennsylvania back country, Philadelphia represented the great metropolis (at the time of the Revolution it was, next to London, the largest English-speaking city in the world); Brackenridge edited a literary magazine in Philadelphia; and it was a Philadelphia audience that he above all aimed to please in his novel *Modern Chivalry*. Bookish and no doubt ambitious, Brackenridge tried his hand at several branches of literature: a heroic poem, 'The Rising Glory of America', written in cooperation with Freneau; two patriotic plays in neoclassic blank verse, in 1776 and 1777; sundry sermons and political discourses; a literary publication, the *United States Magazine*, that ran for twelve months in 1779. He had been ordained as a minister, but having abandoned that and literary editorship, he took up the law as a means of support, was admitted to the bar, and in 1781 moved to Pittsburgh – then a mere frontier village – to practice. He was thenceforth a lawyer, and a judge, and something of a political leader in his district. His literary efforts were mainly confined to his long serial novel, which has something of the character of a private journal or entertainment. It appeared in various parts, at intervals from 1792 to 1815.

*Modern Chivalry* began as another Hudibrastic poem, 'The Modern Chevalier', at the expense of a political opponent of Brackenridge's, an ignoramus with populist appeal. The scheme is to tell the travels of a man of education and leisure, Captain Farrago, who rides about America with his Irish servant, Teague, observing. They are modelled, distantly, on Don Quixote and

Sancho Panza, and Cervantes' influence luckily induced Brackenridge to revert to prose. It is Cervantes as modified by Smollett and Gil Blas, and there are evidences of Swift, too. Chapters of narrative are followed by chapters of comment. Thus Chapter 2 of Vol. 1 is headed 'Containing Some General Reflections' and begins 'The first reflection that arises . . .' There are long interpolated essays on law and constitution-making, and much of the 'action' refers to contemporary political events. Particularly in postscripts, and more and more as the book proceeds, Brackenridge talks directly to the reader – or to himself – about his career, about the book, about its sales prospects, about what he has written so far. He quotes critics' comments on the first two volumes at the beginning of the third.

The main themes of his satire are the excesses of democratic behaviour, the inordinate ambition of the unqualified, and the unintelligent choice the voters usually make. The Irish servant is always the butt; awkward, illiterate, a liar, a coward, a boaster, a sensualist, helplessly dependent on Farrago, he is yet constantly being elected by popular vote, while Farrago, the clear-headed, thoughtful man of principle, remains ignored, if not resented. Yet Brackenridge's attitude is not unqualifiedly conservative. He is committed to democratic institutions as opposed to aristocratic, he is very hostile to Britain and his imagination is plainly engaged by the life of the frontier. He is no Federalist. He is perhaps closer to Cooper in attitude than to anyone else, and indeed in temperament; a dry, detached, idiosyncratic mind, simply and rigidly masculine, judicial as well as judicious, and yet democratic by conviction. 'There is a natural alliance between liberty and letters. Men of letters are seldom men of wealth, and these naturally ally themselves with the democratic interest in a community.' Literature, learning, and the law are very close to each other for him; all are defenders of *real* liberty.

Brackenridge's book was the first work of literature published west of the Alleghenies, and it captures something of the frontier. One must say that he had practically no talents for either narrative or characterization, but the book bears the strong stamp of his personality. His was very much a lawyer's sensibility, curious, humorous, anecdotal, and because so much of South-Western humour was lawyer's work one catches echoes of Brackenridge in Twain and the Gavin Stephens side of Faulkner, as also perhaps in James Gould Cozzens, Louis Auchincloss, and J. P. Marquand. It is also a Scottish sensibility – Edinburgh, like Philadelphia, had a very important lawyer class – and in Brackenridge more than anyone else we see the influence of Scotland fertilizing American literature. He was born in Scotland (came to America when he was five), imbibed his neoclassic literary principles from President Witherspoon of Princeton, and expounds a Scottish commonsense philosophy. Exiled so far west of Edinburgh, even of Philadelphia, he of course repeated old fictional patterns, did not invent the new pattern the world was waiting for, as Scott did, but his eccentric, meandering disquisition has the merits of its idiosyncrasy, is in its way alive.

Brackenridge was a conservative – after the Whiskey Insurrection of 1794 – but a conservative member of the democratic party in American politics. Philip Freneau (1752–1832) was a radical member of that party. Both were involved at different times in newspaper battles with Cobbett, then a conservative, but for Freneau this warfare was a much larger part of his life. He was also much shriller and harsher in his invective than Brackenridge.

Freneau's practical life was divided between this political-literary journalism and commercial sea-going, voyages alternating with editorships. The most famous of the newspapers he ran was *The National Gazette*, which he edited from 1791 to 1793 in the interests of Jefferson and France, and very much against the interests of Adams and England. It mounted a campaign against Hamilton and the Bank of the United States, the symbolic agents of the upper class, and printed extracts from Part 2 of Paine's *The Rights of Man*. Part 1 he had serialized in the New York *Daily Advertiser* when he was editor of that. He was of course an enemy of the Hartford Wits, and his poetry as well as his politics were often attacked in the Hartford *Daily Mercury*, which Barlow had founded in his conservative days. Jefferson credited *The National Gazette* with having averted the threat of a revival of monarchy in America. Whether or not that would have come, politics were then very bitter in Philadelphia. John Adams wrote of 1793 that there were 10,000 people in the streets daily clamouring to drag George Washington from his house (Freneau intimated in his paper that Washington wanted to be made king) and that only the yellow fever epidemic of that year saved the city from bloody revolution. Later in life, when the national excitement had died down, and the balance had settled against his party, Freneau continued his journalism, but it was more literary, and he invested more hopes in his poetry.

As a poet, Freneau clearly had talent, and the group of his poems always anthologized do stand out from the mass of what was being published then. But it is striking that they are so unlike each other.

He never found his own voice, and he was not the sort of virtuoso who could make a significant contribution by sheer technique. He wrote every kind of piece, humorous, satiric, invective, epic, lyric, but he is at his best in the last, when he is most quiet and reflective. In polemic, in any situation of direct comment, his tone is habitually violent and unmeasured. In part, therefore, he was a simple victim of circumstances, of the contemporary whirlpool of controversy. Paine survived that without losing his individuality, but it was harder for a literary man, especially one with radical opinions. Literature, a less sovereign principality of the mind, protected its followers less well from alien conscriptions. One has small sense of what Freneau was like. Even his letters give the sense only of a bundle of opinions, and of ambitions to get into print. His biography by Lewis Leary is subtitled 'A Study in Literary Failure', and that word is again the one we have to record.

Joseph Dennie (1768–1812) stood on the opposite side to Freneau and Brackenridge politically. He was a firm Federalist, so firm in his contempt for democracy that he was indicted by a Philadelphia grand jury for a paragraph deemed actually treasonable. He was a New Englander by birth and training, but his major work was done in Philadelphia, and could be called Philadelphian in style. His migration, in 1799, is a good example of the magnetism of Philadelphia as a literary capital, though that position, which it had held for thirty or forty years, was soon to be lost, never to be recovered.[1] In the next period it was to Boston that literary aspirants would come. Boston was already reading the new and dangerous books, the German books, which Philadelphia never accepted.

Dennie was an essayist, a critic, and above all an editor. The essay was a very popular form in this period. Between 1785 and 1800 a hundred series of light periodical essays appeared briefly in New England journals alone, not counting those reprinted in the larger papers or on special occasions. Dwight and Freneau both wrote several such series; they were usually given some pseudonymous signature, and Freneau made use of forty-four such pseudonyms in his life. I have not discussed these essays because they were not on the whole a success. Their model was Addisonian, above all, and – for the more daring – Laurence Sterne. Dennie's famous series, *The Lay-Preacher*, claimed to combine 'the familiarity

[1] Royall Tyler (1756–1826) is another New Englander who made the same migration. A friend and collaborator of Dennie's, he is most famous for his play *The Contrast*, 1787, the first – Sheridanesque – American comedy.

of Franklin's manner and the simplicity of Sterne's'. Sterne was morally disapproved by the Hartford Wits, but Dennie, on his first appearance as lay-preacher in church, borrowed from one of Sterne's sermons; and it was this ability of his to respond to some of the liveliest writing of his time that enabled him to make a significant contribution to the American literary scene. His essays have some stylistic life, of a very elaborate kind, and curiously resemble passages of Emerson at times.

As a critic Dennie did useful work, of a kind then sufficiently rare in America. He reviewed *Lyrical Ballads* with understanding, and praised Wordsworth's later work. He understood exactly what Tom Moore and Leigh Hunt were doing, and treated them with respect. And he would copy, for example, a paragraph from the New York *Advertiser*, describing the launching of the frigate *President* in high-flown American rhetoric, and follow it by a mockery and a criticism. He trusted his own sensibility.

He went to Philadelphia to become an editor of the *Gazette of the United States*, but in 1801 he founded the *Port-Folio*, America's first successful literary magazine, which ran until 1827 and achieved a circulation of 2,000 largely because of his editing. The contributors, in the early years, included Brown, Charles J. Ingersoll, Royall Tyler, Alexander Wilson, and such eminent Bostonians as John Quincy Adams and Josiah Quincy. The first volume included both Adams's *Tour Through Silesia* and his translation of Juvenal's thirteenth satire; though it did not publish his translation of Wieland's 'Oberon' – a significant venture into the new German literature. Because most magazines in those days derived from clubs composed of the men with literary interests in the city, often lawyers and doctors, editing required a talent for social organization, which Dennie seems to have had. His first such group was called the Tuesday Club; later the Confederacy of Letters, including judges and bishops, banded together to keep the *Port-Folio* in existence.

But beside this talent for bringing men together, Dennie had a real interest in literature, and the *Port-Folio* printed, for instance, hitherto unpublished letters written by Smollett, and others by Boswell. But Dennie's taste, though in some valuable sense authentic, was undeniably narrow. He did not believe in American writing, and though this was a reasonable enough position, it plainly derived in his case from limitations of temperament, just as his mannered politics did. He was a curious man, a dandy both in dress and opinions, declaring himself that he could never be profound, that his talents were superficial but showy. His pseudonym was Oliver Oldschool, and the primness, the perverseness, the pout that the signature suggests are there in the writing too. He showed what could be done for letters in America – and something *could* be done – by adamantly and quick-wittedly following an anti-democratic line. But he as much as anyone made possible Irving and Longfellow, made hard the way of Whitman and Twain.

Charles Brockden Brown (1771–1810) was probably the most talented of these Philadelphia men; one cannot be sure because his opinions were so ambiguous, his temperament so muddy, his career so irresolute, so full of changes of direction, and his life so short. Born of Quaker parents who read French philosophy, he entered a law office at the age of sixteen, but was already planning epic poems on subjects out of American history. He belonged to a Belles Lettres Club in Philadelphia (1786–93), which sometimes met at Franklin's home. At eighteen he had a contribution to the *Columbian Magazine* printed, and in 1793 he left the law to devote himself to literature. He wrote for the magazines with some success, and in 1798 moved to New York, and became a member of the Friendly Club, and editor of their *Monthly Magazine*. That year and the next he published five books: *Alcuin; a Dialogue*, a brief and perhaps unfinished Vindication of the Rights of Women; *Wieland*, a Radcliffean or Godwinian novel which demonstrates the power of education and early associations – as opposed to Original Sin – to shape character; *Ormond*, another such novel perceptibly related to *Clarissa; Arthur Mervyn*, a novel with a powerful description of the yellow fever epidemic in Philadelphia, and a plot like that of Godwin's *Caleb Williams*; and *Edgar Huntly*, a novel showing how wealth and rank pervert the understanding, and involving Indians and panthers. Then there are two later novels, published in 1801, less melodramatic and less interesting, *Clara Howard* and *Jane Talbot*. Brown made something of a reputation as a novelist, especially in England, but no significant income, and the rest of his life he spent as an editor, with an occasional political pamphlet.

He is noted, and justly, for having adapted the Gothic novel to the conditions of democratic America, away from those of feudal Europe, which seemed so indigenous to the form. Instead of gothic castles, ruined abbeys, wicked barons, mad monks, torture cells, ancient manuscripts, we have cruel Indians and savage panthers and the yellow fever, ventriloquism and somnambulism and spontaneous combustion, and men driven out of their moral senses by too much speculative philosophy. And he used the form, as the best European practitioners did, to dramatize or mythify conflicts deriving from commitment to radical creeds. Terror was then what pornography is now, the lowbrow mode highbrow writers love to try. It is not certain how much he had read of German literature, but he wanted the reader to think he was familiar with it; he recommended Kotzebue, Schiller, and Goethe; he made use of Tschink's *Geisterseher*; and he offered the 'German' kind of experience – headlong passions portrayed in wild numbers with terrific energy.

Brown's opinions, or at least his tastes, when he began to write, were artistically radical even by European standards; and he is the only American writer of whom this was true. His early Journal contains notes on a Utopian commonwealth, a new religion, an alphabet, and thirty-two pages of architectural drawings and designs. And an early series for a magazine, called 'The Rhapsodist', defines the author thus: 'The life of the rhapsodist is literally a dream. Love and friendship, and all the social passions are excluded from his bosom. Nature is the mistress of his affections, in the contemplation of whose charms he is never wearied.' The man who writes this in 1798 is plainly in sympathy with the world of letters in Europe as much as Paine and Priestley were with the world of politics. He was ready to read Godwin's *Political Justice* – which had indeed a great effect on him. But by the time be became an editor, almost immediately afterwards, he was avoiding politics and fostering history, declaring himself the ally of Christian morals, praising Hamilton and attacking the French Revolution. The editor's policy shall be, he wrote, that 'His poetical pieces may be dull, but they shall, at least, be free from voluptuousness or sensuality, and his prose, whether seconded or not by genius and knowledge, shall scrupulously aim at the promotion of public and private morals.' What had happened? Plainly something ominous for American literature. Brown was not a thinker, or a fighter; the literary men he knew in New York were Federalists; and after all one may say that the whole world had changed its mind about such matters. But Brown was never able to write any lively fiction in the conservative mode. Perhaps the experience of being turned back, turned around, ideologically, was too discouraging; perhaps his talents were irredeemably oriented towards radical fiction; perhaps he never had real confidence in those talents – it was clear that he never *employed* them confidently – always hurriedly and amateurishly.

The stories are, in certain ways, well written. Brown's neoclassic sentences ring with clarity and with intellect. The clear and forceful statement is a pleasure in its own right, and so is the contact with ideas – the same pleasure as Godwin gives. The details of the narrative are detached from but vividly related to the ideas the author is dealing with. The anecdotes are well controlled for the purpose of narrative suspense. But as far as observation of character goes they are much less satisfactory. There is no minute-by-minute drama of realism, as in Richardson's novels, except in the scenes of terror. The dialogue is sparse in a way that suggests poverty of talent. And there is no controlling, consistent, credible idea behind, for instance, *Ormond*.

It is surely an exaggeration to talk of Brown as a significant novelist. There is, rather, the tantalizing question of whether he might have become one. Still, one can see why he was a favourite author of his contemporary, Shelley (Constantia Dudley of *Ormond* was for Shelley the perfect woman), and had he lived in Godwin's circle in London – had he mingled with Holcroft and Shelley and so on – Brown might conceivably have written more memorably. In Philadelphia however he, as much as Freneau, failed.

In New York during our period one writer overshadowed all others: Washington Irving. He earned over $200,000 as a professional author. During his lifetime hotels, steamboats, cigars and city squares were named after him. When he died New York closed down in his honour. A hundred and fifty carriages accompanied his coffin in the funeral procession, and a thousand people waited outside the church. His career seemed to prove, though in equivocal ways, that an American writer could be a national hero.

Irving was born in 1783, the youngest son of a large family, and his elder brothers protected him, first from his severely religious father, and later from the world at large. Until he was past forty they continued to plan various aspects of his life for him, in the belief that he was delicate in physique and temperament. He began to publish essays under the name of 'Jonathan Oldstyle' in the New York *Morning Chronicle* (1802–3). Five years later he joined with a brother and with his friend James Kirke Paulding in another such series, *Salmagundi*, which commented Tatlerishly on phenomena of the day like waltzing, tea-drinking, and feminine nudity. His contributions were signed 'Anthony Evergreen', and it is worth noticing how often Irving used Dennie-like pseudonyms and how similar their significance was.

In 1809, he produced *Diedrich Knickerbocker's History of New York*, a parody history of the Dutch colony, a whimsical combination of true history (most of the mock research is genuine) and outrageous falsification, with a good deal of reference to contemporary events and personalities, particularly political, and always from a Federalist standpoint. Wilhelm Kieft in Book IV, for instance, is a satiric portrait of Jefferson. This very New Yorkish book about New York is Irving's sprightliest work, at least as originally written; he revised it twice, the second time forty years after it was written, and each time made it tamer.

After this success he was editor of *The Analectic Magazine* for a year, and then in 1815 went to Europe for the family firm. In 1819–20 he produced *The Sketch-Book of Geoffrey Crayon*, which made his reputation on both sides of the Atlantic. This contains a number of stories like 'Rip van Winkle' and 'The Legend of Sleepy Hollow', plus essays like 'Westminster Abbey', meditations on mortality, descriptions of an English Christmas, humorous character sketches, etc. Geoffrey Crayon is a carefully contrived persona: an avuncular bachelor, a sentimentalist, a traveller, an observer, prone to foolish mistakes, irritabilities, rashness of heart, but growing more human and more winsome with each stroke. Irving made use of the eighteenth-century convention of foolish, sentimental, flute-playing strollers and loungers across Europe – Goldsmith, Sterne, Rousseau. But one feels as one reads – as was the fact – that he was much further from that persona than they: a very circumspect person. Goldsmith *was* foolish and rash; Irving only pretended to be for literary purposes.

The two stories mentioned had German originals – are in fact to some degree translations – and this represents the more nineteenth-century side of his offering. Scott, whom Irving much admired, had pointed out to him the importance of German literature as a source of fictional material. Irving spent some time in Germany, mostly in Dresden, which had a large literary circle with a homely social style, the Dresdener Liederkreis. He mixed with men like de la Motte Fouqué, the author of *Undine*, and Kind, the author of *Der Freischütz*, and the whole circle, known in German literary history as the pseudo-Romantics. Longfellow and Hawthorne were both impressed by the *Sketch-Book*, and set their careers to follow Irving's star.

After two more similar books using German material, which were less successful, he began a life of Columbus, compiling it from a collection of documents just made by the Spanish scholar Navarrote. His new book came out in 1828, earning him 3,000 guineas from John Murray, the British publisher. Irving wrote altogether 3,000 pages on Spain, about 1,000,000 words, a third of his total. The subject united the advantages of patriotic interest, for Americans, with those of current Romanticism. Colourful romantic history was one of the new forms of the nineteenth century, and it saved Irving the labour of inventing a plot, always the hardest thing for him to do. He made great use of Bouterwek's *History of Spanish Literature*, and of Schlegel's famous *Lectures on Dramatic Art*, which first aroused enthusiasm for Spanish writers.

In 1832 Irving returned to America, and wrote three books about the West, which also did well, both at home and in Europe: *A Tour of the Prairies*, *Astoria*, and *The Adventures of Captain Bonneville*. The second of these is an account of the millionaire John Jacob Astor's fur-trading empire in Oregon, and all three were in the service of the contemporary exploitive interest in the West, celebrating the adventure of exploring it and the possibilities of developing it. Irving's merchant brothers were quite important figures in the expanding commerce of New York, and through them he remained a citizen of the city.

Irving's taste was essentially conservative. His essay on Thomas Campbell, of 1810, praised him for obeying 'the established laws of criticism' even then, in an age when 'we are overwhelmed by an abundance of eccentric poetry', and when we are 'confounded by a host of poets of vitiated tastes and frantic fancies'. He had no liking for Wordsworth or Coleridge, even declaring that Leigh Hunt was a nobler poet than the first, and Scott a profounder intellect than the second. He admired Scott and Byron, was a friend of the 'society' authors Tom Moore and Samuel Rogers, and preferred the London of Holland House to that of Hazlitt and Lamb, or that of Dickens, whom he found 'outrageously vulgar, in dress, manners, and mind'. 'There could be nothing more humiliating to me,' he told John Murray in 1824, 'than to be mistaken for one of that loose rabble of writers who are ready to decry everything orderly and established – my feelings go the contrary way.' Essentially his work for American literature was to find the formula that combined as much as possible of what was harmless in the new Romanticism with a cautiously genteel sensibility, and to serve up the result with such evident grace and suavity that the American reader would feel culturally reassured. He has certainly been much over-rated; I see no way to avoid the conclusion that he was a bad writer; but he was a phenomenon of the first order in the history of literature. So many writers followed him, such as Hawthorne and Longfellow, just as he had followed others. Scott, and Moore, guided him in what to read and write. They had done the same trick for England, of providing

confections in the new style with – at least in Scott's case – some
genuinely innovatory insights and plenty of hearty substantial common sense in the old style like fruit cake underneath. Irving was a
rather more provincial practitioner in the same line, who continued
it into a later period. His parents after all were Scottish – indeed
one of his brothers was born in Scotland. Irving, like Brackenridge,
was in a sense an exiled Scot as well as an American; but New York
was a different environment from Philadelphia – politics mattered
less, manners mattered more.

In New England the years 1790–1820 were singularly barren,
said Emerson, looking back. He first broached this idea in a letter to
his brother William in 1850, when it was proposed to do something
to honour their father's literary achievement, and he incorporated
the phrase into his 'Historic Notes of Life and Letters in New
England'; there was in those years, he said, not a book or a speech
or a thought in Massachusetts. And indeed it is probably fair to take
Robert Treat Paine (1773–1811) as the emblematic poet for Boston
in that period. His real name was Thomas Paine, but he changed it
to remedy the embarrassing coincidence. He was a friend of
Dennie's and Tyler's, another firm Federalist (he got physically
attacked in the streets for his saucy opinions) and a favourite of the
Federalist gentry. He was rather like Dennie in stature and temperament, small, dainty, and shrill, and one can see that precocity –
of a different kind from the Hartford Wits' – would be likely to
characterize the spokesmen for the Bostonian class in possession of
the culture of the past and on the defensive against an Insurgent
Demos.

Massachusetts in 1800 had 20,000 Republican voters and 25,000
Federalists, and the latter included all the wealth, social position,
and education in the state. Passions ran high; men were murdered
in the streets for their opinions; and even the Rev. Joseph
Buckminster, a man of literary tastes and liberal opinions, preached
that Jefferson's Presidency would bring down the vengeance of God
on the country.

Boston was the most Britishly homogeneous, and socially the
most conservative, of all the large cities. But its conservatism was
not the effect of unbroken continuity. Its chief spokesmen in our
period were not the rulers of pre-Revolutionary Boston. Some of
these had been driven out with the British, and had been replaced
by merchants who had made fortunes privateering during the war,
and who came predominantly from outside the city, from Essex
County (Salem, Marblehead, Beverly, Newburyport) and hence

were known as the Essex Junto or the Country Party. Leading figures were Timothy Pickering (who brought Dennie to Philadelphia when he was Secretary of State), Fisher Ames, and George Cabot. This sort of change happened all over America, of course. As many as 60,000 loyalists may have emigrated during the war, mostly men of property. Unlike the emigrés of the French Revolution, the majority did not return. America was quickly becoming a business civilization; in 1781–90 thirty-three corporation charters were granted, 1791–5 102, 1795–1820 557. But in New England alone was the effect of these changes to stiffen the grip of the conservative upper classes; perhaps because in New England alone the end of the war did not bring the disestablishment of the clergy. The New England Congregational clergy had been leaders in the Revolution, they were still the leaders of their people in the Federal period, and the alliance between them and the other ruling classes was unbreakable. And so, of all big cities, Boston was the most averse to new political ideas.

The Essex Junto effectively silenced the radicals among the old leaders, for instance James Otis and Samuel Adams. They allied themselves rather with men of the old Province House set, which had centred round the Colonial Governor's mansion, those of them who, usually because of patriots in the family, had not been forced to leave. These included Harrison Gray Otis, Charles Bulfinch, William Tudor, and Josiah Quincy. This alliance proved a saving grace to the arts in Boston, for these 'intermediary families' preserved the cultural interests of the old ruling class much more than the new men. In one area, architecture, Boston flourished during our period, and Bulfinch, who invented the Federalist style of building, an adaptation of Robert Adam's NeoClassicism, is the artistic centre of the times much more than any writer.

But signs were not lacking that even in literature Boston had a remarkable future ahead of it. William Tudor, another member of the intermediary families, began *The North American Review* in 1815, which, though always ponderous, set a high standard in its first few years, and was open-minded enough to champion the new romantic fiction and poetry. In this were published several highly interesting essays on the plight of American literature. And before that there was *The Monthly Anthology*, which had pieces by Tudor and Ames and Josiah Quincy and poems by John Quincy Adams and Washington Allston. As Emerson said, his father's real service to literature was that he fostered *The Monthly Anthology*, not what he himself wrote.

But the true omens of the future are the essays by the Channings cited before; not only for their intrinsic intelligence and literary skill, but for the way they foretell Emerson. It was after all Emerson who brought American literature finally out of its doldrums; and stylistically, in Edward Tyrrell Channing, and ideologically, in William Ellery Channing, Emerson is already there, waiting to be born. And how was Boston, through these two, able to produce the writer America had been waiting for? One answer must be because Boston was reading German literature. The escape from the constrictions of the Federalist sensibility and the anti-Federalist sensibility did not come by means of political change but by means of literature itself.

In the general educated consciousness, Germany had scarcely existed before Mme de Staël's book *De l'Allemagne* came out in 1814. Everyone had read *Werther*, but no one had taken Germany seriously, so that when Ticknor decided to go to a German university, he had difficulty finding a German grammar in Boston. He and Edward Everett and Joseph Cogswell and George Bancroft brought back to Harvard in the twenties the benefits of the new German university world, long before the rest of America received them.

But his was philological Germany. Many Germanies were important for nineteenth-century America, some of them in deleterious ways, like the Dresden pseudo-Romanticism of Irving and Longfellow, and the terror novels Brown used. But the most important was the Germany of Weimar, of Goethe, Schiller, and Herder. This was William Ellery Channing's Germany. In England in 1819 he had spent time with Wordsworth and Coleridge, and back in Boston he read Schiller and *Wilhelm Meister* with his disciples, along with Plato and Shelley. He said, 'We want great minds to be formed among us. We want the human intellect to do its utmost here' – that is, in Boston; and as the means to that end, he wanted music and dancing taught in the schools, picture galleries and halls of sculpture opened, festivals fostered. He wanted the arts to educate mankind, in just the ways that Weimar proposed.

Weimar was also the Transcendentalists' Germany. Goethe's life as well as his work were of prime importance to Emerson and to Margaret Fuller. When we read F. H. Hedge in *The Dial* in 1840 saying, 'The work of life, so far as the individual is concerned, and that to which the scholar is particularly called, is self-culture': or when we read his title, 'The Art of Life – the Scholar's Calling'; we both remember Fichte's 'Uber das Wesen des Gelehrten' and Emerson's 'The American Scholar'. The declaration of literary independence itself owes something to Germany.

This is not the place to discuss Weimar as a city of culture, but it was of course the most remarkable one in its period – perhaps in all history. It worked out some striking solutions to the problems of the literary man in a world of revolution and reaction, and these solutions liberated American writers when they found them. To estimate, even to understand, the achievements and failures of Boston, Hartford, New York, and Philadelphia, one should put them beside Weimar. One thing that jumps to mind is the paradoxical apoliticism of the Weimar strategy. Goethe was of course involved in the governing of his state, but he turned his back on the big political ideas of his time, democracy, nationalism, etc. He chose rather to build up a community of first-class minds, interested in every branch of human knowledge and experience. They studied and speculated together about everything from Ossian to osteology, from the metamorphosis of plants to the Thirty Years' War. But among all these interests it is fair to say that literature was primary, for the leading men of Weimar, for Goethe, Schiller, and Herder. The study of literature was pursued just as seriously as that of science and religion, and the creation of literature – a great literature – was the paradoxical achievement of that (politically seen) state of general paralysis.

But Weimar's achievements became relevant to American literature only in the latter's next period. What actually got written at this time invites us to compare the American cities rather with Edinburgh. Here again we can do no more than invite the reader to follow up the idea. Politically, as Henry Cockburn said, Scotland then was dead; it was ruled, on Pitt's behalf, by one man, Henry Dundas, through the Tory Party; it was 'a village at a rich man's gate'. But just because the Tories were so completely in power, the Whigs, nearly all lawyers and so united by training and profession as well as by principle, had all the advantages of being an official opposition, all the moral and intellectual freedom which that can give. They were very close to each other, and yet remained on social terms with their enemies. And social terms, in Edinburgh, meant literary and intellectual terms. Ideas were pursued very seriously, though urbanely, in the society led by Hume and Adam Smith. It was comparable, in that way, with Weimar. Cockburn remarks on 'The extent, and the ease, with which literature and society embellished each other, without rivalry and without ostentation'. Thus Scott, though a Tory, benefited from Edinburgh culture.

Scott's novels and the *Edinburgh Review* do not, of course, compare with the work of Goethe, Schiller, and Herder. On the other hand, they compare very well with Irving's fiction and with the *North American Review*. What Edinburgh had to offer was a distinguished version of eighteenth-century urbanity turning the corner into a still respectable version of nineteenth-century sensibility. The test of a culture city is whether one feels that its artists did the best they could have done with their talents, and clearly one feels that about the Edinburgh writers much more than about the Americans. And some of the best things America did achieve were derived from Edinburgh. That eighteenth-century urbanity, expressed in architecture by Adam, was successfully translated by Bulfinch. The nineteenth-century historical novel was imitated from Scott by Cooper.

Goethe and Scott both died in 1832. So did Freneau, and Trumbull the year before. Goethe was born in 1749, and if we take the five years before and after 1750 we find that Dwight and Barlow and Humphreys and Brackenridge and Freneau and Trumbull were all born then; were all in their twenties during the American Revolution, and their forties during the French Revolution. Dennie and Brown also were born and died between those dates. They formed a generation, one which has to stand beside Scott and Goethe, has to be measured by the standard of their splendid productivity. And measured by that standard, their work clearly reveals a deterrent to creativity, an abortifacient, a blighting influence, the nature of which this essay has tried to define.

In summary, the trouble seems to have been that a provincial culture, hitherto quite flourishing, was blighted by the destructive strains of revolution. The revolution should perhaps be described as threefold, the American, the French, and the literary revolutions, all inter-related. The American Revolution brought with it the strain of needing an American, a non-British, style; and the strain of fearing popular violence directed against men of culture. America's first professional architect, Peter Harrison, had his house sacked and his library destroyed, in 1775, and in the nineteenth century Cooper, an aristocrat by temperament, was the object of vicious attack. Most artists felt to some degree uneasy in America. The French Revolution brought a strain to liberal and progressive opinion all over the world. It acted as a huge object lesson in the dangers of enthusiastic experiment, for all but the most committed. It separated the Browns from the Paines. As event followed event, the king's execution, the Terror, the Directory, the rise of Napoleon, more and more people felt, like Wordsworth, that they had been wrong before. And the literary revolution brought the strain of new genres and modes of feeling for which there were neither safe exemplars nor audience. No audience largely because of the association of the new genres with the dangerous opinions and events of the other two revolutions. As Van Wyck Brooks says, 'The freedom of mind of such good readers as Jefferson, Hamilton and Aaron Burr had all but disappeared by 1830, when the very names of Rousseau and Voltaire, so admired in former days, had become, as an observer said, mere "naughty words"'. When Adams and Jefferson died, in 1826, they were succeeded by Webster, Clay, and Calhoun, who were far from comparable in liberality of mind. The social and intellectual bases of literature suffered badly under these strains; the public became genteel, responding only to consolation and entertainment; and the writers became too confused to constitute themselves each other's audience.

Thus we have Charles Brockden Brown taking very quickly his cue to write the radical Gothic novel, but dropping it almost as quickly, bewildered by the course of events and opinions, including his own. And Freneau, swerving from political virulence to lyrical meditation, unable to marry the two, and thus unable to find his own voice. Thus we have the Connecticut Wits in their conservatism turning the pages of literary history back fifty years to find in Pope and Swift models – necessarily unprofitable models – for a literature of reaction. And Dennie, and Paine, desiring to be setters of standards and arbiters of taste, trapped instead into irritability and condescension. And thus we have Emerson discovering, through Weimar, the strategy of transcendence, which is, I suggest, in part a way of rising above just this dilemma.

The most interesting case, theoretically, is Barlow's revision of 'The Vision of Columbus', after his change of opinions, into a still more neoclassic *Columbiad*. He had plans, just before the revision, for a new original poem; but it was to have been on canals ('A Poem on the Application of Physical Science to Political Economy in Four Books') and after the manner of Erasmus Darwin. He did not know, we must realize, any models for a Romantic radical poem. He had met Blake in London, but he was not ready to understand Blake's poetry; or *Prometheus Unbound*; or even *The Prelude*; not to mention Goethe or Schiller. Hartford had not trained him, and neither would have Boston or New York or Philadelphia, to take literature seriously. These were difficult times for literary men all over the Western world, but also times of wonderful opportunity. In Weimar and Edinburgh, where literature treated with ideas on equal terms, with the living ideas of politics, religion and science, writers found it a golden age. But American cities did not give their writers the best chance.

# 4

# *JAMES FENIMORE COOPER: CULTURAL PROPHET AND LITERARY PATHFINDER*

## *Kay S. House*

Shortly after James Fenimore Cooper's death in 1851, the American historian George Bancroft decided, 'Another like Cooper cannot appear, for he was peculiarly suited to his time, which was that of an invading civilization.' The opportunities and abilities that made Cooper thus 'peculiarly suited' still interest us, for the thirty-two books he produced between 1820 and 1851 have helped shape American literature and the nation's sense of itself. Modern versions and perversions of his fictional characters stalk across our television screens, and those who read Cooper today find that some of the questions he raised about American life are going not only unanswered but unasked.

This is not to say that there are no barriers between Cooper and the modern reader. His 'tales', as he called them, were spun out leisurely to suit the publishing conventions of his time. Many of his heroines, afflicted by other conventions, seem pathologically vapid now. Cooper's interest in special subjects (sailing, agriculture, the American Navy, or constitutional law, for instance) sometimes forces the reader to wade through technical descriptions he would just as soon do without. Cooper made significant changes in his prose style during his career, but was always capable of producing passages that have the consistency of cooling mozzarella cheese. Not only did he write before the American language was born, but he was struggling with problems of craft (in trying to write of American society and ideas) that challenged William Faulkner and Saul Bellow. Finally, he is 'difficult' because of the unorthodoxy of his thought. The modern student who can cope with Faulkner's involutions of plot and language too often finds himself exasperated by Cooper's mind and concludes that Cooper is inconsistent when the real difficulty is that Cooper cannot be fitted into any of those few pigeon-holes that are supposed to represent all sociological or political possibilities. The demand for a simple label that Henry Adams rebuked by referring to himself as a Conservative Christian Anarchist leads, with Cooper as with Adams, to more confusion than clarity. Cooper's political position combines Christianity, the United States Constitution, his knowledge of history, and his observation of human nature. All are behind a statement like the following passage from *The American Democrat*, a book Cooper wrote for elementary-school children in 1838.

All that democracy means is as equal a participation in rights as is practicable; and to pretend that social equality is a condition of popular institutions is to assume that the latter are destructive of civilization, for, as nothing is more self-evident than the impossibility of raising all men to the highest standard of tastes and refinement, the alternative would be to reduce the entire community to the lowest. The whole embarrassment on this point exists in the difficulty of making men comprehend qualities they do not themselves possess. We can all perceive the differences between ourselves and our inferiors, but when it comes to a question of the differences between us and our superiors, we fail to appreciate merits of which we have no proper conception.

Even without the contemptuous chapter on political parties in the same book, it would be clear from a passage like this that Cooper's concern is not really 'political' but moral and cultural.

Robert Spiller's phrase, 'critic of his times', is apt for Cooper, but the nineteenth-century appellation, 'The American Scott', indicates the equally strong strand of romance that he twisted together with the criticism in his best books. It is clear from his work that he was influenced not only by Scott but by the classics, Shakespeare, Byron, Jane Austen, Maria Edgeworth, Smollett and Fielding. When Cooper began to write, Americans were troubled by what James Russell Lowell called 'the appalling question' of Sydney Smith: 'Who reads an American book?' By the time of his death, his works were available in Egyptian, Turkish and Persian as well as in all the languages of Western Europe. The reason for his success was not his mastery of literary techniques but his genius and his knowledge – both broad and intimate – of American subjects and scenes. Not only did he offer exciting American adventures to curious foreigners, but he reconnected – through the Indians, the wilderness, the sea, and the solitary men who are his heroes – his America with the mythical lost continents and the landscape of quest out of which 'America' as an ideal had been formed long before its settlement.

## I *Cooper and His Contemporaries*

Born in 1789, the year the United States Constitution went into effect, Cooper was in an excellent position to observe the changes made in the first half of the nineteenth century and could foresee, long before his death in 1851, the danger that the nation would be divided by a civil war. Cooper's father was a congressman, a judge, and a friend of statesmen like John Jay, George Washington, and Alexander Hamilton.Young Cooper grew up on a 40,000 acre tract of land, in upper New York State, to which his father had led a group of settlers in the 1780s. This boyhood home appeared to be the beginning of an authentic manor life; even the twelfth child in a family of thirteen could expect adequate land from a father who had owned 750,000 acres at one time or another and had controlled still more as the American agent for other investors (including Mme de Staël and her father). Beloved by the settlers for his help to them and his financial fairness, and admired for his services to the infant nation, Judge Cooper was nonetheless struck on the back of the head as he left a political meeting in Albany and died shortly afterward.

The author was twenty years old at the time and had done little to distinguish himself except for being a good student of classical languages and literature. He had gone to Yale at the age of thirteen with an overload of energy, charm, and Latin (compared with the other students) and a shortage of self-discipline and maturity. A series of pranks got him expelled shortly before he was sixteen, and after a year of tutoring at Cooperstown he went to sea on a merchant vessel bound for London and Spain. Returning a year later, he obtained his midshipman's warrant and served with the infant US Navy until May 1810, when he resigned because of his father's death and his wish to marry Susan De Lancey. The De Lanceys' Tory wealth had been confiscated during the American Revolution, but Cooper did not care about fortune, as he told his brother: 'It is enough that she pleases *me* in the qualities of her *person* and *mind*.' Soon after their marriage, however, the depression following the War of 1812 made land unsalable and the claims against Judge Cooper's still-unsettled estate forced Cooper to desperate attempts to save his inheritance. In addition to his own wife and the five children they rapidly produced, Cooper was troubled by the wives and families of his five debt-laden brothers, all of whom died before 1821. Farming, bartering, borrowing, investing in a frontier store, buying a whaleship, Cooper floundered and fought for a decade. Like later writers who also came from prominent but impoverished families (such as Melville, Hawthorne, Twain, and Faulkner), Cooper felt the sense of obligation entailed on 'good' families. Belonging to no church himself, he helped to found the American Bible Society, founded and worked with agricultural societies, supported and served in the state militia, and drew together a number of New York *literati* to form one of the liveliest social clubs of the era. Such activities brought him prominence but no profit, and he finally tried what his biographer, James Beard, calls 'the most quixotic experiment of all, the writing and publishing of fiction'.

His first effort, *Precaution* (1820), is not a good book in spite of Cooper's using Jane Austen's concerns and *Ivanhoe*'s length as a model. Even before it was in print, however, Cooper had started another, informing his publishers,

I take more pains with it – as it is to be an American novel professedly. The task of making American Manners and American scenes interesting to an American reader is an arduous one – I am unable to say whether I shall succeed or not – but my wife, who is an excellent judge in every thing but her partiality flatters me with very brilliant success.

Mrs Cooper was right, as she generally seems to have been. Readers bought 8,000 copies of *The Spy* (1821) in the first four months after publication and, partly on the strength of this success, 3,500 copies of *The Pioneers* were sold on the day it appeared in 1823.

Otherwise, 1823 was not a good year: Cooper's inherited lands were put up for forced sale for taxes and debts in 1822 and 1823; his stone house on one farm burned down before they had a chance to move into it; his infant son died; his household goods were seized and inventoried for debts, and Cooper suffered a sunstroke. In spite of his illness and troubles, he kept writing, however, and after publishing *The Pilot* (1824), *Lionel Lincoln* (1825), and the very popular *The Last of the Mohicans* (1826), he had cleared enough of his debts to go to Europe. After saying that he would be abroad about three years, for his daughters' education and his own health, Cooper stayed almost eight, writing and publishing steadily in spite of the time and energy drained off by travel, social engagements, and a widely varied correspondence.

His letters are a reliable indication of the range of his fiction. To John Jay's daughter-in-law, a woman interested in European society, he sent letters his detractors like to quote since they sound like part of the women's section of a newspaper. To his publishers and some influential friends, he presented arguments for an American copyright law that would treat Sir Walter Scott (and other foreign authors) fairly and help American readers as well. He tried to educate the Duchesse de Broglie (Mme de Staël's daughter) on the subject of Indian tribes, and corrected the *Revue Encyclopédique*'s errors about Negro rights, pointing out that in New York, because of 'blunders' in protective legislation, Negroes had more rights than anyone else. To an American friend charged with negotiating a treaty with the Turks, he sent concise diplomatic gossip. The president of the New York Lyceum of Natural History got the information he wanted about an American frog as well as a description of Paris's new giraffe. The Secretary of the Navy's request that Cooper not forget his 'voluntary obligation often to communicate with me' elicited letters about the organization and management of the US Navy. Cooper's friendship with Lafayette and his disapproval of the conduct of the US Minister and Attaché in Paris during the Finance Controversy of 1828 led to long letters of political and financial analysis, while his involvement with the Polish and Greek struggles for independence caused him to ask Americans for moral and financial support. In the course of commissioning paintings and statues, Cooper wrote not only to the artists themselves but to other Americans who might help them gain as much recognition at home as they were receiving abroad.

His letters show that Cooper could easily adapt his style and tone to fit the recipient and the subject, but he was absolutely uncompromising about matters of principle. He had serious concerns that he wanted to put into his fiction, and he wanted to be read by the widest possible audience. Having discovered that the public demanded tales of young love and of adventure, he got to be an expert at spinning out an adventure but had difficulty in producing what contemporary critics called 'pictures of sentiment and love'. Whether Cooper always shared William Dean Howells's belief that it was an American novelist's *privilege* to protect the innocence of the American girl or whether he reached this conclusion as the result of the escapades of some of his relatives, friends' daughters, and servant-girls, we do not know. We do know that the scenes between the heroine and the young man she will marry (if he turns out to deserve her) before the book is over, such tedious reading today, were too brief and too infrequent to satisfy the reviewers a century and a half ago. Cooper himself finally showed some irritation at this particular requirement, writing in 1842,

The reader will do us the justice to regard *The Two Admirals* as a sea story and not as a love story. Our admirals are our heroes; as there are two of them, those who are particularly fastidious on such subjects are quite welcome to term one the heroine, if they see fit.

By this time, however, Cooper had lost most of his public in any case, and even this testy remark was deleted from the preface to subsequent editions.

Structurally, the love story was invaluable to Cooper. The perils and misunderstandings that separated the young man and the heroine gave Cooper an easily-followed plot line to which he could attach everything else that interested him, and he could generally end the novel with a happy marriage. Few of his American readers seem to have noticed, much less cared, that the true centre of the book is always elsewhere – in a lone man or in a conflict of groups that happen to include the lovers incidentally. From this 'deflected centre', as it were, come all the human problems, cultural paradoxes and mythic emanations for which we read Cooper today. But it is only fair to remember that his brushfire burst of fame in the America of the 1820s was probably based in large part on his offering tales of sentiment and sound advice to the women and adventure to the men – all in a 'real' American setting. As late as 1911, in fact, the anonymous introduction to a textbook edition of Cooper, after criticizing him for 'transgressing the salient laws of accepted grammar' and for 'being inconsistent in his portrayal of character', recommends his work by saying

His best stories have rapid movement and a vivid portrayal of scene. The passions of his characters are elemental and need no critical acumen to discern. He paints with a big brush on extensive canvas in primary colors, so that standing afar and looking only for large effects the daubs do not disturb the casual observer. There is an easy obviousness about it all that lends permanent charm.

This kind of lofty stupidity helps to explain why the history of Cooper's relationship with his countrymen is, finally, a sad one. He knew, if only from the difficulty he had in keeping translations of his novels from appearing in print ahead of the original publication, that his public was international, but he directed himself so relentlessly to American problems and American readers that we cannot question his statement that his reason for writing was America's 'mental independence'.

In a country that 'never knows where it is going, but is always on its way', as the late Yvor Winters used to say, mental independence was proving harder to achieve than political independence. By the time he returned to the United States in 1833, Cooper had made a serious study of European governments and had been uncomfortably close, through his friendship wtih Lafayette, to the results of the July Revolution of 1830. To his dismay, he found that while

European liberals like Lafayette considered the United States the 'polar star of nations pretending to freedom', the Americans themselves seemed to have lost their bearings. 'The great error at home,' he decided, 'appears to me to be a wish to apply European theories to our state of things. We are unique as a government, and we must look for our maxims in the natural corollaries of the Constitution.'

Cooper accordingly became a student of the Constitution and at uncomfortably close range after he was vilified in the local press for closing, after repeated acts of vandalism, a picnic ground the Coopers had let the public use. During the 'excitement', the 'public' demanded the destruction of Cooper's books and three newspapers printed libellous editorials. Cooper answered, 'There is but one legal public, and that acts under the obligation of precise oaths, through prescribed forms, and on constitutional principles. Let "excitement" be flourished as it may, this is the only public to which I shall subject the decision of my rights.' Cooper became an expert, admired by other experts, on Constitutional safeguards, but with each judgment he won the tissue of lies, distortions and innuendoes in the press seemed to increase, and by the time of his publication of *Home as Found* (1838) not only Cooper but his family and his ancestors were under attack. Editors who cared less for the Constitution than for the 'voice of the people' or the 'spirit of the age' closed their pages to mention of him or his work. In some of his last books, as a result, Cooper used his novels to smuggle messages to the outside world, like so many notes corked in bottles.

At the same time, because he was being either carelessly or wilfully misread, Cooper became more explicit in his social criticism. Debates and authorial intrusions bristle from the text and when he appoints one character (never a self-portrait) as spokesman, that person too often appears overly explicit. If, as Henry James said, it is the business of the author to create his readers as well as his characters, we might well conclude that Cooper's weakness had been in creating readers. Yet, as the unpopularity of Melville and of James himself suggests, the American of the nineteenth century wanted primarily to be flattered and entertained. In 1834, Cooper was so discouraged that he wrote that he was going to give up fiction, and he turned for a time to histories and travel books until, seven years after his dismal homecoming, he yielded to the temptation to resurrect Natty Bumppo in a romance that combines the wilderness and the 'inland sea' of Lake Ontario. The resulting romance, *The Pathfinder* (1840), is the weakest of the Leatherstocking tales, but it put Cooper back on his true course, and in the decade of life left to him he produced the haunting *The Deerslayer* (1841), five good sea novels, the Littlepage trilogy (which describes almost a century of settlement and social decline), and *The Crater* (1848), a tale which describes the rise and fall of a republic in less than a generation.

These later books, particularly the sea stories, extend Cooper's moral and cultural inquiry further than his books had gone before, but the reader who begins with the early, better-known, and most available romances can easily follow the final development of Cooper's position, for it was in the first books that he arrived at the methods and materials that were to remain the foundation for his fictional world. Cooper lost his following, but he never lost his genius for juxtaposing myths of possibility (what might be or might have been) with realistic analysis of the American scene. Even when he set the action in the past, his concern was for the present and future, so that he made the romance into a form of cultural prophecy. It was clear, as we shall see, from his very first books that here was a writer capable of constructing a broad and firm base for American prose.

## II *Early Success with 'The Spy'*

With his second book, Cooper set out to be an historian in the sense he quoted from Henry Fielding: 'I am a true historian, a describer of society as it exists, and of men as they are.' The tale is set during the American Revolution, but there is no simplistic division of heroes and villains as there is in American textbooks. Instead, Cooper presents the Revolution, accurately, as America's first civil war. While be believed that the colonists' cause was just, and the thrust of the book shows this, he followed Sir Walter Scott in showing certain characters joining the 'right' side for the wrong reasons while others, for the best of motives (such as loyalty), found themselves committed to the 'wrong' side of the conflict. It is less the side chosen than the motive behind the choice that matters to Cooper. In all his books that touch on the Revolution, we find admirable characters who are loyal to the crown, and in a romance called *Wyandotté*, the head of a family and a minister (both of them well-intentioned and responsible men) spend most of a night arguing their proper allegiance only to find, at breakfast the following morning, that each has convinced the other and that they have exchanged sides. In Cooper's novels, in short, choices of allegiance are often made in what Huckleberry Finn would call a 'close place'.

Trying in *The Spy* to relate historical events and individual lives, Cooper presents the kind of division within the family that we generally associate in American literature, only with stories of the Civil War. The heroine and her sister are newly motherless because Mrs Wharton, already ill, 'sunk under the blow' of having her son called by the British to fight against members of her own Virginia family. The war separates this same son from his best friend (but without destroying the friendship). The head of the family, a weak man that Cooper charges with 'imbecility of character', is trying to appear neutral in order to save his property, and yet Cooper partially offsets his own distaste for Mr Wharton by telling us that he has been imprisoned for a month after 'kind neighbours' tried to get him convicted as a traitor in order to buy his lands. Cooper warns his reader, at the start of the novel, that patriots have died hated as Tories, while 'flaming patriots' have survived affluently on British gold. None of the characters indulges in the sort of rhetoric, Puritanic in its polarization, that Tom Paine used; instead, Cooper realistically and with some humour sketches a spectrum of opinions within the Wharton household. The heroine has a vague feeling that England is 'too distant' and that liberty involves 'the right to change masters' while her sister protests that it is a 'pretty liberty that exchanges one master for fifty' but is really more concerned about the drabness of New York social life if the British troops are withdrawn. The rebel surgeon sees the war as a battle of mercantile and agrarian interests, saying he fights to 'obtain as much freedom as the vicious system of metropolitan rule has left us'; another rebel (a proud Virginian and hence a part of the group Cooper calls 'the hardiest spirits in America') resents America's being a 'satellite of England – to move as she moves, follow where she wists, and shine that the mother country may become more splendid by her radiance'. Aunt Peyton admires the deportment of the British officers but is vaguely inclined to back the rebels because her friends and relatives in Virginia admire General Washington as a man. Meanwhile, a maid is confused by one rumour that the King wants all the colonists' earnings for himself and all the tea for his own family, and another rumour that says Washington himself wants to be King. Cooper even refuses to conclude that the Americans defeated the British, remarking instead that Great Britain 'became disgusted with the war and the independence of the States was acknowledged'.

It is probably safe to say that the average reader missed most of this, as well as the criticism of the management of the war that some colonial officers make. At long last, someone had written an 'American' book – in setting, historical framework, and characterization. John Jay had told Cooper about a patriotic spy, but creating the fictional character, choosing the setting, and picking the precise moment for the action were Cooper's problems. He took his cue partly from Scott and partly from the nature of the war itself; it was a 'war in which similarity of language, appearance, and customs, rendered prudence doubly necessary', and during which 'Great numbers wore masks'.

Cooper placed at the thematic centre of the narrative a peddler, Harvey Birch, who is suspected as a spy but whose allegiances are as impossible to trace as his wanderings. The importance of spies during the Revolution is stressed by Cooper's starting the action shortly after Washington had refused to stop the execution of Major André in 1780, and by his constructing a plot in which the main barrier preventing the marriage of the hero and heroine is the fact that the heroine's brother has been captured and condemned to death as a spy. Once he placed all the characters in a 'borderland', a territory between the two armies where 'the law was momentarily extinct and justice was administered subject to the bias of personal interests and the passions of the strongest', Cooper had all the conditions he needed for a freewheeling adventure.

As Harvey Birch emerges from behind various disguises, is glimpsed gliding across the landscape, or refuses to discuss his activities and beliefs (while the other characters speculate mistakenly about him), he seems not only mysterious but ubiquitous – like some spirit that emanates from the land itself. With the character of Harvey Birch, we get the first glimpse of Cooper's ability to evoke myth from the common man. It would be a number of years yet before Alexis de Tocqueville would make his prediction about the cultural effect of democratic government on man, but Cooper had (in Harvey Birch and Natty Bumppo) two portraits on record by that time. In what Philip Rieff calls 'the greatest single passage describing modern man', Tocqueville would write:

Thus not only does democracy make every man forget his ancestors, but it hides his descendants and separates his contemporaries from him; it throws him back forever upon himself alone and threatens in the end to confine him entirely within the solitude of his own heart.

In trying to account for the motivation of the common man John Jay had told about, Cooper had created a modern character. Credibility demanded, for Cooper, that this lowly peddler should have fallen from a higher state, so we are told of a fire that destroyed the fortunes and lives of all the Birches except Harvey and his dying father. Harvey will have no descendants because his 'blasted' character makes a good marriage impossible. His contemporaries are alien for a reason we have heard from Cooper before: People cannot appreciate qualities or abilities they themselves neither possess nor understand. Once his father dies, the only person to understand Harvey is George Washington, and even that takes explanations. When, after the war is over, Harvey refuses payment and Washington asks how others in the espionage network can be reassured that Harvey will be forever silent, Harvey's answer comes from Cooper's contempt for the man who can be bought: "'Tell them I would not take the gold.'" Washington understands this logic instantly, but a Wall Street merchant stopped Cooper on the street to complain that Harvey had no 'motive' for his actions since he refused payment.

One can imagine Cooper's dismay, particularly since he had taken other precautions against such a misunderstanding. One of his favourite devices was to put in a story a villain who actually is the wretch the hero might appear to be. In the course of making it clear that, while independence was better than colonial status, British rule was better than anarchy, Cooper created a group of characters who actually are as contemptible as Harvey is thought to be. In the absence of government, the inhabitants of the borderland are at the mercy of an irregular group of colonists called the 'Skinners'. Intent on 'relieving fellow citizens from any little excess of temporal prosperity they might be thought to enjoy, under pretence of patriotism and the love of liberty', these barbarians help to define Harvey's character by negation. These 'fellows whose mouths are filled with liberty and equality, and whose hearts are overflowing with cupidity and gall' are the direct opposite of the silent and self-sacrificing peddler. They move only as a mob in contrast to his aloneness. They set fire to a house full of women and wounded men after their leader promises 'plate and money enough to make you all gentlemen' while Harvey, penniless, is acting as a gentleman should. They are cowards, shooting from ambush, in contrast to his unarmed bravery. Like vultures they circle around the weak and dying, and they naturally break their promises and then taunt the victim for being so stupid as to believe them. Cooper is careful to show how the suffering they inflict grinds even harder on the poor than on the rich, and we have, in connection with the 'Skinners', sufficient proof of Cooper's classical belief that the purpose of government was primarily to protect the physically weak and the morally scrupulous from such predators as these.

As portents of the future, the characters in the novel challenge Crèvecoeur's early notion about the 'new man' America would produce and support his later, less familiar, reappraisal. Cooper shared John Jay's belief that love of one's country, particularly in times of national danger, had 'purifying consequences' on everyone's character, and yet Cooper was wary of radical expectations. He clearly did not believe that a Harvey Birch would naturally emerge from the hut in which we find him; patriotism might purify but there were limits to how much it could elevate a man. Cooper consequently suggests that Harvey has once had a 'better station' in life and had known cultivated people. Some American critics worry about Cooper's 'class consciousness', but we see from Harvey Birch and Natty Bumppo that Cooper did not expect the average man to achieve his full stature without education and acquaintance with some culture. As he has a character say of Natty, 'He was a noble shoot from the stock of human nature, which never could attain its proper elevation and importance, for no other reason than because it grew in the forest'. Explicitly denying any Rousseauvian notions about the virtues of primitive life, Cooper wrote that while he had known men who were *physically* like Natty Bumppo, 'in a moral sense, this man of the forest is purely a creation'. Cooper then goes on to add what seems to be a perfectly adequate rationale: 'The idea of delineating a character that possessed little of civilization but its highest principles as they are exhibited in the uneducated, and all of savage life that is not incompatible with the great rules of conduct, is perhaps natural to the situation in which Natty was placed'. Meant to represent 'the better qualities of both conditions', Natty and Harvey are possible Americans in a country that is all frontier. If, Cooper seems to have been saying, the human race was to have a second chance in America, we might reasonably hope for such men as these.

## III *The Leatherstocking Tales*

Before Cooper died, he correctly predicted that he would be remembered primarily as the author of The Leatherstocking Tales. This five-book series grew out of *The Pioneers* (1823), a book Cooper said he wrote to please himself after writing *Precaution* to please his wife and *The Spy* to please his friends. The leisurely beginning of the novel suggests this as the prose lingers fondly over descriptions of the landscape and the history of the region around what is now Cooperstown, New York. The fact that the Templeton of this book is named for Judge Temple, just as Cooperstown is named for Cooper's father, indicates an autobiographical connection even though no character in the book represents the author himself. The text is haunted by memories of the region as it had once been, a region described by Judge Cooper in his own book, *A Guide to the Wilderness*, published in Dublin in 1810.

In 1785 I visited the rough and hilly country of Otsego, where there existed not an inhabitant, nor any trace of a road; I was alone, three hundred miles from home, without bread, meat, or food of any kind; fire and fishing tackle were my only means of subsistence. I caught trout in the brook and roasted them on the ashes. My horse fed on the grass that grew by the edge of the waters. I laid me down to sleep in my watch coat, nothing but the melancholy wilderness around me. In this way I explored the country, formed my plans of future settlement, and meditated upon the spot where a place of trade or a village should afterwards be established.

The self-portrait William Cooper sketches here suggests Hemingway's Nick Adams (of the 'Up in Michigan' stories) as much as it recalls the Book of Psalms, and yet once we read the words 'melancholy wilderness' we must prepare for the destruction of this mood and the shift from first-person narrative to the passive voice beloved by proponents of progress; the words with which the passage jolts to a halt remind us somewhat rudely that we are not in the days of David but in an age of democracy and development. For his own fictional purposes, Cooper added Natty Bumppo to this scene, having him feed and shelter the scouting Judge.

Pleasing himself, Cooper gave a curious structure to *The Pioneers*. After the first chapter, in which a deer and a partridge are killed and the Judge accidentally wounds a mysterious young man in the presence of the Judge's beautiful, unmarried daughter, there are twenty chapters in which, as students complain, 'nothing happens'. And yet it is these very chapters that give resonance to the whole and keep the final twenty chapters from tending to melodrama rather than to myth. The novel opens on Christmas Eve and we have only reached the end of Christmas Day by the beginning of Chapter 19; the next two chapters rapidly telescope the breaking up of winter and the beginning of spring; then the seasons support the action to the end of the book where we find the inhabitants settling in for another winter and the old hunter, Natty, going off into the forest through the autumn leaves. The timing of the novel is appropriate, for in spite of the fact that this was the book that started the long Odyssey of Natty Bumppo, Cooper's subject is really the birth of a settlement.

Rather than create complex characters, Cooper stressed interesting relationships and complex societies. Templeton is a microcosm of America with Judge Temple at the head of a representative group of settlers (mostly of English descent, but including also French, German, Negro and Irish characters) who have invaded the wilderness already occupied by Natty Bumppo, Indian John (Chingachgook) and the mysterious young man. In the scenes of village life, people from various ethnic groups and social levels gather companionably (around a tavern fire, for instance) in a paradigm of the American future. Cooper clearly disapproved of Crèvecoeur's 'new man' who sheds all his old world traits; in *The Pioneers*, the hope of an interesting and balanced community life comes from preserving individual differences within a voluntary association of political equals. Attributes that could not possibly coexist in one man (French volubility and emotionalism with German stolidity and thoroughness), can coexist in the community and enrich it. Most of the book strikes us now, as it struck D. H. Lawrence, as wish-fulfilment literature full of beautiful pictures.

Yet Cooper gives us some disturbing portents of future trouble as well. In the tavern, we find a 'slovenly-looking' lawyer who takes the most comfortable seat, slanders Natty, and tries to stir up trouble against the Judge; he 'slinks' from the room as the Judge arrives and the best seat is appropriated by the Judge's cousin, Richard Jones. The Judge remonstrates futilely with a settler who has 'cashed in' his land and is now drifting, considering teaching school. Natty makes some surly remarks based on something he and the old Indian know and he leaves the tavern after saying, "'I have no heart for singing. If he, that has a right to be master and rule here is forced to squinch his thirst, when a-dry, with snow-water, it ill becomes them that have lived by his bounty to be making merry, as if there was nothing in the world but sunshine and summer.'"

When Cooper finally puts together for us the facts that explain Natty's attitude, we find ourselves confronting a question of rights that has haunted American writers from Cooper to Faulkner and Frost, and which runs through the Leatherstocking tales. The 'natural' rights of the Indians and their heirs have been cancelled by the Revolution and the land now belongs to Judge Temple, a patriotic and progressive non-combatant (being a Quaker) who looks something like a war-profiteer. The Judge is acting within his legal rights, and his attempts to use the land for the benefit of immigrants is clearly a social good. Yet, if might (or arms or of numbers) makes right, then the rifle-toting squatters and the mobs of Cooper's later novels, rapacious people who in no sense are acting for the benefit of society, have some claim to be acting within 'the American tradition'. Indian John, willing his own death in a forest fire somewhat in the manner of a modern protester, underlines this question of the extent to which the claims of the public can properly override the rights of an individual. More importantly, with the deaths of old Major Effingham and Indian John and the exclusion of Natty Bumppo, Cooper had hit upon his great theme – dispossession – that casts a shadow over all the Leather-Stocking tales and most of his other settlement novels.

If our humanitarian heads justify Judge Temple, our emotions are with the heroine and her young man (Oliver Effingham) in feeling that Natty, driven from the community, takes with him much more than his rifle and hounds. Cooper had not yet given Natty, as a character, the clearly symbolic dimensions he achieves in *The Deerslayer* or *The Prairie*, but we have even here a sense of Natty's life as being morally and aesthetically superior to that of the other characters. Living in harmony with nature, taking from it only what he needs to live, making his occupation an art, and obeying his natural sense of propriety, Natty has a classical simplicity, something of the 'Greek spirit' that Cooper found elsewhere in the simple but efficient beauty of the American clipper ship. It somehow seems appropriate that Natty's small hut beside the lovely lake, such an irritant to the greedy and prying settlers that he burns it in a ritual farewell to his old life, will be duplicated by Thoreau on the shores of Walden pond.

How did this illiterate and ungainly old hunter grow to dominate not only this particular book but the imaginations of Americans for generations to come? By comparison with the other white men in the book, Natty represents less a new way to live, by hunting, than a new way to *be*. At the bottom of the village's economic scale, Natty is morally superior not only to the villainous Hiram Doolittle but to another woodsman, Billy Kirby, who looks like Natty but who expresses his notion of democratic rights by laying waste to nature. Our respect for him increases even more as we compare him with the Judge's cousin, Richard Jones. Some of us fear that Richard is the 'typical' American: energetic, 'progressive', self-confident, ignorant of his own ignorance. Having constructed a monstrous mansion boasting not one but four 'fronts' and a porch so structurally unsound that the roof has to support its own columns, having imposed on the virgin land a gridiron pattern of ugly streets, Richard turns his honorary position as sheriff into a burgeoning bureaucracy and loses his head over rumours about silver mines. Effervescent Richard, like a polluted ornamental fountain, divertingly emits bubbles of evil. Having been given the 'petty concerns' of Judge Temple's household, Richard enlists the aid of greedy and stupid men and before long various kinds of pettiness have combined into a power that drives Natty from the settlement.

Weighing Natty's priceless services against the settlement's fines and court costs, we realize that Cooper has smuggled a chivalric hero in buckskin breeches onto the American scene. Cash means nothing to Natty, but character is everything. Having imposed on himself a code of behaviour far more stringent than any laws would dare demand, Natty feels keenly the degradation of being exhibited 'like a beast' in the stocks. His harmonious co-existence with nature, his obsession about privacy, his contempt for vulgar curiosity, his unorthodox friends, and his calm self-sufficiency constitute a set of 'aristocratic' attitudes. The Richard Joneses and others 'with troubled longings after other people's business', as Natty puts it, can account for his behaviour only by convincing themselves that the mysterious young man is Natty's illegitimate son and that his jealously-guarded hut is full of silver. By the time that the 'treasure' proves to be the dying pauper, Major Effingham, we are ready to agree with Natty that exile is necessary. He disappears into the west, a direction that means, in the American mind, both open space and death.

Balzac called Natty a 'magnificent moral hermaphrodite between the savage and civilized states', which makes him sound like a case of arrested development and which is wrong anyway. Natty is not *between* two states, but has selected from both Indian and white cultures the beliefs and standards he wants. Just as his clothing, in *The Pioneers*, combines the best items of Indian and white dress, Natty's instructions for his burial, in *The Prairie*, combine the Indian custom of burying a man's pets with him and a tombstone with 'something from the holy book' engraved on it. The grave itself is to be 'where I have lived, beyond the din of the settlements'. A theist with a sketchy knowledge of Christian thought, Natty tests dogma by common sense and his own experience, deciding that Christian forgiveness of one's enemies may be a good theory but would 'make for an onsartin life in the woods'. Worse, from a Christian point of view, he thoroughly agrees with the Indian system of avenging the deaths of one's friends.

Natty's language is as eclectic as his beliefs, ranging from the worst kind of poetic diction to an abrupt 'Anan'; he speaks with all the inconsistency of the auto-didact. And yet there is a freshness about the auto-didact's viewpoint that makes a character like Natty a natural link between Cooper's contemporary American and the old mythical America that Scott Fitzgerald was to describe as the 'fresh green breast of the new world' where man stood 'face to face for the last time in history with something commensurate with his capacity for wonder'.

It seems paradoxical that the mythical America that was to be the human race's second Eden does not relate as closely to the new settlement, where the opportunites are merely economic and social, as to the westward-moving Natty Bumppo. The paradox fades, however, once we correct Balzac's error of opposing the 'savage' state and the 'civilized' one, for in the Leather-Stocking series they are the same. Cooper made this discovery in the course of writing the series and may never have realized fully what he had done, but the reader is well advised to follow Cooper's own progress, going from *The Pioneers* to *The Last of the Mohicans* to *The Prairie* and finally to *The Deerslayer*. When Natty leaves Templeton at the end of *The Pioneers*, we are not tempted to say that he is leaving 'civilization' since there is really nothing civilized about life in this raw settlement, and we are even less inclined to think of the bounty-hunters, seducers, and renegades that Natty encounters in later books as being products, even the outcasts, of civilization. By contrast, even in *The Pioneers* we have a sense that Natty and Indian John (Chingachgook) are different. Some of us have long argued that Natty and his Indian friends seem pre-Christian, Homeric, but it may be even more accurate (given Cooper's religious faith) to identify Cooper as one of the many Americans who crave a Camelot. The only conceivable source, on this continent, for Natty Bumppo's chivalric ideals was that body of customs and traditions perpetuated by the Indians. There is little point in debating the accuracy of 'Cooper's Indians'; the important thing is that he gives them, the Delawares in particular, the attributes of civilization. Like Tolstoy, Cooper believed that whereas Nature and Society are always at odds (as in *The Pioneers*), Nature and Civilization are compatible. The ability of a people to live in harmony with nature, in fact, is one way of recognizing a true civilization. In *The Pioneers*, Natty and Chingachgook, choosing by a small and steady light the fish they wish to spear, are civilized; the settlers are the barbarians, dragging nets full of fish to shore in the flaring and dying light of a badly built fire. Natty's incredible feat of marksmanship that brings down one pigeon is civilized; Richard Jones's cannon blast into the flock is barbarianism only made worse by technology.

Going back in time to *The Last of the Mohicans*, we get not only the mutual indebtedness of Natty and Chingachgook but also the full orchestration of Cooper's elegiac emotions about the Indians. Here the Delaware nation is shown as the repository of precious traditions so that in a tense moment the oldest chief and the youngest, who have never before met, reach instant accord. Uncas is more than Chingachgook's only son, more than the last Mohican chief; his death breaks the continuity that a civilization requires. Anyone can operate a society, for good or ill, but a civilization must be perpetuated by the children it has fostered. Furthermore, Cooper's Indians live in and through nature, the tribal language, tribal symbols, and tribal legends connecting them, by means of the natural world, with the land and eternity. 'When the Manitou is ready, and shall say "Come",' Uncas explains, 'we will follow the river to the sea and take our own again. Our eyes are on the rising and not toward the setting sun.' The theme of dispossession thus broadened, the hope of reversing the process momentarily raised, the defeat of the Mohicans comes as close to tragedy as anything Cooper ever wrote.

In *The Prairie*, we find that Natty has gone towards the setting sun but is pathetically trying to put together, from plains Indians and the descendants of old friends, the fragments that remain from the civilization he once knew. The young people Natty likes know and care where their forebears lie buried, in marked contrast with Ishmael Bush who has abandoned his own parents, kidnapped a young girl from her family, and governs his own uncouth brood through physical strength and fear. Ishmael is another of those characters who superficially resemble Natty but who are essentially the opposite; Ishmael combines the vices of savage and civilized life as fully as Natty comprehends their virtues.

Finally, with the idyllic *The Deerslayer* (1841) in which the young Natty and Chingachgook ply between hostile, but sometimes admirable, Indians and friendly, but often despicable, white men, we come to the core of Natty Bumppo's character. Again Cooper gives us a brutal oaf who looks like Natty and who undertakes to teach Natty about 'manly' behaviour. Subtitled, 'The First Warpath', the book is a story of initiation in which Natty kills his first Indian, rejects the proposal of a beautiful (but slightly shopworn) girl, fends off the missionary efforts of her feebleminded sister, and worries about the appropriateness, for a man of white skin, of certain Indian customs. Young Natty's confusions, couched in a lot of talk about red and white 'gifts', come from matters of deportment or *mores*, however; where honour is concerned, Natty is no more uncertain than Chingachgook or his fiancée, Hist. Only these three understand the importance to their own characters (as well as to the honour of their people) of keeping their word, although the alacrity with which Judith, the beautiful white girl, grasps this point makes one wish she could have been raised among the Indians. Judith is the first in that long line of American heroines that Henry James said have been 'abandoned and betrayed' by their male friends and relatives. Hist, by contrast, so well understands the obligations of friendship and the psychological cost of disloyalty that she insists they go to Natty's rescue. Of course all three survive to re-enter the companionable solitude of the forest. There is no nonsense about nature reaching out to embrace them, but here, as in the rest of the tales, Natty and his Indian friends so clearly *belong* in nature that their dispossession seems to violate the spirit of the land itself.

## IV Cooper and American Fiction

One of Cooper's imitators, William Gilmore Simms, offered the best description of the formula Cooper had worked out for the books we have just been considering:

The standards of the romance . . . are very much those of the epic. It invests individuals with an absorbing interest – it hurries them rapidly through crowding and exacting events in a narrow space of time – it requires the same unities of plan, of purpose, of harmony of parts, and it seeks for its adventures among the wild and wonderful. It does not confine itself to what is known or even what is probable. It grasps at the possible. . . .

If this very American statement sounds familiar because of what Hawthorne and James were to say later about the romance, it should point equally to the qualities shared by such apparently disparate works as Melville's *Moby-Dick*, Twain's *The Adventures of Huckleberry Finn*, Faulkner's *As I Lay Dying*, and Bellow's *The Adventures of Augie March* or *Henderson the Rain King*.

Cooper kept on producing romances about the process of settlement, often linking characters and generations in a series of works. He included the Dutch settlers in some of these, describing them well, for instance, in *Satanstoe* (1845), the first book of the

Littlepage trilogy. His most interesting book about the Indian-white problem (as well as about American Puritans) is *The Wept of Wish-ton-Wish* (1829) which contains, in addition to Indian and Puritan extremists, the story of the marriage of a white girl and an Indian chief. (The marriage itself is a good one, but the characters' own consciousness of cultural differences creates, under pressure, insuperable doubts about their right to such happiness.)

When he combined the techniques of the romance with what he knew of the sea, Cooper 'invented' (consensus says) the sea novel. His first attempt, *The Pilot* (1824), was praised because it, like *The Spy* and unlike Scott's *The Pirate*, was 'authentic'. It seemed clear to Cooper that Scott, like Defoe and Smollett, used the sea as a backdrop and knew little about the sea or ships. Cooper loaded *The Pilot* with nautical language and shipboard scenes, but was not satisfied with his characterization of John Paul Jones and used historical figures less often and more warily after this. With *The Red Rover* (1828) he produced a successful sea romance and Melville, reviewing the book, found in it a catalyst for *Moby-Dick*. In this work and in other books he wrote after Cooper's death, Melville so obviously had Cooper in mind that we can readily believe his statement: 'The man, though dead, is still as living to me as ever.' Cooper had made his ship a microcosm and his crew representative of all races then living in the United States; his captains are mysterious characters with strangely powerful control of their crews. Modern Americans are not interested in the sea or in their own history, and these books are almost completely unknown. *The Red Rover* itself is so intense as to seem overwrought these days (although it was very popular in Europe when it was published, Berlioz renaming an overture *Le corsaire rouge*), but *The Water-Witch* (1831) is a delightful tale of smugglers sailing around Long Island during colonial times and *Jack Tier* (1848) and *The Sea Lions* (1849) are grimly fascinating books written in Cooper's last years when, as he had feared, the only standard that seemed to matter in the United States was mere money. Where earlier sea novels had contained interesting if enigmatic captains, and *The Water-Witch* and *The Red Rover* were haughty about anything mundane, the captain of *Jack Tier* and one of the captains of *The Sea-Lions* are simply exploiting the ocean. Nothing qualifies these men for command except some technical skill and their ability to finance the voyage. Here democratic opportunity to rise in rank through merit has gone sour; unprincipled men placed in command simply use naval discipline to oppress better men than they are. Both books are studies of greed and cruelty and deserve to be placed with Cooper's political writings along with more obvious examples of social criticism.

Cooper used the familiar device of Utopian novels, the voyage to an unknown land, for two such books of criticism. *The Monikins* (1835) is a Swiftian allegory that grew out of the after-dinner conversations of Cooper and Samuel F. B. Morse when Cooper was living in Europe; the satire is wide-ranging, hitting at England, France, and the United States (as monkey kingdoms of Leaphigh, Leapthrough, and Leaplow) as well as at fashionable political theories. The book is less tedious than many Utopian (or anti-Utopian) novels and more challenging than *The Crater*, the book usually recommended to people who want to 'get at' Cooper's political thought. Published thirteen years after *The Monikins, The Crater* is a simplified summary of political comment abstracted from Cooper's entire political experience, with a cast of stock villains (dissenting ministers, lawyers, printers, demagogues and gossips) who defeat and drive out an Utopian community that has settled on a volcanic island in the Pacific. Cooper, reactivating the volcano, blows the whole island back into oblivion at the end of the tale, and while the book is clear enough, as summary, its connections are with *Gulliver's Travels, Robinson Crusoe*, and Utopian fiction as a genre rather than with the mythic America we have come to expect from Cooper.

Far more telling, consequently, is the satire in the two-volume adventure, *Homeward Bound* and *Home as Found* (1838), in which Cooper connects the Effingham family (of *The Pioneers*) with the land of the Leather-Stocking tales and the legend of Natty Bumppo so that the contemporary scene is superimposed on the vanquished past. Bitter at the betrayal of the old opportunities and ideals, Cooper etched some characters so sharply that Sinclair Lewis's similar figures seem pale and fuzzy imitations. One of Cooper's characters, Steadfast Dodge, is as relevant an irritation today as he was to D. H. Lawrence, who called him by the wrong name but responded correctly to the characterization: 'Ah, Septimus Dodge, if a European had drawn you, that European would never have been forgiven by America. But an American drew you, so Americans wisely ignore you.'

Cooper's contemporaries ignored Steadfast Dodge, but they never forgave Cooper for creating him. One editor called Cooper 'a base-minded caitiff who has traduced his country for filthy lucre and from low born *spleen*' when these books appeared, and it did

William Cullen Bryant no good to object that the Steadfast Dodge characterization was a satire only of that particular type of person. As satire, the two books belong to that kind of humour Twain said we would not need in Heaven, that despairing American humour that James called a 'consolation' and that Faulkner himself uses when the only alternative is to stand speechless before an outrage.

Melville predicted that 'a grateful posterity will take the best care of Fenimore Cooper'. Generally speaking, posterity has done no such thing, and the newspaper editors' revenge has been taken by the librarians who shelve both Cooper and Melville in the children's department where there is little chance of their being found by anyone capable of understanding their criticism or of understanding the metaphysical extensions of their sea novels. The problems of moral navigation that these writers posed are unsuspected by generations whose faith is in The Absurd or who are committed to revolutions without goals.

In marked contrast with the public, however, our writers do know and continue their own heritage. Some of these backward glances are precise: Auden to Audubon, Robert Lowell to Melville or Jonathan Edwards, J. F. Powers' reworking of scenes from *The Pioneers* in *Morte d'Urban*. More generally, Faulkner's Yoknapatawpha County has the historical reverberations and the social breadth Cooper was groping for in his novels of New York State and the frontier. The feeling of the land that we get from Twain (in spite of his scoffing), Hemingway, Fitzgerald, or Faulkner is a legacy from Cooper's literary mythology, as is the haunting sense of continual dispossession found additionally in James and Henry Adams. More than any other early American writer, in short, Cooper discovered and put into print what Van Wyck Brooks called American literature's 'usable past', and he still has a valid claim for attention in our deafening present.

# 5

## EDGAR ALLAN POE

### Ian M. Walker

Poe is one of the most controversial figures in American literature. In his lifetime he achieved modest fame as a poet and short story writer, and notoriety through his reviews and literary quarrels; but the recognition he sought as a man of letters eluded him. His career as a 'magazinist' did not enable him to escape poverty; sales of his books were pitifully small, and the Northern literary establishment of his day was suspicious of him. Emerson dismissed him contemptuously as 'the jingle man', while James Russell Lowell declared in *A Fable for Critics* (1848):

> There comes Poe, with his raven, like Barnaby Rudge
> Three fifths of him genius and two fifths sheer fudge.

Today we are in a better position to appreciate Poe's achievements than were many of his literary contemporaries whose judgments on him were often soured by his own caustic reviews of their work. Moreover, the hopeless, isolated figures who inhabit the claustrophobic world of Poe's fiction, and who are obsessively engaged in exploring the irrational contours of their own minds, have seemed more significant to our self-conscious and neurotic age than they did to Poe's own. But despite continued and widespread popular interest in Poe, his reputation remains uncertain. Some critics, notably Yvor Winters, have found little merit in his writings; others, including T. S. Eliot, value him primarily because he influenced the French symbolists, and through them modern poetry. Poe's reputation as a writer has also suffered at the hands of certain naïve commentators who have confused the man with his writings, and concluded that his tales and poems were a frenzied form of self-exposure. Even some of Poe's most perceptive critics have seemed uncertain about his total achievement. Allen Tate in his influential essay 'Our Cousin, Mr Poe' (1948) declared, 'Poe's serious style at its typical worst makes the reading of more than one story at a sitting an almost insuperable task', while Richard Wilbur in his excellent 'Introduction' to *Poe* (Laurel Poetry Series, New York, 1959) is almost as ambiguous about the value of Poe's poetry and aesthetics as James Russell Lowell had been more than a century earlier; he concludes: 'There has never been a grander conception of poetry, nor a more impoverished one.'

But the reader who seeks to understand Poe and his work has more to contend with than the hesitation of the critics; he must also come to terms with the Poe legends. For many years after Poe's death, scholars and amateur enthusiasts debated with rancour the legends surrounding his personality, and these legends are still current today. On the one hand, he was caricatured by his literary executor, Rufus Griswold, as a drunkard, drug addict and irresponsible misanthrope; on the other, he was seen as Baudelaire's *poète maudit*, the archetypal alienated artist, caring only for Beauty, and struggling with a materialistic world he despised and which was hostile towards him. This legend has some foundation in Poe's life and character, and it would certainly have appealed to his sense of the dramatic more than the image of the hard-working, poverty-stricken literary artisan who emerges from A. H. Quinn's authoritative *Edgar Allan Poe: A Critical Biography* (1941).

Although to some extent Poe has eluded his biographers, the facts in his life are quite well documented. He was born in Boston in 1809, the son of impoverished actors. His father David Poe disappeared before Edgar was born, and when his mother Elizabeth Arnold Poe died in Richmond, Virginia, in 1811, he was taken into the childless home of John Allan, a prosperous tobacco merchant. His childhood seems to have been normal, and he received a sound education at schools in Richmond and England where the Allan family lived between 1815 and 1820, and later at the University of Virginia in Charlottesville. After a quarrel with John Allan about debts he had incurred in Charlottesville, Poe left Boston in 1827; there he enlisted in the US army and published his first book – *Tamerlane and Other Poems* 'By a Bostonian'. This slight volume made no impression on the reading public, and went unnoticed by the critics; but undeterred in his ambition to be a poet he published *Al Aaraaf, Tamerlane and Minor Poems* in Baltimore, December 1829. In 1831 a new volume entitled *Poems* appeared in New York, but by now his relations with John Allan were embittered beyond repair, and connections with his home were severed.

In 1833 he won a fifty-dollar prize offered by the Baltimore *Saturday Visitor* with his story 'MS Found in a Bottle', and this success helped him to an editorial position with the *Southern Literary Messenger* of Richmond. There he found a steady outlet for his poems and tales, and his critical reviews elevated the *Messenger* into the most influential literary journal in the South. Although he spent most of his adult life away from the South, Poe always regarded himself as a Southerner. His reactionary social and political attitudes, his contempt for the opinions of the democratic 'mob', as well as his antagonism towards the New York literary cliques and the Boston 'frog-pond' derive in part from his Southern loyalties. The aesthetic and elitist literary values which he established while he worked on the *Messenger* – he appealed for a literature that would be appreciated by the discriminating 'few', and equated popularity with mediocrity – belong to the conservative milieu of the old South and its ideal of the gentleman-scholar. Poe's own projected magazine, the *Stylus*, was intended for a cultural élite drawn primarily from the South: 'I wish to establish a journal in which men of genius may fight their battles; upon some terms of equality, with those dunces the men of talent' (Letter to Philip P. Cooke, August, 1846.)

In 1836 Poe married his cousin Virginia Clemm who was not quite fourteen. This marriage has puzzled Poe's commentators, though his contemporaries seem to have accepted it without question. In 1838 his only novel *The Narrative of Arthur Gordon Pym* appeared, followed in 1840 by his collected *Tales of the Grotesque and Arabesque*, but neither work brought him much financial return or literary fame. By this time he had parted company with the *Messenger* and moved on to Philadelphia and editorial work with *Burton's Gentleman's Magazine* and *Graham's Magazine*, but his plans to own and edit a superior literary journal based on his own critical principles came to nothing. The year 1845 was Poe's *annus mirabilis* – 'The Raven' caused a brief popular sensation; he owned the *Broadway Journal*; a new volume of *Tales* appeared, followed by his final book of verse, *The Raven and Other Poems*. But at the same time poverty, a dangerous proclivity to drink, and worry about Virginia's health were affecting Poe's unstable temperament. In January, 1846, the *Broadway Journal* collapsed through lack of financial backing, and Virginia was clearly dying from consumption. Poe was always a difficult person to work with as his employers discovered; he was edgy, arrogant and suspicious, and in 1845 he became obsessed with denouncing Longfellow as a plagiarist. There was little justification for Poe's belief that Longfellow had plagiarized him, but in an acrimonious series of articles in the *Broadway Journal* he accused the New England poet of being 'not only a servile imitator, but a most insolent literary thief'.

The death of Virginia in 1847 precipitated a serious crisis in Poe's life from which he never fully recovered. There is a frenetic quality about the last two years of his life: he claimed to be in love with Annie Richmond (a married woman) and Sarah Helen Whitman (a widow with literary pretensions), but while his emotional involvement with these ladies stimulated him to continue writing poetry, his private letters to them reveal a confused, and at times, sick man. In 1848 Poe published *Eureka*, a book-length prose-poem on the nature and destiny of the universe, which he believed to be his greatest achievement. In July 1849 he wrote to Mrs Clemm: 'I have no desire to live since I have done "Eureka". I could accomplish nothing more.' He died in Baltimore in October 1849, at the age of forty. Although Poe's life was scarred by poverty, literary neglect and personal misfortunes, he never wavered in his devotion to the craft of literature, and to his dream of establishing genuine critical standards in American letters. A few months before his death he wrote to his friend F. W. Thomas:

Depend upon it, after all, Thomas, Literature is the most noble of professions. In fact, it is about the only one fit for a man. For my own part, there is no seducing me from the path. I shall be a littérateur, at least, all my life; nor would I abandon the hopes which still lead me on for all the gold in California.

Although Poe is generally classified as a 'romantic' writer, art was never for him a matter of casual inspiration, but a discipline which demanded the highest degree of imagination, and also intense intellectual endeavour. In his essay 'Peter Snook' (1836) he instructed his readers that, 'There is no greater mistake than the supposition that a true originality is a mere matter of impulse or inspiration. To originate, is carefully, patiently and understandingly to combine.' Later in 'The Philosophy of Composition' (1846) he attempted to illustrate that the artist is a highly conscious craftsman who establishes his effect through a variety of literary contrivances:

Most writers – poets in especial – prefer having it understood that they compose by a species of fine frenzy – an ecstatic intuition – and would positively shudder at letting the public take a peep behind the scenes, at the elaborate and vacillating crudities of thought – at the true purposes seized only at the last moment – at the innumerable glimpses of idea that arrived not at the maturity of full view – at the fully matured fancies discarded in despair as unmanageable – at the cautious selections and rejections – at the painful erasures and interpolations – in a word, at the wheels and pinions –

the tackle for scene-shifting – the step-ladders and demon-traps – the cock's feathers, the red paint and the black patches, which in ninety-nine cases out of the hundred, constitute the properties of the literary *histrio*.

The structures of Poe's best tales and poems are not arbitrary, but are determined by a carefully worked out philosophy of literary unity which he derived in part from his reading of Coleridge and the German critic A. W. Schlegel in translation. This philosophy of literature was itself based upon a much wider theory of cosmic unity which Poe elaborated in *Eureka*. In *Eureka* God is the Supreme Artist who created the universe according to an aesthetic principle of unity; each atom in the universe of matter relates to, and is dependent upon, every other atom so that no single part can be removed without destroying the original unity of the 'plot' of creation:

That each atom attracts – sympathizes with the most delicate movements of every other atom, and with each and with all at the same time, and forever, and according to a determinate law of which the complexity, even considered by itself solely, is utterly beyond the grasp of the imagination. If I propose to ascertain the influence of one mote in a sunbeam on its neighbouring mote, I cannot accomplish my purpose without first counting and weighing all the atoms in the Universe, and defining the precise positions of all at one particular moment. If I venture to displace, by even the billionth part of an inch, the microscopical speck of dust which lies now on the point of my finger, what is the character of that act upon which I have adventured? I have done a deed which shakes the Moon in her path, which causes the Sun to be no longer the Sun, which alters forever the destiny of the multitudinous myriads of stars that roll and glow in the majestic presence of their Creator.

The human artist is thus a God-player who mirrors Divine creativity, and in his microcosm of art seeks to emulate the coherence and beauty of the universe. The artist's search for absolute artistic unity is, of course, doomed to failure since the human mind is finite and fallible; yet the example of God's aesthetically perfect creation must always remain the artist's dream and inspiration:

In the construction of *plot*, for example, in fictitious literature, we should aim at so arranging the points, or incidents, that we cannot distinctly see, in respect to any one of them, whether that one depends from any one other or upholds it. In this sense, of course, perfection of plot is unattainable *in fact* – because Man is the constructor. The plots of God are perfect. The Universe is a plot of God.

'The American Drama' (1845)

According to Poe's literary theory the unity of a work of art comprises two important ideas. First, there must be a unity of structure in which each part relates to the whole; and second, the artist must strive to arrange each element in his work in order to emphasize one prevailing idea, and by so doing he creates a psychological 'unity of effect' on the reader. But this essential 'unity of effect' can only be achieved by the artist who understands the psychological basis of his art, and who accepts the limitations of the human mind. The long poem and the novel are misconceived art forms, Poe maintains, because they neglect the all important principle of 'unity of effect' – in a novel the reader cannot hold all the elements of the structure together in his mind. Poe explained this idea in a review of Dickens's *Watkins Tottle and Other Sketches* (1836)—the American title of *Sketches by Boz*:

We cannot bring ourselves to believe that less actual ability is required in the composition of a really good 'brief article' than in a fashionable novel of the usual dimensions. The novel certainly requires what is denominated a sustained effort – but this is a matter of mere perseverance, and has but a collateral relation to talent. On the other hand – unity of effect, a quality not easily appreciated or indeed comprehended by an ordinary mind, and a *desideratum* difficult of attainment even by those who can conceive it – is indispensible in the 'brief article' and not so in the common novel. The latter, if admired at all, is admired for its detached passages, without reference to the work as a whole – or without reference to any general design – which, if it even exist in some measure, will be found to have occupied but little of the writer's attention, and cannot, from the length of the narrative, be taken in at one view, by the reader.

By 1842 when he came to write his famous review of Hawthorne's *Twice Told Tales*, Poe had moved on from merely defending the short story form; by now he was more confident and had more experience in writing, and the example of Hawthorne led him to affirm that the short story was the sole fictional form in which the true artist could fulfil his longing for aesthetic unity:

A skilful literary artist has constructed a tale. If wise, he has not fashioned his thoughts to accommodate his incidents; but having conceived, with deliberate care, a certain unique or single effect to be wrought out, he then invents such incidents – he then combines such events as may best aid him in establishing this preconceived effect. If his very initial sentence tend not to the outbringing of this effect, then he has failed in his first step. In the whole composition there should be no word written, of which the tendency, direct or indirect, is not to the one pre-established design.

Poe's philosophy of the short story deeply influenced his practice as a writer, and an examination of one story, 'The Cask of Amontillado' (1846), will reveal how he embodied his principles of unity in his own art. The revenge theme is commonplace enough, but it is how Poe treats the theme that makes this story interesting. He wastes no time on introductory preambles; the first paragraph establishes the situation, and the reader calls to mind Poe's dictum that not one word in a tale should be wasted:

> The thousand injuries of Fortunato I had borne as I best could, but when he ventured upon insult I vowed revenge. You, who so well know the nature of my soul, will not suppose, however, that I gave utterance to a threat. *At length* I would be avenged; this was a point definitely settled – but the very definitiveness with which it was resolved precluded the idea of risk. I must not only punish but punish with impunity. A wrong is unredressed when retribution overtakes its redresser. It is equally unredressed when the avenger fails to make himself felt as such to him who has done the wrong.

The plot of the story is made up of mutually dependent parts that spring inevitably out of Montresor's craving for revenge. The time of the story is evening, the place Italy during a carnival. Montresor the revenger meets his victim, the ironically named Fortunato, who is drunk and dressed in a clown's outfit with bells that jangle from the top of his cap. We never learn the exact nature of the wrong Montresor alleges he has suffered at the hands of Fortunato, and we never need to know because this is not a part of Montresor's story. We see things only through Montresor's ironic, obsessional mind, and he is not interested in reasons for his revenge if any indeed exist, but only in how he carries it out. The events in the story evolve not out of accidental occurrences, but directly out of the characters of the two protagonists. Once Montresor brooding obsessively over his peculiar revenge meets Fortunato who is drunk, but still self-confident and motivated by an arrogant pride in his knowledge of wines, the dénouement is in sight; Fortunato's foolish complacency is a perfect complement to Montresor's cunning and mock humility. The story's tone derives from the patterns of irony that permeate and unify it. The victim's name and his fool's dress are obvious examples of irony, but the conversational exchanges between the two protagonists are more complex. Montresor encourages Fortunato into the cellar by pretending to discourage him; he tells him of its dangers and inconvenience, and then cunningly suggests that Fortunato's rival Luchesi might be consulted:

'As you are engaged, I am on my way to Luchesi. If any one has a critical turn it is he. He will tell me—'

'Luchesi cannot tell Amontillado from Sherry.'

'And yet some fools will have it that his taste is a match for your own.'

'Come, let us go?'

'Whither?'

'To your vaults.'

'My friend, no; I will not impose upon your good nature, I perceive you have an engagement. Luchesi—'

'I have no engagement; – come.'

'My friend, no. It is not the engagement, but the severe cold with which I perceive you are afflicted. The vaults are insufferably damp. They are encrusted with nitre.'

'Let us go, nevertheless. The cold is merely nothing. Amontillado! You have been imposed upon. And as for Luchesi, he cannot distinguish Sherry from Amontillado. . . .'

'Come,' I said, with decision, 'we will go back; your health is precious. You are rich, respected, admired, beloved; you are happy, as once I was. You are a man to be missed. For me it is no matter. We will go back; you will be ill, and I cannot be responsible. Besides, there is Luchesi—'

'Enough,' he said; 'the cough is a mere nothing; it will not kill me. I shall not die of a cough.'

'True – true,' I replied; 'and, indeed, I had no intention of alarming you unnecessarily – but you should use all proper caution. . . .'

These patterns of irony add a further dimension to the story – that of acute psychological realism, through which we can follow the cruel cunning of Montresor and watch him destroy Fortunato word by word. None of the talk is irrelevant gossip – the discussion about masons, the Montresor family motto and the buried bones are part of Montresor's revenge; the conversation and plot of the story are indistinguishable. Montresor is an artist with words; he knows the exact meaning of what he says, whereas Fortunato does not until the very end when the jangling of the bells on his fool's cap mock his wordless recognition of his fate.

Almost from the beginning of his career Poe was accused by polite literary journals of offences against 'good taste', and his tales of psychological terror were often dismissed as mere gothic melodramas of the 'forcible-feeble and the shallow-profound' school made popular in America by the influential British journals *Blackwood's Edinburgh Magazine, Fraser's Magazine*, and the *New Monthly Magazine*. Although Poe was well acquainted with *Blackwood's* tales of terror, and admired some of their attempts to investigate abnormal states of mind, he was also fully aware of their absurdities and excesses which he satirized in 'How to Write a Blackwood Article'

(1838), 'A Predicament' (1838) and 'A Decided Loss' (1832). In 'A Decided Loss' (later entitled 'Loss of Breath') the hero suffers a series of catastrophes that parody the horrors of *Blackwood's*. During an argument with his wife he literally loses his breath, and thus becomes a figure of 'life in death'. While in this remarkable state he is by turns smothered, eaten by cats, dissected by a physician, hung and finally buried alive. But like a good *Blackwood's* narrator he still keeps his wits about him, and even indulges in philosophical speculations on his sufferings!

In a few of his early tales, however, Poe did experiment with supernatural horror albeit in a playful manner: 'Metzengerstein' (1832) is an absurd melodrama based upon the superstition of metempsychosis, and there would also appear to be supernatural elements in 'MS Found in a Bottle' (1833) and 'Morella' (1835). But Poe's interest in this 'German' or supernatural horror soon waned, and in December 1835 he wrote to Judge Beverley Tucker admitting, 'the "mere physique" of the horrible which prevails in the "MS Found in a Bottle"', but then added, 'I do not think I would be guilty of a similar absurdity now'. By 1838 when he wrote 'The Fall of the House of Usher' his understanding of the psychological basis of terror had matured, and he was annoyed when the story was rejected by the *Southern Literary Messenger* on the grounds that it was too 'German'. This allegation, along with others of a similar nature, provoked Poe to write his 'Preface' to *Tales of the Grotesque and Arabesque* in which he defended the serious nature of his art and material:

But the truth is that, with a single exception, there is no one of these stories in which the scholar should recognize the distinctive features of that species of pseudo-horror which we are taught to call Germanic, for no better reason than that some of the secondary names of German literature have become identified with its folly. If in many of my productions terror has been the thesis, I maintain that terror is not of Germany, but of the soul, – that I have deduced this terror only from its legitimate sources, and urged it only to its legitimate results. . . .
I think it best becomes me to say, therefore, that if I have sinned, I have deliberately sinned. These brief compositions are, in chief part, the results of matured purpose and very careful elaboration.

An examination of 'The Fall of the House of Usher' may suggest that Poe's high estimate of his work was justified.

The opening scene of the tale contains the elements of a conventional Gothic horror story – dilapidated house, blighted landscape, a solitary horseman and black foreboding tarn:

During the whole of a dull, dark, and soundless day in the autumn of the year, when the clouds hung oppressively low in the heavens, I had been passing alone, on horseback, through a singularly dreary tract of country; and at length found myself, as the shades of the evening drew on, within view of the melancholy House of Usher. I know not how it was – but, with the first glimpse of the building, a sense of insufferable gloom pervaded my spirit. I say insufferable; for the feeling was unrelieved by any of that half-pleasurable, because poetic, sentiment, with which the mind usually receives even the sternest natural images of the desolate or terrible. I looked upon the scene before me – upon the mere house, and the simple landscape features of the domain – upon the bleak walls – upon the vacant eye-like windows – upon a few rank sedges – and upon a few white trunks of decayed trees – with an utter depression of soul which I can compare to no earthly sensation more properly than to the after-dream of the reveller upon opium – the bitter lapse into everyday life – the hideous dropping off of the veil. There was an iciness, a sinking, a sickening of the heart – an unredeemed dreariness of thought which no goading of the imagination could torture into aught of the sublime. What was it – I paused to think – what was it that so unnerved me in the contemplation of the House of Usher? It was a mystery all insoluble; nor could I grapple with the shadowy fancies that crowded upon me as I pondered. I was forced to fall back upon the unsatisfactory conclusion, that while, beyond doubt, there *are* combinations of very simple natural objects which have the power of thus affecting us, still the analysis of this power lies among considerations beyond our depth. It was possible, I reflected, that a mere different arrangement of the particulars of the scene, of the details of the picture, would be sufficient to modify, or perhaps to annihilate its capacity for sorrowful impression; and, acting upon this idea, I reined my horse to the precipitous brink of a black and lurid tarn that lay in unruffled lustre by the dwelling, and gazed down – but with a shudder even more thrilling than before – upon the remodelled and inverted images of the gray sedge, and the ghastly tree-stems, and the vacant and eye-like windows.

Yet the landscape described here bears little relationship to any in the natural world; what concerns the narrator is his own feelings and mental processes which are objectified in this landscape of the mind with its imagery of dream, decay and stagnation. From the beginning the terror in the story is psychological – 'not of Germany, but of the soul', and this is dramatized by the narrator when he looks 'with a shudder even more thrilling than before' upon the inverted landscape reflected in the black waters of the tarn. The water that reflects and distorts reality is an image of the mind where the real sources of terror exist. Roderick Usher's mind, like that of the narrator, is also reflected in his environment. The narrator comments on several occasions upon the intimate connections between Roderick Usher and the House of Usher; indeed, in the popular imagination they have become fused into one identity:

'House of Usher' – an appellation which seemed to include, in the minds of the peasantry who used it, both the family and the family mansion.

The House of Usher, we come to realize, has perhaps no objective reality, but may exist as a metaphoric projection of Roderick's disordered and decaying mind, into which the narrator enters. Roderick's artistic creations are compulsive dramatizations of his terror – his painting of the vault clearly foreshadows the identification of his terror with his entombed sister Madeline, and his poem 'The Haunted Palace' is a self-conscious allegory describing his own mental disintegration. Usher is in the agonizing position of watching every stage in his own collapse, while remaining powerless to prevent it. He realizes that his own irrational fears will destroy him.

To an anomalous species of terror I found him a bounden slave. 'I shall perish,' said he, 'I must *perish* in this deplorable folly. Thus, thus, and not otherwise shall I be lost. I dread the events of the future, not in themselves, but in their results. I shudder at the thought of any, even the most trivial, incident, which may operate upon this intolerable agitation of soul. I have, indeed, no abhorrence of danger, except in its absolute effect – in terror. In this unnerved – in this pitiable condition – I feel that the period will sooner or later arrive when I must abandon life and reason together, in some struggle with the grim phantasm, FEAR.'

Yet this terror which he objectifies in his dying sister Madeline uncontrollably attracts him; what he fears most he desires most, and like Poe's other deranged protagonists he actively and perversely seeks the experience of absolute terror that leads to self-destruction.

But 'The Fall of the House of Usher' is also a story about the narrator. We learn of events through his involvement with them, and he is far from being a detached observer – he says of the 'phantasmagoric' furnishings of the house, 'I hesitated not to acknowledge how familiar was all this'. Roderick's encounter with terror is also a part of the narrator's experience, for they both share in the illusion of Madeline's horrific resurrection as they read 'The Mad Tryst' together. Madeline's escape from the tomb seems real only because the narrator believes in it, and tells us about it in such a compelling and dramatic manner, but Poe is also careful to make the whole episode incredible when viewed rationally. Madeline dies from a mysterious disease that wasted her body, and is buried in an airless copper-lined vault deep underneath the house. The narrator also remembers that the coffin lid is screwed down, and the bolt on the 'massive iron' door of the vault is closed after the burial. But the terror that Roderick seeks to bury in the dark underground vault of his mind will not remain hidden, and eight days later he is paralysed with fear:

> And now, some days of bitter grief having elapsed, an observable change came over the features of the mental disorder of my friend. His ordinary manner had vanished. His ordinary occupations were neglected or forgotten. He roamed from chamber to chamber with hurried, unequal, and objectless step. The pallor of his countenance had assumed, if possible, a more ghastly hue – but the luminousness of his eye had utterly gone out. The once occasional huskiness of his tone was heard no more; and a tremulous quaver, as if of extreme horror, habitually characterized his utterance.

At this stage we realize that the narrator's façade of reason is also breaking down: 'An irrepressible tremor gradually pervaded my frame; and, at length, there sat upon my very heart an incubus of utterly causeless alarm.' The shared vision of the resurrected Madeline is an embodiment of 'the grim phantasm, FEAR' in whose clutches Roderick dies, 'a victim to the terrors he had anticipated' and created. At the end the narrator has good cause to say 'I fled aghast', for when he sees the house collapse into the black tarn he is witnessing his own psychic disintegration which had been prefigured in the first paragraph by the image of the house in the water.

Many of the protagonists in Poe's tales of terror are remarkably alike, and although they explain themselves over and over again their personalities never change or develop. Obsessive, isolated and joyless, they adopt fragile masks of reason in order to explore their own irrational cravings for self-destruction. They live in a world where rational cause and effect have ceased to operate, and where human conduct is motivated by 'perverseness':

> In the sense I intend, it is, in fact, a *mobile* without motive, a motive not *motivirt*. Through its promptings we act without comprehensible object; or, if this shall be understood as a contradiction in terms, we may so far modify the proposition as to say, that through its promptings we act, for the reason that we should *not*. In theory, no reason can be more unreasonable; but, in fact, there is none more strong. With certain minds, under certain conditions, it becomes absolutely irresistible. I am not more certain that I breathe, than that the assurance of the wrong or error of any action is often the one unconquerable *force* which impels us, and alone impels us to its prosecution. Nor will this overwhelming tendency to do wrong for the wrong's sake, admit of analysis, or resolution into ulterior elements. It is a radical, a primitive impulse – elementary.

'The Imp of the Perverse' (1845)

In three of Poe's most successful tales – 'The Tell-Tale Heart' (1843), 'The Black Cat' (1843) and 'William Wilson' (1839) – this 'perverseness' takes the form of a murder which also involves an implicit motive of self-destruction within the murderer.

At the beginning of 'The Tell-Tale Heart' the narrator reveals his own disordered mind through his illogical protestations of sanity and his nervous dislocated language:

TRUE! – nervous – very, very dreadfully nervous I had been and am; but why *will* you say that I am mad? The disease had sharpened my senses – not destroyed – not dulled them. Above all was the sense of hearing acute. I heard all things in the heaven and in the earth. I heard many things in hell. How, then, am I mad? Hearken! and observe how healthily – how calmly I can tell you the whole story.

Although he murders his victim in a brutal manner, the narrator offers no rational motive for his crime; indeed he claims to love 'the old man', and then hastily settles upon the old superstition of the 'evil eye' to explain his actions:

It is impossible to say how first the idea entered my brain; but once conceived, it haunted me day and night. Object there was none. I loved the old man. He had never wronged me. He had never given me insult. For his gold I had no desire. I think it was his eye! Yes, it was this! He had the eye of a vulture – a pale blue eye, with a film over it. Whenever it fell upon me, my blood ran cold; and so by degrees – very gradually – I made up my mind to take the life of the old man, and thus rid myself of the eye forever.

Throughout the absurdly contrived and drawn out murder, which the narrator ironically believes reveals the supremacy of his in-tellect, he hears the continual beating of a heart which he ascribes to 'the old man', but which in reality is his own quickened by terror and excitement in the adventure of self-destruction. Even when the victim has been murdered, and the body cut up and buried under the floor boards, the heart beat continues and increases in intensity, until driven to despair the murderer compulsively confesses to his crime. It is now evident that the murderer and his victim are both aspects of the same consciousness, and the 'vulture eye' of the 'old man' is in reality the 'vulture I' who preys remorselessly upon himself. Self-hatred, the subject of this story, is also dramatized in 'The Black Cat' and 'William Wilson'. In 'The Black Cat' the narrator again insists upon his sanity; he presents himself in the guise of a matter-of-fact, basically kind gentleman who grotesquely insists that his terrible story is 'a series of mere household events' motivated by excessive drinking. But behind the façade of rational

cause and effect lies 'the spirit of PERVERSENESS' which com-
pels the narrator to torture and kill his beloved cat, then to murder
his wife with an axe, and finally without remorse or reason to betray
himself to the authorities. He murders only to incur his own destruction. In 'William Wilson' the relationship between the killer and
his victim is still more explicit. In this story William Wilson projects
his conscience into an illusory alter-ego who haunts, torments and
exposes him continuously. When William Wilson is finally provoked
into destroying his self-created tormentor, he is forced into the
realization that his act of 'murder' is one of self-hatred, for he
cannot exist without his conscience:

> *'You have conquered, and I yield, Yet, henceforward art thou also dead – dead*
> *to the World, to Heaven and to Hope! In me didst thou exist – and, in my death,*
> *see by this image, which is thine own, how utterly thou hast murdered thyself!'*

But 'William Wilson' is not a conventional moral allegory, and Poe
refuses to draw the kind of pious conclusion that Hawthorne often
indulged in. The conscience, the 'other' William Wilson, preys on
the ego and precipitates the final disintegration of the personality.

Tension is often created in Poe's tales by the dichotomy between
the rational tone which the narrator adopts, and the perverse,
irrational nature of his unconscious mind which the narrative reveals. In 'MS Found in a Bottle' the narrator presents himself as a
rationalist, a man given to 'habits of rigid thought' and lacking in
imagination. Yet the symbolic voyage which he deliberately undertakes breaks through his fragile mask of reason, and leads him into
the strange, exciting and dangerous world of 'inner space'. The
mundane descriptions of the ship's cargo that begin the story soon
give way to dream imagery of decay, remoteness, stagnation and
annihilation, as he careers on a great black ship past ramparts of ice
like 'the walls of the universe', irresistibly drawn towards the vortex
of the sea which he believes contains 'some exciting knowledge –
some never-to-be imparted secret, whose attainment is destruction'. Likewise when the protagonist of 'A Descent into the
Maelstrom' (1841) peers down into the vortex of the sea, he discovers in this image of his own mind sources of wonder and terror:

Never shall I forget the sensations of awe, horror, and admiration with
which I gazed about me. The boat appeared to be hanging, as if by magic,
midway down, upon the interior surface of a funnel vast in circumference,
prodigious in depth, and whose perfectly smooth sides might have been
mistaken for ebony, but for the bewildering rapidity with which they spun
around, and for the gleaming and ghastly radiance they shot forth, as the

rays of the full moon, from that circular rift amid the clouds which I have already described, streamed in a flood of golden glory along the black walls, and far away down into the inmost recesses of the abyss.

In *The Narrative of Arthur Gordon Pym* the narrator's concern with the phenomenal world is also marginal; the disasters he encounters on his voyage which include murder, mutiny, cannibalism and burial alive are provocations to him to continue to explore the limits of his own perverse nature. By the time Pym reaches the strange island of Tsalal, 'a country differing essentially from any hitherto visited by civilized men', the world has taken on the forms of his own terrors and obsessions. While hanging from a cliff face on Tsalal Pym is overwhelmed by a perverse compulsion to hurl himself to destruction. His perverseness colours all the experience of his voyage, and his awareness of the external world is governed by inner compulsions and terrors. Thus the mutiny, cannibalism, treacherous natives with black teeth, grotesque animals and warm Antarctic regions which he encounters are projections of his unconscious mind which distorts and inverts reality. Pym is totally self-involved and his quest for ultimate knowledge of his own psyche leads him, as with Ahab in *Moby-Dick*, to encounter the meaningless whiteness of annihilation:

And now we rushed into the embraces of the cataract, where a chasm threw itself open to receive us. But there arose in our pathway a shrouded human figure, very far larger in its proportions than any dweller among men. And the hue of the skin of the figure was of the perfect whiteness of the snow.

An aspect of Poe that is often overlooked is the diversity of his work in the short story form. Apart from his studies in the psychology of terror, Poe also experimented with science fiction, hoaxes, satires, philosophical dialogues, surrealist fantasies and detective stories. He was dissatisfied with *Tales* (1845) because the edition did not reveal the full range of his accomplishment, and in August, 1846, he wrote to his friend Philip P. Cooke outlining his plans for a new and more representative collection:

Were all my Tales now before me in a large volume and as the composition of another – the merit which would principally arrest my attention would be the wide *diversity and variety* ... There is a vast variety of kinds and, in degree of value, these kinds vary – but each tale is equally good of its *kind*.

The detective stories – 'The Murders in Rue Morgue' (1841), 'The Mystery of Marie Roget' (1842), 'The Gold Bug' (1843) and 'The

Purloined Letter' (1845) – have been seen as marking the be-ginnings of the genre in English. 'The Murders in the Rue Morgue' is the most interesting and successful tale in the group. The brutal and apparently motiveless murders of two quiet and inoffensive women in a Paris suburb baffle the police who have 'no method in their proceedings, beyond the method of the moment'. Because they have never encountered a crime of this nature before, their dull intelligences are confused, and the 'solution' of the crime is left to the aristocratic amateur detective C. Auguste Dupin. Dupin is a poet *manqué* who cuts himself off from ordinary concerns, and seeks to excite his imagination in the enclosed world of his 'time-eaten and grotesque mansion'. He claims to possess an acutely logical mind together with a highly developed imagination, and the narrator reminds us that 'the ingenious are always fanciful, and the truly imaginative never otherwise than analytic'. Dupin ventures out into the night-time world of crime, and imposes upon it the order of his own mind; he recognizes the bizarre and irrational nature of existence, and solves the crime by arguing from this premise that had been overlooked by the official authorities: he begins by im-aginatively conceiving that the murders in the Rue Morgue were motiveless, and his deductions lead him by seemingly logical steps back to the killer – an unreasoning ape. The world of Dupin is not unlike the rest of Poe's fictional creation; it is a world that is essentially absurd, full of fantasy, pseudo-reason, tricks, anti-climaxes and non-sequiturs. And Poe's method in this tale is not unlike the methods he used elsewhere in his fiction to bring about an appearance of what he termed 'vraisemblance': it consists of bringing together the familiar and the possible with the in-credible and the fantastic.

Poe's experiments with other genres have not withstood the test of time so well. 'The Unparalleled Adventures of One Hans Pfaall' (1835), 'The Balloon Hoax' (1844) and 'The Facts in the Case of M. Valdemar' (1845) were briefly popular in Poe's day, and although they still possess a curiosity value, they seem primitive when compared with the work of modern science fiction writers. His comic stories have fared badly: some like 'Lionizing' (1835) and 'The Literary Life of Thingum Bob, Esq.' (1844) are concerned with forgotten literary problems and personalities; others like 'Bon Bon' (1832) and 'The Spectacles' (1844), which is about a short-sighted man who married his great-great-grandmother, are vulgar and rather silly. The social satires are more important, and they reveal Poe's reactionary and pessimistic attitudes towards human nature and American society. 'Four Beasts in One' (1836), 'Some Words With a Mummy' (1845) and 'The System of Dr Tarr and Professor Fether' (1845) are attacks on politial and social democracy, which Poe despised and feared as an aberration of natural law that results in the tyranny of the 'insolent, rapacious, filthy' monster 'Mob'. In 'Some Words With a Mummy' a group of scientists bring an Egyptian mummy back to life, but in response to their boasts about the progress of civilization in the nineteenth century, the mummy retorts that notions of progress were in the air in his day too, 'and as for "progress", it was at one time quite a nuisance, but it never progressed'. In 'The System of Dr Tarr and Professor Fether' the naïve narrator visits a lunatic asylum famous for the liberal and progressive 'soothing system' initiated by its superintendent. Despite the narrator's professed understanding of the 'metaphysics of mania' he does not at first realize that the superintendent has himself gone mad; the inmates have revolted and taken control, and subjected their former guardians to the American 'system' of tar and feathers. At the evening banquet each of the lunatics reveals his or her particular mania to the narrator, and while the band plays 'Yankee Doodle' the superintendent explains how the lunatics gained control of the asylum:

it all came to pass by means of a stupid fellow – a lunatic – who, by some means, had taken it into his head that he had invented a better system of government than any ever heard of before – of lunatic government, I mean. He wished to give his invention a trial, I suppose – and so he persuaded the rest of the patients to join him in a conspiracy for the overthrow of the reigning powers.

The political and social implications of the story are obvious, though the tone throughout is lighthearted and comic. 'Four Beasts in One', however, is more virulent in its attack on democracy, and the farcical surface of the story with its puns and word plays offers an ironic contrast to the serious meaning suggested by the action, in which Antiochus Epiphanes (who perhaps represents Andrew Jackson) and his brutal mob so offend against the natural order of life that the wild animals rise in revolt and chase them through the streets. This story looks forward to the more abstract futurist fantasies, 'The Colloquy of Monos and Una' (1841) and 'Mellonta Tauta' (1849), in which inhabitants of the future look back with dismay at man's perverse experiments with democracy.

In *Eureka* Poe conceived of God as the Supreme Artist, and the universe as a perfectly unified work of art. In the 'Preface' he describes his book as a 'poem', and addresses it to the 'dreamers' and poets who value the Divine gift of imagination and recognize that Beauty and Truth are one:

To the few who love me and whom I love – to those who feel rather than to those who think – to the dreamers and those who put faith in dreams as in the only realities – I offer this book of Truths, not in its character of Truth-Teller, but for the Beauty that abounds in its Truth, constituting it True. To these I present the composition as an Art-Product alone, – let us say as a Romance; or, if I be not urging too lofty a claim, as a Poem.

According to Poe's cosmic myth man has perversely exalted reason above imagination, and by placing his faith in rationalism rather than in the visionary knowledge of the 'poetic intellect' he has betrayed God, and brought the earth into a corrupt and 'fallen' condition. 'The Colloquy of Monos and Una' dramatizes this situation. The angel Monos tells his partner Una that the world is esssentially mad and humanity is in the grip of a kind of mass 'perverseness':

Man, because he could not but acknowledge the majesty of Nature, fell into childish exultation at his acquired and still-increasing dominion over her elements. Even while he stalked a God in his own fancy, an infantine imbecility came over him ... he grew infected with system, and with abstraction. He enwrapped himself in generalities. Among other odd ideas, that of universal equality gained ground; and in the face of analogy and of God – in despite of the loud warning voice of its laws of gradation so vividly pervading all things in Earth and Heaven – wild attempts at an omniprevalent Democracy were made. Yet this evil sprang from the leading evil – Knowledge. Man could not both know and succumb. Meantime huge smoking cities arose, innumerable. Green leaves shrank before the hot breath of furnaces. The fair face of Nature was deformed as with the ravages of some loathsome disease.

In 'The Conversation of Eiros and Charmion' (1839) and 'Al Aaraaf' Poe imagined the future destruction and purification of the sinful earth by fire. But meanwhile the poets, those guardians of 'Supernal Beauty', live as alien visitors on earth striving to escape the torturing confines of reason and materialism, to enter into the visionary world of the imagination. Building on hints he obtained from reading Coleridge and Shelley, Poe formulated a theory of poetry in which the poet, instead of seeking to order and come to terms with his earthly experience, must reject the world, and strive to transcend phenomena in order to bring 'fallen' man some glimpse of the eternal Platonic idea of 'Supernal Beauty' which is available only to the imagination. In his lecture on 'The Poetic

Principle' (1850) in which he summoned up and clarified his theory, Poe wrote of the poetic endeavour:

We have still a thirst unquenchable. . . . This thirst belongs to the immortality of Man. It is at once a consequence and an indication of his perennial existence. It is the desire of the moth for the star. It is no mere appreciation of the Beauty before us – but a wild effort to reach the Beauty above. Inspired by an ecstatic prescience of the glories beyond the grave, we struggle, by multi-form combinations among the things and thoughts of Time, to attain a portion of that Loveliness whose very elements, perhaps, appertain to eternity alone.

But what Poe says here was not new; he had been saying the same thing in reviews and essays throughout his career. As early as 1836 in a review of the poetry of Halleck and Drake he had described the poet as a visionary traveller into the dream world of 'Supernal Beauty':

If, indeed, there be any one circle of thought distinctly and palpably marked out from amid the jarring and tumultuous chaos of human intelligence, it is that evergreen and radiant Paradise which the true poet knows, and knows alone, as the limited realm of his authority – as the circumscribed Eden of his dreams.

These ideas are of course of major importance in Poe's poetry, yet the poetry, fiction and criticism are parts of a single vision of life and art, and Poe also explored the poet's quest for 'Supernal Beauty' in his fiction – notably in a group of stories that include 'Ligeia' (1838), 'Eleonora' (1842), and 'The Domain of Arnheim' (1847).

'Ligeia', which Poe at one time believed to be his finest story, is both a study of madness and terror, and an exploration of the poet's quest for 'Supernal Beauty'. Despite the surface air of Gothic fantasy, it is not, as has commonly been supposed, a tale of metempsychosis in which the dead Ligeia returns from the grave to possess the body of her rival Rowena. The epigraph at the beginning of the story which speaks of the will 'which dieth not' refers to the narrator rather than to Ligeia. It is his story which we hear, and it is his own obsessed imagination which the narrative explores. In the first paragraph he admits that he cannot remember when he met Ligeia or what her real name was; he recalls her like a dream: 'an airy and spirit-lifting vision more wildly divine that the phantasies which hovered about the slumbering souls of the daughters of Delos'. His incantatory, hysterical description of her is patently artificial and dream-like, and she sounds more like a work of art than a living woman:

I examined the contour of the lofty and pale forehead – It was faultless – how cold indeed that word when applied to a majesty so divine! – the skin rivalling the purest ivory, the commanding extent and repose, the gentle prominence of the regions above the temple; and then the raven-black, the glossy, the luxuriant and naturally-curling tresses, setting forth the full force of the Homeric epithet, 'hyacinthine!' I looked at the delicate outlines of the nose – and nowhere but in the graceful medallions of the Hebrews had I beheld a similar perfection. There was the same luxurious smoothness of surface, the same scarcely perceptible tendency to the aquiline, the same harmoniously curved nostrils speaking the free spirit. I regarded the sweet mouth. Here was indeed the triumph of all things heavenly – the magnificent turn of the short upper lip – the soft, voluptuous slumber of the under – the dimples which sported, and the color which spoke – the teeth glancing back, with a brilliancy almost startling, every ray of the holy light which fell upon them in her serene and placid, yet almost exultingly radiant of all smiles.

In his poetry Poe often symbolized 'Supernal Beauty' in the form of a woman, and in 'The Philosophy of Composition' he went so far as to declare: 'the death, then, of a beautiful woman is, unquestionably, the most poetical topic in the world'. The narrator of this story is also a poet; his imagination is haunted by Beauty which he embodies in his dream woman Ligeia, who significantly possesses the name and characteristics of a goddess of Beauty in the visionary world of Al Aaraaf in Poe's poem. In Poe's poetry the earthly poet's tragedy is that his dreams of beauty are transient, and similarly the death of Ligeia who is perfect in beauty, knowledge and love signifies the narrator's loss of his visionary imagination. The rest of the story tells of his frenzied attempts to recover his lost power, first, by the calculated use of opium, and second, by a deliberate retreat into madness and dreams. The furnishings of his pentagonal magic chamber reveal his disordered mind, and the 'phantasmagoric effect' he seeks to produce with the curtains is a histrionic attempt to excite his imagination into a transcendent state. On the night of Ligeia's resurrection, her return to life coincides with the ebb and flow of the narrator's imagination. Finally, his reason collapses – 'There was a mad disorder in my thoughts – a tumult unappeasable'; his imagination triumphs and he sees the mundane, earthly Rowena transformed into Ligeia, a vision of 'Supernal Loveliness'.

When Poe was a young man he was quite certain about the future course and purpose of his career – he would become a poet. In the 'Preface' to *Tamerlane and Other Poems* he wrote with youthful arrogance:

He [Poe] will not say that he is indifferent as to the success of these Poems – it might stimulate him to other attempts – but he can safely assert that failure will not influence him in a resolution already adopted. This is challenging criticism – let it be so.

Yet most of Poe's poetry was written by the time he was twenty-two, and after 1831 his creative energy went principally into the composition of fiction and critical reviews. He still continued to write poetry, but he tended to be defensive, even derogatory about his achievement. In June 1844 he told Lowell, 'I have been so negligent as not to preserve copies of any of my volumes of poems – nor was any worthy of preservation', and soon afterwards in the 'Preface' to *The Raven and Other Poems* he stated:

Events not to be controlled have prevented me from making, at any time, any serious effort in what, under happier circumstances, would have been the field of my choice.

It has generally been assumed that Poe's efforts to write poetry were curtailed by his obvious need to make a living in the world, and his recognition that his poems would not provide him with an income. Certainly most of his poems were received with indifference by the general public, and even 'The Raven', which was instantly popular, brought him only five dollars when he sold it to the *American Whig Review*. But it is also probable that Poe's interest in writing lyric poetry diminished after 1831 – after this date he seems to have been more concerned with the idea of poetry which he worked out in critical reviews and essays, than with its practice. Moreover, the range of themes and attitudes in his poetry was severely limited by a dogmatic aesthetic which insisted that a poem must be brief, indefinite, musical and infused with melancholy in order to produce the desired effect of a 'Rhythmical Creation of Beauty'. It is perhaps not surprising that Poe wrote so little poetry, considering the narrow field of his vision.

*Tamerlane and Other Poems* is an apprentice work, which by 1829 he was ready to disown; he considered that it had been suppressed through 'circumstances of a private nature'. It is probable that he regarded the pamphlet as being too ephemeral (it was badly produced by a Boston job printer and sold for twelve and a half cents), the poems themselves too private. But he never discarded the poems; instead he revised them thoroughly, cut out the more obvious references to his own thinly veiled personal history, and republished them in later editions. 'Tamerlane', for example, began in 1827 as a poem of 406 lines, but when he revised it for his 1829 edition he cut it to 234 lines, tightened up the verse, and made the whole poem more objective. Poe constantly revised his own work, and each new poem was submitted to unrelenting scrutiny as he strove to achieve technical perfection – 'A Dream Within a Dream' emerged after several revisions as an entirely different poem, with not a single line of the original left in it.

Yet despite its imperfections and an undue reliance on poetic models, especially Byron and Thomas Moore, Poe's first book was an impressive achievement for a boy of eighteen, and the central issues that were to preoccupy him throughout his poetic career are evident here. On the surface 'Tamerlane' appears to dramatize a stock romantic theme – the conflict of love versus ambition. Tamerlane, the speaker in the poem, tells how he deserted his idyllic native home and his beloved Ada in order to conquer the entire world. Having realized his ambition he returns to discover that Ada (for whom the conquests were originally conceived) is dead, and only death can re-unite them. Tamerlane's complaint is not simply that his involvement with worldly ambition has taken away his beloved; it has also destroyed his creative imagination. He regrets the loss of his childhood:

> O craving heart, for the lost flowers
> And sunshine of my summer hours!

a time when harmony and order existed and his imagination revelled in dreams of Supernal Beauty which he embodied in Ada:

> I had no being – but in thee:
> The world, and all it did contain
> In the earth – the air – the sea—
> Its joy – its little lot of pain
> That was new pleasure – the ideal,
> Dim, vanities of dreams by night—
> And dimmer nothings which were real—
> (Shadows – and a more shadowy light!)
> Parted upon their misty wings,
> And, so, confusedly, became
> Thine image and – a name – a name!
> Two separate – yet most intimate things.

Tamerlane's poetic imagination is destroyed through his involvement with materialism, and by Time which robs him of his dream world and leaves him alienated and regretful:

> And boyhood is a summer sun
> Whose waning is the dreariest one.
> For all we live to know is known,
> And all we seek to keep hath flown.
> Let life, then, as the day-flower, fall
> With the noon-day beauty – which is all.

At the end of the poem the sunshine world of childhood has been destroyed by the 'fire within', and Tamerlane the poet is left inert and isolated in the cold sterile moonlight, longing for death which will reunite him with the dream world of his imagination.

The dominant mood of Poe's early poetry is one of isolation and regret for the lost world of the imagination from which the poet has been cast out by Time. In 'Alone' (which was not included in any of Poe's published volumes) the poet describes his sense of apartness in terms of his unique sensibility:

> From childhood's hour I have not been
> As others were – I have not seen
> As others saw – I could not bring
> My passions from a common spring—
> From the same source I have not taken
> My sorrow – I could not awaken
> My heart to joy at the same tone—
> And all I lov'd – I lov'd alone.

In 'Dreams' the poet longs to live continually in a dream world; even though the dreams were sad, they would be more wonderful and meaningful than 'the cold reality/of waking life'. The poet's tragedy is that his visionary dreams are subject to Time, and in 'A Dream Within a Dream' the isolated figure of the poet stands by the ever-changing sea to watch the golden grains of sand (his dreams) slipping relentlessly through his fingers into the water.

'Al Aaraaf', Poe's longest and most ambitious poem, marks a new departure in his work. While it builds upon the themes of the early poetry, it is also more abstract, and is less concerned with exploring the private emotions of the poet than with elaborating an aesthetic theory that insists that Beauty and Truth are one. Al Aaraaf is a far distant star that embodies the idea of 'Supernal Beauty' and is ruled over by the goddess Nesace. She is instructed by God to gather her fellow angels together and warn the unfallen universe of man's perverse folly:

> Divulge the secrets of thy embassy
> To the proud orbs that twinkle – and so be
> To ev'ry heart a barrier and a ban
> Lest the stars totter in the guilt of man!

Man has fallen from Divine Grace in this poem through his intellectual arrogance, and he has failed to perceive what only his imagination could have taught him – the unity of Beauty and Truth. Nesace calls together the angels in her aesthetic paradise; only Angelo and Ianthe neglect the summons because they are corrupted by earthly, physical passion:

> They fell: for Heaven to them no hope imparts
> Who hear not for the beating of their hearts.

Poe revised his earlier work for the edition of 1831, but there were also some new and important poems collected here for the first time including 'The Sleeper', 'The City in the Sea', 'The Valley of Unrest', 'Israfel' and 'To Helen'. In 'Israfel' the earthly poet contrasts his situation with that of Israfel the poet of heaven or perhaps Al Aaraaf, 'who has the sweetest voice of all God's creatures'. Israfel has access to 'Supernal Beauty' but the frustrated earthly poet, haunted by Time, can only make his poetry out of the elements of his 'fallen' world:

> Yes, Heaven is thine; but this
> Is a world of sweets and sours;
> Our flowers are merely – flowers,
> And the shadow of thy perfect bliss
> Is the sunshine of ours.

'The City in the Sea' is a powerful symbolic presentation of the poet's vision of the 'fallen' world as a grotesque and terrifying nightmare overshadowed by Death:

> Resigned beneath the sky
> The melancholy waters lie.
> So blend the turrets and shadows there
> That all seem pendulous in air,
> While from a proud tower in the town
> Death looks gigantically down.

Poe claimed that 'To Helen' was inspired by Mrs Jane Stanard, the mother of one of his school friends, and 'the first ideal love of my soul'. But clearly the Helen of the poem is meant to recall Helen of Troy who rescues the 'way-worn' poet from the 'desperate seas' of life by transporting him into a visionary world of Beauty. In the final stanza Helen is seen as the permanent reality of art who holds the agate lamp through which the poet sees the clear white light of Truth refracted into the colours of Beauty:

Lo! in yon brilliant window-niche
How statue-like I see thee stand,
The agate lamp within thy hand!
Ah, Psyche, from the regions which
Are Holy-Land!

In the edition of 1845 Poe included his most famous poem, 'The Raven'. Unlike many of his poems, 'The Raven' possesses a clear narrative structure which is developed through distinct events to a psychological climax. In 'The Philosophy of Composition' he explained the psychology behind the poem as 'that species of despair that delights in self-torture'. The poet's vision of 'Supernal Beauty' symbolized by the 'lost Lenore' is dead, and he tortures himself with the fear that he will never recover it. He questions the raven in order to receive an answer he knows already, and at the end of the poem he is inert in the despair he has imposed upon himself:

And the Raven, never flitting, still is sitting, still is sitting
On the pallid bust of Pallas just above my chamber door;
And his eyes have all the seeming of a demon's that is dreaming,
And the lamp-light o'er him streaming throws his shadow on
    the floor;
And my soul from out that shadow that lies floating on the floor
                Shall be lifted – nevermore!

'The Raven' possesses more human interest than most of Poe's poems, but the complex rhyme schemes, and the use of parallelism and repetition do not wholly succeed – instead of reinforcing the poem's meaning, they sometimes draw attention away from it. Poe's growing interest in the technique of poetry found more mature expression in the poems he composed during the last two years of his life.

'Ulalume' (1847) describes a debate between the poet's soul and his ego about two kinds of love – one a passion for a real woman (perhaps Mrs Whitman), the other the memory of a lost love (Virginia). The drama takes place within the poet's mind, and the non-rational nature of the arguments is emphasized by the monotonous incantatory rhythm of the poem:

The skies they were ashen and sober;
The leaves they were crispéd and sere—
The leaves they were withering and sere:
It was night, in the lonesome October
Of my most immemorial year:

> It was hard by the dim lake of Auber,
> In the misty mid region of Weir—
> It was down by the dank tarn of Auber,
> In the ghoul-haunted woodland of Weir.

In the midst of this symbolic landscape of bereavement and death, the poet's heart is newly awakened to passion; he forgets his lost love, and fixes his attention on Venus the morning star. Psyche, his soul, mistrusts the hopeful star and warns him away, but he refuses to accept her advice until he confronts the tomb of his lost love, Ulalume. The poet then comes to understand that his new love, indeed life itself, is an illusion, and only death can re-unite him with the reality of his lost visionary world. Similarly the lover in 'Annabel Lee' (1849) seeks release from his frustrations and longings by acting out his death-wish, in the tomb of his beloved:

> For the moon never beams, without bringing me dreams
> Of the beautiful Annabel Lee;
> And the stars never rise, but I feel the bright eyes
> Of the beautiful Annabel Lee:
> And so, all the night-tide, I lie down by the side
> Of my darling – my darling – my life and my bride
> In the sepulchre there by the sea—
> In her tomb by the sounding sea.

In one of his last and most autobiographical poems 'For Annie' (written in 1849 for Annie Richmond), Poe explicitly dramatized an idea that had been implicit in earlier poems and tales: that life is cruel, mad and destructive of beauty, and death is the entry into a perfect form of existence. In 'For Annie' life is seen as a hellish torment, and death is imagined as a joyful experience in which the poet's soul is released from the confines of reason and the body into a realm of peace, love and beauty:

> Thank Heaven! the crisis,
> The danger, is past,
> And the lingering illness
> Is over at last—
> And the fever called 'Living'
> Is conquered at last.

Poe was not a commercially successful writer in his lifetime. The literary milieu in which he wrote, dominated as it was by fervent and uncritical literary nationalism and maudlin sentimentality, had little time for his sophisticated artistry and elitist literary principles. George R. Graham, one of the most astute magazine publishers of the day, wrote after Poe's death: 'The character of Poe's mind was of such an order, as not to be very widely in demand. The class of educated mind which he could readily and profitably address, was small – the channels through which he could do so at all, were few. . . .' In a bitter essay entitled 'Some Secrets of the Magazine Prison-House' (1845) Poe spoke of the predicament of the serious writer in America in terms of his own experience:

Were we in an ill humor at this moment, we could a tale unfold which would erect the hair on the head of Shylock. A young author, struggling with Despair itself in the shape of a ghastly poverty, which has no alleviation – no sympathy from an every-day world, that cannot understand his necessities, and that would pretend not to understand them if it comprehended them ever so well—

For many years following his death Poe was understood better in Europe than in America. His first scholarly biographer, John Ingram, was an Englishman, while the French, inspired by Baudelaire, had no hesitation in acclaiming Poe as a major author with an international appeal. But it was only after the breakdown of the genteel moralistic tradition in American literature that Poe's true significance began to be recognized in his own country. This recognition came initially as much from creative artists, notably D. H. Lawrence and William Carlos Williams, as from the critics; Williams in *In the American Grain* (1925) wrote that Poe brought to American literature 'the sense for the first time in America, that literature is *serious*, not a matter of courtesy but of truth'. The seriousness that Poe displayed in his art is akin to that of his great contemporaries, Hawthorne, Melville and Thoreau; like them he affirmed in his best tales and poems that literature must dramatize man's permanent moral and psychological fears and inspirations.

# 6

# NEW ENGLAND TRANSCENDENTALISM

## George Hochfield

I

The key to the period appeared to be that the mind had become aware of itself.

R. W. Emerson

The movement that came to be called, and to call itself, Transcendentalism originated in a conflict within the communion of Boston Unitarianism. Indeed, most of the important Transcendentalist spokesmen attended Harvard Divinity School, which by the first decade of the nineteenth century had become a Unitarian seminary, and served for greater or lesser periods of time as Unitarian ministers. This group included Emerson, George Ripley and Theodore Parker, as well as such lesser figures as James Freeman Clarke, William Henry Channing, Frederick Henry Hedge, Christopher Pearse Cranch and John Sullivan Dwight. Orestes Brownson, although self-educated, also occupied a Unitarian pulpit for several years. Only Bronson Alcott, Thoreau and the feminine component of the movement, Margaret Fuller and Elizabeth Peabody, fell outside this narrow pattern, but they too were inextricably part of the same intellectual and social milieu. Transcendentalism, then, was an intensely local phenomenon, almost a family affair, and it had its beginnings in the emotional atmosphere of a family quarrel.

The quarrel arose over the state of religion in the Unitarian churches of Boston, but it quickly became a contest of much larger scope involving basic issues of philosophic, theological and social outlook. In the process of exploring these issues, a literary record of considerable volume was built up: this is the Transcendentalist contribution to American intellectual history. Given the circumstances, much Transcendentalist writing has a polemical edge; nor can one overlook the fact that to their contemporaries, especially in the hectic days of the mid-1830s, the Transcendentalists seemed madmen or fools, perpetrators of a harebrained radicalism that threatened the foundations of society. Of the entire group, only Emerson and Thoreau may be said to have written as literary artists, for the sake, that is, of the work, not necessarily for the sake of the controversy. Even in their writing, however, one almost always finds a vein of practicality and an evident intention to persuade. Transcendentalism, after all, was not primarily guided by aesthetic or speculative ends. Rather it was, in O. B. Frothingham's word, a 'gospel', or as Santayana accurately said of Emerson's thought, 'religion expressing itself as a philosophy'. Nevertheless, Emerson and Thoreau had genuine literary careers and left a deep impression on American letters. They deserve separate treatment. The first step, however, must be an explanation of the Transcendentalist–Unitarian quarrel, and a survey of the body of ideas upon which the Transcendentalist group were in substantial agreement.

Boston Unitarianism in the first third of the nineteenth century was an exquisite socio-theological creation. It had no special ties to the tradition of European Unitarianism (as is shown, for example, in its relative lack of concern with the question of the Trinity), but was the product of a slow century-long evolution in certain churches which had been part of the original orthodox Congregationalism of New England. The chief influence on these churches was Anglican rationalism, and the sharpest lines of division between them and New England orthodoxy were drawn on the issues of innate depravity, the place of reason in Scriptural interpretation, and the character of God. By the beginning of the nineteenth century the principal doctrines of Unitarianism had been hammered out and required only a confident and unified interpretation. This was finally achieved in the work of William Ellery Channing, the spokesman of Unitarianism's golden age from 1819 when he delivered his discourse at the ordination of Jared Sparks ('Unitarian Christianity') to his death in 1841.

Channing's grave, mild, infinitely reasonable voice propounded a set of ideas in which, as Henry Adams remembered many years later, it appeared that Boston had 'solved all the problems of the universe'. He began with a typical eighteenth-century insistence on the rationality of the Christian religion and the perfect adequacy of human reason to intepret its meaning. 'God has given us a rational nature', Channing said, and this is the foundation of all subsequent intercourse between Him and his creatures. The Bible, despite its entanglements with the history of a former age and its somewhat primitive figurative style which lacks the 'precision of science', is nevertheless 'a book written for men, in the language of men, and . . . its meaning is to be sought in the same manner as that of other books'. God, in other words, 'when he speaks to the human race, conforms . . . to the established rules of speaking and writing'. It is evident, therefore, that men may confidently rely on these rules in extracting universal truths from the knotty, poetical language of Scripture. Channing uses a telling analogy to suggest the nature of this procedure: 'We reason about the Bible', he says, 'precisely as civilians do about the Constitution under which we live'. Thus doctrinal differences are resolvable on the Highest Authority, just as they are in the Supreme Court, by the exercise of sound reasoning and argumentative skill.

The corollaries are obvious. God, far from being an inscrutable, foreordaining Tyrant as the orthodox would have him, is a benign Parent whose only purpose towards his children is to educate them in the moral conduct necessary for salvation. Nor is man a depraved creature helplessly dependent on God's will. On the contrary, man's reasonable nature is a fundamental ground of unity with God, and in the light cast by reason he may seek to approximate the divine character itself. Christ is the model of perfection towards which he aims, an embodiment of eternal truth in the form of an inspired human teacher. Channing, though he deplored enthusiasm as a false face of piety, was capable of speaking with great warmth on this subject of human capacity and likeness to God:

Whence do we derive our knowledge of the attributes and perfections which constitute the Supreme Being? I answer, we derive them from our own souls. The divine attributes are first developed in ourselves and thence transferred to our Creator. The idea of God, sublime and awful as it is, is the idea of our own spiritual nature, purified and enlarged to infinity. In ourselves are the elements of the Divinity.

But having come so far, almost to the verge of Transcendentalist heresy, Channing was unable to take the further step by which the 'elements' within man were wholly identified with the divine. He was restrained, in part, by the ancient habit of Christian thought which recoiled from pantheism, but more immediately and consciously by his assumptions about the nature of that very reason from which he derived his exalted idea of human dignity. Like a hundred other versions of rational religion in the eighteenth century, Channing's Unitarianism was grounded in the epistemology of Locke, and thus, as the Transcendentalists were quick to point out, could not help but divide man from God as effectually as Calvinism had done.

Locke had taught that the mind was a blank page upon which only sensations could write. Reason synthesized and abstracted from the ideas produced by sensations, as was evident in the formulation of natural laws, but the mind remained essentially passive and dependent on external stimuli as the primary source of all knowledge. The attractiveness of this theory lay in its apparently scientific rigour and in the support it gave to a rational ordering of experience based on the accumulation of hard data. But it created a dilemma for religious writers anxious to preserve some measure of Christian orthodoxy. They were moved, on the one hand, to argue the rationality of Christian faith, its basic agreement with natural law and its consistency as a body of doctrine. In this direction lay deism, to which the Christian revelation was unnecessary or even suspect. At the same time, Locke's premises contained an implicit threat to *all* religion, for they could well lead to a thoroughgoing scientific materialism (Holbach) or pure idealism (Berkeley) or to a devastating scepticism which questioned the possibility of any knowledge beyond what was given immediately to the senses (Hume). Consquently many rational apologists for Christianity felt compelled to insist as well on the divine guarantees of faith provided by revelation. Scripture agreed with reason, but it went beyond reason to record the facts of supernatural intervention in history. Such facts, it was argued – they were summed up in the word 'miracles' – buttressed the authority of reason and at the same time supported the claim of Christianity to unique status as a vehicle of religious truth. This was the sort of balance between reason and revelation which the New England Unitarians learned from enlightened Anglicanism, and they took a great deal of satisfaction in it. Their reliance on Locke assured them of philosophic respectability; judicious resort to the Bible saved them from deism and maintained a bond with traditional Christianity. It was an intellectually sound and serious position: unbigoted, undogmatic, trusting in man and yet careful in its discrimination between what men might know and what they had to take on faith. Nevertheless, it was precisely against this admirable structure that the Transcendentalists declared war, and precisely against those elements about which the Unitarians felt most secure: the Lockian philosophy, and miracles.

II

In the decade before 1836, the year when Transcendentalism burst into public view with a flood of manifestoes, a new sensibility was emerging in the journals and early writings of the young Unitarian ministers. This sensibility was created in response to the new world of European Romantic literature just then finding its way to Boston. The major figures of this period of discovery were Coleridge, Wordsworth and Carlyle in Britain, Cousin and Benjamin Constant in France, Goethe and Schiller in Germany, together with certain of the new German theologians like Strauss and Schleiermacher, and, more dimly, Kant and his philosophic successors. The upshot of all these influences was a turn towards introspection, towards a new awareness of the self as an object of scrutiny and as a source of insight into the meaning of experience. The whole purpose of modern literature seemed to be an investigation of the inner world and an attempt to relate this world to nature, history and the divine. Simultaneously, there was a growing impatience with the presuppositions of Unitarian thought and the cautious style of Unitarian life. The Lockian image of the mind with its apparently mechanical action and its detachment from the emotions came to seem shallow. Was it not standing in the way of a truer awareness of human potentiality? Was it not having a chilling effect on the religious impulse? Was not Unitarianism, as Emerson said, growing 'corpse-cold'?

These tendencies came to a head in 1836 with the publication of a number of striking documents in which Transcendentalism emerged as a full-blown heresy in the Unitarian camp. Emerson's *Nature* remains the most famous of them, but it was by no means the most controversial. In that year Bronson Alcott issued his first important statement on education, 'The Doctrine and Discipline of Human Culture', and Elizabeth Peabody brought out her *Record of a School* in which she described Alcott's teaching methods to the scandal of Boston. Orestes Brownson published an unapologetic summary of Cousin's philosophy, and went on to a sweeping and radical vision of history in a little book called *New Views of Christianity, Society, and the Church*. George Ripley, too, contributed his earnest and heartfelt *Discourses on the Philosophy of Religion*. These works, and a number of lesser ones, made it clear that a new school had arrived on the New England scene, and that the breach with the old was irreparable.

They all began from the assumption that the root of intellectual evil in their time was Lockian empiricism. The immediate point of attack was miracles. Miracles were an anomaly from a true Lockian standpoint (though Locke himself had accepted them as consistent with reason). So long as the truth of Christianity rested on the evidence of miracles, it was subject to question on the same grounds of empirical validity as all other claims to truth. Nothing might stop the critic hostile to Christianity – David Hume, for example – from demolishing the whole notion of miracles as contrary to experience and thus reducing Christian faith to a childish delusion. In that direction lay the death of religion, for a rigorous empiricism could never admit the possibility of supersensual knowledge. It was very simple as the Transcendentalists saw it: if you relied on the senses, you could never believe in miracles; and if faith depended on miracles, there could be no faith. This was the underlying confusion responsible for the drying up of the Unitarian religious spirit.

The Transcendentalist solution was offered in two ways. On the one hand, they were fond of pointing out that talk of miracles was misleading since God was one will and nature a single act of creation – it was all miraculous if looked at properly. The miracles of the Christian churches, Emerson said in his 'Divinity School Address', were a Monster because they were not 'one with the blowing clover and the falling rain'. But more importantly, the way out of the confusion over miracles was to put Locke in his place, to recognize that the senses had an extremely limited role in the acquisition of knowledge and were irrelevant to the problem of religious truth. To achieve this it was necessary to go back to epistemological beginnings and to discard the apparatus of evidence and argument by which men found it necessary to reason themselves into faith.

The new starting point was a simple idea which proved so gratifyingly effective in solving problems that it became the key to nearly all Transcendentalist thinking. This idea, the distinction between Reason and Understanding, was borrowed most immediately from Coleridge – Brownson got his version from Cousin – who had derived it from post-Kantian German philosophy. In its Transcendentalist form, however, the idea had little relation to any of its possible sources, except for the use of Coleridge's terminology. It was, essentially, the American version of the great Romantic rediscovery of the intuitive and creative powers of the mind. By Reason – with a capital R to distinguish it from the eighteenth-century version – the Transcendentalists meant intuition, immediate knowledge independent of the senses, a grasp of

the Absolute arising directly out of the soul or instincts. Understanding was simply the old Lockian knowledge derived from sense
perception, but circumscribed by its relevance to the practical world
and scientific investigation. To Unitarians, of course, Reason was
nothing more than a shameless reversion to the old theory of innate
ideas which Locke had demolished, but this criticism was no longer
frightening. For the Transcendentalists, it was a way out of the trap
of the senses, a fuller, truer description of the powers they knew to
be latent within them. It explained the restless human desire for
freedom, the sense of an immanent unity with nature, the conviction of transcendent values irresistibly present to the soul. 'Man
is conscious', Emerson said, 'of a universal soul within or behind his
individual life, wherein, as in a firmament, the natures of Justice,
Truth, Love, Freedom, arise and shine. This universal soul he calls
Reason: it is not mine, or thine, or his, but we are its . . .'

The first service of Reason was to clear up the question of
miracles by demonstrating their irrelevance to the act of faith. The
reality of divine truth, it appeared, was precisely what Reason
spontaneously confirmed. Such truth emanated from the 'universal
soul' in man; it did not result from his inferences about the relation
of certain unusual events to the ordinary course of nature. George
Ripley, who was inclined to believe in the reality of miracles, saw
them as expressions of the divine character but not in any sense as
evidences. 'Our Saviour', he said, 'explicitly declared that he came
into the world to bear witness to the truth, not to exercise a
marvellous power over the agencies of physical nature . . . In the
final appeal, he rested the claim of his truth on its intrinsic divinity
and power'. And these intrinsic qualities are immediately recognizable to man by virtue of the Reason dwelling within him. Thus
'the true manner in which the evidences of Christianity are to be
understood . . . is the correspondence between the divine spirit of
Christianity and the divine spirit in man . . .'

The claim implicit in words like these extended far beyond the
argument over miracles. The idea of Reason contained a dynamic
force which often drove cautious men like Ripley and Emerson into
positions they had not foreseen but which they arrived at with a
sense of exhilarating liberation. Having begun by seeking a way out
of the Lockian impasse, they discovered that Reason was not simply
a mode of thinking but a fact of consciousness that required a
complete redefinition of the nature of man. When they spoke of a
'universal soul within or behind [the] individual life' or of 'the
divine spirit in man', the redefinition that was going on in their work

becomes apparent. It was carrying them to the point from which Channing had drawn back: the recognition that God was in man, that man was 'a god in ruins', in Emerson's phrase, but a god waiting to be resurrected. Brownson came to this revelation through his reading of Cousin: 'As [Reason] reveals spontaneously in every man's consciousness the vast world of reality, the absolute God, the cause and substance of all that *appears*, it follows that every man has the witness of the spiritual world, of the absolute, the infinite, God, in himself'. And Ripley, in his effort to show that the message of Christ proved itself by its intrinsic divinity and did not depend on inferences from miracles, asserted that 'reason though within us is not created by us; though belonging to human nature, originates in a higher nature; though shining in the mind of man, is an emanation from the mind of God . . .'

The divinity of man was one of the fundamental affirmations of Transcendentalism. Growing out of the idea of Reason, it led directly to the various forms of social, religious and political criticism undertaken by the whole school. This use of Reason differentiated it sharply from Coleridge's and all others'; it was astonishingly naïve, peculiarly American, and its implications were revolutionary. The divinity of man was, in effect, an answer to the problem the Transcendentalists had not even known was troubling them but which was, nonetheless, the most important stimulus of their thought. The problem was the meaning of democracy. Transcendentalism sprang up when the eighteenth-century sources of the democratic revolution were running dry. Just as Lockian empiricism no longer satisfied their needs, Lockian contractualism no longer provided an adequate basis for understanding the changed nature of modern society. It was a society in which monarchies and aristocracies had been overthrown, of equality and individualism and freedom, of science and industry. Men's chains had been struck off, and enormous material appetites and energies had been released. Democracy had triumphed – but what was democracy? What was the spirit animating it, and towards what goal?

The answer lay in the nature of man revealed by the idea of Reason. If men indeed shared a 'universal soul' and an inborn 'power of perceiving truth', then the acknowledgement of their value and dignity was a sort of religious obligation. This had been instinctively recognized when, for example, the Declaration of Independence spoke of 'unalienable rights [to] Life, Liberty, and the pursuit of Happiness'. Democracy, it appeared, had its root in a proper estimation of human nature, 'in the sacred truth', as Emerson put it, 'that every man hath in him the divine Reason, or that, though few men since the creation of the world live according to the dictates of Reason, yet all men are created capable of so doing'. Their unrealized capacity for living according to the dictates of Reason, furthermore, defined the ultimate purpose of Democracy. It must be the release and full expression of man's latent powers, his final emancipation from the bondage of historical evil – in a word, his deification. Naturally, the Transcendentalists believed American society to be farther along this path than any others. Although it was already a familiar idea that America was a new beginning for a 'new race of men', the Transcendentalists brought to this dream of national destiny an intensity of hope and a confidence in human nature that have made their statements a *locus classicus* of American idealism. Orestes Brownson had a special penchant for this theme, but his thought was typical when, at the beginning of his essay on Cousin, he justified the new philosophy as serving the needs of the American dream:

We are beginning to perceive that Providence, in the peculiar circumstances in which it has placed us, in the free institutions it has given us, has made it our duty to bring out the ideal man, and to prove, by a practical demonstration, what the human race may be, when and where it has free scope for the full and harmonious development of all its faculties.

Democracy was thus the link connecting the inner world of man's consciousness with the outer world of his conduct and social relations. It brought into plain view the image of man which the Transcendentalists had discovered in their attempt to restore a 'spiritual' religion, and it provided them with the impetus for a radical criticism of institutions and a utopian view of history that were the first real flowering of democratic ideology produced by the heirs of the American revolution.

III

At the heart of this ideology was a demand for freedom perhaps more insistent and absolute than any made in American history until recent times. The very act of talking about 'Reason', of imagining its fulfilment in some perfected human individual, compelled the Transcendentalists to see that freedom was an essential condition for them. What they were calling for, in effect, was the *liberation* of mankind, the release of a power everywhere latent but everywhere suppressed or unawakened. The principal cause of human failure seemed obvious to them: it was society, that mass of forms and conventions and institutions by which men were held captive, alienated from their true selves. In the early stages especially, there is an underlying drama in the literature of the Transcendentalist rebellion which gives it its infectiousness. The drama is that of the single individual engaged in a struggle to free himself from the bonds of society. This struggle is intense in Emerson; it comes to a powerful, even ferocious, climax in 'Self Reliance': 'if I am the Devil's child, I will live then from the Devil', and, 'What I must do is all that concerns me, not what the people think'. In Thoreau the same passion for a true identity acquired a relentless and all-consuming force; Thoreau's work is the summit of the Transcendentalist idea of individual freedom.

In part, the pressure behind this idea derived from two other sources. First of all, the movement was nourished in Puritan soil, and it gave vent to some of the most deeply ingrained characteristics of the Protestant temperament. Like their ancestors, the Trans-cendentalists believed that the essence of religion was an immediate personal relation with the divine, a contact that transformed and sanctified men, purging them of worldliness and infusing them with an ardent, joyful piety. Of course, they cared not at all for the legalism which was the other side of the Protestant mind; in this respect they resembled the antinomians of an earlier day. Reason was their 'grace', and the triumph of divine instincts over social conformity was their 'election'. Although they gave the idea of freedom much wider scope than their Puritan forebears, it still had the central purpose of allowing a return to the primitive source of religion: direct, unmediated apprehension of God's majesty and power. And just as the Puritan longing for a Community of Saints grew out of the extraordinary valuation they placed upon this apprehension of God, so 'democracy' for the Transcendentalists reflected the same impulse to renew society on the basis of the individually redeemed human soul. In this light, Transcendentalism can be seen to have repeated many of the typical features of Protestant schism. Brownson, who became a Catholic in the 1840s and a violent critic of his own earlier positions, was at least partly right when in 1846 he characterized the Transcendentalist movement as a desperate attempt to revive the religious spirit in a Protestantism that had been badly weakened by the Age of Reason.

Another source of the radical demand for freedom made by the Transcendentalists was the purely Romantic idea of organicism.

This was both a metaphysical and psychological principle, on the one hand an alternative to the Newtonian world-machine and on the other an escape from the Lockian mechanism of idea-formation. Because of their obsessive concern with the evils of 'sensualism', the Transcendentalists were especially drawn to the psychological implications of the organic viewpoint. In general, this meant that they understood the development of the mind by analogy with living creatures, as a process of growth, unfolding and ripening, a gradual realization of inherent qualities latent in the organism from its very birth. As early as 1826 Sampson Reed, the proto-Transcendentalist and Swedenborgian, had said that 'The mind is originally a most delicate germ whose husk is the body, planted in this world that the light and heat of heaven may fall upon it with a gentle radiance and call forth its energies.' Such a view helped the Transcendentalists interpret their own experience in having outgrown Unitarianism, but more importantly it explained how Reason emerged in consciousness, how the mind out of its own elements and independently of the senses could achieve a harmony with nature and an intuition of divine truth.

The organic theory of mental growth was responsible to a considerable extent for the dynamic quality of Reason and inevitably contributed to Transcendentalist radicalism. The 'germ' Reed spoke of was both active and vulnerable. It sought to expand according to the law implanted in it, and hence an impulse was generated in the soul that moved men relentlessly towards awareness of the divinity within them. But needing 'the light and heat of heaven', it was thwarted in its development by a materialistic and conformist society. A sort of biological necessity therefore urged men into conflict with the institutions that surrounded them, and as Reason quickened into life under such influences as nature and the 'Gospel of Christ' the conflict evolved into a full-fledged struggle between individual and society.

A combination of factors then – Reason, the organic metaphor with which it was conceived, and an atavistic Puritanism – pushed the Transcendentalists to an unprecedented demand for individual freedom. In this demand was the burning core of their social criticism. From a somewhat diffident band of ecclesiastical reformers hoping to reawaken the piety of the New England churches, they found themselves transformed by the issue of freedom into radical antagonists of society at large. In a sense, they were compelled to enact the drama which they had first discovered intellectually, the drama of liberation from all that stood between them and 'the dictates of Reason'.

IV

Being churchmen, they turned first to the church. In the contro-versy over miracles the Transcendentalists had placed their main reliance on the doctrine of Reason which provided them with a new basis for the certainty of religious truth. Ripley, in typical fashion, had insisted that the truth of Christianity was not proved to the Understanding but given immediately to the Reason. The Gospel of Christ which corresponded to 'the divine spirit in man' was its own verification; it did not require learned expositors. But this line of thought cast doubt not only on the rational methods of Unitarian theorists, but on the very idea of a church. If the Christian message and the nature of man were in perfect correspondence, what need was there of an external authority on matters of ritual and theology? Was not such an authority bound to clash with the divinity innate in human consciousness?

Three discourses on these questions are especially memorable: Ripley's 'Jesus Christ, the Same Yesterday, Today, and Forever', Emerson's 'Divinity School Address' and Parker's 'The Transient and Permanent in Christianity'. The burden of all three was that the Word of God had always and necessarily been at odds with the institutions of religion. Between Christ, who had spoken the eternal and immutable truths of Reason, and 'historical Christianity' with its contradictory dogmas and violent idolatries, there was a gulf which no theological casuistry might bridge. In making this dis-tinction the Transcendentalists saw themselves as heralding the ultimate purification of religion: the separating out of the simple Gospel of Christ from the forms which had corrupted it through the ages. It was a task which, they frequently said, was the 'mission of the age', an anarchistic and millennarian dream which had a powerful hold over them, at least in the first flush of their en-thusiasm. But it was also closely related to a more immediate social end: the broadening of democracy in the churches and society as a whole. When Andrews Norton, the 'Unitarian Pope', attacked Transcendentalism as 'The Latest Form of Infidelity' on the ground that it claimed a degree of religious certainty beyond the power of human attainment, Ripley replied that Norton's real motive was to keep sacred truth the exclusive possession of a priestly caste. He accused Norton of removing 'Christianity from its stronghold in the common mind, and [putting] it into the keeping of scholars and antiquaries'. But 'The sword of the Spirit', Ripley went on, 'is not wielded after the tactics of a university', and

Christian truth would irresistibly continue to make itself known to the 'intuitive perceptions' of ordinary men. Brownson was even more vehement against the evils of priestcraft. In his essay on 'The Laboring Classes' he denounced the priesthood as an instrument of human subjugation, and in the name of 'Christian law' asserted that the first remedy for slavery and inequality was 'to be sought in the destruction of the priest'. In this manner the old quarrel in the church between those who thought man depraved and helplessly dependent on the will of God and those who thought him capable of acting to save himself was converted into a struggle between religious authority and the democracy of universal Reason.

But a new Reformation was only the first step in a much broader prospect of social change. The church was no longer so pivotal an institution as to absorb all the dreams of democratic radicalism. In fact, the very nature of American society had made economic and political relations the dominant interests of masses of men, and the Transcendentalists had from the start been pulled by the same forces that were at work in the world around them. For the sake of economy, we may give special attention to two social questions in which the Transcendentalists were particularly interested because of their bearing on individual freedom: education and work. Education had been a sensitive issue in America ever since the Revolution, when Republican thinkers like Jefferson had proclaimed the necessity for a new system in keeping with the changed political status of the country. Education in this view was to be publicly supported, universal and secular; its subject matter, the real world (as opposed to the classics); its outlook, scientific and practical; and its aim, to create useful and virtuous citizens, able to govern themselves and to share in the government of the nation. To the Transcendentalists this ideal represented a sort of educational Unitarianism, degraded by its compromise with 'sensualism' and barely attuned to the needs of democratic man. The discovery of Reason made it possible to imagine a new kind of education, the basic purpose of which was to elicit from the scholar the truths hidden in his own consciousness. As early as 1828, Bronson Alcott, who was to become the chief Transcendentalist spokesman on this subject, wrote in his journal that

The province of the instructor should be simple, awakening, invigorating, directing, rather than the forcing of the child's faculties upon prescribed and exclusive courses of thought. He should look to the child to see what is to be done, rather than to his book or his system. The child is the book. The operations of his mind are the true system. . . . Let him follow out the impulses, the thoughts, the volitions, of the child's mind and heart, in their own principles and rational order of expression, and his training will be what God designed it to be – an aid to prepare the child to aid himself.

Here is the kernel of Transcendentalist educational thought and the starting point, in effect, of American 'progressive education'. The focus is shifted from subject matter or social outcome to the child as an end in himself; the inner world takes priority over the outer; and the teacher's function is to stimulate the independent growth of his pupil rather than force upon him an extraneous burden of learning.

In 1834 Alcott began the Temple School in Boston, an experiment as important in its way as Brook Farm for its revelation of the utopian motives at work in Transcendentalism. The school, in fact, was better served so far as history is concerned than the commune, for its rationale and methods were recorded in great detail by Elizabeth Peabody and Alcott in two books: *Record of a School*, and *Record of Conversations on the Gospels Held in Mr Alcott's School*. As Miss Peabody pointed out, 'Contemplation of spirit is the first principle of human culture', and Alcott's job was to make his pupils aware of spirit 'as it unveils itself within themselves'. His method was a cultivated introspection in which the chief task was an analysis of language. Like Emerson, Alcott believed that 'Words are signs of natural facts', and since nature is the embodiment of spirit, words are ultimately links between mind and matter. Through words the spiritual content of nature is disclosed, as the imagination grasps in them the divine meanings hidden in facts. The primary activity of the imagination, for Alcott, was to form language out of nature; hence in the analysis of words the mind is revealed to itself in the mirror of nature as the grand repository and instigator of spiritual insight.

Alcott's teaching was thus designed to be a complete survey of human consciousness, the elements of which he distinguished under such general headings as Love, Conscience, Will, Faith, Judgment, etc. Over and over the lesson was conveyed that in the operations of the soul, as in those of external nature, a divine power was at work which was the fundamental reality of the self and which linked the self to the outer world. A new point of view was thereby inculcated based on man's awareness of 'the true idea of his being', namely that he is divinity incarnate; he commands a spiritual power capable of recovering his lost Edenic sovereignty over the earth and the flesh.

In [man's] nature [Alcott said] is wrapped up the problem of all power reduced to a simple unity. The knowledge of his own being includes, in its endless circuit, the alphabet of all else. It is a universe wherein all else is imaged. God – nature – are the extremes of which he is the middle term, and through his being flow these mighty forces, if, perchance, he shall stay them as they pass over his consciousness, apprehend their significances – their use – and then conforming his being to the one, he shall again conform the other to himself.

Alcott's school lasted for about five years. Brook Farm had only a slightly longer life, but its much larger share of public attention and its fame as a communal experiment have seemed to lift it out of the narrow realm of purely Transcendentalist manifestations. Nevertheless, especially in its earliest days before ideological confusion set in, Brook Farm was a direct expression of Transcendentalist concerns. Even in the sharp disagreements that attended its birth, such as that between Emerson and Ripley, we may find an interesting clarification of certain basic Transcendentalist motives and assumptions.

Brook Farm was intended to solve the problem of work, or labour, which was raised in the first place by the Transcendentalist theory of human nature. No one voiced its hopes more simply and eloquently than did George Ripley:

Our objects, as you know, [he wrote to Emerson] are to insure a more natural union between intellectual and manual labor than now exists; to combine the thinker and the worker, as far as possible, in the same individual; to guarantee the highest mental freedom by providing all with labor adapted to their tastes and talents, and securing to them the fruits of their industry; to do away with the necessity of menial services by opening the benefits of education and the profits of labor to all; and thus to prepare a society of liberal, intelligent, and cultivated persons whose relations with each other would permit a more simple and wholesome life than can be led amidst the pressure of our competitive institutions.

The most important point was the first: 'a more natural union between intellectual and manual labour'. By such a union Ripley intended a good deal more than 'the simple performance of both kinds of work. He meant that at Brook Farm work would be an integral expression of the soul, an action of the self upon nature consistent with the Transcendentalist vision of organic inter-relatedness between man and nature. Work would not be reduced to a mere economic activity as it was in the world outside, where men cunningly exploited dead matter for the sake of physical survival or material reward. Such work only forced man and nature apart; it turned man either into a machine or, as Thoreau said of the ordinary New England farmer, a 'robber'. At Brook Farm, on the contrary, mind and matter would inter-penetrate; work would be what Emerson had demanded of the American Scholar: 'a total act'.

Emerson, nevertheless, was repelled by the whole idea; 'this scheme of arithmetic and comfort', he called it in his journal – 'a room at the Astor House hired for the Transcendentalists'.

I do not wish to remove from my present prison to a prison a little larger. I wish to break all prisons. I have not yet conquered my own house. It irks and repents me. Shall I raise the siege of this hencoop, and march baffled away to a pretended siege of Babylon? . . . Moreover, to join this body would be to traverse all my long trumpeted theory, and the instinct which spoke from it, that one man is a counterpoise to a city, – that a man is stronger than a city, that his solitude is more prevalent and beneficent than the concert of crowds.

Emerson's language was ill-tempered because he was on the defensive before people who thought of him as an ally or even a potential recruit. But he saw them as putting their faith in a new institution no better than the old ones and shirking their primary responsibility to free themselves. Emerson's conviction of human separateness was profound. Each man's relation to the universe, he felt, was so absolute that all other relations were essentially trivial. Only through communion with the divine could a man identify himself with other men, since they too possessed divinity within them. To unite with others was possible 'when all the uniters are isolated. . . . The union must be ideal in actual individualism'.

Ripley was the last man in the world to yearn for 'a room in the Astor House', and he was as deeply suspicious as Emerson of institutions. His passion, he said, was 'for being independent of the world and of every man in it'. What, then, induced him to plunge into a communal undertaking like Brook Farm? Why did the problem of work have to be resolved in precisely this way? At bottom, there were three reasons: utopianism, revulsion against capitalism and technology, and the powerful attraction of the American 'pastoral ideal'.[1]

(1) The utopianism of the Transcendentalists was closely related to the millenarian spirit which infused their minds when the core ideas of Reason and democracy were in process of taking shape. Millennialism is evident in a number of enthusiastic passages

[1] For a brilliant study of American pastoralism, see Leo Marx, *The Machine in the Garden* (New York, 1964), esp. Chapters III and IV.

celebrating the emergence and prospects of divine man; it comes as a burst of vision, a sudden glimpse into the future when the 'god in ruins' shall recover himself and enter into the 'kingdom of man over nature'. These words are from Emerson's *Nature* where they are spoken by the 'Orphic Poet', a persona by means of which the writer is enabled to give vent to the millennialist mood. If so normally restrained a man as Emerson was subject to fits like these, no wonder that others were even more susceptible. Brownson, for example, ended his *New Views* with a rapturous prophecy:

> Man is hereafter to stand erect before God as a child before its father. Human nature . . . will be clothed with a high and commanding worth. It will be seen to be a lofty and deathless nature. It will be felt to be divine . . . Man will be sacred in the eyes of man. . . . Slavery will cease. Man will shudder at the bare idea of enslaving so noble a being as man. . . . Wars will fail. . . . Education will destroy the empire of ignorance. . . . Civil freedom will become universal. . . . Industry will be holy. . . . The universe will be God's temple . . . religion and morality will be united, and the service of God and the service of man become the same. . . . Church and state will become one. . . . God and man will be one.

Millennium, to be sure, is not necessarily the same as utopia either on the plane of thought or of action; but in the progressive climate of nineteenth-century America the two could be, and often were, drawn close together. Brownson's foretaste of the holiness of industry was essentially what Ripley had in mind by 'a more natural union between intellectual and manual labour', and Ripley proceeded to carry the idea into practice. Furthermore, the millennial vision with its characteristic promise of reconciliation, peace and universal love naturally inspired, as it had for centuries, a longing for redemptive brotherhood, either as a portent of the new age or its actual initation. Hence the inevitably communal pattern. Brook Farm was thus, in part at least, a translation of millennial vision into utopian experiment, an attempt to 'combine', as Ripley said, 'the enchantments of poetry with the facts of daily experience'.

(2) Like most utopias, it was also conceived as a remedy for the ills of contemporary society. In diagnosing these ills the Transcendentalists made important contributions to American social analysis. At the heart of their diagnosis was a fear of the growing influence in American life of the twin forces of capitalism and industrialism. This fear probably had its origin in the old Jeffersonian distrust of urban economic concentration, but it was also grounded in a new awareness of the internal contradictions of democratic society. The very freedom on which democracy was

based had unleashed an acquisitive power capable of endangering freedom itself. The Transcendentalists rightly saw that this contradiction was the central issue of American history. Since the Revolution a new class had emerged, not merely of rich men but of men who controlled society's means of production, and their economic strength was already undermining the equality and self-sufficiency so crucial to democratic hopes. Brownson saw the growth of the factory system as the most ominous development of the period, and he bitterly compared the dependent condition of the northern workman to that of the southern slave: 'Wages is a cunning device of the devil, for the benefit of tender consciences who would retain all the advantages of the slave system, without the expense, trouble, and odium of being slave-holders'. In these circumstances the necessity for a second revolution was becoming apparent (at least to Brownson):

Now the great work for this age and the coming is to raise up the laborer, and to realize in our own social arrangements and in the actual condition of all men that equality between man and man which God has established between the rights of one and those of another. In other words, our business is to emancipate the proletaries...

Economic inequality had further implications for the critique of capitalism. When labour is a commodity, both buyer and seller are degraded; commercial relations dominate human intercourse and men are reduced to the status of things. Competition becomes a prominent feature of life, and the barbarism of primitive days is revived under the guise of civilization. Political corruption sets in, for the monied class, as Theodore Parker pointed out, 'buys up legislators when they are in the market; breeds them when the market is bare. It can manufacture governors, senators, judges, to suit its purposes, as easily as it can make cotton cloth'. Parker also observed what might be called a general trivialization of consciousness in society. It was manifested in a growing consumer materialism and a hostility to the disinterested culture of science and art. Even the promise of technology was betrayed by its industrial exploitation. The Transcendentalists were theoretically inclined to welcome the machine as an expansion of human power and a relief from drudgery, but they found the actualities of factory production horrifying. Their ambivalence is strikingly illustrated in an article by Parker that appeared in *The Dial* called 'Thoughts on Labor'. Parker begins by deploring the unnatural state of society in which work brings neither self-fulfilment nor the leisure that permits cultivation. One of the remedies available is the machine, and Parker launches into a conventional celebration of the instruments which 'Genius' has devised to make the river 'turn his wheel' or to 'fetch and carry at his command'. Parker is quite carried away. 'The Fable of Orpheus', he says, 'is a true story in our time', and he suggests that the machine has brought man to the last stage of 'progress in regard to labour' when 'he has dominion over the earth and enjoys his birthright'. But in the next breath he turns to the actual influence of technology as it is felt in the 'village of Humdrum'. Here the machine brings no relief from labour: 'the common people of Humdrum work as long as before the machines were invented, and a little harder'. They are rewarded with the tawdry gratifications of mass-produced consumer goods: 'red ribbons' for their bonnets, 'French gloves', and 'tinkling ornaments' in their ears. The social gulf between them and the vastly richer owners of property has widened, and atomization has increased as men struggle to hold or gain advantage over others. The social state of Humdrum is in fact degenerate, and the mill towns of Massachusetts which are its prototypes seem headed not towards a bright democratic future but a new 'tyranny', a 'feudalism of money'. Brook Farm was thus a remedy for the contradictions of American society and an alternative to capitalism, a political gesture as well as a dream of perfection.

(3) The shape both of the dream and the gesture were determined to a considerable extent by an American ideal that was already, in the 1830s and 1840s shifting its location to the past rather than the future. The American imagination had been haunted from the beginning by the image of a pastoral society in the new world, and it was this image more than anything else that guided the founders of Brook Farm. Pastoralism consisted of a few simple elements, although they might be woven into a variety of complex patterns: a rural location midway between the wilderness and the complex city, an agricultural economy, a general condition of equality and independence among men, a prevalence of homely virtue derived from simplicity of life and harmony with nature. These elements belonged primarily to literary tradition, but in America during the eighteenth century they were converted into the stuff of politics. The virgin continent, remote from civilization and untouched by the past, seemed the appropriate place to establish a living pastoral society. Jefferson, in his ambivalent way,[1] was the

---

[1] Marx, pp. 116–44.

most influential exponent of this view of American destiny. In his hands the materials of the pastoral tradition were fused with the democratic ideology of the Enlightenment into a permanent symbolism of the American farmer, rooted in his own soil, indebted to no one and the equal of all, his breast 'a peculiar deposit for substantial and genuine virtue'.

The American pastoral ideal was one of the sources of Transcendentalism to begin with, and its symbols were perfectly suited to the individualism and nature-romanticism of the fully developed movement. Thus when Ripley and his friends set out to provide an alternative to capitalist society it was practically foreordained that they would revert to the Jeffersonian model. Instinctively, for example, they turned to the countryside as the proper setting of their utopia, and they did so with the traditional moral associations in mind which came from the ancient pastoral antagonism – given contemporary relevance by Jeffersonian republicanism – between farm and city: innocence vs corruption, 'naturalness' vs artificiality, stability vs disorder, etc. Likewise, agriculture was the form of labour most appropriate to the mission of Brook Farm. As a basis of life, Miss Peabody said, it was 'the most direct and simple in relation to nature'. Agriculture had the double virtue of bestowing physical and spiritual sustenance; it made men independent, and capable of cherishing their independence. The intended effect, therefore, was a heightening of freedom, while the cooperative plan escaped the abuses of freedom induced by capitalism. In all these ways the pastoral idea dovetailed with Transcendentalist attitudes to create a peculiar blend of nostalgia and visionary hope. At Brook Farm, for a brief moment, the American Adam was superimposed on the American farmer; here, perhaps, is the secret of the community's long persistence in the national memory.

v

The Transcendentalist heyday lasted for a little more than ten years, from 1836 to the collapse of Brook Farm in 1847. Even before that time, perhaps in 1844 when *The Dial* ceased publication and Brook Farm went over to Fourierism, Transcendentalism had begun to lose coherence and force. But it remained a strong influence at least until the coming of the Civil War, emerging marvellously in the new forms invented by Thoreau and Whitman. And just as Poe and Hawthorne, contemporaries of Emerson, grew up in an intellectual atmosphere conditioned by the presence of

Transcendentalism and were forced to take account of it in their works, so Melville in the late forties and fifties exhibited how deeply it had entered and affected his own mind. Indeed, both to enemies and friends Transcendentalism seemed to strike the keynote of the age. Moreover, the Transcendentalist position exerted its claim not merely on philosophical grounds, but because it had achieved a truly original and impressive literary formulation in the writings of Emerson. When Hawthorne and Melville thought about Transcendentalism, it was primarily Emerson they had in mind. Despite his efforts to avoid publicity and his refusal to assume leadership, Emerson stood at the centre of the movement, brilliant and somewhat ambiguous, compelling a degree of attention well beyond that demanded by his ideas alone. Emerson's distinction was that his writing was more than the sum of his ideas, that in style and spirit he grasped something more profound than the abstractions which for the most part satisfied his colleagues.

Emerson emerged from the same Unitarian cocoon as Ripley, Parker, and so many others. He was born in Boston in 1803, the son of a Unitarian minister and descendant of a long line of New England clerics. His father died when he was young, leaving an impoverished family; his mother ran a boarding-house and educated her sons. In 1821 he graduated from Harvard and spent a few years teaching in a girls' school conducted by his brother. He was sickly, threatened by tuberculosis; in his journals he frequently accused himself of lack of vigour, aimlessness, shyness. Nevertheless, he was ambitious and imagined himself as thriving in the ministry on the strength of his imagination, his love of eloquence and moral truth. In 1825 he entered the Harvard Divinity School and in 1829 became the pastor of the Second Church in Boston. In the same year he married his first wife, Ellen, who was to die only sixteen months after their marriage.

By the time Emerson was ordained the forces were already at work in him and in the Unitarian church which were to make his career in the ministry a brief one. He was ill at ease with the historical evidences and rational proofs of Christianity on which Unitarianism rested. 'Modern philosophy', as he sensed it, was becoming inimical to 'Bare reason, cold as a cucumber', and was turning to 'blushing, shining, changing Sentiment'. The feelings that welled up in him and could not be denied, the intuitions of the soul – these were more and more the springs of his religious faith. In 1831, during the months succeeding his wife's death, Emerson experienced a profound psychological and intellectual crisis which issued in what ought properly to be called a conversion. As a result, he resigned his ministry in the following year – 'The profession is antiquated', he said – and struck out on a new path, the path of 'self-reliance'.

Emerson's conversion involved a total abandonment of the old props of faith and a surrender to the conviction that the divine was immanent in his own motives – his yearning towards moral purity, for example – and in his capacity to envision the beautiful coherence of nature, a perfect matching of his mind with the great, throbbing order that lay all about him. This identification of himself with God, or absorption of God into himself, filled Emerson with an exultant sense of power and freedom. He had only to trust himself now, brushing aside all intermediaries of church or law or custom, and speak his latent conviction for universal truth to flow from him. In the same month that his resignation from the Second Church became final, he put his daring new credo into blunt verse:

> I will not live out of me.
> I will not see with others' eyes;
> My good is good, my evil ill.
> I would be free; I cannot be
> While I take things as others please to rate them.
> I dare attempt to lay out my own road.
> That which myself delights in shall be Good,
> That which I do not want, indifferent;
> That which I hate is Bad. That's flat. . . .

From this point of view Emerson saw that his way of thinking must be completely reoriented. The cardinal principle, as he told his journal in 1834, was 'Nothing less than to look at every object in its relation to myself'. Just as Alcott had sought a new way to train the attention of his pupils on the spiritual reality that underlay all experience, so Emerson required a mode of perception by which the divinity within him was linked to 'the absolute order of things' in the world outside. But Alcott was essentially a dogmatist; he had only to peel back the skin of phenomena in order to find spiritual reality in its place and waiting. Emerson's insistence upon looking at 'every object in its relation to myself' was a far more demanding intellectual exercise. It required not merely the assertion of metaphysical truths, but a continual re-enactment of the process by which divine man apprehends metaphysical truths. Here was Emerson's real task as a writer: to demonstrate a way of seeing in which the individual eye, free of the constraints of history or culture, achieves ultimate meaning through its perception of the sensible data of the world. Ultimate meaning, for him, was latent in the act of perception, in the link which perception realizes between the self and objects, not in a systemization of abstract ideas derived from the analysis of perception. This is why Alcott's mind seemed at last sterile and monotonous – it had come to rest in ideas. To Emerson rather, 'the one thing in the world, of value, [was] the active soul', that is, the soul engaged in seeing. When he called for 'self-reliance', then, he meant primarily this inward activity; 'self-reliance' was not so much a moral injunction as the beginning of vision.

Another way of putting this would be to say that Emerson was a symbolist and that his chief effort was to recreate the symbolic mode of perception. He was trying, that is, to redeem thought from the empiricism and dualism of the previous century by substituting for them the integrative method of poetry.[1] His use of the idea of Reason, therefore, is more complicated than that of the other Transcendentalists. It is not simply a means of registering intuitive certainties but the power of symbolic insight itself. In symbolic perception the irreconcilable elements of eighteenth-century philosophy – mind and matter, the inner world of value and the outer world of fact – have no separate existences but are ways of talking about a single, unitary act. The distinction between subject and object vanishes, and in its place is an immediate grasp, through the symbols of nature, of the organic relation between human consciousness and what is outside of it, or of the organic unity of all parts of Being. In this way faith is restored as a source of knowledge, and the meaningless universe of atoms projected by the eighteenth-century philosophers is transformed into a vital, coherent order, glimpsed by the imagination in images of a re-covered Eden.

Emerson's first major work, *Nature*, illustrates the centrality of the symbolic method to his thought, despite the fact that he seems not to have fully understood what he was driving at. His form betrays his intention in its parody of logical argument, and a vocabulary borrowed from Plato, Plotinus, and Bronson Alcott frequently creates a strong flavour of idealism. But *Nature* is at bottom neither a logical argument nor a case for idealism. Its true motive is clearly stated at the very beginning: 'Why should not we also enjoy an original relation to the universe?' Emerson, in other words, is undertaking 'to look at every object in its relation to

[1] Charles Feidelson, *Symbolism and American Literature* (Chicago, 1953), p 121. Chapter IV of this book is a superb analysis of Emerson's symbolistic outlook.

myself'. In Section 1, 'Nature', he dramatizes the visionary stance which is both key and culmination of his quest. He is alone and under the stars; a mood of 'reverence' is awakened in him which is equivalent to a 'most poetical sense in the mind'. This sense is what enables him to draw his impressions together, to 'integrate all the parts'. A feeling of closeness with nature envelops him to the point of 'exhilaration'. And then his power of insight reaches its climax:

Standing on the bare ground, – my head bathed by the blithe air and uplifted into infinite space, – all mean egotism vanishes. I become a transparent eyeball; I am nothing; I see all; the currents of the Universal Being circulate through me; I am part or parcel of God.

This seems very near to mysticism, but not quite; or to pantheism, but not quite. It is essentially a vision of nature as symbol, in which the eye has pierced the veil of surfaces to discover the organic unity of Being. Emerson's identity is not wholly dissolved; he becomes 'part or parcel of God' in the act of perception. Nor is nature dissolved. It remains itself, but transparent and meaningful: 'the present expositor of the divine mind'.

The next six sections of *Nature* are devoted to a semi-analytic recreation of the vision with which the book begins. From 'Commodity' through 'Spirit' the brute stuff of nature is gradually metamorphosed until the ordinary world has been made identical with the world of thought. The lesson we arrive at when we finally ask, 'Whence is matter? and Whereto', is that 'the dread universal essence, which is not wisdom, or love, or beauty, or power, but all in one' creates and animates all Being, hence 'does not act upon us from without, that is, in space and time, but spiritually, or through ourselves . . . does not build up nature around us, but puts it forth through us. . . .' So we come back in the end to the divine soul of man, on the energy of which everything depends. 'The problem of restoring to the world original and eternal beauty,' Emerson says, 'is solved by the redemption of the soul'. The conclusion of *Nature*, filled with the music of the Orphic Poet, is a call for such redemption rather in the style of a Puritan preacher exhorting his congregation to seek the grace of God. But the Puritans knew that grace was given arbitrarily; Emerson was soon to discover that the symbolic method was no more certain than any other means of salvation known to his ancestors.[1]

---

[1] Emerson's religious development, his lapse into scepticism and ultimate resignation to a Fate as uncontrollable and absolute as the Puritan Jehovah, cannot be dealt with here. In any case, it is very well treated in Stephen Whicher, *Freedom and Fate: An Inner Life of Ralph Waldo Emerson* (Philadelphia, 1953).

What he came to realize was that, if he remained true to his own experience, symbolism posed a difficult challenge to the aspiring mind. Emerson, of course, was not always true to his own experience. His conviction of unity was so fundamental and necessary to him that he often permitted himself to touch the spring of faith by which nature's gates were automatically opened. But when he was at his best, when he 'set [his] heart on honesty', he recognized the elusiveness, transiency, and vulnerability of his most satisfying moments. This is Emerson's most impressive theme: not the triumph of insight, but the struggle to recapture and hold it amid the complex antinomies of life. Almost simultaneously with his bold appeal for men to trust their deepest selves, he was forced to admit that the very conditions of human existence interposed obstacles on the way to self-fulfilment. The basic difficulty lay in the indestructible fact of identity; experience always broke apart into the 'bipolarity' of the One and the many. Not long after he published *Nature* he accused himself of being a 'wicked Manichee!' for 'A believer in Unity, a seer of Unity, I yet behold two . . .' There seemed to be an incredible irony at the heart of life:

A certain wandering light comes to me which I instantly perceive to be the Cause of Causes. It transcends all proving. It is itself the ground of being; and I see that it is not one, and I another, but this is the life of my life. That is one fact then; that in certain moments I have known that I existed directly from God . . . and in my ultimate consciousness am He. Then, secondly, the contradictory fact is familiar, that I am a surprised spectator and learner of all my life. This is the habitual posture of the mind – beholding . . .
Cannot I conceive the Universe without a contradiction?

This contradiction, since he was unable to conceive the universe without it and unable to accept it as an ultimate fact, provides the dramatic tension of Emerson's work. His mind was always seeking to relate the particular to the whole, to convert, that is, every object into a symbol, and so he found himself engaged in a perpetual dialectic in which, as Feidelson says, 'the genesis of symbolism is enacted over and over'.[1] Dialectic is the heart of his method and his style. His essays, especially those written after 1840, are a repeated confession that the world lies about him in disorder, and a repeated struggle to make discernible through the fragments of his experience the order of which they are part. Here lay Emerson's greatness. Although he comforted himself with the knowledge that

[1] *Symbolism and American Literature*, p 123.

the irony of 'contradiction' was not absolute, he did not flinch from confronting that irony with its threat of scepticism and despair. Consequently, his work has real literary and moral distinction. At its best it is a courageous effort to deal with the whole of his experience, not merely those preferred truths which he shared with his fellow Transcendentalists. In his quest for unity he was willing and able to entertain the contradictions engendered by his own thought. In so doing he vindicated his ideal of the 'active soul' and offered a profound insight into the very nature of its activity. Perhaps Melville was thinking of this when, after hearing Emerson lecture for the first time and finding him an 'uncommon man', he said, 'I love all men who *dive*'.

## VI

After his resignation from the ministry, a trip to Europe in 1833 during which he was befriended by Carlyle and met Wordsworth, and his remarriage in 1835 to Lydia Jackson, Emerson's life settled into a regular dual pattern. On one side was his home at Concord, his study, and the surrounding woods and fields where he meditated and wrote steadily in his journal, accumulating the material for his lectures and essays. On the other side was his public life of regular forays to the lecture platforms which were springing up all over the country. In this career he visited such provincial outposts as Buffalo, Cleveland, Cincinnati, and St Louis, and endured the hardships of stagecoach and riverboat travel as well as the courtesies of his often mystified hosts. Gradually his reputation became popular and national, his heresies were forgotten or ceased to matter, and after the Civil War until his death in 1882 he enjoyed the status of an eminent man, the 'American Sage', a representative in the spiritual realm of American progress and success.

Twenty years earlier Thoreau had died of tuberculosis, still relatively unknown as a writer and only forty-five years old. Emerson had given the funeral oration in which, among many words of praise, he expressed his disappointment with Thoreau's accomplishment, and for his condescension history seems to have exacted revenge. In the twentieth century Thoreau's reputation has eclipsed that of his master. Emerson has become blurred to us; his moralism, his personal aloofness, and his association with such vaguely oppressive entities as the Oversoul have contributed to obscure his intellectual distinction. Thoreau, on the other hand, has been ever more deeply etched on our minds, especially in postures of resistance and defiance. He is the writer as hero, whose work and life form an inseparable whole and whose integrity makes every heart vibrate as to an iron string. He has, that is, become an actor in the drama of cultural mythology – a not unsuitable fate for one who was so sensitive to the inner drives of his culture.

Thoreau was born in 1817 in Concord, Massachusetts, the son of a pencil maker. He attended Harvard College where he may have been among the audience of graduating students who heard Emerson deliver his 'American Scholar' address in 1837. After college he returned home and taught school with his brother until 1841 when he joined Emerson's household as a companion and handyman. Though he lived with the Emersons for only two years, and though he came to regard his friendship with the older man as a 'long tragedy', this relationship which began in the mid-1830s and lasted to the end of his life was central in Thoreau's development. He grew eventually to be more than a disciple, which was hard for Emerson to acknowledge, but his indebtedness to works like *Nature* and to the personal stimulus and encouragement of Emerson (which some partisans of Thoreau have questioned) is un-questionable.

In 1845 Thoreau began the adventure which he made exemplary in *Walden*. He settled by Walden Pond on some land belonging to Emerson and passed about two and a half years there, living not as a hermit – that was not his intention – but essentially as a scholar disengaged from worldly affairs. The time at Walden was an opportunity for communion with nature, but also, and perhaps more importantly, an opportunity for study and a great deal of writing. Thoreau, like Emerson, had kept a journal for many years; at Walden Pond he added to it extensively, and mined it for the composition of his first book, *A Week on the Concord and Merrimack Rivers*, which was published in 1849. Only after he left Walden did he deliberately undertake a book about his experience there, re-turning to his journals, adding later observations, revising, com-pressing and shaping his material into an extremely artful record of a single year. *Walden* was published in 1854; Thoreau wrote no other books. In his later years he lived mainly with his family, visited various parts of New England and Canada, and acquired a certain notoriety for his passionate defence of the abolitionist John Brown. The last two years of his life were marked by declining health and in 1862 he died.

Thoreau's fame rests almost entirely on two works, 'Civil Dis-obedience' and *Walden*. 'Civil Disobedience' was first published in

1849 in the one and only number of *Aesthetic Papers*, a journal edited by Elizabeth Peabody. Its doctrine is that individual conscience takes precedence over all external sources of moral decision: 'The only obligation which I have a right to assume is to do at any time what I think right'. From this Thoreau deduced the necessity, on critical occasions, of civil disobedience such as refusal to pay taxes. (Later, in defending John Brown, he seems to have had no qualms over Brown's acts of violence.) The power of the essay does not arise from its reasoning; indeed Thoreau makes little effort to argue his position. It derives rather from the intensity of his conviction, the courage of his defiance, and the vitriol of his contempt for mere power and numbers. Underlying his attitude is the Trans-cendentalist image of the self-reliant man, with which Thoreau was prone to identify himself. He conveys this, as he was later to do in the opening chapters of *Walden*, by threading 'Civil Disobedience' with the reiterated use of the word 'man' in a normative sense: 'I think that we should be men first, and subjects afterwards'. The effect is to imply that most men are not men – in Thoreau's imagery they are primarily machines, the passive instruments of state or social power – but that an ideal of manhood remains which will be instantly recognizable when it is appealed to. The doing of 'what I think right' depends almost exclusively upon the acknowledgement of this universally available ideal, for Thoreau does not take great pains to define, except by negation, what he means by 'right'. Yet, despite the great rhetorical force which he achieves by relying on the notion of 'manhood', it seems true that Thoreau no longer shares the older Transcendentalist faith in the divinity of man although it has a strong vestigial influence on his mind. Enough is left of it to goad him to scorn, even fury, towards mankind, but it is evident that he feels himself alone with his burden of conscience, and he slips, somewhat against his own principles, into the role of a Jeremiah crying out against a humanity constitutionally sunk in sloth, habit, cynicism, and docile obedience to the laws.

Thoreau's abandonment of one of Transcendentalism's central affirmations about the nature of man is an important reason for several of the distinctive qualities of his work. Because he is fundamentally sceptical of human nature, his self-reliance is less a means of redemption, as it was for Emerson, than a personal obsession or compulsion, and his moral outrage carries a strong flavour of egotism. The standards of human failure and success are never so clear to his reader as they are to Thoreau himself. This tends to place him beyond the range of criticism, or even of dialogue; one of the peculiarities of Thoreau's books is that they seem to have been written in a world uninhabited by other people. A second consequence of his scepticism was that Thoreau was forced to revert to what, with deliberate paradox, might be called 'Transcendentalist empiricism'. He could not assert the reality of Reason, yet nature remained to him basically the same as it had been for Emerson: 'the present expositor of the divine mind'. His approach to nature, therefore, laid heavy stress upon the senses as the means of receiving precise communication from the natural world. He consciously reversed the terms of censure which had been used by earlier Transcendentalists: 'We need pray for no higher heaven,' he said in the *Week*, 'than the pure senses can furnish, a *purely* sensuous life'. Yet the emphasis indicates that something more was at stake than sensory experience in and for itself. A '*purely* sensuous life' was one in which the senses were pure and so made it possible to '*see* God'. What Thoreau wanted to say was that nature was not 'merely' symbolic, but divine in itself, the actuality of God – God was visible and audible. Without the instrument of Reason, nature was not the rather generalized medium of intuitive vision it had been for Emerson. It was a host of particulars from which the eye and the ear, by an alert and disciplined passivity, caught hints of the divine presence. Thoreau's object, then, was a sort of mystical illumination via the senses. He thought that the fact in its very particularity could be induced to yield the secret of its cause and meaning, to 'flower in a truth'. The main concern of *Walden* is just such illumination. It is a book about the attempt to '*see* God'.

Even the most sophisticated readers of *Walden* tend to treat it as literal autobiography, a record of what actually happened to Thoreau while he was living at Walden Pond. There can be no more fundamental mistake, although making it is a tribute to Thoreau's art. *Walden* is an *imagined* work; it is a re-creation of experience in the form discovered by conscious intent. The actual moments of Thoreau's life are quite inaccessible. He is as much, or as little, to be identified with the voice who speaks to us in *Walden* as Henry Adams is with the hero of *The Education of Henry Adams*, or as Whitman with the hero of 'Song of Myself'. *Walden*, then, is not to be read as a validation of Thoreau's hypothesis about the relation of mind to nature, but as an imaginative statement of the hypothesis and an attempt to persuade us of its truth. Only from this perspective can criticism hope to measure Thoreau's achievement without descending into cultural mythology.

So excellent a critic as Perry Miller, for example, writes of

*Walden* as if it provided a test of the truth or falsity of the 'Romantic aesthetic':

If at one and the same time Nature is closely inspected in microscopic detail and yet through the ancient system of typology makes experience intelligible, then Thoreau will have solved the Romantic riddle, have mastered the destructive Romantic Irony. Seen in such a context, his life was an unrelenting exertion to hold this precarious stance. In the end the impossibility of sustaining it killed him. But not until, at least in *Walden*, he had for a breathless moment, held the two in solution, fused and yet still kept separate, he and Nature publishing each other's truth.[1]

The upshot of these remarks is that Miller wishes to admire Thoreau without believing his 'questionable thesis', and he feels constrained to take the thesis seriously in order to admire. Trying to accommodate his conflicting impulses, he talks as if the 'Romantic riddle' were more or less soluble, and as if *Walden* were a successful solution to it. In this light Thoreau takes on the aura of a prophet, and his book the authority of a revelation.

But it is patently absurd to speak of Nature publishing its truth (this language comes from Thoreau himself), or of anyone else doing so on Nature's behalf, for that matter. Only writers publish, and whatever truth they manage to convey is their own. The 'truth' that *Walden* conveys is the truth of Thoreau's attempt to create a language which would embody the mystical illumination he found in natural facts.

In this attempt he was only partially successful. Like other of his contemporaries whose writing began from symbolist premises, Thoreau soon learned that the flowering of fact into truth was an extremely elusive literary subject. The difficulty arose in Thoreau's case chiefly as a result of his unusual fidelity to natural facts. Emerson had, in a sense, stepped back from the issue which Thoreau was determined to face by concentrating on the subjective dilemma of the mind vacillating between unity and duality. Melville, on the other hand, was free to invent a world in which natural symbols were wholly converted into literary symbols. But for Thoreau Concord was his given, and he was committed to making of it what he could. His problem, as he conceived it, was to distil poetry – in practice this meant moral intuition – out of the nearest and most ordinary materials without violating their integrity or superimposing upon them the law of his own imagination.

---

[1] 'Thoreau in the Context of International Romanticism', *Nature's Nation* (Cambridge, Mass., 1967), pp 177–8.

The limitations inherent in this predicament may be suggested if we compare *Walden* for a moment with *Moby-Dick*. Both are narrated by an Ishmael who has deliberately removed himself from conventional life in order to confront the truth of direct experience. Both narrators are pursuing a quest in a microcosmic world aimed at penetrating to the 'lower layer' of meaning which is assumed to inform the symbolism of 'visible objects'. Both are impressed by the unexplored territory of the self which this quest reveals, and both are drawn to the sources of religion in the Orient as a way of restoring the sense of divine omnipresence. But Melville's Ishmael has a mind endowed with enormous associative energy; it draws visible objects into itself, releases their capacity for almost infinite suggestiveness, and finally creates a network of relations that binds them, despite the dissonance or contradictoriness of parts, into a unified whole. Melville makes imagination the furnace and anvil where the materials of the sensuous universe are melted and recast. His white whale is thus the most completely developed symbol ever realized in the pages of a book. All the meanings of the physical world conceivable to Melville are present in *Moby-Dick*, and yet they do not create an impossible incoherence but a grand multi-faceted design.

By comparison, the natural scene in *Walden*, though brilliant in detail and often luminous with an aura of meaning that seems to emanate from within, is thin and fragmentary. The landscape of Concord remains external to Thoreau and finally inorganic. Its major symbol, for example, Walden Pond, fails to exert the unifying and deepening influence on *Walden* that Thoreau's patient attention to it leads us to expect. Thoreau's procedure with respect to the pond is not unlike Melville's: he drinks from the pond, bathes in it, rows on it, fishes in it, measures its dimensions and records its changes of depth, observes its colour and surface and its seasonal variations. All of this scrutiny, so richly expressive of Thoreau's love, leads in Chapter IX of 'The Ponds' to moments of celebration like the following:

In such a day, in September or October, Walden is a perfect forest mirror, set round with stones as precious to my eye as if fewer or rarer. Nothing so fair, so pure, and at the same time so large, as a lake, perchance, lies on the surface of the earth. Sky water. It needs no fence. Nations come and go without defiling it. It is a mirror which no stone can crack, whose quicksilver will never wear off, whose gilding Nature continually repairs; no storms, no dust, can dim its surface ever fresh; – a mirror in which all impurity presented to it sinks, swept and dusted by the sun's hazy brush, –

this the light dust-cloth, – which retains no breath that is breathed on it, but sends its own to float as clouds high above its surface, and be reflected in its bosom still.

This passage is fairly typical of Thoreau's sensuous mysticism. It is basically an image heightened by metaphor – the pond as mirror – in which the qualities of brightness, clarity, and incorruptible purity are emphasized. These qualities hint at a meaning which is held in suspension by the metaphor, namely that in the waters of the pond man may see reflected the inconstancy and 'meanness' of his own nature. There is, in other words, a moral standard implied by Walden Pond, or a 'truth' referable to man which the divine presence in nature manifests through the symbol of 'sky water'.

Yet when we ask how convincing this symbol is, the answer is in doubt. Can a body of water really offer us moral instruction? Or, to put the question more fairly, has Thoreau succeeded in making his image a vehicle of the relation between man and nature which his whole book implies? For many readers a gap remains between the image and the purpose it is intended to serve. 'Purity' of water and 'Purity' of the moral life are essentially so different, and the latter concept remains so vague despite the brilliance of Thoreau's rhetoric in depicting the pond, that the two finally remain unassimilated. The symbol is, so to speak, only half-created, and it tends to resemble an allegorical device to which a spiritual meaning has been arbitrarily fastened. The cause of this weakness lies in Thoreau's devotion to fact. Although he is willing to employ metaphors in his rendering of the natural scene, these serve chiefly to reinforce the local impact of sensuous imagery. Thus the descriptive material of *Walden* fails to define the 'higher' reality (spiritual or divine) which is supposed to be present in sensory experience. If it were not for the sermons scattered throughout *Walden* in which Thoreau explicitly states his moral convictions, the reader would be at a loss to find his bearings among the particular details of the book.

Nevertheless, *Walden* achieves another kind of triumph. Taken as a whole, as a fable rather than as an attempt to validate what Perry Miller calls the 'Romantic aesthetic', the final impression made by *Walden* is like that of a myth. In this perspective its basic theme is self-renewal, and its elements are withdrawal from society, isolation, the discipline of poverty, communion with the sacred (nature), and the recovery of a unified and revitalized self. It is an exceedingly simple story that Thoreau tells, and even if the 'Romantic' aspiration of his hero goes unrewarded, a mythic design remains which links his story to other narratives of intense and lonely purpose. The purpose at last dominates the details of *Walden*. In the end one is forced to acknowledge something heroic about Thoreau. His passion to affirm the limitless possibilities and infinite worth of the self, with all his egotism, his facile scorn, and his blindness to the social fabric of life, led him to tell what has proved to be a quintessentially American tale.

# 7

# NATHANIEL HAWTHORNE

### Agostino Lombardo

Nathaniel Hawthorne's art has been studied, often with keen insight, by a great many critics, but the most illuminating words are still probably those written by Herman Melville, before he met Hawthorne and established a firm friendship with him, in a review of *Mosses from an Old Manse*:

Where Hawthorne is known, he seems to be deemed a pleasant writer, with a pleasant style, – a sequestered, harmless man, from whom any deep and weighty thing would hardly be anticipated – a man who means no meanings. But there is no man in whom humor and love are developed in that high form called genius; no such man can exist without also possessing, as the indispensable complement of these, a great, deep, intellect, which drops down into the universe like a plummet.

And further on:

. . . spite of all the Indian-summer sunlight on the hither side of Hawthorne's soul, the other side – like the dark half of the physical sphere, – is shrouded in a blackness, ten times black.

The same concepts can be found in the eloquent, impassioned letters which the great author of *Moby-Dick* (which was dedicated to Hawthorne), wrote to him after they had met and got to know each other, for instance in a reference to *The House of the Seven Gables*:

This book is like a fine old chamber, abundantly, but still judiciously furnished with precisely that sort of furniture best fitted to furnish it. There are rich hangings, wherein are braided scenes from tragedies! There is old china with rare devices, set out on the carved buffet; there are long and indolent lounges to throw yourself upon; there is an admirable sideboard, plentifully stored with good viands; there is a smell of old wine in the pantry; and finally, in one corner, there is a little dark black-letter volume in golden clasps, entitled 'Hawthorne: A Problem'.

And in fact there could be no better aid to understanding Hawthorne than these words. It is true that sometimes Melville assumes an attitude towards him streaked with a kind of mysticism, not hesitating to compare him to Shakespeare or to make rather surprising assertions, like the one in another letter: 'I shall leave the world, I feel, with more satisfaction for having come to know you. Knowing you persuades me more than the Bible of our immortality'; but while Melville's enthusiasm here arises from the sense of an 'infinite fraternity of feeling' towards the friend who had been able to understand *Moby-Dick*, it should also be pointed out that his critical judgment is well-founded and exact, and his view of Hawthorne's art penetrates deep into its very nature and its finest qualities.

It is indeed difficult to find a way of writing which looks, for the most part, so 'harmless' and 'pleasant'; at first glance, the reader might even ask himself what ever could have attracted Melville in a writer who seems so much nearer to the enjoyable but limited Washington Irving than to the impetuous, exuberant, tragic bard of the White Whale. Remembering the tumultuous openings of Melville's novels we find ourselves reading, instead, the opening paragraph of *The House of the Seven Gables*:

Half-way down a by-street of one of our New England towns stands a rusty wooden house, with seven acutely peaked gables, facing towards various points of the compass, and a huge, clustered chimney in the midst. The street is Pyncheon Street; the house is the old Pyncheon House; and an elm-tree, of wide circumference, rooted before the door, is familiar to every town-born child by the title of the Pyncheon Elm. On my occasional visits to the town aforesaid, I seldom failed to turn down Pyncheon Street, for the sake of passing through the shadow of these two antiquities – the great elm-tree and the weather-beaten edifice.

It might even be said that there is not a single point in common between these two writers. Melville's language ('Call me Ishmael . . .') reflects at once the temper of a writer from whom we might expect anything, a writer who might make mistakes but will at all events take us a long way, out of conventionality, towards possibly unlimited horizons. That paragraph by Hawthorne would lead us to believe that a calm, traditional, conventional novel will follow, basically an example of Victorian prose; our impression is that such a writer will not make mistakes but will not take us very far either, will never hurl us, like Melville does, into those depths in which great poetry constantly plunges us.

In fact, even Hawthorne's life story is totally without the exciting or at least unusual events which characterize the first part of Melville's life and the lives of so many American writers. To outward appearances, his life could not be more tranquil, middle-class and actually monotonous. Born in Salem on 4 July 1804, he passed a serene childhood in spite of his father's early death, and an adolescence in which an open-air life and irregular studies did not prevent him from reading certain books which were essential for his formation as a writer (at least Bunyan, Spenser and Shakespeare should be mentioned). From 1821 to 1825 he attended Bowdoin College at Brunswick in Maine, where the decision to devote himself to writing was gradually taking shape in his mind. This decision was finally put into practice during those 'solitary years' which saw Hawthorne, from 1825 to 1837, living with his mother in Salem, totally immersed in his reading and in his own literary activity. After 1837, the year in which *Twice-Told Tales* appeared, and after his meeting with Sophia Peabody, his 'intercourse with the world' became closer and more constant, but his life continued to lack colour and excitement. Marriage to Sophia, the birth of his children, Una, Julian and Rose, his posts at the Boston and Salem customs-houses, his stay at Concord and at Lenox, his encounters with the principal literary figures of his time, from Emerson to Thoreau and Melville: these are the salient events of Hawthorne's life in the period when his greatest works appeared: the short stories of *Mosses from an Old Manse* (1846) and *The Snow-Image and other Twice-Told Tales* (1852) and the novels: *The Scarlet Letter* (1850), *The House of the Seven Gables* (1851), *The Blithedale Romance* (1852). As to the ensuing years, tied up with his stay in Europe from 1854 to 1859, first as American consul to Liverpool, then as a tourist in France and Italy, they do not distinguish themselves for other characteristics than those derived from his inner experience, as is proved by *The Marble Faun*, the novel of 1859 in which his European experience is condensed. Only his last years – he died in 1864, while on a journey – are tinged with drama, but it is significant that this dramatic quality belongs to the sphere of art, not life, deriving as it does out of Hawthorne's inability to finish the four different works he was trying to write: *The Dolliver Romance, The Ancestral Footstep, Septimius Felton*, and *Dr Grimshawe's Secret*.

A life, then, which has the same external features of Hawthorne's art and to which the same words may be applied that the writer used in the preface to the 1851 edition of *Twice-Told Tales* to define those fruits of his imagination: 'They have the pale tint of flowers that blossomed in too retired a shade ... the coolness of a meditative habit, which diffuses itself through the feeling and observation of every sketch. . . . Whether from lack of power, or an unconquerable reserve, the Author's touches have often an effect of tameness. . . . The book, if you would see anything in it, requires to be read in the clear, brown, twilight atmosphere in which it was written; if opened in the sunshine, it is apt to look exceedingly like a volume of blank pages.' But such a judgment touches only the surface of Hawthorne's art and life. If we look deeper, if we really get inside the exquisite lines of his prose, and the orderly lines of his life, we realize that beneath the elegant, almost motionless surface there lies one of the most disturbed, tormented and problematical worlds possible to imagine. Hawthorne's true light is not twilight but rather dark, tragic night. This calm, reserved, refined man is obsessed by the problems of evil, sin and death. He cannot look upon any aspect of reality, either human or natural, without burrowing in beneath it and eventually finding the germ which corrupts and destroys. Of particular importance, with regard to this, are the *Note-Books*, not so much the ones which are limited to noting down events, but those to which the writer confides his own mental processes, his method of observing reality, the ideas to be elaborated and transformed into fiction. Here are some of the earliest entries:

The world is so sad and solemn, that things meant in jest are liable, by an overpowering influence, to become dreadful earnest, – gayly dressed fantasies turning to ghostly and black-clad images of themselves.

There is evil in every human heart, which may remain latent, perhaps, through the whole of life; but circumstances may rouse it to activity.

A story to show how we are all wronged and wrongers, and avenge one another.

An ornament to be worn about the person of a lady – as a jewelled heart. After many years, it happens to be broken or unscrewed, and a poisonous odour comes out.

To symbolize moral or spiritual disease by disease of the body; as thus — when a person committed any sin, it might appear in some form on the body, – this to be wrought out.

Many other examples could be added, taken from the *Note-Books* as well as from the stories and novels themselves. But it will be quite clear by now that the world, for Hawthorne, is not a calm, immobile landscape to be contemplated and sketched with the most suitable, elegant words, it is an abyss into which the writer must continually peer and probe, and which presents, to his appalled gaze, images of sin and mystery.

Although he had been meeting Emerson and his group for a long time, and had actually taken part in one of the utopian ventures of the Transcendentalist movement, namely the communistic farm project of Brook Farm, Hawthorne did not share the optimism of the Transcendentalists, nor their passionate certainty in human and American destinies, exalted by Emerson in his *Essays* and eloquently praised in Whitman's *Leaves of Grass* – and this lack of enthusiasm is amply demonstrated in *The Blithedale Romance*, that ironical work of 1852 inspired by his stay at Brook Farm. Evil and sin do not touch Emersonian humanity; nothing can break or even threaten the harmony, the communion and the loving brotherhood which regulate the life of the cosmos. For Hawthorne this harmony, although possible, is much harder to achieve and it is always opposed, deformed and threatened by the evil hiding away in the heart of the world – like the snake in a man's body in one of his stories. For Hawthorne, as for Emerson, external reality, nature, objects, tangible forms are merely symbols of a deeper, more inward, ultimately spiritual reality, and Hawthorne's language, like Emerson's, Thoreau's, or Whitman's, is an attempt to extract the secret meaning from reality, to render the sense of life in visible terms. But while for Emerson, as for Thoreau and Whitman, the result of such a quest is nearly always positive, a joyous revelation or rather a confirmation, for Hawthorne it is far more frequently a revelation of evil, of death in life, of the mystery and ambiguity which surround us.

The fact is that we must look for the origins of Hawthorne's view of life not so much in Transcendentalism as in the great spiritual movement at the roots of American tradition, Puritanism. It must be immediately pointed out that Hawthorne is not a Puritan. He has a tolerance and understanding of life which set him quite apart from the harsh discipline of that particular culture and religion. It is enough to remember the many stories in which the Puritan concept of life is condemned and the negation of life is seen in it, or *The House of the Seven Gables*, where the Puritan past is shown in an almost totally negative light, or *The Scarlet Letter*, where Puritan inhumanity is counterposed to the vitality and emotional wealth of love. In the introduction to *The Scarlet Letter* – where Hawthorne gives us a vivid portrait of the Salem customs-house and at the same time many useful points towards an understanding of his own formation – one famous passage is dedicated to the author's Puritan ancestors:

He was a soldier, legislator, judge; he was a ruler in the Church; he had all the Puritanic traits, both good and evil. He was likewise a bitter persecutor, as witness the Quakers, who have remembered him in their histories. . . . His son, too, inherited the persecuting spirit, and made himself so conspicuous in the martyrdom of the witches, that their blood may fairly be said to have left a stain upon him.

There are no doubts about Hawthorne's rational approach, about the judgment which he passes on the Puritans here as in the rest of the novel and elsewhere. And yet, that same passage continues with a sentence no less significant because of its gentle irony: '. . . let them scorn me as they will, strong traits of their own nature have intertwined themselves with mine'; and, before presenting and judging his ancestor, he has this to say about Salem:

. . . there is within me a feeling for Old Salem, which, in lack of a better phrase, I must be content to call affection. The sentiment is probably assignable to the deep and aged roots which my family has struck into the soil. . . . But the sentiment has likewise its moral quality. The figure of that first ancestor, invested by family tradition with a dim and dusky grandeur, was present to my boyish imagination, as far back as I can remember. It still haunts me, and induces a sort of home-feeling with the past, which I scarcely claim in reference to the present phase of the town. I seem to have a stronger claim to residence here on account of this grave, bearded, sable-cloaked and steeple-crowned progenitor, – who came so early, with his Bible and his sword, and trod the unworn street with such a stately port, and made so large a figure, as a man of war and peace, – a stronger claim than for myself, whose name is seldom heard and my face hardly known.

What is, however, more important, is that the bonds of feeling and blood by which the writer declares that he is tied to the Puritans are also spiritual and cultural bonds. Hawthorne is attracted in every way, as a writer, to the Puritan world, even though he condemns its less humane manifestations. First of all it provides him with a subject. In the critical study of 1879 which is still one of the keenest analyses of Hawthorne, Henry James rightly observed that Hawthorne 'had, as regard the two earlier centuries of New England life, that faculty which is called nowadays the historical consciousness'; and, considering the stories with Puritan themes, James described them as

the only successful attempts at historical fiction that have been made in the United States. Hawthorne was at home in the early New England history; he had thumbed its records and he had breathed its air, in whatever old receptacles this somewhat pungent compound still lurked. He was fond of it, and he was proud of it, as any New Englander must be, measuring the

part of that handful of half-starved fanatics who formed his earliest pre-
cursors, in laying the foundations of a mighty empire.

But if the history of the Puritans is of primary importance in
Hawthorne's writings, and has its place, directly or indirectly, in
most of his short stories and novels (even in those with a contemporary setting), it is not the only element in the relationship
between the author and Puritanism. It is actually the material
background against which a deeper, more inner relationship is set
up that colours Hawthorne's approach to reality (and consequently
implies a search for a narrative language which can express it).
Where else, if not in Puritan culture and historiography, can we find
the roots of a vision of the life of man and of human history, which
interprets this essentially as a moral episode? Considering the
stories which are usually defined as 'historical', we can note that
perhaps only 'Endicott and the Red Cross' is an exclusively
historical representation; in the other stories the historical purpose
is secondary to the portrayal of the moral elements of which the
story, as in the Puritan writers, is the outward expression. An
example of this is 'The Gray Champion', where the figure of the
mysterious old man who succeeds, merely through the authority of
his physical presence, in making the Governor's troops retreat,
takes on symbolic dimensions. An even more marked example is
'The Maypole of Merry Mount', where an episode of Puritan
history moves, as Hawthorne himself wrote, 'almost spontaneously,
into a sort of allegory', and the elimination of the too laxly tolerant
'settlement' of Mount Wollaston, thanks to the Puritans and Endicott, becomes a pageant not too far removed from the morality play.
Yet another example may be found in the four stories under the title
of 'Legends of the Province House': 'Howe's Masquerade', for
instance, shows the struggle between English and Americans as a
conflict of moral forces, and in the image of the political tyranny
exercised by the English, the idea of the universal tyranny of evil
takes shape.

At the same time, where else can we find the roots of that sense
of evil running through all Hawthorne's works if not in the bitter,
tormented religiosity which inspired a Jonathan Edwards to compose the terrifying words of his sermons and made him see men,
Calvinistically, as 'sinners in the hands of an angry god'? Where else
if not in a society whose spelling book began with the stern reminder 'In Adam's Fall we sinned all' and whose culture was
steeped in images from the Old Testament and *Pilgrim's Progress*? It
is on this base, more than on any other, that the major contribution

of Puritanism to Hawthorne's art takes shape. And even if this art can make play with other strings (like the delicate, ethereal chord struck in many parts of *The House of the Seven Gables*; and the elegiac, even idyllic chord in many sketches), there is no doubt that it reaches its most memorable notes, the notes which make Hawthorne a classic of modern narrative art, in the passionate and yet lucid, the pitiless yet tolerant portrait of human conscience in the face of sin.

For Hawthorne, then, as for the Puritans, human life is essentially a moral story; and the great theme of the author, the one on which his talents are most fully expended, is the great theme of the Puritans. Hester Prynne and the Reverend Dimmesdale in *The Scarlet Letter*, Donatello, Miriam and Hilda in *The Marble Faun*, to mention only the psychological portraits thanks to which Hawthorne really belongs to the 'great tradition' illustrated by F. R. Leavis, all derive their wealth and beauty from the fact that the writer considers and analyses them as consciences in the face of sin. They are not complete figures and they have no previous lives, one might say; their lives only really begin with their guilt, or with their knowledge of guilt, and with their sufferings. Their reality is all in their crises (and in this sense Hawthorne's heroes are the heroes of a tragedy which in America, right up to the twentieth century, is not expressed on the stage but in the novel). A significant example is *The Marble Faun*. This novel is marred by many weaknesses, especially by an insistence on the picturesque which Hawthorne himself recognized ('In rewriting these volumes, the author was somewhat surprised to see the extent to which he had introduced descriptions of various Italian objects, antique, pictorial, and statuesque. Yet these things fill the mind everywhere in Italy, and especially in Rome, and cannot easily be kept from flowing out upon the page when one writes freely, and with self-enjoyment.') However, the quality of the novel improves when the author concentrates on the ground which he knows best and examines the consciences of his characters, analysing the problem of sin and its consequences. From this comes the rich, intense beauty of a figure like Donatello, the happy, ingenuous, even primitive Italian who, after committing a crime (he kills the man pursuing Miriam), undergoes a profound transformation (*Transformation* was the title of the novel when it appeared in England). He droops, and loses that pagan freshness which had inspired the comparison between him and Praxiteles's Marble Faun. This transition (clearly symbolic of original sin) from a state of pure joy to a state of guilt, the progressive darkening of that happy nature, and the sadness which suffuses it, above all the new maturity of intelligence and behaviour that comes to Donatello through an awareness of his own sin, are treated with extreme delicacy and penetration by Hawthorne. This is true also of Miriam. Her ambiguity, her solitude, the mystery surrounding her, the fate which seems to be pursuing her for no reason, or perhaps for a deeper reason than we can know, combine to form a memorable figure, a portrait of a woman, precise in its particular concreteness but which also takes on universal qualities. And Miriam becomes more completely alive when Hilda is set beside her. The virginal Hilda, pure as certain characters from James, such as Milly Theale from *The Wings of the Dove*, breathes innocence and virtue; and yet, through being touched by evil (she was present during Donatello's crime) she is through no fault of her own so contaminated that she closes into herself like a wounded flower and almost withers away until she learns new strength and new maturity from her experience.

But the most illuminating example is also the greatest. *The Scarlet Letter* derives its exceptional expressive force from many elements, as we shall see, but undoubtedly one of the most important is the subtlety with which Hawthorne probes into the consciences of his main characters. So Hester Prynne, the adultress who is punished, is followed in every almost imperceptible movement of her psychological progress: in her proud, but desperate isolation; in her slow reconquest of society; in the renewed outbreak of feelings through which, although years of apparent expiation have gone by, her passion for the Reverend Dimmesdale can appear in undiminished strength; and in the dignity which she shows when she takes up her rightful place in the world again after the minister's death. Hawthorne also studies Hester's husband, Roger Chillingworth, with the same close attention with which the latter studies Dimmesdale to revenge himself, but it is the pastor who gives Hawthorne a chance to reach what is perhaps the finest achievement of his literary career. He penetrates as deeply as possible into this conscience tormented by guilt, whose pain is increased by extreme awareness, by a full knowledge of his own position and his own responsibility to himself, to other men and to God. The gradual physical and moral decline of the pastor; the oppression of his remorse, rendered even more agonizing by Roger Chillingworth's hounding of him; the desperate need to reveal his true self, which leads him, at the end of the novel, to a public confession and a death which is a liberation but which has impelled him to make the tragically absurd gesture of his nocturnal confession on the scaffold: all these are aspects of a moral portrait that opens the way to the great introspective visions of the modern novel. And it is precisely the scene of the nocturnal confession that seems to prove this perfectly:

Walking in the shadow of a dream, as it were, and perhaps actually under the influence of a species of somnambulism, Mr Dimmesdale reached the spot where, now so long since, Hester Prynne had lived through her first hours of public ignominy. The same platform or scaffold, black and weather-stained with the storm or sunshine of seven long years, and foot-worn, too, with the tread of many culprits who had since ascended it, remained standing beneath the balcony of the meeting-house. The minister went up the steps.

It was an obscure night of early May. An unvaried pall of cloud muffled the whole expanse of sky from zenith to horizon. If the same multitude which had stood as eye-witnesses while Hester Prynne sustained her punishment could now have been summoned forth, they would have discerned no face above the platform, nor hardly the outline of a human shape, in the dark gray of midnight. But the town was all asleep. There was no peril of discovery. . . . No eye could see him, save that ever-wakeful one which had seen him in his closet, wielding the bloody scourge. Why, then had he come hither? Was it but the mockery of penitence? A mockery, indeed, but in which his soul trifled with itself! A mockery at which angels blushed and wept, while fiends rejoiced, with jeering laughter . . .

And thus, while standing on the scaffold, in this vain show of expiation, Mr Dimmesdale was overcome with a great horror of mind, as if the universe were gazing at a scarlet token on his naked breast, right over his heart. On that spot, in very truth, there was, and there had long been, the gnawing and poisonous tooth of bodily pain. Without any effort of his will, or power to restrain himself, he shrieked aloud; an outcry that went pealing through the night, and was beaten back from one house to another, and reverberated from the hills in the background; as if a company of devils, detecting so much misery and terror in it, had made a plaything of the sound, and were bandying it to and fro.

'It is done!' muttered the minister, covering his face with his hands. 'The whole town will awake, and hurry forth, and find me here!'

But it was not so. The shriek had perhaps sounded with a far greater power, to his own startled ears, than it actually possessed. The town did not awake . . .

The full significance of the scene can only be grasped when it is seen in its context. Here, however, the emblematic quality must be pointed out. In this tangible representation of a moral reality, in this man, in this human soul torn by guilt and on whose tragic crisis such an intense, all-revealing light is projected, in this physical landscape which is all one with the moral situation, background, part and symbol of it, lies the essence of Hawthorne's art, of his themes and his language.

In this scene there is also, in dramatic relief, a central aspect of Hawthorne's world: the identification of guilt and its consequence with solitude. Not only *The Scarlet Letter*, in fact (where the minister's solitude in that tragic square has its counterpart in the solitude of the other characters, from Hester to Roger and even little Pearl), but all Hawthorne's works may be considered as a profound, compassionate study of human loneliness. His first character is solitary, the Fanshawe of his first, rejected novel, *Fanshawe* (1828), and so are Ilbrahim, the pathetic hero of 'The Gentle Boy', a victim of religious intolerance; Robin, the boy in the magnificent story 'My Kinsman, Major Molineux', who reaches maturity through his own, solitary discovery of evil; Reuben, the central figure of 'Roger Malvin's Burial', oppressed by remorse because he has abandoned his dying friend; and the main characters of *The Marble Faun*, Donatello, Miriam, even Hilda:

> Hilda's situation was made infinitely more wretched by the necessity of confining all her trouble within her consciousness. To this innocent girl, holding the knowledge of Miriam's crime within her tender and delicate soul, the effect was almost the same as if she herself had participated in the guilt. Indeed, partaking the human nature of those who could perpetrate such deeds, she felt her own spotlessness impugned.
> Had there been but a single friend, – or not a friend, since friends were no longer to be confided in, after Miriam had betrayed her trust, – but, had there been any calm, wise mind, any sympathizing intelligence; or, if not these, any dull, half-listening ear into which she might have flung the dreadful secret as into an echoless cavern, – what a relief would have ensued! But this awful loneliness! It enveloped her withersoever she went. It was a shadow in the sunshine of festal days; a mist between her eyes and the pictures at which she strove to look; a chill dungeon, which kept her in its gray twilight and fed her with its unwholesome air, fit only for a criminal to breathe and pine in! She would not escape from it. In the effort to do so, straying farther into the intricate passages of our nature, she stumbled, ever and again, over this deadly idea of mortal guilt.

Nor could it have been any different, in a fiction which centres on the relationship between man and sin, because solitude is closely linked to sin for Hawthorne. It does not have the 'heroic' quality evident in so much Romantic literature, but on the contrary is a negative condition, is guilt, a sin itself, or else is a punishment, a penalty that must be endured – the worst penalty that can be inflicted on man.

Through this conception of solitude as guilt and pain, we are brought to a realization of the positive element of Hawthorne's vision, to the discovery of the instrument of salvation, the possible alternative. The alternative lies in the opposite of solitude, that is, in social harmony, in love, in that 'intercourse with the world' which Hawthorne insists that he wants to establish through his writings. It is found in a life where man accepts his own limitations, thus realizing his own humanity without destroying the humanity of others, and drawing on that in order to live fully himself. So in 'Wakefield', where Hawthorne tells the story of a man who voluntarily cut himself off from the world and, when he decides to go back, finds the most squalid emptiness around him, we read:

Amid the seeming confusion of our mysterious world, individuals are so nicely adjusted to a system, and systems to one another, and to a whole, that, by stepping aside for a moment, a man exposes himself to a fearful risk of losing his place forever. Like Wakefield, he may become, as it were, the Outcast of the Universe.

In his relationship with the world, in social harmony, in love, man can find the true expression of himself. Whoever turns his back on that love, whoever tries to prefer himself to society, not only becomes an outcast, but loses that wealth of feeling which makes life possible. Fullness of life, 'ripeness', lies for Hawthorne in the harmonious balance of mind and heart. When mind predominates, the heart withers, and to Hawthorne there is no worse suffering than this, as he shows in 'The Christmas Banquet', where the unhappiest man in the world is Gervayse Hastings, with his cold heart:

'It is a chilliness – a want of earnestness – a feeling as if what should be my heart were a thing of vapour – a haunting perception of unreality! Thus seeming to possess all that other men have – all that men aim at – I have really possessed nothing, neither joy nor griefs. All things, all persons – as was truly said to me at this table long and long ago – have been like shadows flickering on the wall. It was so with my wife and children – with those who seemed my friends: it is so with yourselves, whom I see now before me. Neither have I myself any real existence, but am a shadow like the rest . . . Mine – mine is the wretchedness! This cold heart – this unreal life! Ah! it grows colder still.'

The behaviour which produces this withering of the heart more than any other, and which Hawthorne therefore points to with horror as 'the Unpardonable Sin', is that of the person who not only tends to cut himself off from the world, breaking off the 'intercourse' and rejecting love, but also, like Faust, tries to reach a higher knowledge, modify natural order and put himself in God's place. So we may read in 'Ethan Brand':

'I have looked,' said he, 'into many a human heart that was seven times hotter with sinful passions than yonder furnace is with fire. But I found not there what I sought. No, not the Unpardonable Sin!'

'What is the Unpardonable Sin?' asked the lime-burner; and then he shrank farther from his companion, trembling lest his question should be answered.

'It is a sin that grew within my own breast,' replied Ethan Brand, standing erect with a pride that distinguishes all enthusiasts of his stamp. 'A sin that grew nowhere else! The sin of an intellect that triumphed over the sense of brotherhood with man and reverence for God, and sacrificed everything to its own mighty claims! The only sin that deserves a recompense of immortal agony!'

Like Ethan Brand, all who commit Faust's sin are punished. Many of the characters which have already been mentioned can be interpreted in this light, from young Fanshawe, who wants to know too much, to Roger Chillingworth, who sins in having neglected Hester Prynne for science and also in trying to set himself up in God's place by punishing the two adulterers. Yet another case is 'The Man of Adamant', in which the inhuman discipline and religious fanaticism of the Puritan Richard Digby corresponds to the material hardening of his heart. When he pursues his abstract ideal of purity, he cuts himself off from the world and shuts himself away in a cave, and then not merely does his heart become stony but his whole body seems like a statue to the person who finds it. In *The Blithedale Romance*, where Hawthorne criticizes Transcendentalist utopianism, sometimes genially, and sometimes harshly, the 'reformer' Hollingsworth (in whom we can perhaps detect certain features of Emerson) is criticized for the Faust- element which is hidden within his ambition:

. . . I began to discern that he [Hollingsworth] had come among us actuated by no real sympathy with our feelings and our hopes, but chiefly because we were estranging ourselves from the world, with which his lonely and exclusive object in life had already put him at odds. Hollingsworth must have been originally endowed with a great spirit of benevolence, deep enough and warm enough to be the source of as much disinterested good as Providence often allows a human being the privilege of conferring upon his fellows. This native instinct yet lived within him. . . . But, by and by, you . . . grew drearily conscious that Hollingsworth had a closer friend than ever you could be; and this friend was the cold, spectral monster which he had himself conjured up, and on which he was wasting all the warmth of his heart, and of which, at last, – as these men of a mighty purpose so invariably do, – he had grown to be the bond-slave. It was the philanthropic theory . . .

And further on:

I loved Hollingsworth. . . . But it impressed me, more and more, that there was a stern and dreadful peculiarity in this man, such as could not prove otherwise than pernicious to the happiness of those who should be drawn into too intimate a connection with him. He was not altogether human. There was something else in Hollingsworth besides flesh and blood, and sympathies and affections and celestial spirit.

This is always true of those men who have surrendered themselves to an overruling purpose. . . . They have no heart, no sympathy, no reason, no conscience. They will keep no friend, unless he make himself the mirror of their purpose; they will smite and slay you, and trample your dead corpse under foot. . . . They have an idol to which they consecrate themselves high-priest and deem it holy work to offer sacrifices of whatever is most precious.

Many other examples could be cited, since this theme is treated by Hawthorne from start to finish of his literary career. The most interesting one is probably provided by the story 'The Birthmark', in which a scientist, Aylmer, succeeds in removing a tiny birthmark shaped like a hand from his wife Georgiana's cheek, as he considers it 'the visible mark of earthly imperfection'; Georgiana is thus made 'perfect', but this is achieved at the cost of her life:

The fatal hand had grappled with the mystery of life, and was the bond by which an angelic spirit kept itself in union with a mortal frame. As the last crimson tint of the birthmark – that sole token of human imperfection – faded from her cheek, the parting breath of the now perfect woman passed into the atmosphere, and her soul, lingering a moment near her husband, took its heavenward flight.

In 'The Birthmark' the Faust theme is expressed with a straightforwardness equal to its high artistic level. It is also a perfect example of Hawthorne's use of an instrument, the symbol, which he took from the Puritan tradition (here is another fundamental element of that relationship) and which he bequeathed to American literature in revivified form. If we look closely at the tiny, persistent blemish on Georgiana's cheek, we see that it seems as changeable, ambiguous and indefinable in its material form as in its meaning. While its actual colours vary (usually 'the mark wore a tint of deeper crimson, which imperfectly defined its shape amid the surrounding

rosiness' but sometimes, when Georgiana blushed, 'it gradually
became more indistinct', to finally become, after a moment of
unexpected pallor, 'a crimson stain upon the snow') and while it
seems 'now vaguely portrayed, now lost, now stealing forth again
and glimmering to and fro with every pulse of emotion that
throbbed within her heart', the meaning given to it fluctuates and
varies. Beside the meaning guessed at by Aylmer, there is the one
given to it by women, who consider the birthmark ugly, and at the
opposite pole, the one given to it by many men who 'would have
risked life for the privilege of pressing [their] lips to the mysterious
hand'. In other words, we are faced with something mysterious and
ambiguous that throws mystery and ambiguity over the entire story,
that is, over the entire reality in whose context the author has placed
it.

Another story, 'The Minister's Black Veil', is fully indicative of
the functions of the symbol in Hawthorne. The story is about a
clergyman named Hooper, who one day appears in the pulpit with
his face covered by a black veil. From that moment on he never
again removes it, in public or in private. The veil cuts him off from
other men and arouses terror in them, and he refuses to be parted
from it even on the point of death, crying out to his fellows:

'Why do you tremble at me alone? . . . Tremble also at each other! Have
men avoided me, and women shown no pity, and children screamed and
fled, only for my black veil? What, but the mystery which it obscurely
typifies, has made this piece of crape so awful? When the friend shows his
inmost heart to his friend; the lover to his best beloved; when man does not
vainly shrink from the eye of his Creator, loathsomely treasuring up the
secret of his sin; then deem me a monster, for the symbol beneath which I
have lived, and die! I look around me, and lo! on every visage, a Black Veil!'

The symbol here is the true protagonist of the story which, dealing
with the themes of sorrow and sin, also suggests through that black
veil, the mystery and ambiguity of life itself. We do not actually
know what the veil symbolizes, what that 'mysterious emblem'
represents. What we do know is the effect produced by it – the
emptiness which it creates around the minister, the terror it arouses
in the faithful he turns to. So we learn that when he preaches, the
veil seems to fill his words with 'a subtle power' and that 'each
member of the congregation, the most innocent girl, and the man of
hardened breast, felt as if the preacher had crept upon them,
behind his awful veil, and discovered their hoarded iniquity of deed
or thought'; and we learn that the veil creates a sort of communion
between the minister and the dead, and throws a dark shadow over

even the happiest circumstances. But we do not know its meaning: whether it is the symbol of a sin committed by the minister or by mankind; or whether it is a sign of expiation or of sacrifice, a gesture of humility or of pride, an offence or a punishment; whether its origins lie in good or evil: all this remains a secret because no one meaning can cancel out another, in the same way that with Melville's whale and the whiteness of its enormous body, all meanings are possible, and the symbol, whether the black veil or the white whale, absorbs them all and goes beyond them. On the other hand, it is because of this ambiguity, as opposed to the mathematical clarity and lucidity of allegory (which Hawthorne uses in several places) that the symbol has its reason for being as well as its artistic validity. This ambiguity is actually the image of life itself, of the universal mystery towards which the writer is moving: a mystery that cannot be defined in words, that cannot be summed up in the short space of a sentence, or in the architecture of a logical construction, but only guessed at and poetically suggested.

The symbol, as defined above, can be found in most of Hawthorne's short stories and novels – one thinks of the cloak in 'Lady Eleanor's Mantle', the picture in 'Edward Randolph's Picture', many objects and the house itself in *The House of the Seven Gables*, the flowers in *The Blithedale Romance*, the statues, pictures and the actual landscape in *The Marble Faun*, the spiders which crowd the unfinished *Dr Grimshawe's Secret*. The same theories of narrative writing that Hawthorne expresses in the prefaces to *The House of the Seven Gables, The Blithedale Romance, The Marble Faun*, with the famous choice of 'romance' instead of 'novel', seem to arise in the main from the need to justify the inclusion of a symbolic object in the fabric of the narrative:

When a writer calls his work a Romance, it need hardly be observed that he wishes to claim a certain latitude, both as to its fashion and material, which he would not have felt himself entitled to assume had he professed to be writing a Novel. The latter form of composition is presumed to aim at a very minute fidelity, not merely to the possible, but to the probable and ordinary course of man's experience. The former – while, as a work of art, it must rigidly subject itself to laws, and while it sins unpardonably so far as it may swerve aside from the truth of the human heart – has fairly a right to present that truth under circumstances, to a great extent, of the writer's own choosing or creation. . . .

Italy, as the site of [*The Marble Faun*] was chiefly valuable to [the author] as affording a sort of poetic precinct, where actualities would not be so terribly insisted upon as they are, and must needs be, in America. No author, without a trial, can conceive of the difficulty of writing a romance about a country where there is no shadow, no antiquity, no mystery, no picturesque and gloomy wrong, nor anything but a commonplace prosperity, in broad and simple daylight, as is happily the case with my dear native land. It will be very long, I trust, before romance-writers may find congenial and easily handled themes, either in the annals of our stalwart republic, or in any characteristic and probable events of our individual lives. Romance and poetry, ivy, lichens, and wall-flowers, need ruin to make them grow.

But once again, Hawthorne's masterpiece, *The Scarlet Letter*, is the work which provides the most conclusive proof. The symbol here is omnipresent, as the title implies, and we find it already in the Introduction, in which the author, whilst brilliantly and vividly recalling his own experiences in the Customs House refers to the finding, among old things, of the story of the scarlet letter and the letter itself:

. . . . the object that most drew my attention . . . was a certain affair of fine, red cloth, much worn and faded. There were traces about it of gold embroidery, which, however, was greatly frayed and defaced; so that none, or very little, of the glitter was left. It had been wrought, as was easy to perceive, with wonderful skill of needlework; and the stitch (as I am assured by ladies conversant with such mysteries) gives evidence of a now forgotten art, not to be recovered even by the process of picking out the threads. This rag of scarlet cloth, – for time and wear and a sacrilegious moth had reduced it to little other than a rag, – on careful examination, assumed the shape of a letter. It was the capital letter A. By an accurate measurement, each limb proved to be precisely three inches and a quarter in length. It had been intended, there could be no doubt, as an ornamental article of dress; but how it was to be worn, or what rank, honour, and dignity, in by-past times, were signified by it, was a riddle which (so evanescent are the fashions of the world in these particulars) I saw little hope of solving. And yet it strangely interested me. My eyes fastened themselves upon the old scarlet letter, and would not be turned aside. Certainly, there was some deep meaning in it, most worthy of interpretation, and which, as it were, streamed forth from the mystic symbol, subtly communicating itself to my sensibilities, but evading the analysis of my mind.

After the Introduction, there is not a single page in the actual novel where the letter does not appear, placed in every possible light, examined from every angle. Here it is for the first time on Hester Prynne's dress: 'On the breast of her gown, in fine red cloth, surrounded with an elaborate embroidery and fantastic flourishes of gold-thread, appeared the letter A. It was so artistically done, and with so much fertility and gorgeous luxuriance of fancy, that it had all the effect of a last and fitting decoration to the apparel which she wore . . .' Further on it is even reflected on a piece of armour, where Hester sees it 'in exaggerated and gigantic proportions, so as to be greatly the most prominent feature of her appearance. In truth, she seemed absolutely hidden behind it.' When Hester and Dimmesdale meet, the letter is given as much importance as the two protagonists: 'So speaking, she undid the clasp that fastened the scarlet letter, and, taking it from her bosom, threw it to a distance among the withered leaves. The mystic token alighted on the hither verge of the stream . . . there lay the embroidered letter, glittering like a lost jewel, which some ill-fated wanderer might pick up.' And the book ends with the letter, which we see for the last time on the grave of Hester and the minister:

All around, there were monuments carved with armorial bearings; and on this simple slab of slate . . . there appeared the semblance of an engraved escutcheon. It bore a device, a herald's wording of which might serve for a motto and brief description of our now concluded legend; so sombre is it, and relieved only by one ever-glowing point of light gloomier than the shadow: – 'ON A FIELD, SABLE, THE LETTER A, GULES'.

The author's insistence on the use of this object might seem (and has seemed to some critics) excessive, the more so since the letter has a human analogue in the figure of Hester and Dimmesdale's daughter, little Pearl, who 'was the scarlet letter in another form', and it also extends to Pastor Dimmesdale himself, of whom it is rumoured that he bears a similar letter on the skin of his chest. But the fact is that Hawthorne insists on the letter not from any poverty of literary inventiveness but because of a necessity intrinsic in the narrative: the letter becomes a tool, used with extraordinary ability, to show the inconstancy, the ambiguity and the incomprehensibility of what is real. So, like the minister's black veil or Georgiana's little hand, it constantly takes on a different appearance parallel to its ever- changing meaning. It is certainly a sign of guilt, a 'scarlet token of infamy' that arouses terror in the beholder, 'seeming to derive its scarlet hue from the flames of the infernal pit', and that gives Hester 'a sympathetic knowledge of the hidden sin in other hearts'. But when, for example, Hester devotes herself to looking after the sick, the meaning of the letter changes completely:

There glimmered the embroidered letter, with comfort in its unearthly ray. Elsewhere the token of sin, it was the taper of the sick chamber. It had even thrown its gleam, in the sufferer's hard extremity, across the verge of time. . . . The letter was the symbol of her calling. Such helpfulness was found in her, – so much power to do, and power to sympathize, – that many people refused to interpret the scarlet A by its original signification. They said that it meant Able; so strong was Hester Prynne, with a woman's strength.

On the other hand, this new meaning is soon cancelled by other meanings. Further on the letter symbolizes Hester's intellectual independence:

She had wandered, without rule or guidance, in a moral wilderness. Her intellect and heart had their home, as it were, in desert places, where she roamed as freely as the wild Indian in his woods. . . . The scarlet letter was her passport into regions where other women dared not tread.

To sum up, when used in this way the symbol creates a complex, enigmatic plot within the narrative, turning the novel into a dramatic mirror of the conflicts, tensions and contradictions of life, destroying and creating, pointing out mysteries and trying to unravel them, expanding the meanings and tones of the narrative to then replace them with a more secret thread. It is thanks to the symbol that *The Scarlet Letter* reveals its true nature, which is far more ambiguous and contradictory than might at first appear. If the novel looks like a tale of guilt and retribution expressed in clearly defined moral terms, the symbol shows that in reality Hawthorne's judgment is suspended; the terms of the moral question are extremely uncertain for him and the novel does not come to any definite conclusion. It is not by chance that one of the finest pages, in which the author's participation seems most genuine and compassionate, is the one which describes how, after their apparent expiation, love blossoms once again between Hester and the pastor:

. . . there lay the embroidered letter, glittering like a lost jewel, which some ill-fated wanderer might pick up, and thenceforth be haunted by strange phantoms of guilt, sinkings of the heart, and unaccountable misfortune.

The stigma gone, Hester heaved a long, deep sigh, in which the burden of shame and anguish departed from her spirit. Oh exquisite relief! She had not known the weight, until she felt the freedom! By another impulse, she took off the formal cap that confined her hair; and down it fell upon her shoulders, dark and rich, with at once a shadow and a light in her abundance, and imparting the charm of softness to her features. There played around her mouth, and beamed out of her eyes, a radiant and tender smile, that seemed gushing from the very heart of womanhood. A crimson flush was glowing on her cheek, that had been long so pale. Her sex, her youth, and the whole richness of her beauty, came back from what men call the irrevocable past, and clustered themselves, with her maiden hope, and a happiness before unknown, within the magic circle of this hour. And, as if the gloom of the earth and sky had been but the effluence of these mortal hearts, it vanished with their sorrow. All at once, as with a sudden smile of heaven, forth burst the sunshine, pouring a very flood into the obscure forest, gladdening each green leaf, transmuting the yellow fallen ones to gold, and gleaming adown the gray trunks of the solemn trees. The objects that had made a shadow hitherto, embodied the brightness now. The course of the little brook might be traced by its merry gleam afar into the wood's heart of mystery, which had become a mystery of joy.

Such was the sympathy of Nature, – that wild, heathen Nature of the forest, never subjugated by human law, nor illumined by higher truth – with the bliss of these two spirits! Love, whether newly born, or aroused from a death-like slumber, must always create a sunshine, filling the heart so full of radiance, that it overflows upon the outward world. Had the forest still kept its gloom, it would have been bright in Hester's eyes, and bright in Arthur Dimmesdale's!

But the symbol in *The Scarlet Letter*, as in most of Hawthorne's works, has an additional function. Whereas allegory constitutes more of a defence, an attempt to hold fast against the crushing blows of reality, than a weapon to attack and penetrate it, the symbol is actually that weapon. We are faced with a representation, but also with a quest. Georgiana's birthmark, the pastor's black veil, the scarlet letter represent an attempt on Hawthorne's part to pierce the heart of reality, to explore it with a tool capable of putting the mystery into words and probing within it. In this way the narration also becomes the starting point for a personal, exploratory search by the author, which sometimes quite literally coincides with the characters' quest, is sometimes autonomous, but is permanently taking place. An example, fundamental in several senses, is provided once again by 'Ethan Brand'. Here also is a complex, fictional *and* personal symbol – the fire burning in the furnace. The fire, which gave rise to Ethan's wild quest and to which he returns, is also the object of the author's quest. Throughout the story Hawthorne tries to define and portray it, no less fascinated by it than Ethan is: 'Within the furnace were seen the curling and riotous flames, and the burning marble, almost molten with the intensity of heat; while without, the reflection of the fire quivered on the dark intricacy of the surrounding forest.' The fire is as much at the centre of this story as the other symbols which have been mentioned. It is the fierce, sinister light that allows the faces of the characters to be seen, and whose very absence is significant, because when the fire is not burning, the world seems to reveal an undreamt-of sweetness. The fire is said to be the actual cause of Ethan's guilt: it is hell, evil, and Ethan throws himself into it to escape and find relief from his desperate awareness of sin. And while he addresses his last words to the fire – to which he is bound by his very surname—: 'Come, deadly element of Fire, – henceforth my familiar friend! Embrace me, as I do thee!', the fire appeases his painful existence by reducing his body (except for the heart, which is as stony as that of the 'Man of Adamant'), to a bare skeleton lying 'in the attitude of a person who, after long toil, lies down to long repose'. And it is the intensity with which the author explores his symbol; the vehement, questioning language he uses in trying to follow the movement of those flames, trying to keep to their flickering movement, to immerse himself in their infinitely changing and variable light and colour; the awareness that such an effort, although desperate, is necessary, because in the fire (as in the birthmark, or the black veil, or the scarlet letter, or the 'great carbuncle' of another celebrated story) the mystery, the cause and the reason of life is hidden, just as it is hidden in Melville's sea, in the water into which Narcissus dives to grasp at 'the ungraspable phantom of life': all this brings about a much closer identification than Hawthorne explicitly states, between the artist and his character. Ethan Brand's quest (like Captain Ahab's) corresponds to Hawthorne's (or Melville's). The moment he describes and rationally condemns Ethan Brand's sin, he commits it himself (and it must be remembered that Melville referred to *Moby-Dick* as his 'wicked book'). Probing into the mystery, trying to eat forbidden fruit, he himself, like Ethan Brand, Dr Aylmer and the other sinners in his works oversteps the limits conceded to man. Wrapped up in his quest, he in turn runs the risk of forgetting other people and seeing his heart dry up. Trying, like Lucifer, to take over the place and function which are given to God alone, he also can speak of the Unpardonable Sin, like Ethan Brand. This is the ultimate result of Hawthorne's use of the symbol: it does not only extend, enrich, put in doubt and even refute the narration, but it puts the artist himself among the characters, and adds his own drama and quest to theirs.

How far the situation of the artist and his drama give Hawthorne a motive to consider and represent, and how far they reflect, and even identify themselves with, the situation and drama of his characters, may be seen in certain stories dealing with this theme. These stories are interesting both as biographical evidence (for example, the writer in 'The Devil in Manuscript' burns his writings as Hawthorne burned many of his, after having tried in vain to find a publisher), and as proof of the state of isolation of the American artist. The chief interest, however, is the portrait of the artist which can be obtained from them and which, although it is linked to Hawthorne's own experiences and background, assumes universal qualities because it is based both on a constant reflection on the nature of art and on the feelings and ideas which inspire his work. Such a portrait is certainly not serene. The price that an artist must pay is extraordinarily high: 'intense thought, yearning effort, minute toil, and wasting anxiety, succeeded by an instant of solitary triumph' are not enough, nor is the burden of the mistrust and incomprehension of society, so much more serious for the American than for the European artist ('The Artist of the Beautiful'), nor the delusion of finding oneself, after a momentary state of grace, totally lacking in true creative qualities ('Drowne's Wooden Image'). In any case, whether he succeeds or fails, the artist must risk the condition which Hawthorne attributes to all those who desperately pursue an ideal: loneliness and a dried-up heart. As he says in 'The Artist of the Beautiful':

To persons whose pursuits are insulated from the common business of life – who are either in advance of mankind or apart from it – there often comes a sensation of moral cold that makes the spirit shiver as if it had reached the frozen solitudes around the pole. What the prophet, the poet, the reformer, the criminal, or any other man with human yearnings, but separated from the multitude by a peculiar lot, might feel, poor Owen felt.

And if the successful writer of 'The Devil in Manuscript' feels himself being carried far 'from the beaten path of the world' and led into 'a strange sort of solitude – a solitude in the midst of men, – where nobody wishes for what [he does], nor thinks nor feels as [he does] . . .', the successful painter of 'The Prophetic Pictures' is in a condition of no less tragic solitude:

Like all other men around whom an engrossing purpose wreathes itself, he was insulated from the mass of human kind, he had no aim – no pleasure – no sympathies – but what were ultimately connected with his art. Though gentle in manner and upright in intent and action, he did not possess kindly feelings; his heart was cold; no living creature could be brought near enough to keep him warm.

But in the portrayal of the painter Hawthorne indicates the further risk implicit in the condition of being an artist: that of committing the Unpardonable Sin. Painting the portraits of Walter and Elinor does not mean, for the painter, reproducing their appearance but piercing to their hearts, exploring their souls. As he himself says to them when they do not fully recognize themselves in the painting:

'The artist – the true artist – must look beneath the exterior. It is his gift – his proudest, but often a melancholy one – to see the inmost soul . . .' But seeing 'the inmost soul' means possessing it, so that he does not confine himself to being the exposer of the truth hidden in his models but feels that he is their actual creator: 'He almost regarded them as creations of his own', giving himself up to a truly Faust-like exaltation of his own powers:

'O glorious Art! . . . thou art the image of the Creator's own. The innumerable forms, that wander in nothingness, start into being at thy beck. The dead live again. Thou recallest them to their old scenes, and givest their gray shadows the lustre of a better life, at once earthly and immortal. Thou snatchest back the fleeting moments of History. With thee there is no past, for, at thy touch, all that is great becomes forever present; and illustrious men live through long ages, in the visible performance of the very deeds which made them what they are. O potent Art! as thou bringest the faintly revealed Past to stand in that narrow strip of sunlight, which we call Now, canst thou summon the shrouded Future to meet her there? Have I not achieved it? Am I not thy Prophet?'

This is what the painter in the story has in common with Ethan Brand, with Dr Aylmer, and with all those people who renew the great sin of mankind in Hawthorne's stories and novels. His sin is also pride, he too tramples over 'the sense of brotherhood with man and reverence for God', sacrificing everything to the 'mighty claims' of an intellect reaching out towards a knowledge and a power which are more than human. Therefore, if he touches on such knowledge and power, he is punished on the one hand by loneliness and the icing up of his heart, and on the other by the evil that his paintings produce: almost in order to be true to the guilty expression which the painter has seen in him, Walter would be ready to kill Elinor if the painter were not there to stop him, if 'like a magician', like Prospero, he did not restrain 'the phantoms which he had evoked' (although the crime does not take place, the happiness of the young couple is shattered nonetheless, and the two will lead a life without love, filled with hatred and suspicion).

A work of art is, then, linked to evil (here is yet another Puritan element in Hawthorne), because in revealing the truth, it shows up the evil which, for Hawthorne, is contaminating the world, and also beause there is a Lucifer-element in the artist which might lead him beyond revelation, towards the very creation of evil. Not only in 'The Prophetic Pictures', therefore, but in many more of Hawthorne's works the artistic object has negative or even diabolic qualities intrinsic in it. Such is the case of 'Lady Eleanor's Mantle', in which the embroidered cloak of the main character, 'which had been wrought by the most skilful artist in London', brings about a deadly plague; of the statues and paintings in *The Marble Faun*, where the problem of the artist is obviously of crucial importance (significantly, the most virtuous character, Hilda, decides to abandon her career as a creative artist to take up the humble position of a copyist). It is also the case of the scarlet letter, which Hawthorne depicts as a true work of art, in which 'much fertility and gorgeous luxuriance of fancy' can be seen. Considering *The Scarlet Letter*, it should also be noted that all the main characters have qualities not far removed from the artistic. Hester is said to have 'in her nature a rich, voluptuous, Oriental characteristic, – a taste for the gorgeously beautiful, which, save in the exquisite productions of her needle, found nothing else, in all the possibilities of her life, to exercise itself upon . . .' Emphasis is laid upon Dimmesdale's powers of oratory and the characteristics of his voice which 'was in itself a rich endowment; insomuch that a listener, comprehending nothing of the language in which the preacher spoke, might still have been swayed to and fro by the mere tone and cadence', while a reflection of Hawthorne's own introspective art must surely be seen in Roger Chillingworth's pitiless analysis of Dimmesdale, as he delves 'into the poor clergyman's heart, like a miner searching for gold; or, rather, like a sexton delving into a grave'.

But of particular importance is one great, complex story, 'Rappaccini's Daughter', where the magnificent flowers 'created' by the 'perverted wisdom' of the scientist, Rappaccini, destroy and corrupt the physical and moral life of man. This story is not explicitly about art, it is a Faust-tale, where the presence of the garden in which Dr Rappaccini cultivates his 'flowers of evil' establishes a direct relationship with the theme of original sin and the Garden of Eden, thus throwing light on the moral significance and the cultural and religious undercurrents of all Hawthorne's 'Faust- writings'. In any case, at the back of the tale of Rappaccini it is not hard to see, more clearly than elsewhere, the theme of the artist, and at the back of his flowers it is not hard to discern the features of the work of art. The following description is from the scene where the young Giovanni Guasconti, a university student in a Padua to which Hawthorne attributes elements of the sinister Elizabethan Italy, sees the flowers for the first time:

Giovanni still found no better occupation than to look down into the garden beneath his window. . . . All about the pool into which the water subsided grew various plants, that seemed to require a plentiful supply of moisture for the nourishment of gigantic leaves, and in some instances, flowers gorgeously magnificent. There was one shrub in particular, set in a marble vase in the midst of the pool, that bore a profusion of purple blossoms, each of which had the lustre and richness of a gem; and the whole together made a show so resplendent that it seemed enough to illuminate the garden, even had there been no sunshine.

But the quality of evil that their artificiality instills in the flowers is explicitly stated further on; they are in fact 'the production . . . no longer of God's making, but the monstrous offspring of man's depraved fancy, glowing with only an evil mockery of beauty'. And because they are not a natural creation of God's, but only the fruit of man's desire to put himself in God's place and imitate him, the flowers conceal a lethal snare behind their extraordinary beauty, the perfume they give off dulls and stupefies the senses, and one drop of their sap can bring death. Moreover, they are linked to Beatrice with close ties, with a similarity 'which Beatrice seemed to have indulged a fantastic humour in heightening, both by the arrangement of her dress and selection of its hues', and which becomes direct identification when we learn that Beatrice, like the flowers, spreads death around herself. The truth is that Beatrice is also fruit of the 'perverted wisdom' of Rappaccini (in a relationship which recalls, in a negative way, the one between Prospero and Miranda in *The Tempest*). As she herself says: 'I, dearest Giovanni – I grew up and blossomed with the plant and was nourished with its breath. It was my sister, and I loved it with a human affection.' And because of this, love between the two young people is impossible. Vitality of feeling and of the heart cannot flower where the mind is exerting its supremacy without restraints; the story ends with Beatrice's death.

A solitary, troubled man, endowed with unusual power but nevertheless condemned, through its use, to lose his own humanity and violate the humanity of his fellow men; a man trusting in his own capacities to reach knowledge, but also aware that it is, on the one hand, the knowledge of evil, and, on the other, the sin of pride; master, at the price of an inexhaustible search and reununciation, of his own precious tools, but terrified by the abysses that these might open up for him; able 'to achieve the beautiful' but also compelled to see the concrete expression of that beauty violated, despised and even destroyed: these are the essential elements of the artist's portrait which Hawthorne composes in his works. These are the outlines of the shadow that always attends the scientists, prophets, reformers and sinners whose painful experiences are being recounted. This is, finally, the portrait of the character who is never described but who is nevertheless extremely concrete, whom we have seen living his own drama alongside the protagonists of the plot, the portrait of Hawthorne himself while writing and, in so doing, exploring the mystery; of Hawthorne who condemns Rappaccini but follows in his footsteps, repeating his sin, as he reaches out towards the control and knowledge of a world which he himself has, proudly, created. The figure of the artist is so deeply present in Hawthorne's works, in the stories as in *The Scarlet Letter, The House of the Seven Gables* (where the problem of the artist is approached through the daguerreotypist, Holgrave), *The Blithedale Romance* (where the artist is the narrator, Coverdale), *The Marble Faun*, and up to the unfinished works, that a danger arises that his work may be interpreted merely as a study of the artistic experience (although a very important study, anticipating modern and contemporary writers such as James and Proust, Joyce and Thomas Mann and Moravia). But dispelling such an interpretation, denying that Hawthorne's works remain shut in the limits of an investigation into the nature of art – as might have happened if the writer had been less engaged in his moral quest and search for knowledge – lies the fact that in the portrait of the artist, as in that drama in which the artist is the hero, a more universal portrait and a vaster drama, those of modern man, find poetic form. This man can be defined, using the words that Shakespeare – a pervasive presence in Hawthorne's works – gave to Hamlet: 'What a piece of work is man, how noble in reason, how infinite in faculties ... and yet, to me, what is this quintessence of dust?' But probably the most suitable words, which point to a whole realm of American experience, are those that Hawthorne uses to describe his artist – scientist Rappaccini:

Nothing could exceed the intentness with which [he] examined every shrub which grew in his path; it seemed as if he was looking into their inmost nature, making observations in regard to their creative essence, and discovering why one leaf grew in this shape and another in that, and wherefore such and such flowers differed among themselves in hue and perfume. Nevertheless, in spite of this deep intelligence on his part, there was no approach to intimacy between himself and these vegetable existences. On the contrary, he avoided their actual touch or the direct inhaling of their odours with a caution that impressed Giovanni most disagreeably; for the man's demeanour was that of one walking among malignant influences, such as savage beasts, or deadly snakes, or evil spirits, which, should he allow them one moment of license, would wreak upon him some terrible fatality. It was strangely frightful to the young man's imagination to see this air of insecurity in a person cultivating a garden, that most simple and innocent of human toils, and which had been alike the joy and labor of the unfallen parents of the race. Was this garden, then, the Eden of the present world? And this man, with such a perception of harm in what his own hands caused to grow, – was he the Adam?

(translated by Susan Bassnett)

# 8

# HERMAN MELVILLE

## Martin Green and Bernard McCabe

### A. The Formation of a Nineteenth-century American Novelist

#### 1. His heritage

Herman Melville was born in 1819, in Lansingburgh, New York, to Allan Melville, a merchant, and Maria Gansevoort Melville, the daughter of General Peter Gansevoort, who had been a military hero of the Revolutionary War, and later sheriff of Albany County and regent of New York University. The Gansevoorts were of Dutch origin, and belonged to the Dutch Reformed Church, which professed a severe form of Calvinism, while the Melvilles were Scottish by origin, and associated themselves with the more romantic and aristocratic and cultured avatars of Scotland. They cherished a relationship with the Earls of Melville; Allan had a brother, Major Thomas Melville, who had brought back from his years in Europe a French wife and French elegance, while Allan himself wrote heroic couplets and cultivated a very literary prose style in his letters. He was not a successful businessman, and had to appeal to his wife's family for assistance and protection. He failed financially in 1830, and again in 1832, and this time took to his bed, with the kind of nervous and psychological symptoms that were then called insanity, and died, leaving his widow with eight children to bring up.

General Gansevoort's sons came to the aid of Maria Melville and her children, not only on that occasion but for the rest of her life, which was a long one. She lived until 1872, by which time Herman's career as an author was effectively over. Indeed, as late as 1876 we find the publication of *Clarel* being made possible only by the charity of Uncle Peter Gansevoort. The Gansevoorts were more solid than the Melvilles, financially, and in other ways too. Maria Melville was more solid than her husband, and certainly counted for more – and worse – in her son's life. (After her death he said

that she had hated him.) The failure and subsequent absence of his
father was a large but negative fact for the writer. Resemblance
threatened him. He too failed to provide for himself, his wife, and
his children; he too was dependent on the charity of the
Gansevoorts and of his wife's father, Judge Shaw. And in his
writing it is easy to trace the effects of an insecure sense of himself
as a man.

He was a timid boy socially, hiding his timidity beneath stolidity.
His father described him as 'very backward in speech and slow in
comprehension, but you will find him as far as he understands men
and things solid and profound and of a docile and amiable disposition'. But the mind he acquired as he grew up was far from docile or
solid. The mind we meet in his books is nervous, irritable, volatile,
intoxicated by rhetoric and speculation. He tells us that he was
always quickly discovered by his fellow sailors to be a gentleman
because of his literary language with them; 'because of something in
me that could not be hidden; stealing out in an occasional
polysyllable; remote unguarded allusions to belles-lettres affairs'.

Other Melvilles of his generation were literary and unsuccessful.
His elder brother, Gansevoort, first took over the father's business
until that failed again, and then made himself a new, political
career, spouting some of the fiercest party and patriotic rhetoric of
that era of fierce language. But in London, appointed secretary to
the American legation there as a reward for party services, he quite
suddenly became overwhelmed by melancholy and lassitude, by a
revulsion from the stress and competition of life, and died, at the
age of twenty-nine. His elder brother had been a much more
picturesque and brilliant figure than Herman, a bundle of frenetic
energy, political fervour, and personal ambition. It was on
Gansevoort Melville that the family pinned its hopes for a revival of
fortunes, and indeed he did do something to start Herman's literary
career.

The first two published pieces by Herman Melville appeared in
the Lansingburgh *Advertizer* in 1839, under the title 'Fragments
from a Writing Desk'. The second described an allegorical quest
for female loveliness, not unlike Tom Moore in style. Melville
admired Moore in those days, grouping him with Hafiz, Byron, and
Ovid, and more loosely with the Arabian Nights and romances in
general.

This was a well-known minor Romantic mode, one which
Tennyson practised at the beginning of his writing career; and in
fact there are some similarities between Tennyson and Melville.

Both were the sons of failed fathers, overshadowed by an alien male power-figure – 'in Tennyson's case, his grandfather, in Melville's the corporate Gansevoort uncle. Both came from families with aristocratic pretensions and literary leanings. Both had older brothers with apparently more brilliant gifts and unstable temperaments, on whom the family hopes focused, but who burned themselves out early, and left to the apparently duller second son the chance to realize – in *literary* terms – the true potential of the family, the depth of feeling, the peculiarity of taste, the intensity of imagination, which the family fate had promised.

This psychological heritage clearly has something to do with the aptitudes of the sensibility, with the nature of the talent, which resulted in the two writers. That preternatural fluency of language, combined with an inner inarticulateness, an inability to utter the self, to take one's stand, to convincingly render one's identity, derives from a fundamental insecurity about one's role as a man. Both were great pipe-smokers, sea-voyagers, night-walkers of city streets, propounders of moral and metaphysical conundrums. Both were averse to clear, sharp, definite rationalist solutions to problems, or formulations of problems. They preferred the grand and the misty. They liked to lose themselves in an *O altitudo* or *O profundo*. Neither, it could be argued, possessed the ability to reason. Their minds were intuitive rather than logical. Both were notably unsuccessful at portraying human relationships, and especially intimate relationships between a man and a woman, in their writings. And in real life the relations of both men with their wives and close friends were notably lacking in fruitful tension, in challenge, self-discovery, and fulfilment.

But at the age of nineteen Herman went to sea, and during a subsequent voyage to the South Seas had deserted the ship and had spent some time, with a companion, in a native village. He wrote an account of this in book-form, called it *Typee*, and Gansevoort got Washington Irving to read it and the British publisher, Murray, to accept it. After that, as was often the case then, an American firm was willing to risk publishing it. Herman had arrived back in Boston in 1844, and he finished writing his manuscript in time for Gansevoort to take it with him when he sailed as the nominee of the newly elected Democratic President. It was – to some degree – as the work of Gansevoort Melville's brother that *Typee* was first praised or blamed. There was doubt in the minds of some reviewers, both as to its truth, and as to the propriety of its tone about Christian missionaries; and it tended to be Gansevoort's enemies who attacked the book, and his allies who defended it. But by the time of the next book Gansevoort was dead, and Herman was part of another family, the literary coterie of Evert Duyckinck, which was to be much more important to his work as a writer.

The degree of similarity between Melville and Tennyson can perhaps be best shown by putting the two of them together in contrast with, say, William Cullen Bryant and James Fenimore Cooper. Cooper seems to have been, of all American writers of the nineteenth century perhaps, the most simply and singly masculine, the most completely oriented towards his father. And in his work we get the masculine traits of clearness, firmness, thoroughness, logic, simplicity and health of feeling, fondness for adventure, so un-adulterated by any feminine feeling for shades of emotion and nuances of relationship, for ambiguities and passions, that he re-mains, for all his virtues, a dull novelist. And in Bryant, too, we get a remarkably determined and unequivocal concentration on the stoic and the heroic and the ascetic, the marmoreal virtues associated by the age with masculinity. This is not so simple with Bryant as it is with Cooper. Bryant's father was a violin-player and poetry-fancier, and his mother was a stern moralist; and Bryant's language, in early poems like 'To a Waterfowl', has a purity and freedom of lyricism which bears testimony to a profound mixture of masculine and feminine elements in his sensibility. But it was his father who made a man out of the over-sensitive boy, with a regimen of daily cold baths, etc. And Bryant's career as a whole, as successful news-paperman and militant editorialist, bears witness to his single-minded fostering of the masculine element in his potential; as does also the paucity and dryness of so much of his adult verse.

Bryant and Cooper were then writers who had made a direct and vigorous act of identification with male images of their times, both in the terms of their family life and in the terms of their literary enterprises; a very successful act, measured by the only standards feasible for ordinary psychological appraisal, though it is not hard to see the price they paid in literary spontaneity and vividness, richness and variety. Melville (like Tennyson) we are suggesting, was a writer who made insistent, but unsuccessful, acts of that kind, whose identity as *man* remained indefinite, and whose brilliant rhetoric is recognizably the function of an inarticulate personality, a talent released from ordinary expressive controls.

Moreover, we are arguing, this 'psychological' fact about them is also a cultural fact. Within a given age the results of certain psycho-logical choices, or rather fates, resemble each other remarkably, and may differ equally remarkably from the results of the same choices in other ages and cultures. For instance, the pressures of speculative capitalism (notably its recurrent commercial crises) acted on both the Melville and the Tennyson families with the same results of intensified anxiety and strenuous competitiveness and revulsion from the world and self-accusations of ineffectuality and neuroticism. Both families were genteel poor in the writers' earliest memories, and Melville was prevented from going to college by his father's financial failure. (That Tennyson *did* go explains many of the differences between the two men's fates, for his Cambridge connections, for instance with Hallam, played a crucial part in his later success.) There was also the heritage of Calvinism in both cases, which remained both a threat and a lure, a promise of profounder but more dangerous and above all forbidden truths and feelings, a reminder of a sterner moral and theological creed, seemingly outmoded by contemporary thought.

Perhaps the most striking of these common cultural conditions, however, was the form that literacy and literariness took in the early nineteenth century. It seems to have been then that the psychological and philosophical influences which McLuhan attributes to printing in general had their intensest effect. Families like the Tennysons and the Brontës in England, like the Melvilles and the Hawthornes in America, all children of the genteel poor, and most typically the children of the vicarage, seem to have been driven towards literature, towards the sort of imagination 'romantic' literature promotes, more than at any other time. Alienated equally from neurotic parents and from illiterate villagers or brutal proletarians, they retreated into romance. The world of words and of fancies, set in conscious opposition to the world of realities, was a refuge to these young people. They conducted their relations even with each other in the terms of that world. The Brontë children retired to different corners of the house, or even of the one room, to *write* things they would then show to each other. The Tennyson children walked on either side of a hedge *composing* verses they would then shout to each other. Melville's case of the disease was even acuter, in that – so far as we know – his brothers and sisters did not constitute for him a private protecting world.

All three of these cultural factors had the same 'psychological' effect, of linking the writer's vocation with passive and feminine roles in life. Perhaps the worst consequence of this was the fabrication of correspondingly fake masculine images; fake even by contrast with that marmoreal masculinity of Bryant's; fake in that they satisfied no high standards of feeling for what masculinity is. This was the worst consequence for Melville because he fell victim to one of those deceptions, and assimilated himself to one of those false images. Melville had small contact with any high standards of taste. Unlike Tennyson, he did not go to the university, nor did he become the friend of anyone comparable with Carlyle.

## 2. His training

Melville came to know intellectual New York around 1845. He said 'Until I was twenty-five I had no development at all. From my twenty-fifth year I date my life'. And in terms of intellectual and literary development this improbable statement has a good deal of truth in it. It was within the two years following 1845 that *Typee* and *Omoo* were published, that Gansevoort died and Herman was married. Unfortunately, that development took place under the aegis of Evert Duyckinck and his New York. As Perry Miller puts it, Melville's America 'consisted almost entirely of the city of New York'. And, 'His failure was not alone his private failure. He was one of a particular generation of New Yorkers.' the disadvantage of this environment we can again let Perry Miller define. 'Herman Melville had a mind, but nobody to educate it; on his own he acquired a passion for ideas, and then tried to enter a world where taste was respected, wit admired, erudition praised, but ideas themselves – well, those might turn out to be "German" and "transcendental"!' To which one would only want to add that a taste for 'ideas' *did* constitute one element in that world, and did shape Melville's own taste for them and in them, but in largely unprofitable ways.

The New York he came to know in those years was above all the city of Lewis Gaylord Clark and Evert and George Duyckinck, the leading literary editors. New York had of course many other aspects, its commerce, its politics, its portlife, its hugely growing immigrant population. But Melville was determined to become a *writer*, and the literary circle was his university, the taste of these men and their magazines was his training. And he was peculiarly susceptible to such training because he was the kind of man we have described, the kind his culture had made him. He had no real self-confidence, intellectual or personal. He was the most evasive and enigmatic of men, to all who pierced the jovial surface; none of his friends felt they really knew him; and in his writing we find an extraordinarily cloudy, suggestive, rhetorical fecundity which offers

anything rather than precise statement or clear tone. He dealt with
things always from an oblique and averted stance, facing away from
them; and influences that enter one's mind from over one's
shoulder, like that, evading scrutiny and confrontation, are in many
ways the most powerful.

The world of Lewis Gaylord Clark and the Duyckincks is described in Perry Miller's *The Raven and the Whale*, a book full of
useful information, though not easy to read. Clark bought the
moribund *Knickerbocker Magazine* in 1834, brought it to life again,
and edited it until 1861. By 1840 it was the most influential literary
organ in America, with a circulation of 4,000 to 5,000. Irving wrote
his *Geoffrey Crayon Papers* for it in 1839–41. Longfellow and
Hawthorne wrote for it from early in their careers. Its characterizing
feature was The Editor's Table, a section which gave gossipy news
items about the circle of real-life (but pseudonymous) bons viveurs
who wrote for the magazine, and who smoked and dined and drank
and joked together, ostentatiously civilized, unbrutalized by commerce. There was Henry Cary, 'John Waters', known as the
American Elia, whose recipe for a clam chowder is echoed in *Moby-
Dick*; C. F. Briggs, 'Harry Franco', who gave the other recipe so
echoed, and wrote sea stories like Melville's; and Dr Francis, a
minor Doctor Johnson and bawdy wit. The *Knickerbocker Magazine*
published a great deal about the sea and ships, including, in 1839, a
tale called 'Mocha Dick, the White Whale of the Pacific'; including,
also, extracts from the sermons of Father Taylor, the real-life
original of Father Mapple in Melville's novel.

Clark's values were Whig, which is to say Establishmentarian. In
religion he was an Episcopalian, in politics he followed Daniel
Webster. Melville's political loyalties, via first his family and later
Duyckinck, were to the opposite party. Partly for that reason, Clark
was one of those who attacked *Typee*, but there were more literary
reasons for his dislike of Melville. He detested in every writer
anything that smacked of 'Transcendentalism', which is to say,
romantic-enthusiastic speculativeness. The literature he approved
of he called 'Rabelaisian', and the crucial taste conflict of the time
was between Rabelaisianism and Transcendentalism.

What they meant by Rabelaisian is perhaps best exemplified by
the emphasis on eating and drinking and yarn-spinning in The
Editor's Table. Also, in private together they were bawdy, though
they denounced the sexual license of the France of their time, and
the novels which bore that taint, such as George Sand's and Victor
Hugo's. Moreover they had a clear grasp of the literary-genre

meaning of the term, as we can see in this quotation from Clark himself, praising a book by comparing it with Rabelais:

there is the same extraordinary display of universal learning, the same minute exactness of quotation, the same extravagant spirit of fun, the same capricious and provoking love of disgression, the same upsetting of accepted ideas, by which trifles are seriously descanted upon, and bolstered up with endless authorities, until they expand into gigantic proportions, while time-honoured truths are shuffled by with the most whimsical contempt.

The effect this taste had on Melville is obvious to every reader of *Moby-Dick* and it was doubly unfortunate. It made him claim mastery over a huge world of learning, and affect large and empty intellectual gestures. And, worse, it offered him a masculine persona with no serious content. The clubman anecdotalist, with his cigar and his hints of bawdry, is asserting his masculinity all the time without any challenging self-definition.[1] This was one of the vulgarities of the age, and it proved irresistible to Melville. But we need not attribute it to his reading of Clark, because in New York everybody was Rabelaisian, no one was Transcendentalist.

Evert Duyckinck had read Goethe, Herder, and Jean Paul, but was fundamentally as hostile to Emerson, to Nature, and to ideas, as Clark himself; as devoted to the values of Episcopalianism and (in theory) the pleasures of the table and the smoking room. Duyckinck, Melville's chief protector, was a less long-time literary editor than Clark, but he was just as much a centre of literary life. Born in 1816, he inherited a private income and accumulated a large library – from which Melville borrowed often. He had scholarly tastes, particularly for neglected seventeenth-century authors. His younger brother, George, was even more of a scholar and an Episcopalian – he was semi-clerical. Neither were men of acute mind, but Evert had a gift for acquiring literary friends and a stubbornness in promoting them which made him finally a figure in intellectual history. His circle wrote for *Arcturus*, a short-lived magazine he edited, later for *The Democratic Review* and its satirical offshoot. *Yankee-Doodle*, and finally for *The Literary World* (1847 on) which Duyckinck again edited. He and his friends formed alliances with Edgar Allan Poe and with the Southern novelist. William Gilmore Simms (both important magazine editors themselves)

---

[1] It was the shy, slight, refined, non-Rabelaisian Bryant who horse-whipped a rival newspaper editor on the streets of New York over a political quarrel. Melville never had either the passionate conviction or the inner self-confidence to do that.

against Clark and his allies, for instance, Poe's enemy, Rufus Griswold, and Bostonians like James Russell Lowell and Oliver Wendell Holmes.

There was no large ideological content to the hostility between these two groups, but such as there was derived from the idea of Duyckinck's friend and Clark's enemy, Cornelius Mathews. This man, though also Rabelaisian, was as close to being Transcendentalist as a New Yorker could get. Not that he was a follower of Emerson, but that he had large ideas about the nature of American genius, and about what American literature should be like. These ideas, which he called 'Young America', can be indicated by this quotation:

Something of a lusty strength – the vigor of a manly and rough-nurtured prime – should have seized upon the soul and driven it afield. A certain grandeur of thought, a wild barbaric splendour it may have been, should have shot forth its fires on every side, and made the wilderness to glow in the forge-light of high passions and thoughts.

It will be clear that this enthusiasm was something that Clark could not endorse – and that Melville could not resist. Mathews was not a talented writer, but some of his novels embody the ideas which later shaped Melville's efforts. The most striking case is *Behemoth*, published in 1839, which is about a mythic and enormous land-animal of pre-Indian America, the last survivor of its huge race, and about its tragic pursuit and destruction by an intrepid band of early Americans, under the inspiration of a fiery leader.

Despite the sharp enmity between Clark's and Duyckinck's magazines, and – to some extent – between their two policies in literature, their two programmes for America, there were strong similarities. Both stood opposed to New England Transcendentalism. As Rabelaisians, they hated anything Puritan. At the same time, as orthodox Christians, they suspected the German elements in Transcendentalism, the pantheistic strain. Above all, they – with the partial exception of Mathews – stood for traditional and humorous self-possession, and so detested the enthusiasm of the Emersonians. Among New Englanders, they admired Longfellow, Hawthorne, Lowell, Holmes, the mellow stylists, the ample, genial spirits.

Among New York writers, both schools showed a rather perfunctory respect for Cooper and Bryant. They were not really devotees of Nature or solitude, prairies or mountains, forests or promontories. Their enthusiasm went rather to Lamb, Hazlitt, and Leigh Hunt, companionable city authors, with gusto. Even socially,

Cooper and Bryant moved in a world of their own (they were personal friends) above the heads of Clark and the Duyckincks. For what the two schools had in common above all was a mediocrity of taste and talent. In all but Mathews, this mediocrity expressed itself in the way most typical of the century, in the clubman shirking of Romanticism, both its ideas and its enthusiasm for Nature.[1] Mathews did not evade that challenge – and consequently Melville learned from him – but Mathews was not to be compared with Emerson. Melville did finally read Emerson, but his letters to Duyckinck about the experience are sad examples of what one critic calls his 'double-talk'. There is something in Emerson 'elevated above mediocrity', but at the same time he 'cannot drink the ale and eat the cake of jolly fellows'. Melville's Rabelaisianism would not let him respond fully to what he read in such a writer.

The effect of this literary education naturally shows itself more in Melville's later books than in his first, though *Typee* was in fact read and edited for Putnam's by Duyckinck. Thereafter Duyckinck and his friends constituted themselves Melville's sponsors. They printed extracts from his books in their magazines, they defended him against attacks, they kept mentioning his name in print, giving the public details of his life and works. They gave him books to review, they lent him books to read, they introduced him to their allies, above all they made him one of their club, their social punch-drinkings, etc., which were, given their idea of culture, the sacramental core of the literary life for them.

When *Typee* and *Omoo* were published, in 1846 and 1847, the Duyckincks praised them for their exciting adventures, and presented their author to the world as a hearty, simple, sailorman, jovially at home in the pleasures of the world, though capable of exalted enthusiasm and melancholy on occasion. (Indeed, it is clear, from their journals and their letters among themselves, that that is really how they saw him.) And as such he had a pronounced though minor vogue. The literary journalism of the time is full of references to Melville, and it was on the strength of that success that he got married.

*Mardi* (1849) was an attempt in a much more ambitious genre of the time, and received much more doubtful response. *Typee* and *Omoo* had both been accounts of a young American sailor's adventures on the islands of Polynesia, where he meets both picturesque white drifters and native tribes, some alluringly gentle

[1] See *The Problem of Boston* by Martin Green for a fuller treatment of this idea.

and beautiful, some frighteningly fierce and cannibal. In the first book, the stress had been more on the young man's isolation from white culture in an erotic South Seas paradise; in the second it had been more on his white companions and their travels. But the new book soon abandoned any pretence of realism and became an exotic and elaborate and obscure allegory. It gave the anti-Duyckinck critics reason to speak of German mysticism and farragos of rhetoric. Several reviewers still called it Rabelaisian, but the hostile ones, like Clark and the Boston *Morning Post*, said it was Rabelais 'purged of everything but prosiness and puerility'. However, the French critic Philarète Chasles had written an article on Melville for the *Revue des Deux Mondes*, and had called him the American Rabelais, so Duyckinck of course reprinted this in his own magazine. He himself defended the book nervously as 'a happy genial production but a book of thought, curious thought and reflection'.

'Thought' meant as usual 'Germany'; though the kind of thinking in question owed nothing to Kant and Hegel, everything to Jean Paul and Novalis. If one tries to read the American efforts in this genre of romance, one gains sympathy for Clark's programmatic hostility. One also sees more clearly what Melville was aiming at, and how he failed. Take for instance William Starbuck Mayo's *Kaloolagh*, or *Journeyings in the Djébel Kumri* (1849), which described the adventures, in North Africa this time, of a man in quest of a mysterious blonde maiden, adventures which begin as realistic but become allegorical. *Kaloolagh*, published the same year as *Mardi*, had its fourth edition by 1852, while *Mardi* never reached a second. Richard Burleigh Kimball's *St Leger*, also published the same year, reached a sixth edition by 1852. This novel, which had appeared serially in *The Knickerbocker Magazine*, portrays a hero who flirts with German metaphysics but returns to solid sentimental English nature. And most important, still in the same year, came Longfellow's novel *Kavanagh*, again treating the seductions of 'German' romanticism, and including a debate directly about Americanism in literature. Longfellow's representative in the debate spoke for the natural rather than the national, and many reviewers commented favourably on this and unfavourably on the Mathews' nationalism to which Melville was affiliating himself. Most notably, Lowell joined in on Longfellow's side in *The North American Review*.

The reception of *Mardi* was therefore very unfavourable to Melville, both in the disapproval of his enterprise by men of judgment, and in the great success in that enterprise of other competitors. He was suffering from having made the wrong alliances in the intellectual and literary world of his time. And because of his general insecurity, an unfavourable reception was more bewildering to him than to most men. He produced, in quick succession, *Redburn* (1849) and *White-Jacket* (1850), which were of the kind his public expected from him and for which they did indeed praise him. *White-Jacket* is the story of a young seaman's service on an American man-of-war, and discusses aspects of naval life like flogging. *Redburn* recounts the experiences, as Melville informed his English publisher, of 'the son of a gentleman on his first voyage, from New York to Liverpool and back, with descriptions of England and of the fo'c'sle life of the sailors'. Even Clark approved *White-Jacket* and *Redburn* was said to belong to 'the great school of Nature'.

## 3. His application

But Melville still wanted to write something much more ambitious, and there were echoes of 'Young American' ideas even in these books. In *White-Jacket* we read, 'Americans bear the ark of the liberties of the world. . . . In our youth is our strength; in our inexperience, our wisdom.' Clearly, he was ready to produce that giant American book, full of wild rhetoric and profound questionings, and yet dealing directly and realistically with the humblest forms of American democracy – *Moby-Dick*.

But before we go on to discuss the writing of Melville's great work, it will be useful to review some more biographical facts. In 1847, he married Elizabeth Shaw, the daughter of Chief Justice Lemuel Shaw of Massachusetts, who was an old friend of the Melville family (he had wanted to marry Allan's sister, Nancy, who died) and long one of the paternal figures in Herman Melville's life. Elizabeth Shaw Melville was an unremarkable person, both in her impact on contemporaries, and in such of her dealings as are recorded for us to judge by. She made no vivid impressions, and the nature of her relations with her husband is entirely shrouded in conventional phrases. In Melville's fiction the relations between man and woman are not portrayed with any intensity of imagination (the relations between two men, on the other hand, call forth striking phrases and scenes) so that we are bound to suspect that there was not much to shroud. The inarticulateness of personality we spoke of seems to have extended into intimate relationships.

The one relationship which we know he embarked on with enthusiasm, and which promised some imaginative profit, was with Hawthorne. He read *Mosses from an Old Manse* in 1850, got to know Hawthorne, and flung himself into a would-be friendship of the talents – a Goethe–Schiller relationship. But Melville had chosen the one man who was more evasive and enigmatic than himself. One might guess that he had chosen him just because he was so, in the sense that much of what excited him in Hawthorne's work and presence was his silence, his ambiguity, the hint – as Melville saw it – of appalling depths of negation. Hawthorne in effect rejected these overtures of friendship, and their last significant interview, on the sand dunes outside Liverpool in 1856, marks a stage in Melville's decline. Hawthorne was then American consul in Liverpool, and Melville was on his way to Palestine. The trip had been paid for by his father-in-law as an attempt to shift his burden of melancholy and nervous depression. (This condition had become so bad that his family – it is believed – had him examined for insanity.) That last sandy unavailing interview is an apt symbol of Melville's defeat in the realm of human relations, and of the solitude in which he was to spend the remaining thirty-five years of his life.

Hawthorne, though almost mawkishly attracted to his wife, found other personal relations difficult; and his last years may have been as desolate as those of Melville. During the first years of his marriage he felt he had defeated the dangers of spiritual isolation which he had glimpsed in Salem (Sophia Hawthorne was a more powerful personality than Elizabeth Melville) but in the 1860s, after his return from Europe, he was again plunged into a despair almost beyond the reach of human companionship. Though Hawthorne and Melville lived within reach of each other again in those years, they did not see each other.

This despair was a threat which hung over all the 'feminine' writers of the age, and again the person most strikingly like Melville was Tennyson. Tennyson became engaged as a promising young poet, but did not marry till twelve years later, after a ten years' break in the engagement. Those ten years, the 1840s, were a black period for the poet as poet (he was generally ridiculed in the Reviews) and in his family relations, and he acquired habits of life that disturbed his friends as much as Melville's habits disturbed his. Tennyson's marriage and his literary success (both of which resulted from the publication of *In Memoriam*) 'saved' him, as perhaps similar success would have 'saved' Melville. But each man remained painfully shy and solitary behind his bluff masculine persona. Melville had several hours each day set apart for solitude, and even in the family's evening gatherings he had a special licence to say nothing.

In contrast one could cite the married lives of Bryant and Cooper, both of whom married young girls they were clearly (though decorously) in love with, and whose careers moved steadily forward to significant degrees of success. Bryant went to New York in 1825 to edit the *New York Review*, at the age of thirty-one, and in 1826 moved to the *Evening Post*. He became its editor at the age of thirty-five, and remained so for nearly fifty years, till his death in 1878. He made a position of great power and influence out of it (his Civil War editorials were particularly noted) and also a good deal of money. He soon owned a third of the paper's stock, which in the 1840s paid annual dividends that averaged $10,000, and in the 1850s was a gold-mine. His career, whatever its austerities and inhibitions, was a model of clean, firm, dignified directedness, compared with Melville's. Such were the rewards the culture offered for successful masculinity.

*Moby-Dick* was written 1849–51, and like *Mardi* it underwent a large expansion in design, a large infusion of 'ideas', part way through the writing. It seems to have been in the summer of 1850, after Melville had reported to Duyckinck being more than half way through a book on whaling, that he began to incorporate into it that mass of elaborate symbolism and metaphysical speculation and romance melodrama and Jacobean theatre, which make up half of the book we know. This was the summer he met Hawthorne, and read into *Mosses* and *The House of the Seven Gables* the most profound and secret negations of hope and comfort. He made out of Hawthorne, not inappropriately but still by force and against Hawthorne's intentions, a predecessor for himself, a progenitor, and sponsor of his own half-acknowledged miseries, his own half-understood impulses to protest against the nature of things.

The immediate reason for the change of plan, or – to stick to the demonstrable – for that essay on Hawthorne which is generally agreed to be continuous with the new material in *Moby-Dick*, was a visit paid by Evert Duyckinck and Cornelius Mathews to Melville. This, at least, is Perry Miller's theory, and he makes a good case for it. The visit of Duyckinck and Mathews became the occasion for a number of parties and picnics for nearby literary people, including Hawthorne and Oliver Wendell Holmes. The most famous of these expeditions was one to Monument Mountain, which the group climbed, and on the top of which Mathews declaimed Bryant's poem about the mountain to the rest. It is neatly symbolic that Bryant's poem, so publicly performed, so pompously approved, dealt discreetly with the very theme (incest) which was to get Melville into so much trouble with the public for his handling of it in *Pierre*.

It is clear, from the different accounts of this expedition written later by the participants, that there was mutual animosity in the air. The two poles of this ideological electricity were Mathews, the bombastic spokesman for Young America and for *The Literary World*, and Holmes, the Brahmin ironist from Harvard and *The North American Review* and – implicitly – from *The Knickerbocker Magazine*. It is also clear that Melville's review of *Mosses* was an espousal of Mathews' side in the quarrel, and a claim to find Hawthorne among the heroes of Young America, to win him away from the companionship of Holmes and Longfellow and Irving, away from the sunny virtues he was usually said to exemplify. Melville revised this essay under Duyckinck's supervision during this visit, and when Duyckinck got back to New York, he sent him a present for Hawthorne, which Melville delivered without knowing that it was a set of his own works. Duyckinck was – typically – trying to promote that alliance between the two which Melville had set his clumsy heart on. Perhaps, if Hawthorne had been able to respond emotionally, or if he had been able to understand Melville and his problems intellectually, the second half of the latter's writing life might have been richly and maturely productive. In which case the record of American literature would look very different.

In any case, it is quite clear how closely *Moby-Dick* corresponds to that idea of the great American book which Young America had worked out. 'A big book, crowded with epic figures . . .' Perry Miller defines it. 'American figures, sprung from native soil, big as the mountains, large as the lakes, oratorical as Niagara. It could not be done in the novel . . . The great American book had to be big, and it had to be a romance.' This Mathews idea, actualized according to the taste of New York Rabelaisianism, in a version particularly influenced by those seventeenth-century essayists and dramatists whom Duyckinck recommended; this formula explains a good deal of that puzzling conglomeration which is all we may see at first in *Moby-Dick*.

It is striking how many features of the book can be traced back to this literary milieu. The very name Ishmael, for instance, the concept of the writer as outcast and wanderer, was a standard term in Duyckinck's group. The comic-grotesque idea of boisterous

Nantucket (which Melville had never visited) was treated in their magazines. The idea of a book about whaling may well have derived from the books on that subject which he had reviewed – he covered everything to do with the sea – for *The Literary World*. And the description of the chowder (Chapter 15) derives from the much-publicized controversy over the two kinds and their best recipes, in *The Knickerbocker Magazine*.

When published, *Moby-Dick* (1851) was not immediately or dramatically a failure, but it was far from a success. Several reviews complained of the bombast of the language and the cloudiness of the ideas, and, for the sake of money if for no other reason, Melville had to begin immediately to write another novel. *Pierre* (1852) he intended to be a popular romance, for the feminine market, but what he produced provoked outright repudiation. Pierre Glendinning's ambiguous relations with his mother, his sister, and his sweetheart – for each he has feelings that would be more appropriately directed to one of the others – disturbed the readers of the time. So did the complicated plot, and the grandiloquent language and wild speculation introduced into the novel.

With *Pierre* Melville began to be a literary failure. For the last ten years of his life he was so completely forgotten that readers thought he had been long dead. But he lived forty years after writing *Pierre*, and the decline during that time was fairly steady. The decay of Duyckinck's literary fortunes, which began when Harper's *New Monthly Magazine* finally showed what kind of literary magazine America really wanted, brought Melville some new, temporary opportunities. *Harper's* began in June 1850, selling 7,500 copies a month, in six months sold 50,000, and by 1860 200,000. This magazine itself printed mainly articles imported from England, but *Putnam's*, founded in imitation in 1853, made a feature of American, and particularly New York, writing, and solicited and published quite a few things by Melville, including 'The Encantadas', 'Bartleby', and 'Benito Cereno'. The first (all three were published in a book called *The Piazza Tales* in 1856) was a description of the Galapagos Islands off South America. The second was a short story, strikingly symbolizing the loneliness and anonymity and passivity of little men in big cities. The third was a novella about a ship whose black slave cargo mutiny and hold their captain a terrorized hostage, a hollow figurehead of white authority.

Melville continued to profess a 'Young American' literary creed. In *Israel Potter* (1855) John Paul Jones, rather than Benjamin Franklin, represents the true America, because he is the spirit of the

West, and of wildness. This is another short novel based on an actual memoir of an unlucky American who loses, in a sense, both his own identity and his country. But both in the quantity and the quality of what he wrote, one can see that Melville had lost faith in himself. *The Confidence Man* (1857) reveals this most clearly by its embitterment. It plays on all the meanings of the title in such a way as to express complete scepticism, moral and metaphysical, by the author. The 1840s had been the decade of Young America. The 1850s seemed to be the decade of the Brahmins. *Leaves of Grass* of course came out then, which Mathews and Melville should have admired, but it did not have the kind of success that could redress the balance for them. Melville needed – what Whitman had but he did not – the faith in himself, the courage, the mere persistence, to keep at his task another forty years.

His family sent him to Europe, perhaps tried to discourage him from writing, and finally found him a job in New York as a customs officer. There he spent the last twenty years of his working life, from 1866 to 1885, producing, after *Clarel*, only *Billy Budd* (which was not published at all till he had been dead for over thirty years). In the last, he returned to the setting of the sea and sailors, and to the theme of a conflict between innocence and corruption, each embodied very purely in a separate individual, a conflict which man's laws fail to adjudicate. It is one of the saddest of careers. There were two sons of his marriage, Malcolm and Stanwix. Both died before their father did, and in circumstances so pathetic as to verge on the tragic. The elder was found dead in his bedroom at home with a gun in his hand after a quarrel with his father. This happened in 1867, when Malcolm was eighteen. The other, who had left home and wandered the world, disappearing for a year in Central America, finally died in a hospital in San Francisco, in 1886, alone and penniless. Melville's relations with his sons, as with his mother, were unhappy.

One need not compare this with Bryant's slow and stately decline amid gathering honours, to feel its sadness. Bryant died in 1878, after addressing a huge assembly in Central Park, dedicating a statue to Mazzini, at the age of eighty-four. Melville may have been one of the crowd that listened. While Tennyson was sufficiently favoured by fate to die – in 1892, one year after Melville – Poet Laureate of the British Empire, personal friend of the Queen-Empress, and to be buried with full honours, the world's great men mourning his passing. And yet Melville wrote things that fascinate and reward our attention more than anything Bryant or Tennyson wrote.

MG

## B. Themes and Styles

One may begin with a passage from the fourth book he wrote in four years:

I very well remembered staring at a man myself, who was pointed out to me by my aunt one Sunday in Church, as the person who had been in Stony Arabia, and passed through strange adventures there, all of which with my own eyes I had read in the book which he wrote, an arid-looking book in a pale yellow cover. 'See what big eyes he has,' whispered my aunt, 'they got so big, because when he was almost dead with famishing in the desert, he all at once caught sight of a date tree, with the ripe fruit hanging on it.' Upon this, I stared at him till I thought his eyes were really of an uncommon size, and stuck out from his head like those of a lobster. I am sure my own eyes must have magnified as I stared.

Melville's Redburn as a child. The pleasant freshness of this writing – Dickensian –, with the lobster eyes, the whispering aunt and the arid-looking book in the pale yellow cover – is something that Melville can often surprise us with. He is at every turn a surprising writer. And *Moby-Dick* is of course the biggest surprise of all. It is surprising that such a powerful and original book should have come from such a prolific yet painfully uncertain writer, surprising that Melville could so suddenly achieve a work of such wide range, resuming as it does, and with such large, confident and authentic gestures, so much of the spirit of the age.

*Moby-Dick* triumphs again and again by yoking together heterogenous voices, temperaments, moral positions, states of mind. But earlier attempts in this mode, in *Typee, Omoo, Mardi, Redburn* and *White-Jacket* too often resulted only in uneasy and artificial tryings-on of costumes and masks, and the striking of various poses. Always there was uncertainty: 'So the product is a final hash, and all my books are botches', Melville said to Hawthorne in 1851, and, typically, of 'beggarly *Redburn*' (in its unpretentious way the most interesting of the early books): 'I wrote it to buy tobacco'. He was the most diffident of great authors. One recalls those poignant passages in his letters to Hawthorne after he had finished *Moby-Dick* itself and dedicated it to him and eagerly and anxiously waited for Hawthorne's comments. The correspondence movingly reveals Melville's impulsive investments in a friendship that the withdrawn Hawthorne could not or would not sustain. But particularly poignant is his *cri de coeur*: 'A sense of unspeakable security is in me at this moment on account of your having understood the book.' And he was to go on worrying about Hawthorne, who nearly a quarter of a century later turns up as

'Vine' – in his long, painful, dusty verse-journey to the Holy Land, *Clarel* (1876). Here Melville probes again at that uncertain writers' relationship, complaining of Hawthorne's 'non-cordialness'.

> Prior advances unreturned
> Not here he recked of, while he yearned
> .......................
> ............Ah, call me *brother*!
> So feminine his passionate mood
> Which, long as hungering unfed
> All else rejected or withstood.

One way out of literary uncertainty for Melville was documentary: his habit of heaping up factual information to strengthen or guarantee his texts. Another way out, as we have seen, was to follow the fashions and the authority of New York genteel belles-lettres and New York Rabelaisian joviality. This habit is responsible for most of the Carlylean thumpings and the quizzicalities from Browne or Sterne that Melville felt it necessary to work up, notably in *Mardi*.

The documentary method works effectively in *Moby-Dick* to establish the necessary large authoritative tone. The rhetoric is still patently literary in the sense that it is an artificial language, consciously divorced from the colloquial. Yet in *Moby-Dick* it works admirably to establish the strenuous energy and adventurousness, the sense of heightened and permanent excitation, of the pressing significance of what is happening.

Of course, the whaling facts can weigh us down, and Melville's other bad habits can be a great nuisance: the weighty musings on insoluble problems – 'Heed it well, ye Pantheists' – manly pipe-puffings – 'I like to feel something in this slippery world that can hold, man' – forced melodrama – '"The black vomit wrench thee" and "Curses throttle thee!" yelled Ahab,' – Melville's coy sex jokes – the 'Cassock' chapter in *Moby-Dick*, for example – or the various dutiful shufflings towards allegory – 'Methinks it pictures life' – along the lines of a tiresome moment in *White-Jacket*: 'We mortals are all on board a fast-sailing, never-sinking, world-frigate of which God was the shipwright'. In the same book, though, when White-Jacket falls into the ocean from the masthead, we hear clearly the distinctive language, the heightened rhetoric that Melville uses so effectively in *Moby-Dick* where realistic and factual details of his whaling adventure story assume that sense of general human significance that lifts the whole narrative on to an epic level:

Time seemed to stand still, and all the worlds seemed poised on their poles, as I fell, soul-becalmed, through the eddying whirl and swirl of the maelstrom air. . . . As I gushed into the sea, a thunder-boom sounded in my ear; my soul seemed flying from my mouth. The feeling of death flooded over me with the billows. . . . Purple and pathless was the deep calm now around me, flecked by summer lightnings in an azure afar. . . . But of a sudden some fashionless form brushed my side . . . some inert, coiled fish of the sea; the thrill of being alive again tingled in my nerves, and the strong shunning of death shocked me through.

'Maelstrom air' – 'I gushed into the sea' – 'the strong shunning of death'. The language deliberately calls attention to itself but is undeniably striking, surprising. Melville gets a similar effect in the marvellous action scenes in *Moby-Dick*, especially when he juxtaposes this extravagance of language with the matter-of-fact plainness of men at work. So in this extraordinarily powerful account of a whale-killing where a wide range of feeling is evoked:

'Haul in – haul in!' cried Stubb to the bowsman! and, facing round towards the whale, all hands began pulling the boat up to him, while yet the boat was being towed on. Soon ranging up by his flank, Stubb, firmly planting his knee in the clumsy cleat, darted dart after dart into the flying fish; at the word of command, the boat alternately sterning out of the way of the whale's horrible wallow, and then ranging up for another fling.

The red tide now poured from all sides of the monster like brooks down a hill. His tormented body rolled not in brine but in blood, which bubbled and seethed for furlongs behind in their wake. The slanting sun playing upon this crimson pond in the sea, sent back its reflection into every face, so that they all glowed to each other like red men. And all the while, jet after jet of white smoke was agonizingly shot from the spiracle of the whale, and vehement puff after puff from the mouth of the excited headsman; as at every dart, hauling in upon his crooked lance (by the line attached to it), Stubb straightened it again and again, by a few rapid blows against the gunwale, then again and again sent it into the whale.

'Pull up – pull up!' he now cried to the bowsman, as the waning whale relaxed in his wrath. 'Pull up! – close to!' and the boat ranged along the fish's flank. When reaching far over the bow, Stubb slowly churned his long sharp lance into the fish, and kept it there, carefully churning and churning, as if cautiously seeking to feel after some gold watch that the whale might have swallowed, and which he was fearful of breaking ere he could hook it out. But that gold watch he sought was the innermost life of the fish. And now it is struck; for, starting from his trance into that unspeakable thing called his 'flurry', the monster horribly wallowed in his blood, over-wrapped himself in impenetrable, mad, boiling spray, so that the imperilled craft, instantly dropping astern, had much ado blindly to struggle out from the phrensied twilight into the clear air of the day.

And now abating his flurry, the whale once more rolled out into view;

surging from side to side; spasmodically dilating and contracting his spout-hole, with sharp, cracking, agonized respirations. At last, gush after gush of clotted red gore, as if it had been the purple lees of red wine, shot into the frighted air; and falling back again, ran dripping down his motionless flanks into the sea. His heart had burst!

'He's dead, Mr Stubb.' said Daggoo.

'Yes; both pipes smoked out!' and withdrawing his own from his mouth, Stubb scattered the dead ashes over the water; and, for a moment, stood thoughtfully eyeing the vast corpse he had made.

Such spectacular passages are the great successes of *Moby-Dick*. Almost everything to do with the sea, ships and whaling is success-ful, with a fine balance maintained between the small details of seamanship and ship-management, such as the hard-headed bar-gaining of the profit-minded Quaker owners ('Don't whale it too much a' Lord's days, men, but don't miss a fair chance either, that's rejecting Heaven's good gifts'), and the grand excitements and ferocities of the pursuit, where we are made to feel the immense-ness, the nightmarish hugeness, but also the simple beauty of the whale, and we feel all the terrors and exhilarations of men bringing their complex skills and tempers to bear upon the forces of nature. Here Melville writes not only with great and surprising energy but with full confidence.

Great energy also goes into the delineation of Ahab: Melville seems to be willing him into life. But it is a symbolic existence only. The story of this aspect of *Moby-Dick*'s composition is well enough known. Looking for ways to bring his obsessive preoccupation with moral and metaphysical ambiguity into play he became, as his letters show, excited about 'the mystical depth of meaning' and 'the pro-found, nay, appalling moral' to be found in Hawthorne's *Mosses From An Old Manse* – 'shrouded in blackness, ten times black'. His habit of half-depressed though also half-jocular enquiry into 'the deeper and unspeakable meanings of life', together with his sub-missive readiness to be formed by more powerful personalities ('This Hawthorne has dropped germinous seeds into my soul') led him to write or rewrite large parts of his great whaling book in a Hawthornian mode. Ahab becomes a luridly mysterious romantic hero, a relative of Chillingworth or Rappaccini, full of 'wild vindic-tiveness' or 'frantic morbidness', whose literary forebears weigh heavily upon him, as does Carlyle's heavy prose.

Melville's intentions are clear enough, but the loud literary hints, the invitations to see Ahab as another Lear or Hamlet are not sustained by anything other than melodrama and grand rhetoric of an almost definitively un-Shakespearian kind. Hints about Cain or

Manfred or Teufelsdröckh perhaps come a little nearer the mark. It has been pointed out that the stridently romantic mode in which Ahab is conceived runs counter to and stifles the kind of response that the epic mode so successfully evokes. It also eliminates him as a character in a novel. Romantic Ahab hardly exists for us as a man alive and for himself, or in contact with other men. As he orates – it seems the only suitable term for his highly-wrought speech – at Starbuck, and as Starbuck orates back, we have no impression amidst these Jacobean exchanges that either person is in contact with himself or with the other.

So we lose something of Melville in *Moby-Dick*. With Ahab he gives up trying to write intimately and imaginatively about human relationships. He abandons the novel, and the special intimacies that even the most formal novelist characteristically establishes with his reader. In a real sense, then, we lose touch with Melville in *Moby-Dick*. For the autobiographical early books do show signs of Melville's serious interest in writing novels, of attempts to present and explore, for instance, the inner life of the narrator, and to make creative projections from it. They are worth looking at again in this light. His successes are not large, partly perhaps because he lacked the traditional novelist's technical equipment – he was careless or insensitive about manipulating point-of-view, for example. But he was interested in trying to be a novelist – something that critics fresh from the impossibility of categorizing *Moby-Dick* as a novel, or eager to recognize Melville's success as an exponent of the romance, have tended not to talk about. Melville clearly made his own decisions, quite consciously made this adventurous shift away from the novel towards epic and, especially, romance. But one need not therefore accept the shift as a total triumph of originality and self-renewal. One can recognize also a self-limiting, even evasive retreat from the real and concrete into the abstract and fanciful, a retreat that makes a part of that sad pattern of frustration and failure that Melville's life presents.

In his earlier books Melville had used his own uncertainties and fears in a personal, almost confessional, way that brought his narrators to fictional life. The narrators in *Typee, Omoo, Redburn* and *White-Jacket* (*Mardi* will not help much here) are clearly closely related versions of Melville himself. In *Typee* the narrator feels 'wronged and outraged', in *Omoo* he is 'weighed down by a melancholy that could not be shaken off'; Redburn believes that 'upon his young soul the mildew has fallen', and so on. This composite narrator is an Ishmael figure, scorned for example in *Redburn* and

*White-Jacket* because he wears outmoded or inappropriate clothes, uneasy in *Typee* because he is an alien among both his own kind and among the savages. But this is more than the standard romantic outsider popular in post-Byronic England or America. He is a wandering adventurer of a paradoxically different stamp. It is impressed upon us that we are meeting a passive, 'feminine' personality, easily dominated, insecure, alternately frightened and fascinated by the domination of others.

So from behind the literary affectations, the earnest religious and social commentary, the dogged documentation and the hearty jocularity common to all the early books, there emerges the idiosyncratic sensibility of a depressed and frightened man. And Melville can bring his sensibility alive to us so that we assent to its authenticity, recognize the lived experience. The claustrophobically enclosed communities he chooses to write about, ships and islands and, in *Typee*, a narrowly circumscribed tribal territory become contexts where he can explore in an almost exclusively male world these timidities in front of life, his fitful but persistent interest in the ways human beings establish dominations over one another, and submit to them.

*Typee* looked at in this light has something more to offer than its promised 'Peep at Polynesia' or its rattling good adventure yarn. In his first book Melville's uncertain narrative voice veers between various extremes, from liberal schoolmarm: 'A high degree of refinement does not seem to subdue our wicked propensities so much', to an occasional rather surprisingly vulgar clubman's wink – the long-lost ship that is still 'regularly tacking . . . somewhere off Buggerry Island, or the Devil's Tail Peak'. But the immediate attractions are of an obvious kind:

From the verdant surfaces of the large stones that lay scattered about, the natives were now sliding off into the water, diving and ducking beneath the surface in all directions – the young girls springing buoyantly into the air, and revealing their naked form to the waist, with their long tresses dancing about their shoulders, their eyes sparkling like dew in the sun, and their gay laughter pealing forth. . . . But the tranquillising influences of beautiful scenery and the exhibition of human life under so novel and charming an aspect, were not my only sources of consolation. Every evening the girls of the house gathered about me on the mats and . . . would anoint my whole body with a fragrant oil squeezed from a yellow root, previously pounded between a couple of stones, and which in their language is denominated 'aka'. And most agreeable and refreshing are the juices of the aka when applied to one's limbs by the soft palms of sweet nymphs whose bright eyes are beaming upon you with kindness; and I used to hail with delight the daily recurrence of their luxurious operation, in which I forgot all my troubles, and buried for the time every feeling of sorrow.

D. H. Lawrence read his own intensities into these after all rather prim fancies about life in a cannibal isle ('the tranquillising influences of the beautiful scenery and the exhibition of human life') because Melville's programme preoccupied him; he wanted to realize and to reject the attractions of the primitive for himself, so he imagined that Melville had done the same. But Melville's typically inert, passive narrator gives only a travelogue kind of life, or at best a decoratively picturesque life, to the dusky maidens. Although there is a certain light and sprightly charm about Melville's narrative, the centre of interest is not in Lawrence's warm flesh and warm uncreate mud. Fayaway, taking off and spreading out her only garment as a sail for Tommo's canoe – 'a prettier little mast was never shipped aboard of any craft' – becomes less warm flesh than plastic ornament.

Melville does not come alive among the Gauguin maids (in truth the only persons he unequivocally shares a bed with in *Typee* are Kory-Kory, his body-servant, and his mate Toby, with whom he establishes a relationship anticipating Ishmael and Queequeg's – 'We then ratified our engagement with an affectionate wedding of palms'). Nor does he live as a social philosopher. Some comfortable, unstrenuous Knickerbocker moralizing goes on: 'Thrice happy are they who, inhabiting some yet undiscovered island in the middle of the ocean, have never been brought into contaminating contact with the white man'. But Tommo as a homespun son of the Enlightenment is hardly a deeply imagined personality.

The book comes most imaginatively alive as a novel about the narrator's obsessive urge to escape. On the surface Melville's escapism merely indulges the kind of taste that Tennyson's speaker invokes in *Locksley Hall*, for 'Summer isles of Eden lying in dark purple shores of sea', though Melville's version is more prosaic, domestic: 'Life is often little else than an often interrupted luxurious nap'. Civilization is to be rejected for a very drowsy kind of renewal in the virgin lands. But the firmest note in *Typee* is one of fear and uncertainty. Tommo is full of 'dismal forebodings' and 'profoundest melancholy'. So he is afraid all the time: 'what furtive and anxious glances we cast into those dim-looking shades'. His Eden turns out to be as claustrophobic and as threatening as the ship-world he originally fled from. His escape turns into continuous flight. He is imprisoned physically by a mysterious disease. His Typee friends too, become in some uncertain way his captors. It is hard for him to tell whether they are 'good' or 'bad'. They appear to have power over him but he is uncertain of the limits of this power. He has a curiously submissive attitude towards his personal body-servant Kory-Kory, who nurses him, feeds him, and even carries him about on his back. (In *White-Jacket* the narrator becomes the favoured 'pet' of a strong handsome sailor, Jack Chase.) The chief, Mehevi, at times awes and dominates him with his 'inflexible rigidity of expression'. The Typees in general, though at times jolly, feasting comrades can be 'wayward and passionate spirits against whom it was vain to struggle'. Tommo is obsessively afraid of cannibalism. And at one point the men of the tribe hold him down and 'desecrate' his skin with a tattooer's needle.

Lawrence, who clearly sees *Typee* as centrally an invitation to the reader to interest himself in the personality of the narrator, said Melville hated life. What Melville brings before us in *Typee* specifically is fear, doubt and a submissiveness occasionally punctuated by fearful revolt. Much the same atmosphere is generated in *White-Jacket*, where the narrator shifts between a hearty admiration for the hardy sailors and a horror at their threatening bestiality or savagery, and where, having seen the cat-o- nine tails torturing the 'dazzlingly white back' of a young seaman he himself 'swallowed his own heart' as he is summoned before the mast:

a dimness was before my eyes. But through that dimness the boatswain's mate, scourge in hand, loomed like a giant . . . but the thing that swayed me to my purpose was not altogether the thought that Captain Claret was about to degrade me. . . . No, I felt my man's manhood so bottomless within me that no word, no blow, no scourge . . . would cut me deep enough for that.

In *Typee* Melville is already working out imaginatively, if in rather inchoate forms, the themes that emerge in all his work, the ambiguities and paradoxes in human experience, the intolerable burdens that uncertainty places upon the individual, whether it is uncertainty about ultimate truth and ultimate reality, about right and wrong, or about the fears of the individual faced with his own self, the *Underground Man* sort of vacillation between extremes of self-degradation and self-assertion. From the beginning Melville clearly wanted to write about these things. The development from Tommo's troubles in distinguishing between good Happars and cannibal Typees to the Luther-like puzzling in *Moby-Dick* over what behind the pasteboard masks is the Devil's and what is God's is hardly fortuitous. In the early books, though, Melville writes about these problems in the plainer terms of his own lived ex-perience.

This is true even of *Omoo*, where Melville attempts a different kind of projection in the character of Doctor Long Ghost, an educated man of sly sexuality, of 'humorous desperation' and of self-destructive irony. Melville plays hard at urban whimsicality, yet *Omoo* is still a novel about imprisonments and escapes. The narrator sails away from the cannibals in a decaying ship full of rotting stores, with a demoralized crew half of whom are sick or dying. Its destination is uncertain. Everyone on board is dominated by the powerful personality of Jermin, the mate. And although the book moves into light fantasy, involving imprisonment on the isle of Tahiti (where the narrator falls for a while in love with a fickle young man), the anarchic ship has first been the scene of a series of male challenges and victories and defeats of a kind that fascinated Melville and puts him in line with all the other American novelists from Fenimore Cooper through Hemingway to Saul Bellow and Norman Mailer (not excluding the crime writers and the script-writers for Westerns) who are concerned with creating exemplars of tough masculinity. (Male force and beauty is also an occasional theme in Melville's Civil War poetry, his most interesting verse. In his 'Ode on the Photograph of a Corps Commander', for instance:

> Ay, man is manly. Here you see
> The warrior-carriage of the head,
> And brave dilation of the frame. . . .)

Melville's claustrophobic contexts present in his own insistent way versions of the same kind of male challenge and response that Mailer presents in *his* knowing way in *The Time of Her Time* or *An American Dream*:

'Man you can take care of yourself,' he said with glee. 'I don't know about that,' I answered, obeying the formal minuet of the *macho*. 'I don't like to mess with anybody,' I told him. 'But a man messes with me – well, I wouldn't want him to go away feeling better than he started.'

The battles in the forecastle in *Omoo*, between Bembo and Salem, are in this tradition, although Melville is characteristically more interested in submissions than in duels. He projects and can give startling immediacy to a series of dominating characters, dangerous men, evil yet fascinating: Jermin, the mate in *Omoo*, Jackson in *Redburn*, and the master-at-arms, Bland in *White-Jacket*. Here is Jermin:

He was the very beau-ideal of the efficient race of short, thickset men. His hair curled in little rings of iron grey all over his round, bullet head. As for his countenance, it was strongly marked, deeply pitted with small-pox . . . his large mouth, and great white teeth, looked absolutely sharkish when he laughed. For the rest, there was a fierce little squint out of one eye. He was always for having a fight; but the very men he flogged loved him as a brother. . . .

Jackson in *Redburn* is a much more sinister version; with his bald head, broken nose and squinting eye, he is physically repulsive and also physically weak. He is dying, presumably of consumption, perhaps of syphilis, too. He is a bitter, envious railer and sneerer, and a total nihilist:

He was spontaneously an atheist and an infidel; and during long night watches, would enter into arguments, to prove that there was nothing to be believed; nothing to be loved, and nothing worth living for; but everything to be hated, in the wide world. He was a horrid desperado . . . he seemed to run amuck at heaven and earth.

But Jackson wins all the forecastle battles. With his fierce will and fierce tongue he establishes total ascendancy over the crew, who cringe before him, laugh sycophantically at his jokes, hurry to adjust to his overbearing, changeable moods.

Redburn himself becomes a special target of his sneers and insults. He hates and fears Jackson's 'degradation' – Jackson boasts all the vices of cruelty and corruption – yet Redburn also admires him:

He had such an overawing way with him; such a deal of brass and impudence, such an unflinching face. . . . And besides all this, it was quite plain, that he was by nature a marvellously clever, cunning man, though without education, and understood human nature to a kink, and well knew whom he had to deal with; and then, one glance of his squinting eye was as good as a knock-down. . . .

In this frightened world with its contrasting or complementary kinds of personality Melville is evidently confronting powerful feelings of his own. The theme persists in very sharply defined terms in the best-known and more interesting of his later works. 'Benito Cereno' and *Billy Budd.* Any feeling of real human encounter in 'Benito Cereno' is stifled in its Hawthornian complexities of symbolic elaboration, but the story is about Don Benito's complete submission to the powerful domination of his tyrant-servant, Babo, in a ship which has become a prison run by fear. In the last book Melville wrote, the Claggart–Billy Budd relationship is analogous. But both Don Benito and Billy Budd are loaded down with symbolic decoration, so much so that they, like

Claggart and Babo, exist for us only on the symbolic level. For in the life-and-death charade that is played out on board the *San Dominick* and the crime-and-punishment charade on the *Indomitable* Melville has so totally distanced us from the protagonists as virtually to refine them out of existence. They are almost as uncommunicative as Bartleby the Scrivener: Cereno at first is too terrorized to be able to speak directly, and when he is freed from his persecutor all we hear is a long, formal, legal deposition. Billy Budd, the beautiful young sailor, despite the vivid detail of 'the ear small and shapely, the arch of the foot, the curve in mouth and nostril', is an even more tenuous presence with his 'more or less of a stutter or even worse'. We are not pressed to believe in his reality. Melville in fact insists that he is making this evasive version of the Jackson–Redburn relationship into a mystification:

And yet the cause, necessarily to be assumed as the sole one assignable is in its very realism as much charged with that prime element of Radcliffian romance *the mysterious*, as any that the ingenuity of the author of the *Mysteries of Udolpho* could devise. For what can more partake of the mysterious than an antipathy spontaneous and profound such as is evoked in certain exceptional mortals by the mere aspect of some other mortal however harmless he may be, if not called forth by this very harmlessness itself?

Returning to *Moby-Dick* one sees a similar mystification. Ishmael's affinity with Melville's earlier narrators is obvious enough. He is more confident and talkative, but his first encounters with the whaling world still cast him in the depressed role of the nervous innocent who 'stumbles against the walls of solitude and derision'. This is true not only of his dealings with the inn-keeper Peter Coffin and with the whaling captains Peleg and Bildad, but also of his association with Queequeg the harpooner. Although Melville treats these encounters largely in a comic frontier-humour style there are serious overtones too. Before and after Queequeg caresses Ishmael and takes him in his 'bridegroom clasp', the narrator is frightened and apprehensive of this strange, powerful and compelling presence: 'I shudderingly remembered it all . . . the awful fear'.

Ishmael's interesting relationship with Queequeg fades out of the book, returning only symbolically at the end, when he survives the wreck of the *Pequod* in Queequeg's coffin. He has no relationship at all with Ahab, who is another bully, but now a transcendental bully. The very success of the early scenes, where Melville engages us directly with Ishmael and Queequeg and sets us asking never-to-be-answered questions about them, underlines the note of retreat, of evasion, or (the erotic overtones in so many of these encounters are surely relevant) a failure of nerve – with Melville resorting to a sublimation of those pressing feelings into the safe mystifications of romantic rhetoric.

Perhaps the sensibility that emerges in the early books announces itself as too limited and disabled to be that of a major novelist. When he did try again, for a few chapters in *Pierre*, it was a half-hearted and uneasy affair. And of course the non-novel, *Moby-Dick*, is a great book. Yet when he was dealing on a human plane with human experiences Melville could be an absorbing writer, too, and there is room for regret that he did not keep that magnified eye of his on the human object as steadily as he kept it on his white whale.

BMcC

# 9

## *WALT WHITMAN*

### *Denis Donoghue*

It is proper to declare that we are concerned with Whitman the poet; allowing, with whatever degree of irony, that it is permissible to reflect upon Whitman the prophet, the laureate of Democracy, the good grey messenger of revolution, the American, Lincoln's elegist, champion of Freedom, and so forth. But it is easier to avow this scruple than to act upon it. Whitman lives in his poems, we say, or he does not live at all. True, in one sense; but the poems do not reach us in such purity. It is disingenuous to maintain that the words 'Walt Whitman' mean the collected works of a certain poet as the words 'T. S. Eliot' mean the collected works of a certain poet. Walt Whitman in a myth, as Eliot is not: that is, whatever Eliot means is to be found, definitively secreted, in the poems themselves, but the meaning of Whitman sprawls far beyond his lines. We see this in the first stanza of Wallace Stevens's poem 'Like Decorations in a Nigger Cemetery':

> In the far South the sun of autumn is passing
> Like Walt Whitman walking along a ruddy shore.
> He is singing and chanting the things that are part of him,
> The worlds that were and will be, death and day.
> Nothing is final, he chants. No man shall see the end.
> His beard is of fire and his staff is a leaping flame.

It would be absurd, or a merry quip, to compare the sun, in the first two lines, with any other figure in American literature: try inserting, for instance, the names of Emily Dickinson, Henry James, T. S. Eliot or Robert Frost. Melville is the only other writer who might survive the comparison. This does not mean that to Stevens or to us, Whitman is obviously the greatest American writer; but rather that, in a peculiar degree, he occupies a special place in the landscape of American feeling. He is an emblem, a moral force, a personage: the poetry, in certain respects, does not matter. This is why Whitman has a particular profile in the iconography of

American literature; his status is heroic, whether the poems are good or bad. He lodges in the mind as a certain gesture, a stance; the last line of Stevens's invocation makes it clear. That line is not offered as description or notation: it testifies, rather, to Whitman's epic character, as if he were a certain feeling, personified. If feelings had proper names, one of them would be Whitman. He is, in Emerson's sense, a Representative Man. So if we say of the words on the page that they alone matter, we can hardly say it until, late in the evening, we have disengaged ourselves from considerations which, in other respects, matter more.

Whitman was born on 31 May 1819 at West Hills, Long Island, New York: 'well-begotten', as he writes in 'Starting from Paumanok', 'and rais'd by a perfect mother'. His father, less than perfect, meant little to the boy. In 1823 the family moved to Brooklyn where the father tried his luck as a builder. Walt's education was vague and random. At the age of seventeen, he attached himself to a printer in New York, and thereafter, for many years, he lived in close touch with printing rooms, newspapers, editorial desks. In 1848 he spent some months in New Orleans, working on a newspaper, the *Crescent*. In 1862 he went to Washington and attended upon Civil War soldiers as a 'wound-dresser': as he wrote in the 'Song of Myself':

> I am he bringing help for the sick as they pant on their backs,
> And for strong upright men I bring yet more needed help.

To support himself, he took a job as a clerk in the Army Paymaster's Office, but in 1864 his health failed and he went back to his mother's house in Brooklyn. Later, he worked again, as a clerk in the Indian Bureau of the Interior Department, where he spent nine years, but after 1873 he was never to recover his health. He left Washington and went to live with his brother George in Camden, New Jersey: in 1884 he moved to his own house in Mickle Street. In the last seven or eight years of his life he lived as a sage, visited and admired by a succession of literary men: he was now famous. He had published the first edition of *Leaves of Grass* in 1855; thereafter, several larger books appeared under that title until the famous 'deathbed' edition of 1892. He had also published *Drum-Taps* (1865), *Democratic Vistas* (1871) and *Specimen Days* (1882). He died on 26 March 1892.

The life was not, indeed, as diverse as the poems claim: many of the ostensibly autobiographical moments in the poems are the work of fancy and desire. The rhetoric of the poetry required a sustaining experience multitudinous and free: confinement to the facts would have impeded the flow. It may be argued that Whitman found, in the way of experience, whatever he needed for the good of the poems; but at the same time the poems often give an impression of cultural emaciation, as if desire and fancy were not enough. Some passages are written, apparently, on the assumption that to say a few things well it is necessary to say everything anyhow: if there is enough of it, some of it is bound to be good. Whitman's culture may have given him what he needed, so that the poems became what they are; but there is the other possibility, that the culture did not give him what he needed to make the poems greater than they are. It is often necessary to say of Whitman what R. P. Blackmur said of Hart Crane, that he represents 'every ignorance possible to talent when it has genius, every wilfulness tolerable because of expressive intention'. Certainly, Whitman's culture gave him material enough for his grandest purposes, but it did not force him to survey those purposes, to criticize his high intention: his individual talent was not, in any profound sense, curbed or rebuked by a critical tradition.

But these are premature questions. We must allow to Whitman's 'expressive intention' at least this; that we take him at his own word and on his own terms before we insinuate other words, other terms. Reading poets like Whitman and Crane, who pursue the American Sublime, we have to take the will and the deed as making a continuum; or at least we have to give these poets the benefit of every doubt, until the doubts are resolved or transcended. Eliot's intention does not offer itself as interesting apart from the deed, but to engage with Whitman and Crane at all, we have to strike a liberal bargain with them: a word is to be justified by the line, the line by the stanza, the stanza by the poem, the poem by the whole work, *Leaves of Grass*; and even then we are not released, there is still the larger *oeuvre*, the life.

'Of all mankind,' Whitman writes in the introduction to the first edition of *Leaves of Grass*, 'the great poet is the equable man.' He may have been encouraged in this sentiment by Emerson who said, in the essay 'The Poet', that the poet is representative: 'he stands among partial men for the complete man, and apprises us not of his wealth, but of the commonwealth'. To Whitman, the poet is seer, arbiter, standard, and key; the self, so far as the self is complete and expressive. In 'Song of Myself' he speaks of 'the Me myself', saying that it is not 'contain'd between my hat and boots': it is not even the sum of its experiences, but rather than sum, apprehended:

Apart from the pulling and hauling stands what I am,
Stands amused, complacent, compassionating, idle, unitary,
Looks down, is erect, or bends an arm on an impalpable certain rest,
Looking with side-curved head curious what will come next,
Both in and out of the game and watching and wondering at it.

The pulling and hauling: that is, the events of life, one thing after another, the matter of relevant things. But the self is not identified with its casual contents; the contents are transfigured by the imagination. Poems are 'psalms of self' if in thinking of song we mark the singer. The poet's theme is 'my own diversity', the range and plenitude of those experiences which the self has apprehended. Ultimately, the self is identified with 'the soul', and that with God. 'To be this incredible God I am!', Whitman exults in 'Song at Sunset'. In the 'Song of Myself': 'Divine am I inside and out, and I make holy whatever I touch or am touched from'. Man is God in the measure of his senses and his imagination: it makes little difference whether we think of divine attributes and then ascribe them to man, or think of certain human powers and equate them, transfigured, with God. All roads lead to that romantic Rome. The idiom is philosophically idealist, to begin with; as Coleridge thought of the human imagination as the finite counterpart of God's creative power, the infinite I AM. But Coleridge did not press the analogy to the pitch of identifying God and man; Whitman's pitch, in fact. Whitman speaks of God as of man in his most extreme reach of imagination.

The pattern is clear in 'Passage to India' and other poems. Whitman cannot think of God and the universe as separate from himself; such a thought would leave him wrecked, dissociated. So he refutes the thought by thinking of himself, 'the soul', and endowing that phrase with divinely creative attributes: at that stage there is no longer any need to use an idiom of divine things or divine powers; the soul is God:

Swiftly I shrivel at the thought of God,
At Nature and its wonders, Time and Space and Death,
But that I, turning, call to thee O soul, thou actual Me,
And lo, thou gently masterest the orbs,
Thou makest Time, smilest content at Death,
And fillest, swellest full the vastnesses of Space.

It is a characteristic curve of feeling: the poet redeems himself, constantly renews himself, until he fills the world. This partly explains why, to Whitman, poetry consists in the entire life of feeling. Feeling is the divine spirit, the great poem is the great life, and the mere words on the page are only one form of this activity. The ultimate poem is life itself; the poems are merely one part, consistent with other parts. Ideally, poems intervene between one great silence and another. What is crucial is the process, the continuity and diversity of feeling; process rather than product. Look after the process and the product will look after itself. The enemy is 'stagnation'. The poet never stagnates: 'if he breathes into any thing that was before thought small it dilates with the grandeur and life of the universe'; like God.

So the poet is, in Emerson's phrase, the secretary. 'I find a provision, in the constitution of the world,' Emerson writes in *Representative Men*, 'for the writer or secretary, who is to report the doings of the miraculous spirit of life that everywhere throbs and works.' Add to this the further assumption that the miraculous spirit is most clearly found in 'the Me myself', and we have the gist of Whitman's rhetoric. It is given, implicitly, in the last paragraph of Emerson's book:

The secret of genius is to suffer no fiction to exist for us; to realize all that we know; in the high refinement of modern life, in arts, in sciences, in books, in men, to exact good faith, reality, and a purpose; and first, last, midst, and without end, to honour every truth by use.

There is enough here for Whitman's purposes. The idealist slant of his aesthetic need not be extreme, there is no need of solipsism. It is possible to assimilate the Romantic imagination to intimations of divine purpose and power, but it is also possible to act as secretary, writing the miraculous truths of nature and self. There is no contradiction, especially if the post of secretary is not restricted to mere transcription. The secretary reports what he sees, hears, touches, tastes, and smells, but these impressions are related and, indeed, transfigured by the imagination: what the secretary writes is the imaginative record, not a blunt paraphrase. The secretary has his own diversity.

To use a standard philosophical idiom: the object is qualified by the subject's reception of it. The point, in relation to Whitman, must be enforced. There is a sense in which he is nonchalant about the self: as if the self were the sum of its experiences and could safely, beyond that, be taken for granted. 'I become as much more as I like,' he says in 'Song of Myself', reciting several experiences to display his possessions. 'A shroud I see – and I am the shroud', he says in 'The Sleepers'. Whitman's sense of self may often be defined as a sense of its possessions. But a complete merging of subject and object is rare in his poetry: there are dangerous moments in certain meditations upon death and the sea. Nearly always, subject and object are held in poise, each is itself. 'Clear and sweet is my soul . . . and clear and sweet is all that is not my soul.' The characteristic act of the self is to attract appearances and impressions, the chosen objects of experience:

> And I know I am solid and sound,
> To me the converging objects of the universe perpetually flow.

The fuller the flow, of course, the better: the self lives well, never short of converging impressions. What happens to these impressions when they converge is the history of Whitman's imagination.

The language is idealist in the sense that the primary act is deemed to be the act of feeling: normally, there is no quarrel between subject and object, but if a quarrel should break out, subject must be asserted. 'All architecture is what you do to it when you look upon it', Whitman says in 'A Song for Occupations'. Everywhere the governing idiom is personal, subjective: what is objective is acknowledged, but Whitman emphasizes the subjective force of attraction and perception, the force of convergence towards a centre. Poetry is great because it is personal, it comes from the person, the self, the soul:

> My words are words of a questioning, and to indicate reality;
> This printed and bound book. . . . but the printer and the printing-office boy?
> The marriage estate and settlement. . . . but the body and mind of the bridegroom, also those of the bride?

In 'Song of the Answerer', 'Every existence has its idiom. . . . every thing has an idiom and tongue'. In 'To a Historian' Whitman distinguishes between historian and poet, the historian celebrates 'bygones', the poet, 'Chanter of Personality', projects 'the history of the future'. If we ask the secretary whether his text contains more subject than object, he is likely to reply that objects are, indeed, acknowledged but, finally, they minister to the subject. As in 'Out of the Cradle Endlessly Rocking', 'the sea whisper'd me'.

If the poet is God, poetry is everything, it encompasses everything, religion, science, fact, life, everything. Poetry is Being: so the idiom of Being is superior to all other idioms, as the poet is superior to all other persons, complete where they are partial. It it typical of Whitman to use one idiom to refute another, as the single category of Being refutes all other categories. The distinction between good and evil vanishes, at least in this stringent theory, when both terms are dissolved in the higher language of Being. Hence Whitman's ethic is his aesthetic: his sense of the world is an aesthetic sense, in which good and evil are featured as neutral terms. William Carlos Williams wrote, in the essay 'Against the Weather', that 'the blessed and the damned are treated by Dante, the *artist*, with scrupulous impartiality. . . . Pan is the artist's patron'. This is in Whitman's spirit. It was William James, I think, who brought into critical currency the notion that, in practice, Whitman lacked a sense of evil. In a lecture of 1895 he spoke of 'our dear old Walt Whitman's works' as the handbook of that 'temperamental optimism' which is 'incapable of believing that anything seriously evil can exist'. What James started, Yeats continued, in a famous passage in *A Vision*. But it will not do. Some of the most haunting passages in 'Song of Myself' are apprehensions of sickness and pain, 'the silent old-faced infants and the lifted sick'. The fact is that Whitman was determined to erect one terminology and place it above all: in that terminology, such words as feeling, poetry, and being would be strong enough to put any rival terminology down. The conventional distinction between good and evil, respectable and illicit, would be dissolved, on the superior ground that anything which exists and is felt is good. Any object which exists and converges upon the subject is good. This is why Whitman says, in 'Starting from Paumanok':

Omnes! omnes! let others ignore what they may,
I make the poem of evil also, I commemorate that part also,
I am myself just as much evil as good, and my nation is – and I say there is in fact no evil,

(Or if there is I say it is just as important to you, to the land or to me, as any thing else.)

In a battle, success and defeat are good: all things which exist are equal in their perfection, each is miraculously itself. Whitman recognizes every thing for what it is, good or bad, but he is not daunted by its nature. *Etiam peccata*. The reasoning in these passages is not severe, and it entirely depends upon the governing rhetoric in which existence is the only and greatest good. If that rhetoric is deemed to fail, the case is lost, and Whitman the loser is humiliated as a fool.

Taking precautions against this fate, Whitman tries to make the language of Being so compelling that resistance is discouraged: only an extraordinarily wilful reader is likely to resist. 'The flush of the known universe' is his theme, if we allow that, equally, the divine powers of the 'knower' are engaged. 'He brings everything to the text of himself': who does not? To ease the strain of belief, Whitman sometimes translates the ostensible terms of good and evil into the language of the Hero, so that the rivals may each appear as heroic. The account of the frigate-fight in 'Song of Myself' is a case in point; another is the levelling ethic of 'A Song for Occupations'. Or again, as in 'To Think of Time', Whitman posits a perspective so lofty that the distinction between good and bad, from that height, is invisible:

> The vulgar and the refined.... what you call sin and what you call goodness ... to think how wide a difference;
> To think the difference will still continue to others, yet we lie beyond the difference.

Later:

> What is called good is perfect, and what is called sin is just as perfect.

Another procedure is to assimilate the language of poetry and Being to that of irrefutable things – stones, trees, animals – in which the distinction between good and bad hardly arises. In the introduction to *Leaves of Grass* Whitman says that 'to speak in literature with the perfect rectitude and insouciance of the movements of animals and the unimpeachableness of the sentiment of trees in the woods and grass by the roadside is the flawless triumph of art'. I will have purposes,' he continues, 'as health or heat or snow has.' The rhetorical trick here – to speak of it in these sullen terms – is to take advantage of the several meanings of 'perfection'; the state of being complete in its own kind, and – a separate meaning – the state of moral excellence. The first meaning is neutral, according to the dictionaries; the second is of course eulogy. Whitman's strategy is to use the word as a term of praise, to prevent the second meaning from assuming any airs. Anything may be perfect, in its kind: so pious folk may not preen themselves. But meanwhile, animals know how to live; they toil not, neither do they spin, sweat, whine, worry, weep, kneel, or discuss. In 'Me Imperturbe' Whitman says:

> Me imperturbe, standing at ease in Nature,
> Master of all or mistress of all, aplomb in the midst of irrational things,
> O to be self-balanced for contingencies,
> To confront night, storms, hunger, ridicule, accidents, rebuffs, as the trees and animals do.

Like Thoreau in this respect, Whitman counsels: 'Simplify'. We are to live as little children: between children and natural forms there is a 'wooing both ways'. In this version of pastoral the liaison of subject and object is continuous; objects converge upon the subject, and in reply the subject directs his feeling towards the objects:

There was a child went forth every day,
And the first object he looked upon and received with wonder or pity or
    love or dread, that object he became,
And that object became part of him for the day or a certain part of the
    day . . . or for many years or stretching cycles of years.

Finally, everything ministers to the subject, the child: objects willingly celebrate the child, incorporating themselves in him. But the supreme analogy for poetry is the human body itself, simple, uncompounded, stark, but capable of everything. 'I sing the body electric.' 'And your very flesh shall be a great poem,' Whitman promises the reader, 'and have the richest fluency not only in its words but in the silent lines of its lips and face and between the lashes of your eyes and in every motion and joint of your body.' 'If life and the soul are sacred the human body is sacred.' In turn, the canonical terms in Whitman's vocabulary are those which are drawn immediately from a bodily source: many are phrenological terms. A short list includes: adhere, inhale, respiration, adhesiveness, meeting, inspiration, acceptation, realization, give, receive, press, swallow. The poet distrusts abstract terms not because of a fussy cult of 'the concrete', but because the best words are continuous with the intimate life of the body.

Naturally, the great moment, then, is the moment at which subject and object meet; in bodily terms, the moment of contact. 'I am mad for it to be in contact with me', he says in 'Song of Myself', and the object might be anything. Of the great poet, he writes in the Introduction of Leaves of Grass: 'What balks or breaks others is fuel for his burning progress to contact and amorous joy.' Sight is good, but not as good as touch: touch is immediate, indisputable, perhaps erotic. 'The press of my foot to the earth springs a hundred affections.' 'Is this then a touch,' he asks later, 'quivering me to a new identity?' In 'A Song for Occupations' he writes: 'I pass so poorly with paper and types. . . . I must pass with the contact of bodies and souls.' So he tries to use paper and types as if they, too, were modes of contact. Sight is good, but it holds the object of sight at a distance. This is scandalous to Whitman, who resents distance: things are certified by touch. In the passage about the 'common farmer' in 'I Sing the Body Electric' the proof of intimacy is touch, 'that you and he might touch each other'.

As there is no conflict, ideally, between one body and another, so there is none, ideally, between body and soul. 'I am the poet of the body,' Whitman says, 'and I am the poet of the soul.' Yeats speaks of body being bruised to pleasure soul, and he often thinks of these terms in incorrigible rivalry. True, there are moments in which he, too, thinks that the body in splendid animation might certify a great 'unity of being'. But more frequently the poor soul is 'fastened to a dying animal'. Whitman starts with the body and makes the soul at home there: if all else fails, he is prepared to make the body the chief term, but he sponsors amity. 'Behold, the body includes and is the meaning, the main concern, and includes and is the soul.' If a more elaborate definition of soul is demanded, he is ready to say:

Was somebody asking to see the soul?
See, your own shape and countenance, persons, substances, beasts, the
    trees, the running rivers, the rocks and sands.

So there should be no quarrel: let the soul be the shine upon the face of nature, the animation of the human body.

The optimism is part of Whitman's time, since he chose to take it from his time. In 'Great Are the Myths' and other poems the leading terms are evolutionary, excelsior-terms, promissory notes: the earth's progress is unlimited. A two-line poem, 'Roaming in Thought', was written in Hegel's light:

Roaming in thought over the Universe, I saw the little that is Good steadily
    hastening towards immortality,
And the vast all that is call'd Evil I saw hastening to merge itself and
    become lost and dead.

After talking to a German spiritualist, Whitman wrote 'Continuities', celebrating the myth of the eternal return, promising that 'nothing is ever really lost'. Even life and death may be reconciled:

Great is life . . . and real and mystical . . . wherever and whoever,
Great is death. . . . Sure as life holds all parts together, death holds all parts
    together;
Sure as the stars return again after they merge in the light, death is great as
    life.

In 'Out of the Cradle Endlessly Rocking' the sea whispers to Whitman 'the low and delicious word death'. But this is not the Romantic swoon of death: Whitman sets up, in full lucidity and daylight, those great opposites which he then proceeds to reconcile; the opposites are invoked for the sake of the reconciliation. The imagination must be declared, exhibited: its characteristic act is to accept whatever experience offers, but to make the acceptance a strikingly personal act. The personal gesture redeems the content of experience, reconciles all dichotomies. The process is Hegelian.

The political equivalent is democracy, the American version.

'The United States themselves are essentially the great poem', Whitman claims, because the American democratic style is the greatest style, the most liberal, the most capacious. It may be maintained that Whitman's cult of 'the common people' is, in the limiting sense, a 'literary' gesture. It is certainly true that he derived his politics from his aesthetic, as he derives his ethic from the same source. He did not start with democracy or even with 'these States': his sense of these matters was, in the first instance, an aesthetic sense, governed by the primacy of Being. 'The Americans . . . have probably the fullest poetical nature'; not on the demonstrable strength of American poems already written, but on the promising strength of a society in tune with an aesthetic feeling, a certain way of life, a style. At this stage, that is, before the Civil War, Whitman did not look very closely at the practical versions of democracy, local politics, the detailed organization of wards, cities, and states. He sponsored the idea of democracy, regardless of its local manifestations. After the War, he became disenchanted, as the sharp prose of *Democratic Vistas* indicates: his critique of practical democracy is as vigorous as, say, Henry Adams's image of the Age of Grant in his novel, *Democracy*. But that was far ahead. In the first editions of *Leaves of Grass* America was presented as God's new Eden, where every diversity is received, every contradiction reconciled, 'her athletic Democracy' a wonderful invention. The terms of praise are poetic terms, in the sense that they may be applied, with equal conviction, to poetry and to America; the metaphors are the same. The possibility of poetry is the possibility of America: the great poet is the American Adam, the secretary. So at this stage there was no need to ask hard questions, as Adams would ask those questions in one way, Henry James in another. Whitman's concern was the metaphorical congruity of American democracy and a correspondingly liberal poetry. So he celebrates this largesse, and it is hardly wonderful that, in this mood, he blurred the difference between the actual and the possible, promiscuous in his attendance upon the future tense.

But we must not exaggerate. Every self-conscious country needs an apostle: if he serves that purpose, it is irrelevant if he serves any other. For many years, Whitman offered himself as the American bard, chanter of democratic personality: at first the offer was spurned, but gradually it was accepted. American agreed to take him at his proffered word; he was received as the spirit of unity, force, diversity, cohesion. So it has taken readers a long time to realize that this image of Whitman is partial. We are still encouraged to think of him as representing a simple, honest unity; with the further implication that this is a better thing than its rival, a Jamesian image of irony, critique, and sophistication. That is, we are invited to read the poetry as if it were politics, all the better for a vulgar touch, proof of honesty and unity. It must be conceded that Whitman lends himself to these purposes: if a politician needs a slogan, he is bound to find what he needs in Whitman, perhaps on the first page. But the truth is more complex. Whitman was never entirely the unified man of popular legend, liberal, androgynous, available; he was not completely liberated from the common anxieties and divisions of his time. Even when his poems end in reconciliation, they begin, many of them, in division: 'wandering and confused . . . lost to myself . . . ill-assorted . . . contradictory'. Often the division can be healed only by pointing to a happier future implicit in Whitman's terminology. 'Do you suppose I could be content with all if I thought them their own finale?' he asks in 'Faces': one face is 'a dog's snout sniffing for garbage', but it is a human face; Whitman rages against it, but he contents himself by thinking of a future in which that man, too, will be a true man. In such a future, all things are possible. But meanwhile there are poems like 'As I Ebb'd with the Ocean of Life', in which Whitman is just as confused and dispirited as any of his contemporaries:

O baffled, balk'd, bent to the very earth,
Oppress'd with myself that I have dared to open my mouth,
Aware now that amid all that blab whose echoes recoil upon me I have not
   once had the least idea who or what I am,
But that before all my arrogant poems the real Me stands yet untouch'd,
   untold, altogether unreach'd,
Withdrawn far, mocking me with mock-congratulatory signs and bows.

The poem does not end there: Whitman never leaves such feelings as his last word, he tries again until, by force of will, the reconciling motives begin to assert themselves. But the evidence is indisputable: Whitman lives, at least on certain days, in the world of Arnold's 'The Buried Life', Hopkins's 'terrible sonnets', Clough's *Amours de Voyage*. If they are divided, so is he. In Whitman, theory is one thing, practice another. Sometimes he is the chanter of fellowship, but again he seems dissociated, alien, 'withdrawn far'. Sometimes he is open, expansive, a comrade; at other times, secretive, furtive. Now clear, now ambiguous; now healthy, now morbid; singing the 'song of companionship', proclaiming his exile. Even in *Calamus*, where the leading figures are moved in Whitman's direction, there are moments in which the entire structure of his world seems doomed:

Of the terrible doubt of appearances,
Of the uncertainty after all, that we may be deluded,
That may-be reliance and hope are but speculations after all,
That may-be identity beyond the grave is a beautiful fable only,
May-be the things I perceive, the animals, plants, men, hills, shining and
    flowing waters,
The skies of day and night, colors, densities, forms may-be these are (as
    doubtless they are) only apparitions, and the real something has yet to be
    known,
(How often they dart out of themselves as if to confound me and mock me!
How often I think neither I know, nor any man knows, aught of them!)
May-be seeming to me what they are (as doubtless they indeed but seem)
    as from my present point of view, and might prove (as of course they
    would) nought of what they appear, or nought anyhow, from entirely
    changed points of view;
To me these and the like of these are curiously answer'd by my lovers, my
    dear friends. . . .

It is a characteristic movement: the slide from 'appearances' to
'apparitions', and then, the beginning of the return to solid ground,
the 'real something' conceived now not in terms of philosophical
thought but in terms of 'contact'. The effort to disengage himself
from one terminology and to grasp another is mimed in the poem
itself: a crucial moment is 'yet', 'and the real something has yet to be
known'. The word is seized as if with physical strain, and the return
begins. Now the only truth is physical, human in that sense, erotic:

When he whom I love travels with me or sits a long while holding me by the
    hand,
When the subtle air, the impalpable, the sense that words and reason hold
    not, surround us and pervade us,
Then I am charged with untold and untellable wisdom, I am silent, I
    require nothing further,
I cannot answer the question of appearances or that of identity beyond the
    grave,
But I walk or sit indifferent, I am satisfied,
He ahold of my hand has completely satisfied me.

This may appear simple, merely an abdication of judgment, the
terrible doubt resolved by turning away from it; but in fact the
resolution at the end is not achieved, in the poetry, without strain.
In life, such a resolution may be easy or hard, but in poetry it is
achieved only by exerting great pressure upon certain crucial terms.
Notice, for instance, what is done with the sequence, holding/hold/
ahold: the lovers, holding hands, surround the middle word, 'the
sense that words and reason hold not', with the force of their own

rhetoric. In the presence of physical certainty, the uncertainty of words and reason seems more extreme than ever. These poor things are bound to break. In the physical context, now, even the impalpable is redeemed: 'then I am charged with untold and untellable wisdom', the body electric again, driving its hero beyond all doubt. He is now indifferent, 'I am satisfied'; a word rescued from a context in which he suffered, intellectually, always dissatisfied. Now 'satisfied' means answered as well as fulfilled; but the answer has reached Whitman, as always, from an alteration of terminologies.

The decisive moment in these matters is the moment at which one terminology shifts towards another: often the change is begun with an important word, used now in a slightly odd sense, pointing to the new area of feeling. It is like the change from the present to the future tense. The exemplary occasion in Whitman is the moment when the present even is seized, fully acknowledged, and all the relevant energies are directed towards the future. 'The direct trial of him who would be the greatest poet is today,' Whitman writes: such a poet must 'flood himself with the immediate age', must 'attract his own land body and soul to himself'. In 'Song of Myself' everything converges upon the present:

> There was never any more inception than there is now,
> Nor any more youth or age than there is now;
> And will never be any more perfection than there is now,
> Nor any more heaven or hell than there is now.

Or in 'A Song for Occupations':

Happiness not in another place, but this place ... not for another hour, but this hour.

But the conclusion is not merely: seize the day. Whitman is bringing everything to bear upon this moment, 'now', because this is the turning point, the start of a new age. If new terminologies are to be enforced, they must be enforced now: or at least a start must be made now.

Inevitably, the past is ambiguously treated. Emerson said that 'man is explicable by nothing less than all his history', but his account of history is self-centred, history as a gathering of man's affinities, no more, nor less. Emerson does not value the past for its critical force or its objectivity; the modern self is the centre of all circles. Indeed, a sense of the past as different from ourselves and therefore compelling is rare in American literature. Henry James writes of his Ralph Pendrel in *the Sense of the Past*:

He was by the turn of his spirit oddly indifferent to the actual and the possible; his interest was all in the spent and the displaced, in what had been determined and composed roundabout him, what had been presented as a subject and a picture, by ceasing – so far as things ever cease – to bustle or even to be. It was when life was framed in death that the picture was really hung up.

James would not propose such a sense of the past for everything: the deathliness of the figure makes that clear enough. But James, more than any other American writer, values the composition, the picture, and therefore the frame in which it is set. Nothing is really understood, and therefore nothing is really appreciated, he seems to say, until it is framed for vision and contemplation. He is pleased with the bustle of things, but only as relevant actions and materials; the human process is incomplete until the bustle is stilled, the relationships composed in the picture. Whitman is utterly different: he is so devoted to process, to bustle and miscellany, that pictures seem to him monstrous, dead things, beyond human contact. The eye, at that extreme, is doing the devil's work. Rather than take such a risk, Whitman is prepared to disengage himself altogether from the past: by definition, in any event, the past is beyond redemption, so let it go. Out of the past, objects converge upon the present, and that is good: better still, the movement of feeling towards the future may now begin.

Whitman has often been rebuked for this. George Santayana's rebuke is famous, especially the versions which he included in his *Interpretations of Poetry and Religion* and *The Last Puritan*. The complaint has many aspects, but they bear upon one, finally, Whitman's scanting the past. In the *Interpretations* Santayana says that Whitman reduces experience to a succession of moods: in this the poet is a barbarian, one 'who regards his passions as their own excuse for being'; the passions are not to be understood or controlled, they are merely to be entertained. This is Whitman's primitivism: he has gone back 'to the innocent style of Adam, when the animals filed before him one by one and he called each of them by its name'. He has tried 'the imaginary experiment of beginning the world over again': no past is acknowledged as in any degree a restraint. Whitman ignores 'the fatal antiquity of human nature', thereby indulging himself in a manner fostered by liberalism and American transcendentalism. To him, the past was an alien place, and, comparing his own world, he declared the latter a fresh creation. The first result was that he confirmed himself in his chief interest, his own sensations: nothing else was really alive. The world is all surface, no depth: impressions pass before Whitman's senses and he yields himself to each. He sees common life 'not in contrast with an ideal, but as the expression of forces more indeterminate and elementary than itself'. So the vulgar appears to him sublime. In the discussion of American literature which Santayana inserts in Chapter 13 of *The Last Puritan*, Jim insists that Whitman is 'the great, the best, the only American poet'; and, to make a grand claim, he hands Oliver a copy of *Leaves of Grass*. The book opens of itself at at passage heavily scored in the margin, from 'Song of Myself':

I think I could turn and live awhile with the animals . . . they are so placid
    and self-contained
I stand and look at them sometimes half the day long.
They do not sweat and whine about their condition,
They do not lie awake in the dark and weep for their sins,
They do not make me sick discussing their duty to God.

Oliver's reaction is immediate:

*Dope*, thought Oliver, himself a little somnolent in the noonday heat and the soft air, *dope* in another form. A lazy refusal to look backward, or to look ahead. A hatred of reason, a hatred of sacrifice. The lilies of the field. Work wasn't worth while.

He reads the passage aloud, then asks his father, 'Don't you like that?' 'I like the first three words: *I could turn*,' his father answers:

I should have liked it well enough if he had said he could turn and *no longer* live with the animals, they are so restless and merciless and ferocious, possessed with a mania for munching grass and gnawing bones and nosing one another, when they don't make me sick saying they are God's chosen people, doing God's work.

It is sharp: Oliver's father ridiculing the Franciscan Walt Whitman:

He doesn't see that human conventions are products of nature, that morality and religion and science express or protect animal passions: and that he couldn't possibly be more like an animal than by living like other men. His rebellion is no conversion, no deliverance. He pretends to turn – for it is largely affectation – only from the more refined devices of mankind to a ruder and more stupid existence. He is like Marie Antoinette playing the shepherdess.

The critique then moves into other terms, but it is clear that Whitman's indifference to the past is, in Santayana's eyes, his mortal sin. To Santayana, the past is available as critique, as ideal, as sacrifice: bluntly, the past provides the standard by which present and future acts may be judged. Santayana accepts history as he accepts the difference, once for all, between animals and men. 'I could turn'; but he wants the turning to be a real conversion. He wants Whitman to accept the sacrificial record of the past, accept it as critique and, if proper, as rebuke. As a European, Santayana bitterly resents the American facility which sets the past aside, 'making it new' with a vengeance directed upon the old.

Perhaps it would not matter, or at least it would not be disastrous, if Whitman were prepared to put any other critical power in place of the past. What Santayana means to force upon Whitman is an acknowledgment that the world was not made today for his sole benefit and pleasure. The trouble is that in freeing himself from the burden of the past Whitman plans to free himself from every other burden: he will not be rebuked, he will be his own free man. In this respect he is far more extreme than Emerson; even the Emerson of 'Circles' who wrote:

Do not set the least value on what I do, or the least discredit on what I do not, as if I pretended to settle anything as true or false. I unsettle all things. No facts are to me sacred; none are profane; I simply experiment, an endless seeker, with no Past at my back.

In 'Starting from Paumanok' Whitman claims:

> I conn'd old times,
> I sat studying at the feet of the great masters.

But he made no commitment to the past; and for that, Santayana berated him.

But we have to ask what Whitman's freedom gave him, besides ease. In one sense he was, indeed, free; he put down burdens which other men sustained. But it may be argued that in another sense he was bound, because he was ignorant of what he disowned. There is no evidence that he conn'd old times sufficiently to know them as sturdy and different from his own: certainly, he did not propose a relation to the past based upon that knowledge. So it is necesssary to say that he freed himself from human history without taking the precaution, in the first instance, of thoroughly understanding it. Whatever worth we ascribe to his freedom, it must allow for that limitation, that its facility was not profoundly earned. That is why his message, so far as it may be described as such, is dispensable. He was, by his own assertion, a prophet and a sage, but his prophecy was somewhat meretricious, his wisdom untested. What matters, after all, is the poetry.

To get the beauty of Whitman's poetry hot, one must read it in long, rolling stretches. No poet is less revealed in the single phrase, the image, or even the line. The unit of the verse is indeed the phrase, a loose-limbed structure of several words easily held together and moving along because the cadence goes with the speaker's breath. This is what William Carlos Williams learned from Whitman, the natural cadence, the flow of breath as a structure good enough for most purposes and better for humanity than the counting of syllables. For both poets the ideal is what Williams called 'a redeeming language', a language to bridge the gap between subject and object, thereby certifying both and praising bridges. Again in both poets the function of language is to verify an intricate network of affinities and relationships, contacts, between person and person, person and place, person and thing. In Whitman, the number of completely realized poems is small: many poems contain wonderful passages, but are flawed, often by a breach of taste, a provincialism. Where the poem fails, it fails because Whitman thought too well of his excess to curb it; the words converge upon the poem, and he will not turn them aside. Some of his greatest writing is in 'Song of Myself', but on the other hand that poem, too, is often provincial, awkward. The best of Whitman, certainly one of his greatest achievements, is a shorter poem, 'Crossing Brooklyn Ferry'. William Carolos Williams once praised a poem by Marianne Moore as an anthology of transit, presumably because the words secured a noiseless progression from one moment to another: they did not sit down to admire themselves. Whitman's favourite subject is movement, process, becoming: no wonder he loved bridges and ferries, which kept things moving while defining relationships, one thing with another.

The first stanza of the poem, in its final version, is a direct invocation to the water, the clouds, the crowds of people crossing on the ferry. But the first requirement in this stanza is to recite these things in personal terms: water and clouds must be translated into personal terms, sharing in that feeling. The translation is effected by the sensory verbs: any object, however resistant, is amenable to the poet's senses, and, once sensed, is rendered personal. Hence: 'Flood-tide below me! I see you face to face!'; face to face, marking the personal meeting, equal with equal. The last line of the stanza points the feeling towards a future ('And you that shall cross') and establishes a kinship which the subsequent stanzas will enrich. The second stanza defines the exemplary moment as the confluence of present and future; it is Whitman's version of Blake's sentence, that Eternity is in love with the productions of Time. Here, for Whitman, the present moment is certified by its continuity with the future. The specific occasion of this stanza is the poet's sense of 'the scheme of things', the unity among instances of diversity. In the light of the scheme, every single object seems 'disintegrated', but, a second later, is seen as part of the scheme and therefore redeemed: without the scheme, everything would be mere flotsam. The personal version is the poet's kinship with those 'others' who, ages hence, will see and feel the same things. In the third stanza the standpoint is moved directly to the future; from which, now, the present is seen as a shared past, the shared history of feeling: 'Just as you feel ... so I felt'. The result is that the present moment is enchanted by being part of an enchanted past, magically sensed and recalled. The work is done, for the main part, by the verbs 'watched', 'saw', 'looked', and so forth. It is typical of Whitman that the only 'past' he is willing to acknowledge is the 'present', seen from the standpoint of the 'future'. He does not, in general, acknowledge a past now, in some sense, distinct from his own present feeling: there is no stanza in this poem, for instance, which links the 'present' speaker to the 'past'. It is as if Whitman resented any gone time in which he did not participate. He is quite willing to see the present recede, since he has played his part in it, and to be incorporated in a future which he had done something to entertain. But the past is intolerably alien, from the standpoint of a man who has not lived it. In the fourth stanza Whitman is still in a projected future, the language caressing its objects in repeated phrases. The fifth stanza is an anthology of sharing: 'I too lived . . ', the experiences proved by reference to the body: 'I too had receiv'd identity by my body'. The sixth stanza is a change, a dark place of confession. Whitman looks at himself, his own work, his thoughts, and finds them 'blank'. He confesses to evil and ambiguity:

> I am he who knew what it was to be evil,
> I too knitted the old knot of contrariety,
> Blabb'd, blush'd, resented, lied, stole, grudg'd,
> Had guile, anger, lust, hot wishes I dared not speak.

At the same time Whitman strains towards the idiom of acceptance, the secular equivalent of forgiveness after confession. The movement is effected by the line. 'Was one with the rest, the days and haps of the rest', coming immediately after the lines of confession. Individual guilt is incorporated in universal guilt, and the movement towards forgiveness and unity begins. By the end of the stanza, the poet has been received into amity. But it may be argued that, in fact, the forgiveness was implicit even in the lines of confession. Whitman does not simply confess, 'I was evil', with an implication, 'I repent': what he says is, 'I am he who knew what it was to be evil', and in this version the fact of evil is balanced by the fact of knowledge. Evil is bad, let us say, but knowledge of evil is good, especially if the evil is one's own. Whitman is looking at himself as if he were a separate person; a procedure highly respectable in the Emersonian tradition of American literature. In the chapter on Goethe in *Representative Men* Emerson says:

An intellectual man can see himself as a third person; therefore his faults and delusions interest him equally with his successes. Though he wishes to prosper in affairs he wishes more to know the history and destiny of man; whilst the clouds of egotists drifting about him are only interested in a low success.

Whitman is speaking of himself as a third person, but he assimilates everything he says to the language of knowledge; according to this rhetoric, every sin committed and acknowledged adds to the sum of personal knowledge. Every acknowledged fall is fortunate. There is a certain complicity, therefore, in Whitman's rhetoric here: the stanza as a whole allows him to find a way out, but the way out is already implicit in the dark detail. The result is that the catalogue of sins, bad as ethics, comes to appear good as experience. In the next stanza, forgiveness takes the form of communion, a conspiracy of feeling: 'Closer yet I approach you . . .' In the eighth stanza the same mood is given in terms of tying, fusing, and pouring, self and self. The poem ends with the long stanza of exaltation, beginning 'Flow on, river! flow with the flood-tide . . .' The stanza is a sequence of imperatives, until a change near the end; but the imperatives are designed not to change the direction of their object but to endorse each object in its natural direction: 'Live old life!'; 'Sound out, voices of young men!'; 'Fly on, sea-birds!' This is the form in which world-harmony is heard, the natural action, continuous, flowing, un-questionable. The function of Whitman's lines is not to describe each action, but to encourage it, giving it an endorsing hand. The poet's energy is to answer the energy of the world: this is the form his Sublime takes. Near the end, the mood changes, beautifully, into the indicative: I quote the last two imperative lines and the change:

Expand, being than which none else is perhaps more spiritual,
Keep your places, objects than which none else is more lasting.
You have waited, you always wait, you dumb, beautiful ministers,
We receive you with free sense at last, and are insatiate henceforward,
Not you any more shall be able to foil us, or withhold yourselves from us,
We use you, and do not cast you aside – we plant you permanently within us,
We fathom you not – we love you – there is perfection in you also,
You furnish your parts toward eternity,
Great or small, you furnish your parts toward the soul.

This is Whitman at his best. The clue is in the line: 'We fathom you not – we love you –'. It is Whitman's delicacy, his sense of limits, his fine decorum, which prevents him from fathoming the world, moving in upon it to steal its secret. There is always something in an object which Whitman prefers, at last, to leave untouched: he is content to sense its presence, but he does not grasp it. When this delicacy is present, the proof is in the style. In 'Crossing Brooklyn Ferry' Whitman and his style are one, there is no gap when we think of the words on the page and then, by an effort, think of his presence behind the words. He is identical with his style. This happens only when the poetic concern is eminently congenial to his talent, to his sense of the world, and his sense of a corresponding language. It is time to remark that, in these best moments, he has a remarkable feeling for life, for the world as it reaches him through the senses: the world, given to him in appearances, impressions, images, sounds, the press of things. But it is necessary to make a distinction. There are poets who excel in description, in giving a particularly vivid impression of the surfaces of life. Whitman is not one of these; though his descriptive power, when he chooses to use it, is at least good enough for the local purpose. In his greatest poems the world is not given to us, minutely, as *sensibilia*, one apprehended thing and then another: rather, Whitman receives the contents of his experiences as certain great gestures, great cadences of feeling. He touches the world in time, and the experience is enacted as a cadence. The detail is not lost or buried: it is incorporated in the rhythm, contained there like juice in an apple. That is: the detail is not given to the reader as a separable event, but as one phase in the movement of feeling. It is an error, therefore, to speak of his catalogues as if they were lists of undifferentiated things, each one ticked off. The things which are listed are there for the wave of feeling which, in that exact form, they sustain: different things would mean a different wave of feeling, a different feeling or a different direction. Wallace Stevens wrote to Joseph Bennett, 8 February 1955 of Whitman's catalogues:

I can well believe that he remains highly vital for many people. The poems in which he collects large numbers of concrete things, particularly things each of which is poetic in itself or as part of the collection, have a validity which, for many people, must be enough and must seem to them all opulence and elan. For others, I imagine that what was once opulent begins to look a little threadbare and the collections seem substitutes for opulence even though they remain gatherings-together of precious Americana, certain to remain precious but not certain to remain poetry. The typical elan survives in many things. It seems to me, then, that Whitman is disintegrating as the world, of which he made himself a part, disintegrates.

But this is to read the lines as lists of things, *sensibilia*, and to find poetic value in those things. If they have grown threadbare, the reason is that we have become weary of them, we know them too well, they cannot change. This is, indeed the fate of objects, congealed. But the way to read Whitman's catalogues is to attend to the rhythm, their flow and ebb, the cadences of feeling which they embody. Poetic value does not depend, then, upon the self-renewing power of objects but upon the self-renewing power of feeling. Theodore Roethke's sense of Whitman is, I think, more accurate than Stevens's for this reason. In 'The Abyss' Roethke invokes Whitman after a stanza in which he speaks of himself as 'neither in nor out of this life':

> Be with me, Whitman, maker of catalogues:
> For the world invades me again,
> And once more the tongues begin babbling.
> And the terrible hunger for objects quails me:
> The sill trembles.
> And there on the blind
> A furred caterpillar crawls down a string.
> My symbol!

Clearly, Roethke does not need Whitman as maker of catalogues: it is impossible to think of Roethke as having much to do with catalogues. Whitman is needed because the poet feels himself 'invaded' by the world, those objects which overwhelm him in their demand: answering in himself the 'terrible hunger for objects'. Whitman the maker of catalogues is also the Whitman who genially disposes the objects listed; genially, so that they are not too demanding and, in turn, his hunger is not too demanding. To Roethke, Whitman's catalogues testify to an agreeable sense of the world, but that sense reaches him, it is clear, through the feeling beneath and between the objects. The phrase we need is in 'Crossing Brooklyn Ferry': 'We receive you with free sense at last'; free sense, not demand or hunger. In 'The Abyss' Roethke's third stanza begins:

> Too much reality can be a dazzle, a surfeit;
> Too close immediacy an exhaustion.

Whitman would answer: only if you insist on possessing every piece of reality your senses deliver; only if immediacy brings out the hunger in you. What Roethke prayed for, calling upon Whitman's intercession, was tact, a certain last propriety. Of Whitman's catalogues he seems to have felt that they, in an obvious sense so material, were in a deeper sense so spiritual, so undemanding. What matters is the feeling. Someone says in *The Last Puritan* that there is no poetry in identifying things that look alike, 'but the most opposite things may become miraculously equivalent, if they arouse the same invisible quality of emotion'. In 'Crossing Brooklyn Ferry', 'Song of the Broad-Axe', 'Song of the Exposition', and other poems particular things are invoked in a particular order for the feeling they define; not for the miscellany; not for the objects as possessions. Whitman does not claim to possess those objects; what he possesses is a flowing sense of them, of their interest, their value, their amazing existence.

The proof is in the delicacy. Almost at random in the 'Song of Myself' we read:

A child said *What is the grass?* fetching it to me with full hands,
How could I answer the child? I do not know what it is any more than he.

It is beautiful; mainly because of the transparent language. Whitman lives up to the feeling by giving it in undemanding words, he puts the words in that order to reflect the figure of the feeling, the shape it makes. Neither too much nor too little; not even an excess of moderation: the words do not claim to be interesting, in their own right, but to serve their master, the feeling itself. Again, in 'Out of the Cradle Endlessly Rocking':

Yes my brother I know,
The rest might not, but I have treasur'd every note,
For more than once simply down to the beach gliding,
Silent, avoiding the moonbeams, blending myself with the shadows,
Recalling now the obscure shapes, the echoes, the sounds and sights after
   their sorts,
The white arms out in the breakers tirelessly tossing,
I, with bare feet, a child, the wind wafting my hair,
Listened long and long.

Even here, we are not encouraged to sink to rest upon a word or a phrase: we are to go with the feeling in the long sentence. The meaning is the history of the sentence, the qualifying phrases slowing the movement but not impeding it, since the structure is never in danger. In the last line the feeling is fulfilled, the repeated 'long' not an indulgence but a celebration. It is not fanciful to find, in this delicacy, Whitman's chief value, since delicacy is only the short name for many qualities which run together. The delicacy may be felt to require his doubt as well as his certainty, his trouble as well as his peace, his fear and his assertions: it is all there in the achieved lines and poems.

What the work does not give, however, is proof of development. I suppose our ideal *Collected Works* would feature the wonderfully complete fulfilment of possibilities dimly discerned in the early poems. The career of such poets as Eliot and Yeats is a great consolation in this respect. It is easy to see that in *Prufrock and Other Observations* Eliot laid down, barely knowing what he did and certainly not knowing its implications, seeds of growth and development which would flower, eventually, in the great middle and last poems. *Four Quartets* is continuous with *Prufrock* and *The Waste Land*: every poem seemed to be accomplished in itself and yet to require a further poem for complete lucidity. With the entire work at hand, in poems, plays, and criticism, we think of Eliot's achievement as a major development of the early hints and guesses. With Yeats we feel that somewhere along the line of his work he discovered, perhaps in theatrical metaphors, possibilities which the collected poems and plays fulfil; notably possibilities of drama, one voice answering another, a continuous action. With Whitman, we feel that the first edition of *Leaves of Grass* is, in fact, the whole story. Thereafter, the editions were enlarged, but new possibilities were not discovered; later editions, larger, were not in any important sense different. It is as if Whitman found for himself a settled poetic stance, and discovered that it might be held: there was no reason why it should be questioned. He did not question the basis of his faith. It is possible to argue that the third edition (1860) has special importance, but the categories disposed in that book are not really different from those of the first edition. After the War, a difference is clear, but the difference arises from the failure of Whitman's faith, its practical misfortune. There is no evidence of possibilities being worked out, challenged, questioned, from one book to another. The reason is that Whitman defined himself, at an early stage, in relation to the world, and the definition was so resolute that it did not call for revision. The later editions present more material, but not different senses of its value. This partly explains how Whitman came to represent, perhaps all too easily, a definable relation to America and to the world: that relation was powerful, engaging, indeed inescapable, but its chief mark was its resistance to change. It did not contain within itself the reason why, under different circumstances, it might be otherwise: more experience merely served to confirm it or to trouble it, not to change it. In a famous moment Yeats distinguished between poetry and rhetoric: rhetoric is made from the quarrel with others, poetry from the quarrel with ourselves. Whitman's aesthetic does not allow for a quarrel with himself: a quarrel with himself would bring his poetry to an end. The poetry contains its own basis, its own strength, but it is the mark of that poetry to make any alternative basis impossible. Whitman may choose, but the choice is limited: either to write that kind of poetry, or remain silent. We often feel that the poet of the first edition of *Leaves of Grass* secured the great advantages of that poetry too easily: he did not have to labour in its cause. He laboured, indeed, with the detail of the lines, but not with the incorrigible burdens attendant upon poets: the problematic relation of the poet to his past, to the life and history of his world. A man must labour to possess a tradition, as Eliot warned. But Whitman secured his first necessity once for all. It has often been maintained that the crucial Whitman is the poet of the first edition of *Leaves of Grass*; everything thereafter being a decay. The argument is not conclusive. But it has at least this merit, that the first effect of reading Whitman is an effect especially akin to that of a poet, this poet, writing his first book. Thereafter, the effect may be greater or less, but there is a sense in which the gist of the case has already been presented. This does not lend support to the common view that Whitman is a naïf, producing one book and spending his life trying to repeat its success. Indeed, Whitman is, if anything, more a decadent than a naïf. But his real problem is to justify to himself the composition of poems which are, in their real nature, merely further expositions of what has already been declared. There are a few remarkable moments in the later editions: sometimes a certain wry wit is audible, the irony directed upon himself. There are transitions which mark Whitman as a comic poet of great merit. But these are local charms. The essential Whitman is already defined, set in his landscape.

Finally, we acknowledge the myth, and the values it declares. To some poets, Whitman is the American inventor of free verse, destroyer of the iambic pentameter. William Carlos Williams thought of him in this context, praised him for helping American poets to free themselves from Europe, rebuked him for not going further. To other poets, Whitman is the spokesman of America as Promises, a doubtful hero in the twentieth century, a sentimentalist smelling of duplicity. But perhaps the permanent strength of Whitman is what Hart Crane saw, especially in that part of *The Bridge* called 'Cape Hatteras', virtually an ode to Whitman:

> ... O, something green,
> Beyond all sesames of science was thy choice
> Wherewith to bind us throbbing with one voice,
> New integers of Roman, Viking, Celt—
> Thou, Vedic Caesar, to the greensward knelt!

# 10

# NEW ENGLAND: THE UNIVERSAL
# YANKEE NATION

## Marcus Cunliffe

In 1815, at the end of the War of 1812, the New England states were curiously defensive and alienated. They had been the stronghold of the quasi-conservative Federalist party, and as such the upholders of the nearest thing to an American version of conservatism: an ideal, that is, of gentlemanly conduct in a political and cultural realm controlled by gentlemen. They had also, in opposing the war with Britain, somewhat incompatibly fallen back upon anti-Federalist doctrines: doctrines exalting the rights of the states over the central government.

In 1815, the year of the establishment in Boston of the *North American Review*, New England Federalism was shattered and discredited. The war, never universally popular, was suddenly converted into an apparent triumph, in fact a providential confirmation of the rightness of Americanism in general and the wisdom of the administration in particular, by the rout of a British army by General Andrew Jackson outside New Orleans. In this unlooked-for culmination to a seemingly shapeless and pointless conflict, the New England ideal was all at once made to look un-American: disloyal, erring, anachronistic. It was as if the proud New England region, led by Massachusetts, no longer had a claim to lead the nation. And the decline seemed manifest in the increasing tempo of movement out of the state, in the great tide of western settlement. Why remain in a land of incorrect principles and infertile soil?

This decline was of course soon arrested. New England, or at least its cities and its manufacturing towns, became rich from a new blend of manufacturing and trading enterprise. Boston was by 1850 asserting an extraordinary prominence as a cultural centre. New England authors were the pride of the nation – and still more of New England.

It is instructive to consider why this happened. One familiar explanation is the power of the Puritan heritage, with its emphasis on activity, introspection and moral commitment. This nurtured a curiously expansionist form of regional patriotism. The South subsequently annexed some of the attributes of the New England mentality of the era of the War of 1812, especially the conviction that the federal government was a force to be combated. The South, in other words, turned inward upon itself, cherishing anachronism as its way of life. New England, however, sought – and with great success – to universalize its own regional creed. Instead of trying vainly as the South did to close its frontiers to alien vices, New England strove to become culturally as well as economically a sort of Scotland – an exporter of produce that ranged from textiles to schoolteachers.

In accordance with this talent for expansion, New Englanders again and again consoled themselves that it was their mission to transform the rest of the country into their own image. A Boston editor of 1815 manfully insisted that the heavy emigration out of Massachusetts was a concealed blessing. 'The emigrants,' he said, 'will inoculate with correct principles those they may sojourn with. It will be the vaccination of Federalism, annihilating the smallpox of Democracy.' When Federalism itself had been annihilated as a coherent political party, within a few years, something of its cultural vehemence remained. The process of transference and annexation was perhaps most evident in religion. The 'burned-over' district of western New York, the birthplace of Mormonism and a scene of intense religious ferment, was largely settled from New England. So were many of the townships of Ohio. The *Western Messenger* (1835–41), a periodical edited by the Reverend James Freeman Clarke, was consciously modelled upon the transcendentalist spirit of Boston and Concord. The Reverend Lyman Beecher of Connecticut, explaining why he felt a call to remove himself to the fringes of civilization in Ohio, spoke of 'New-Englandizing' the West. 'The moral destiny of our nation,' he wrote, 'and all our institutions and hopes, and the world's hopes, turns on the character of the West.' President Edward Everett of Harvard used similar language in an address to Boston emigrants. 'Go with the Bible in one hand and your New England civilization in the other', he enjoined them, 'and make your mark on the people and the country.' Neither he nor Beecher had any doubt that New Englanders were a chosen people, endowed with a vast responsibility for the betterment of mankind. While such assurances did not always endear them to other Americans, it invested them with an exceptional and advantageous zeal of temperament.

In the political context, this inner-directed New Englandism was expressed in a popular phrase of the early 1820s coined by a journalist: 'the Universal Yankee Nation'. It referred to the problem of whether John Quincy Adams of Massachusetts had a wide enough constituency of New England and New England-minded citizens to be elected as president. Politically speaking, the concept of this Nation, 'moved by the same great moral causes and impulses', certainly underlay the anti-slavery movements of 1830–60, including the new Republican party of the 1850s, although the phrase itself soon passed into the limbo of all *ad hoc* political slogans.[1] It is useful enough to be resurrected in a wider context, as the conviction of a moral–cultural climate in which New England claimed to be the *fons et origo*. The Universal Yankee Nation was both a geographical region and an exalted state of consciousness.

This condition of consciousness eludes precise definition because of its largeness, and because the largeness incorporated attitudes as various as the oracular-mystical fringes of transcendentalism or the breezy, no-nonsense clubmanship of Boston Brahmins like Oliver Wendell Holmes, the practical piety of Harriet Beecher Stowe and her educator-sister Catharine Beecher or the bluestocking unorthodoxy of a Margaret Fuller, the generous egalitarianism of a Theodore Parker or the elitist severity of a Francis Parkman. What is beyond question is that the Universal Yankee Nation exerted a disproportionate influence over the culture of nineteenth-century America. Of a comprehensive listing of one thousand American writers born up to 1850, no less than 487 have been credited to New England. The closest figure below this is 316 for natives of the Middle Atlantic States (including New York, New Jersey and Pennsylvania). The South Atlantic states furnished only ninety-nine; the East North Central, fifty-three; Canada, eighteen; the East South Central, fifteen; and so on. Of the thousand, information on religious affiliation was available in 460 cases. Of these over a quarter (119) were Congregational in upbringing, and forty-nine Unitarian. The Congregational church and Unitarianism were *par excellence* New England institutions; and relative to the actual size of these denominations, Boston-centred Unitarianism generated a higher proportion of writers than any other creed, with Congregationalism in second place.[2] Nor was this

[1] Shaw Livermore, Jr, *The Twilight of Federalism: The Disintegration of the Federalist Party, 1815–1830* (Princeton, 1962), 95–7.

[2] Edwin L. Clarke, *American Men of Letters: Their Nature and Nurture* (New York, 1916), 47–8.

culture exclusively parochial. We need to take into account, for instance, the activities of secondary figures like Thomas Bulfinch, son of the eminent architect of Boston's State House and the US Capitol. Young Bulfinch, a shy product of Boston Latin School and Harvard College, held a minor post in a local bank. His literary avocation though – pursued with relish and zeal, and a good deal of success – was to re-tell the great stories of ancient and mediaeval legend (*The Age of Fable*, 1855; *The Age of Chivalry*, 1858).

And in the nineteenth century New England drew other writers into its orbit, for it could provide them with a sense of an historic past, rich in names like Lexington and Bunker Hill, with a pleasing countryside, and with access to libraries, museums, orchestras, clubs and publishing houses. Though Mark Twain's best work dealt with the Missouri of his boyhood, much of his mature professional life was spent in New England. The magnet of Boston and the *Atlantic Monthly* brought the Ohio-born novelist William Dean Howells to settle there, though he eventually forsook Boston for the more metropolitan dazzle of New York. Henry James, Senior, domiciled his family for a while in the Boston area. His novelist-son displayed close understanding of the New England mind in such novels as *The Europeans* and *The Bostonians*, even if he preferred to live in Europe. Another son, William James the psychologist–philosopher, became a New Englander through adoption from his long stay as a member of the Harvard faculty. Mid-century, as Van Wyck Brooks justly maintained, brought a *Flowering of New England*, and the subsequent *New England: Indian Summer*, which furnished the title of another of his books, displayed another half century of productive talent in the years 1865–1915, whatever the intimations of decline.

One of the features of this triumph of the Yankee Nation was an ingrained respect for moral culture. Moral culture implied and stemmed from an old preoccupation with the word of God, and by extension the word of any of God's intelligent, metaphysically inclined creatures. New England was a land of clerics, of unusually good private and public schools, and of colleges. True, the nineteenth-century college – Harvard, Yale, Dartmouth, Bowdoin, Amherst, Williams – was often parochial and slack; Harvard did not begin to become a great centre of scholarship until the last third of the century, under the reforming presidency of Charles W. Eliot. Nevertheless, whether or not they thought they might be destined for the church, nearly all unusually gifted youths New England seemed to secure a college education – and this too even if they derided the results, as in the case of Henry Adams, who explained in his autobiography that Harvard had begun his vain, lifelong quest for an education by denying him one. For Adams, after all, was as zealous as any seventeenth-century forebear in pursuing the quest. From Harvard, following on the heels of scores of earnest young Americans, he passed straight to the lecture-halls of the German universities. In comparison with their English contemporaries, who both amused and depressed Adams for their congenital inability to train their intellects, the Americans of his generation were a band of dedicated seekers-after-truth. Oxford and Cambridge were in their eyes casual and eccentric to the point of absurdity; the real challenge was to be sought in Berlin or Heidelberg.

One might remark that certain of the Bostonian *literati* were in fact eccentric in a somewhat English manner. That is to say, they were sure of themselves, and of their place in the best society that America offered, and so felt free to behave according to their own lights. Henry Adams, for example, was in the fourth generation of a highly distinguished American family. His great-grandfather John Adams and his grandfather John Quincy Adams had been presidents of the United States. His father, Charles Francis Adams, was American minister to Britain during the Civil War. The Adamses, Henry said, gravitated to Washington as if by natural instinct. By the third generation, through marriage into wealthy families, they were also in comfortable financial circumstances. The temperament absorbed from their heritage was high-minded, and often contrary. In Henry's words, about himself and about his region:

Resistance to something was the law of New England nature; the boy looked out on the world with the instinct of resistance; for numberless generations his predecessors had viewed the world chiefly as a thing to be reformed, filled with evil forces to be abolished, and they saw no reason to suppose that they had wholly succeeded in the abolition; the duty was unchanged. Boys naturally look on all force as an enemy, and generally find it so, but the New Englander, whether boy or man, in his long struggle with a stingy or hostile universe, had learned also to love the pleasure of hating; his joys were few.

Despite the muted language this is a ferocious statement. The Adamses are perhaps a special case. The two presidents had each only a single, rather unsuccessful term in office. They and their descendants felt that they had been punished by a growingly corrupt America for their own rectitude. Henry, and his clever, quirky brother Brooks Adams, now and then revealed a half-conscious conviction that they were wiser than their generation. Fastidious and occasionally petulant. Henry persisted in describing himself as a failure. By publishing several of his books anonymously or in private editions, he ensured his own lack of fame, while perhaps secretly yearning to be discovered and thrust into the limelight.

All of these tendencies can however be detected, if sometimes in only minute traces, among New England men of letters. One of the most gentle of them, the poet John Greenleaf Whittier, was unable to forget that his beloved region had once bitterly persecuted his Quaker ancestors; and like the equally gentle Emerson, he was moved to pronouce a terrible anathema upon the 'dim, dishonoured brow' of Daniel Webster, once to them the 'godlike' Webster, the peerless spokesman of the Yankee Nation, but after 1850 – in their view – a moral coward ready to come to terms with the slaveholders of the South. They criticized themselves – their diaries are full of self-castigation – and they criticized one another. Their enmities were entangled with their friendships, and often carried tribal overtones. Andrews Norton, related to the Adamses and connected by marriage to President Eliot, became professor of sacred literature at Harvard. He was mightily offended by Emerson's 'Divinity School Address' of 1838. His son Charles Eliot Norton became one of New England's most refined scholars. In 1873 Charles Norton happened to be voyaging homeward from Europe on the same ship as Emerson. Norton's diary commends Emerson as 'the greatest talker in the ship's company'. Yet the praise carries a rebuke:

His serene sweetness, the pure whiteness of his soul, the reflection of his soul in his face, were never more apparent to me; but never before in intercourse had I been so impressed with the limits of his mind. His optimistic philosophy has hardened into a creed, with the usual effects of a creed in closing the avenues of truth. . . .

Other men – Henry James, Sr, Santayana – expressed similar reservations about Emerson. Norton's were of a piece with his whole position, which was far more sceptical than Emerson's. But it may not be fanciful to suppose that something of old Andrews Norton's Unitarian orthodoxy – a sort of so-far-and-no-farther liberalism – lingered on in the son, supporting one of the many oppositions that characterized the spare, prickly New England mind.

The essence is wonderfully caught in the scene at Hawthorne's funeral in 1864. Among the pallbearers were Emerson, Norton, the poets Longfellow and J. R. Lowell, the professor of medicine and proper Bostonian Oliver Wendell Holmes, Bronson Alcott the transcendentalist (father of Louisa May Alcott), the critic Edwin P. Whipple, James T. Fields the publisher and the Harvard scientist Louis Agassiz – a group-portrait of the famous men of the Boston–Cambridge world. The sermon was dignified and felicitous, and the whole occasion (Emerson noted) 'so bright and quiet that pain or mourning was hardly suggested, and Holmes said to me that it looked like a happy meeting'. But Emerson acknowledged that there *was* an immensely sad lesson for himself. He and Hawthorne had long been neighbours in Concord. They had been on amiable terms, but somehow always distant terms. Emerson had believed that 'I could well wait his time, – his unwillingness and caprice, – and might one day conquer a friendship. . . . Now it appears that I waited too long.'

In other words, the spokesmen of the Yankee Nation tended to be solitary. They were not incapable of friendship, and the Boston 'Brahmin' gentry had a distinct appetite for social gatherings. A Holmes or a Lowell were celebrated for after-dinner speeches and for witty *vers d'occasion* and impromptu epigrams. But most of them ritualized their gregariousness, fending off close intimacy. The cultural life of New England was conducted in salons and clubs, not taverns and bohemias. There was something abstemious, even parsimonious in their personal relations. Less malicious and coterie-ridden than the literary circles of London or Paris (or New York), they were also less capable of uninhibited affection. In New England, as a later poet said, the wind was always nor' nor' east. Men and women buttoned themselves against an anticipated chill. They would not risk exposure to the elements, or to their fellows.

Their treatment of Margaret Fuller is characteristic. Emerson admired her intellect and scholarship. New England acquaintances were prepared to approve her reformist involvement in the Europe of the 1848 revolutions. But her marriage to an Italian of unclear social status embarrassed them. After her death by drowning in 1850, Emerson dutifully acted as Fuller's literary executor. But he and his associates, including Hawthorne, tended to perceive her career as a shame verging upon a scandal.

The result was a literature of inhibitions, tending either to operate on the social surfaces of life (as with the Brahmins) or inwardly, hypertensely (as with Thoreau, Emerson and Hawthorne) – the confessional of men who by worldly standards have almost nothing to confess: they wish to make a clean breast of things but have clean breasts to start with.

Of no New England writer are these remarks more applicable than of Emily Dickinson, the little spinster of Amherst, Massachusetts. In the words of Roy Harvey Pearce: 'She is the Puritan diarist who no longer has to believe that her acutely sensed private experiences are valuable and explicable only as types of something larger than they – something given from above, from outside herself. Which is to say, she is the extreme Protestant self' – living in a town remote from Boston, relatively untouched by metropolitan Unitarianism, and still outwardly dominated by the sterner creed of orthodox Calvinism. Emily Dickinson wrote a continuous fragmented 'letter to the world' in the shape of a stream of tiny, aphoristic poems – only a handful of them published during her lifetime. Though she was well-read, seminary-educated, and had some contact with men of learning and men of letters, notably the Bostonian Thomas Wentworth Higginson, her activity was by choice almost reclusively withdrawn. She was an intensely private person. She presents a paradox in extreme form: that of a modesty so inward that it is immensely egocentric. Somewhat like Henry Adams, she shunned recognition yet was on her own curious terms vastly ambitious. It was she who took the initiative in sending some poems to Higginson, and then maintained a correspondence with him extraordinary in its gnomic candour. Perhaps she liked the idea of public recognition almost as much as she feared it. One feels in certain of her poems the danger of a distressing feyness, a pretence of being tiny and delicate and sensitive – an unconscious parody of Victorian femininity. In such poems her language is apt to seem unduly whimsical, as with people who give 'charming' or 'original' nick-names to their animate and even inanimate possessions. If poor Higginson found her embarrassing – both evasive and importunate – he is not altogether to be blamed.

Nor can he be entirely faulted if, in common with her sister Lavinia who edited a partial collection of her poems for publication after her death in 1886, he thought her verse eccentric in prosody and diction. Her range of expression was wayward and, in appearance, restricted. Many of her stanzas metrically carry echoes of the hymns that she sang in her childhood, when churchgoing was obligatory. Yet in these deficiencies, if they were deficiencies, lies the astonishing strength of Emily Dickinson. Her system is her own; she does not find, indeed does not seek, the consolations of formal religion. She is interested in the unmediated, unvarnished truth, a truth discerned in some nuance of an everyday event from which she extracts an individual significance:

> For Occupation – This—
> The spreading wide my narrow hands
> To gather Paradise.

But Paradise is hedged with agonies; grief is even more valuable than ecstasy because it brings us closer to understanding:

> I like a look of Agony,
> Because I know it's true—
> Men do not sham Convulsion,
> Nor simulate, a Throe—

Some truths are to be hidden, including the love she seems to have felt for certain men, one of whom was a married clergyman. Other truths, such as her distaste for her overbearing father with his 'pure and terrible' heart, had to be expressed obliquely. Other truths again were minor by-products of domestic life in Amherst, with its round of 'hollyhocks and puddings'. But again and again she returns to the shock of selfhood, the probing not for certitude but for insight – the inner reality of a death, the necessary pain of remaining silent when a spoken declaration might do harm. So in her muted, diminished scale the tiniest incident can become enormous: fear at the sight of a snake, inducing 'zero at the bone'; the bitter humour of the reflection that 'Denial is the only fact received by the denied'; or the statement, which might well have struck her in the first instance not in reading a newspaper account of social cataclysm but through observing a plant in the garden, that 'Revolution is the pod systems rattle from'.

Few of the authors of the Yankee Nation were as prolific as, say, James Fenimore Cooper, or as Walter Scott, of whom it was remarked that he had written more books than any other man could read. One or two such as Hawthorne might have published more if they had not been obliged to turn to other work in order to guarantee a sufficient income. Some, such as the historians William H. Prescott and Francis Parkman, were cushioned by private incomes that gave them leisure in which to study and write. What is remarkable about their careers as a whole is the habit of steady industry. Henry Adams, protesting that he was a man of no discernible career, produced more than a dozen volumes of history and two novels, as well as his brilliant exercises in a personal–impersonal diagram of the story of mankind, *Mont-Saint-Michel and Chartres* (1904) and *The Education of Henry Adams*. Longfellow, whom Anthony Trollope considered the most English of poets, seemed outwardly an embodiment of the English gentleman-littérateur. Yet as a young man he had qualified for a professorship by an arduously crowded apprenticeship in modern languages, and never acquired a taste for indolence even when he could well afford it.

In the Yankee culture idling was impermissible. The experiences of the New England historians furnish a remarkable psychological testimony in support of this observation. George Bancroft, the first to gain fame, graduated from Harvard in 1817, at the age of seventeen, achieved a doctorate from Göttingen three years later, and returned to Harvard to teach. He published a volume of verse and some learned essays on German life and literature; he immersed himself in democratic politics and became a chief intellectual spokesman for Jacksonianism; and he busied himself with a huge comprehensive history of the United States from the discovery of the American continent. The first of its ten volumes (which eventually took the story down to the end of the Revolution) appeared in 1834. He was Secretary of the Navy in the 1840s and then American minister in Britain, when he seized the opportunity to amass a then-unrivalled collection of source-material from the British and French archives. After the Civil War he served for seven years as American minister to Prussia and the newly unified Germany. He died at the age of ninety-one, convinced to the last that he had been privileged to be a citizen of the best country in the world, still more privileged to be its chronicler, and only unfortunate in not having been able to add several more volumes to the ten that had occupied him intermittently for forty years.

Still more remarkable, however, was the career of Prescott, for this depended upon an exceptional fortitude of spirit. Prescott was blinded in one eye while he was a Harvard undergraduate, and the sight of his other eye was so weakened that for long spells he was in effect totally blind. His health was too weak to allow him to travel as much as he needed for his research. For actual writing he had to rely upon a noctograph – a frame strung with parallel wires which guided the pen across the page. He composed by shaping whole chapters at a time in his mind, arranging them in his memory and finally transferring them to the paper held by the noctograph. Of course he could not have produced any notable work without aid from his family. But, to reiterate, the impressive thing is that he did not surrender to adversity. Eyestrain and various nervous ailments beset many writers of the period, including Prescott's contemporary, Longfellow. Longfellow provided the anthems of undauntedness for them in such poems as 'Excelsior!' and above all 'The Psalm of Life', which enjoined men to be 'up and doing':

> Life is real! Life is earnest!
> And the grave is not its goal;
> Dust thou art, to dust returnest
> Was not spoken of the soul.[1]

For Prescott, to be up and doing meant to settle to historical scholarship, with a high sense of the narrative drama and the moral significance of his subject. After some false starts he found his theme in the early Spanish exploration and settlement of the new world. More than ten years of patient toil preceded the publication in 1837 of his three-volume *History of the Reign of Ferdinand and Isabella*. He was forty-one years old, and seemingly on the verge of a frail middle age, when the enthusiastic reception of his history on both sides of the Atlantic brought him fame. Vastly encouraged, though still compelled to work at an apparent snail's pace, he pushed forward with his next two still more successful works, *A History of the Conquest of Mexico* (1843) and *A History of the Conquest of Peru* (1847). In 1855 two more volumes were published, of a *History of the Reign of Philip the Second* which he did not live to complete. He conceived them as monuments of patient research, but also and more importantly as pieces in the great cumulative march of mankind out of savagery and oppression towards the ultimate destination of a moral landscape much like that of New England – libertarian, resourceful, decent, Protestant. Prescott's histories were in addition intended as literature – so as to combine the narrative momentum and the excitement of character-clash of a great novel (and the romantic charm of the far-away in time and space) with the soberer satisfactions supplied by actuality and by a good sermon. In these respects they paralleled the achievement of Macaulay's *History of England*, and exhibited some of the same confidently Whiggish sentiment. They were part of the same sequential world-history of liberty, in which (as Bancroft had also implied) America was in the vanguard, and New England in the van of the vanguard. Christianity would infallibly triumph over paganism (Mexico and Peru), Protestantism over Catholicism (as in

---

[1] Compare some favourite lines of William James's, from the *Greek Anthology*:

> A shipwrecked sailor, buried on this coast,
> Bids you set sail.
> Full many a bark, when we were lost,
> Weathered the gale.

James had a period of breakdown, before establishing himself in his professional career, that brought a terrible paralysis of the will. He recounts the visitation as if it had happened to someone else in his *Varieties of Religious Experience*.

Macaulay's account of the Glorious Revolution of 1688–9), pure American doctrines of liberty and equality over the flawed British version of these (Bancroft's central thesis). The same lesson was extended by another New England historian, John Lothrop Motley, in his somewhat inferior though very popular *Rise of the Dutch Republic* (1856) and his *History of the United Netherlands* (1861–8), though with an even stronger emphasis on an auxiliary conclusion – that the 'Anglo-Saxon' or Germanic peoples were destined to triumph over the 'Celtic' or Mediterranean races. It should be emphasized that they did not claim that all American virtue was confined to New England, or directly derived from New England precept and performance. Their assumptions were more diffused – and perhaps the more influential for that very fact. They regarded the history of mankind, as, generally speaking, providential and progressive; even Henry Adams, despite the quasi-scientific detachment of his nine-volume *History of the United States of America During the Administrations of Jefferson and Madison* (1889–91), conveyed a firm belief that the energies of the new world were in every way more significant than the stultifications of the old world. 'Should history ever become a true science', he asserted in the final chapter, 'it must expect to establish its laws, not from the complicated story of rival European nationalities, but from the methodical evolution of a great democracy.' Human endeavour, thought Bancroft, moved in an ascending spiral, though its loops were sometimes so gradual and large that men could not always discern that there was an ascent. America represented the latest and highest coil of the spiral. All prior history could thus be seen as a prelude; and thus the New England scholar annexed the whole of history, subduing it to his purposes, much as in other ways other New England men of letters subsumed the entire realm of American and indeed of European culture.

The grandeur of aim, and its accompanying personal history of a fight against odds, is also exemplified in the career of Francis Parkman – yet another Bostonian, educated at Harvard, who sought his own identity and that of his region in a large sweep of bygone events. While he was still a boy Parkman conceived a lifelong passion for the old backwoods North America of the sixteenth, seventeenth and eighteenth centuries. As an undergraduate, with 'injuns on the brain', he undertook compulsively arduous journeys into northern New England and New York. 'My favourite backwoods,' he later memorably recalled, 'were always on my mind. Before the end of the sophomore year my various schemes had crystallized into a plan of writing the story of what was then known as the 'Old French War' . . . – later enlarged to include the whole conflict between France and England; in other words, the history of the American forest'. He was, he said, 'haunted by wilderness images day and night' a fascination that exerted a similar pull in those Harvard graduates of a later generation, Theodore Roosevelt and Owen Wister, who also sensed an almost mystic rapport amid the hard simplicities of frontier existence.

Parkman's language – 'on the brain,' 'on my mind', 'haunted' – reveals an obsessive preoccupation; and indeed there was a kind of desperate fervour in his absorption with the trails and archives of a vanished era. In common with Motley he tried his hand at writing fiction. In company with other well-to-do young Americans he travelled to Europe – where incidentally he saw his cousin succumb to the spell of Roman Catholicism, and where he had to summon up an ancestral horror of Papist wiles in order to fight off their temptations for himself. But his prime passion was for the 'American forest'. At the age of twenty-five, in 1846, he set out westward, along the Oregon trail, in search of the first-hand atmosphere of Indian life. It was characteristic of him that he disapproved of the Indians among whom he lived almost as strongly as he did of the miscellaneous, unkempt waggonloads of white emigrants along the trail. It was equally characteristic that this disenchantment made no difference to his scheme of work, even though the mental and physical hardships he had endured almost broke him. On returning to Boston in 1848 he collapsed. He was able to write *The California and Oregon Trail* (1849), but for many years thereafter he was the victim of a recurrent neurotic malady which he called 'the Enemy' and to which he attributed a satanic force that would probably not have seemed strange to his Puritan forebears. One of his problems was that he half-despised the literary life as an evasion of manliness and of American reality. He was an author who suspected authorship was not a proper occupation for a masculine New Englander. At any rate, the Enemy almost destroyed him. He described the symptoms of each onset in a letter of 1864:

Labor became a passion, and rest intolerable. . . . The stimulus rapidly increased. . . . The condition was that of a rider whose horse runs headlong, with the bit between his teeth, or of a locomotive, built of indifferent material, under a head of steam too great for its strength, hissing at a score of crevices, yet rushing with accelerating speed to the inevitable smash.

His method of dealing with it was 'counter-attack': insistence upon working at his histories until the moment when he was obliged to capitulate, in pain and half-blinded, and resumption of work as soon as he felt capable of picking up his pen again. He would be the captain of his own fate; he would fight on, in the spirit of Emerson's poem on 'Character':

> The Stars set, but set not his hope:
> Stars rose; his faith was earlier up:
> Fixed on the enormous galaxy
> Deeper and older seemed his eye;
> And matched his sufferance sublime
> The taciturnity of time.

Concentrating; forcing himself even when he could only produce six lines a day and was dependent on others to copy out the source materials he needed; turning aside now and then for distraction to his hobby horticulture (even this pursued with an almost grim commitment): Parkman kept the Enemy at bay in the realization that he could never entirely vanquish it – the creature was inside himself, an *alter ego* as implacable as in one of Hawthorne's kindred fantasies. In 1851 he managed to bring out his *History of the Conspiracy of Pontiac.* The death of his wife and of his only son, later in the decade, were victories for the Enemy, and so it seemed was the outbreak of the Civil War, which Parkman was forced to watch from an armchair, helpless and fuming as tangible enemies – the South, the traitorously weak elements in the North – threatened the survival of his nation. A visit to an army encampment in 1862 drew from him a cry of anguish at 'the banners I was not to follow, – the men I was not to lead. . . . I thought I had known what deprivation is, but I had not. It was the lamentation of the moth, in despair, because, being burned already, he cannot fly into the candle.' He poured out his frustration in angry newspaper articles. 'Where Are Our Leaders?' he asked, lashing at the 'worthless young imbeciles' strolling on Beacon Street when they should have enlisted to fight for the Union.

The war did end at last, in 1865, in the Union's favour; and Parkman, though he was never again very sanguine as to the future of American democracy, was able to resume his researches. In fact, though his theme embraced the triumph of Yankee qualities over those of France, and though as a good New England Protestant he was glad at the outcome, he sensed added depths in the story. From the end of the Civil War to the year before his death in 1893 he published seven works: *Pioneers of France in the New World* (1865), *The Jesuits in North America* (1867), *The Discovery of the Great West* (1869, revised subsequently as *LaSalle and the Discovery of the Great West*), *The Old Régime in Canada* (1874), *Count Frontenac and New France under Louis XIV* (1877), *Montcalm and Wolfe* (1884), and *A Half-Century of Conflict* (1892). Most of these in fact dealt with the French, as explorers and scientists, missionaries and administrators. He admired the best among them, such as LaSalle[1] and Frontenac, for their courage, initiative and intelligence. He saw them as natural aristocrats, flowers of a handsome civilization borne down by the sheer mass of Anglo-Saxon numbers and equipment. So there was a doubleness underlying Parkman's vigorous narrative structure. The downfall of the French was inevitable, one might say deserved. Yet the civilization that replaced them was imperfect; and as individuals, a LaSalle or a Frontenac were perhaps finer than any of their Anglo-American supplanters. One of the great vignettes of American literature, recalling Melville's *Moby-Dick* in its blend of irony and heroism, comes at the climax of LaSalle's journey down the Mississippi. LaSalle, 'grand type of incarnate energy and will' (here Parkman somewhat bends the evidence) claims the huge tract he has explored for France. The personal achievement is on the same giant scale. But LaSalle is doomed to be murdered by his followers, and the voice in which he reads his proclamation, in the forlornly gallant little wilderness ceremony, is 'inaudible at half a mile'. There is here for Parkman more than the charm of romantic pathos, and more than an intimation of *vanitas vanitatum*, though both are present. There is a consciousness of his own torment, and a bleak suspicion that no civilization in the new world, including New England's, is fated to endure very long. In advancing, to the extent that they *do* advance, each weakens in primal hardihood.

From about 1850 to 1880, to recapitulate, the principal spokesmen for American literary culture were either New Englanders or domiciled in New England; and for the next twenty years New England, though its dominance was passing, could still take pride in the momentum of its influence. Of the two wings of New England culture, the Transcendental and the Brahmin, the latter with its genteel overtones seemed the more ubiquitously attractive. The major Brahmin men of letters had a fame that spread far

---

[1] Parkman first became attracted to LaSalle through reading a biography (1844) by the Harvard historian Jared Sparks. Their versions of the true LaSalle may have been somewhat fanciful: see Peter Wood, 'La Salle: Discovery of a Lost Explorer', *American Historical Review* 89 (April 1984), 294–323.

beyond New England, or indeed the United States. In addition to the historians, there was Longfellow, whose reputation in the English-speaking world rivalled that of Tennyson. There was the poet-essayist Lowell, whose cosmopolitan charm served him well as American minister to Britain (and ensured him – the supreme mark of recognition in the realm of Anglo-American culture – a commemorative plaque in Westminster Abbey). And there was the no less versatile Oliver Wendell Holmes, author of a quantity of much-admired Bostonian light verse, some novels, and the celebrated *Breakfast-Table* volumes of genial essays. Collectively, then, the Brahmin men of letters appeared at the time as the summit of American achievement in the literary arts. The 'genteel tradition' that they embodied seemed to the majority of educated Americans of all regions the appropriate expression of a national style. Only in retrospect did the qualities of a Melville or a Whitman begin to appear more profound, or more genuinely American.

This polite culture, it should be emphasized, was not merely a product of the New England milieu. The literature emanating from the Boston area appealed to the middlebrow American reader because this national public wished to be reassured that it was cultivated, urbane, able to catch an allusion or a joke as quickly as anyone in the metropolitan centres of Europe. Longfellow and Lowell both assumed that their nation needed a great literature, and no doubt both dreamed of contributing to it. But both doubted whether patriotism was a proper motive in itself. Any literature, said Lowell, 'as far as it is national, is diseased, inasmuch as it appeals to some climatic peculiarity, rather than to the universal nature'. Longfellow made the same point in his novel *Kavanagh*. The legends recounted by Thomas Bulfinch, or in Hawthorne's *Wonder Book* and *Tanglewood Tales*, treated such material not as outlandish or un-American, but as elements in a cultural heritage that also embraced Shakespeare, Milton and Pope – not to mention Scott, Thackeray and Dickens. Nor was the Brahmin style consciously Anglophile, nervously deferential though it sometimes seemed. Lowell was furious when someone in Britain complimented him on his excellent pronunciation and asked him where he learned to speak so well. He replied, in the spirit that led him in his Harvard 'Commemoration Ode' to describe Abraham Lincoln as the 'first American', that he owed his accent to his own heritage: it was honestly and anciently come by, not an imitation. 'English' speech was as American as it was English.

The problem is complicated. Lowell, Holmes and their ilk felt no need to apologise for their Americanness. They were capable of tart responses to Europeans, especially Englishmen, who struck them as supercilious. But they felt themselves to be citizens of the world; and in particular – almost despite themselves – their context was Anglo-American. Owen Wister, an upper-class Philadelphian, was so to speak Bostonized by a Harvard education. At Harvard he had become friendly with young Theodore Roosevelt, a New Yorker who was later president of the United States. The atmosphere of the Boston of 1880, when Wister, Roosevelt and their student-contemporaries mingled with the city's society, is well brought out in Wister's biography of his distinguished classmate:

Pinafore [Gilbert and Sullivan] had recently blazed its trail of tune and laughter all over our map, pretty and witty comic operas from Paris and Vienna drew crowded houses, not a musical show had yet been concocted by the Broadway Jew for the American moron, clean cut muscular light music hadn't yet rotted into the fleshy pulp of jazz. . . . [Stevenson's] Long John Silver was soon to become our favorite villain, [Kipling's] Mulvaney had not yet risen out of India to warm our hearts, the great grey genius of *War and Peace* and *Anna Karenina* had not yet loomed up as the highest peak in fiction. . . .

There were arguments over the poetic standing of Browning and Tennyson, though most Bostonians preferred Tennyson; and at Harvard 'quarrels could still arise hotly over the relative merits of Dickens and Thackeray'.[1]

Owen Wister went on to say of Boston's gentlefolk: 'English they were by their colonial names, by their decent standards, by their stable characters.' But 'not one of them', fifteen years after the end of the Civil War, 'had forgiven England or what her spokesmen said or did against our Union when our Union was fighting for its life, and on the edge of losing it.'

His final thrust serves to indicate how ambivalent was the Anglo-American connection. The two cultures overlapped so much as to seem almost identical in tastes, yet their relations were emulative and tinged with subtle hostilities. It is therefore inaccurate to portray the Brahmin mode as 'un-American'. It was not the voice merely of some snobbish Bostonians, but of an entire national orientation toward the genteel. Nor was it an indication merely of a provincial mimicry of the culture of the mother country, though such deference did persist.

[1] Owen Wister, *Roosevelt: The Story of a Friendship, 1880–1919* (New York, 1930), pp 17–20.

It was however vulnerable for other reasons, as we may perceive from the tone of Wister's reminiscence, or from Parkman's despair at what he took to be a pervasive decline in America's moral civilization. Such men regarded themselves as guardians of this national civilization. Their snobbery was minor and defensive in comparison with that of high society in Europe. They still felt that they were democrats, even with reservations, and that American ideals if not always the actuality of American life were morally superior to those of the old world. But their defensiveness had taken on a sourly disdainful and even proprietorial tinge. By the closing years of the century the guardians were no longer sure that their role was appreciated, or that the newer, immigrant America, the America-to-be of the 'Broadway Jew' in Wister's disagreeable terminology, could be included with the old moral universe. They thought of themselves as sentinels, but suspected the enemy had already breached the Yankee fort and might before long have overrun it. Culture and democracy, as Matthew Arnold and other English thinkers were arguing, could not easily be reconciled, though the task was important. At least the Europeans were still able to benefit from the traditional aristocratic sanctions in support of high culture. No such residue was available for the Americans. They had evolved a formula which for a while sounded like an acceptable compromise, by differentiating the wholesomely from the dangerously democratic. In *Democracy Unveiled* (1805) the Federalist writer 'Christopher Caustic' (Thomas G. Fessenden) said:

By 'people' I mean the great body of American farmers, merchants, mechanics, etc., who possessing habits of industry, and our primitive New England manners, may be considered as the *stamina* of republicanism. . . . I would make a distinction between the *people* and the *mob* or *populace*. By the latter I would designate certain of the lowest class in the community, who are alike destitute of property and of principle, and may emphatically be styled the *rabble*.[1]

A couple of generations later the formula had broken down. Puritan New England was being transformed by Irish immigration.

[1] Compare a similar statement by Charles J. Ingersoll, from *Inchiquin, the Jesuit's Letters* (1810): 'There is no populace (plebs). All are people (populus). What in other countries is called the populace, a compost heap, whence germinate mobs, beggars, and tyrants, is not to be found in the towns; and there is no peasantry in the country. Were it not for the slaves of the south there would be but one rank.' In 1850, Melville's *White-Jacket* distinguished between 'the public' ('a monster . . . with the head of a jackass, the body of a baboon, and the tail of a scorpion') and 'the people' ('let us hate the one and cleave to the other').

Boston was governed by Roman Catholic politicos. The guardians of culture felt challenged by the mob spirit, and by *nouveaux riches* who were equally vulgar. They could lament the transformation, as writers like Thomas Bailey Aldrich did.[1] They could generalize their fate, like Henry Adams, into a theory of cosmic degradation. Or they could withdraw, along with Oliver Wendell Holmes, into the comforting sanctums of Brahminism – the club, the literary dinner, the college reunion. They could seek to resurrect the old Federalist conviction that culture was, as it always had been, the preserve of gentlemen. The very notion of a 'Brahmin' level of society in Boston – Holmes's contribution – was distinctly elitist in equating social with intellectual eminence.

The battle was not entirely lost, and Boston was not entirely isolated. In every large American city – New York, Philadelphia, Chicago, San Francisco – and in every college enclave the genteel tradition seemed to gain rather than diminish in strength. The Brahmins had genuine virtues of scholarship, sensibility and cosmopolitanism. And they were not the only ones to express alarm at the shoddiness of the burgeoning business culture of the Gilded Age. Though Mark Twain considered himself a robust republican, he increasingly lost faith in the capacities of ordinary Americans to lead the good life or even recognize it when they saw it. But Boston, and the rest of New England, was after 1880 gradually losing its pre-eminence. The newer, rawer America was groping for other ways of recording reality. The entrenched upholders of the genteel tradition no longer acknowledged the primacy of the Universal Yankee Nation. In 1877 the *North American Review*, that prim yet solid cultural organ which had been a Boston mouthpiece for educated opinion ever since 1815, moved to New York. It was, Longfellow sadly observed – and with a nice touch of unconscious parochial pride – 'as if Troy had lost her Palladium'. A few years later William Dean Howells, the nation's most respected critic – novelist, likewise transferred his operations from Boston to New York. The shift was partly economic. Even a large nation can only have one cultural capital, where the arts and their associated trades can concentrate. This tends to be also the financial capital of the

---

[1] 'It has been a pathetic experience for me,' Charles Eliot Norton wrote in old age, 'to live all my life in one community [Cambridge, Mass.] and to find myself gradually becoming a stranger to it.' A late example of rather cranky Boston behaviour is revealed in selections from the immense *Diary of Arthur Inman*, ed. by Daniel Aaron (2 vols, Cambridge, Mass., 1985). Inman, a reclusive Southern millionaire transplanted to New England, wrote privately and incessantly: a labour of love, or of intense antipathies?

nation. By the 1880s New York was beyond question the leading city of the United States, magnetizing talent and resources into Manhattan. And as Boston's hegemony gradually faded, its spokesmen were too intelligent not to know what was happening: to know too that there had always been something inadequate in the Yankee outlook. 'How narrow Boston was! How scant a pasture it offered to the imagination.' The words are those of J. R. Lowell. They reveal the Yankee talent for self-scrutiny, the admirable incapacity (which was also a limitation) to be wholly convinced that Boston truly was what Holmes called it in a slightly ironical boosterish moment – the hub of the universe. Seen subjectively, every place on the world's surface is the centre of the world. Awareness of cosmopolitan culture, and awareness that nothing stayed still in the United States: these factors preserved genteel culture in New England from total sterility, yet also meant that the Brahmins could never again be quite exuberant enough to maintain the old expansionist drive. Little by little they shifted from fervour into dilettantism, even though they were *serious* dilettanti, never mere dandies of literature. Henry James's tribute on James Russell Lowell provides a subtle epitaph for the closing days of a half-formidable, half-flawed tradition. Lowell, says James, 'carried style – the style of literature – into regions where we rarely look for it: into politics of all places in the world, into diplomacy, into stammering, civic dinners, and ponderous anniversaries, into letters and notes and telegrams, into every turn of the hour – absolutely into conversation, where indeed it freely disguised itself as intensely colloquial wit.' The implication is that, in the literature produced by late nineteenth-century New England, the good became the enemy of the great: professional competence and a mastery of the best authors, ancient and modern, had supplanted the lonely old Puritan obsessiveness. By 1900 the genteel tradition, so variously and on the whole so ably represented by the Universal Yankee spirit, was about to yield to another cultural order which would be both better and worse.

# 11

## HENRY JAMES:
## THE PREY OF ALL THE PATRIOTISMS

*Howell Daniels*

Henry James remains one of the most fascinating 'cases' in American literature. Long ago the commentaries upon his writings must have surpassed his own remarkable output, prodigious even by the Balzacian standards of the nineteenth century: twenty-two novels and one hundred and twelve short stories, of which some are in the region of 50,000 words and in a less fastidious critical terminology than that of James would qualify as novels. In addition to a volume of plays, there are numerous collections of critical essays, some of which James brought together in his own lifetime; several travel books, including *The American Scene* which remains one of the most perceptive accounts of the United States; collections of letters, notebooks, autobiographical volumes, art criticism and journalism. Although interest in James has never exactly been lacking, since the observation of the centenary of his birth in 1943 he has been comprehensively treated as moralist, psychologist, prophet and allegorist, as a typical nineteenth-century author and as a modernist writer and, not least, as a highly skilled and entertaining novelist. These are but a few of the many responses which have been made to James's work; their extent and variety cumulatively testify to the magnitude of his achievement and the complexity of his art.

The facts of James's long and productive life are briefly told. He was born in New York City on 15 April 1843, the son of Henry James Sr, an unorthodox follower of Swedenborg, and the younger brother of William James, the future philosopher. The nature of the sometimes tense fraternal relationship has been skilfully and convincingly related to the fiction by James's principal biographer, Leon Edel. After a haphazard and peripatetic education, including attendance at schools in Geneva, London and Paris and a year at Harvard Law School, Henry began in the early 1860s to publish his first essays and reviews. Several visits to Europe culminated in his decision in 1875 to settle initially in Paris and then permanently in London where, with the exception of brief forays to the Continent and the United States, he remained until his move to Lamb House in Rye in 1898. It was here that he wrote his last novels, which in turn were profoundly influenced by his earlier and ultimately unsuccessful attempts to write for the stage, and it was at Lamb House that he revised much of his work for the selective twenty-four volume New York Edition of his writings. In 1915 he became a British subject and a year later died in London, leaving two unfinished novels, *The Ivory Tower* and *The Sense of the Past*.

I

In the years immediately after James's death perhaps the most memorable tributes were paid by his two distinguished fellow-expatriates, Ezra Pound and T. S Eliot. Writing in a memorial issue of *The Little Review*, Pound described James's work as 'this labour of translation, of making America intelligible', as the 'whole great assaying and weighing, the research for the significance of nationality'.[1] Similarly, in a note of 1924 Eliot emphasized the essential unity of James's work in that he 'was possessed by the vision of an ideal society; he *saw* (not fancied) the relations between the members of such a society'. No one, he maintained, 'has ever been more aware – or with more benignity, or less bitterness – of the disparity between possibility and fact'.[2] Earlier, in the 1918 essay which contains the famous judgment that Henry James had 'a mind so fine that no idea could violate it', Eliot had remarked that the 'real hero, in any of James's stories, is a social entity of which men and women are constituents' and, with remarkable prescience considering the theses which were soon to be advanced on the disastrous consequences of James's expatriation, he had pointed out with some acerbity that neither of the principal components of this social entity had reason to feel smug about their reflection in his work.[3]

These comments provide an opportunity to examine an aspect of James's work which in recent years has been swamped by studies

---

[1] *Literary Essays of Ezra Pound*, ed. T. S. Eliot (London, 1954), p 296.

[2] 'A Prediction in Regard to Three English Authors.' Reprinted in *Henry James: A Collection of Critical Essays*, ed. Leon Edel (Englewood Cliffs, NJ, 1963), p 54.

[3] 'In Memory.' Reprinted in *The Shock of Recognition*, ed. Edmund Wilson (London, 1956) p. 856.

devoted to formal and technical considerations: his role as cultural mediator or, to use Pound's phrase, as a translator of one country to another. This central concern of his life and art inevitably invokes two related subjects which have provoked much debate: James's expatriation and his use – indeed invention – of the international subject.

There is no need at this date to attempt to refute the twin theses of Van Wyck Brooks and V. L. Parrington – succinctly summarized by F. O. Matthiessen as 'flight, frustration, and decline' – that James's decision to live abroad was to vitiate much of his later fiction. Certainly the facts of his expatriatism are not simple, and James's own attitude was not without its contradictions, inconsistencies and tensions.[1] But whether James exemplified what has been called 'dispatriation' – the 'disattachment from any single measure of values' – or the ideal of cosmopolitanism, he was, as we know from his comments on such representative predecessors and contemporaries as William Wetmore Story and Henry Harland, always aware of the essentially factitious nature of an American's relationship with Europe. Yet he knew what he wanted. To his brother William he confidently asserted, 'I know what I am about, and I have always my eyes on my native land', and he reassured his mother, worried by English criticism of one of his stories, in similar terms: 'I know too perfectly well what I intend, desire and attempt . . . I know what I want – it stares one in the face, as big and round and bright as the full moon.' His fiction is finally a triumphant vindication of the intelligence with which he analysed and dramatized his own position.

James's own comments on the international element in his fiction are for the most part confined to the prefaces which he wrote when revising his work (and which were conveniently assembled by R. P. Blackmur under the title *The Art of the Novel*). It is worth stressing that in no way did he attempt to construct a specific aesthetic of the international novel and he never really defined his use of the word 'international' as applied to his own work. His critical observations usually take the form of retrospective glances at the origins, the salient features of and the conditions giving rise to the novels and stories under review, although some of his discussions – on, for instance, the opposition of manners and the use of the innocent protagonist – are of general interest and value. In the relevant

[1] There are useful discussions of this complex topic in Christof Wegelin, *The Image of Europe in Henry James* (Dallas, 1958), particularly pp 141–51, and in Alan Holder, *Three Voyagers in Search of Europe* (Philadelphia, 1964).

prefaces, however, it is made quite clear that James's international fiction was intimately related to his own observation of his fellow-countrymen and women in Europe in the post-Civil War period and that for negative as well as positive reasons he deliberately placed his American characters in a European context (and to a lesser extent reversed the movement) in order to examine the behaviour of certain representative individuals in an environment at once familiar and alien.

In that continent the individual American was open to change and modification in a way in which the English traveller was not. And their frequently dissimilar reactions attest ultimately to a significant difference in the cultural assumptions of the societies of which they were products, a difference which also offers an explanation of why the international novel should have been an American rather than an English phenomenon. The 'closed' nature of the English national character contrasted remarkably with its 'open' American counterpart, a fact recognized by James as early as 1867 when he wrote to his friend Thomas Sergeant Perry: 'We have exquisite qualities as a race, and it seems to me that we are ahead of the European races in the fact that more than either of them we can deal freely with forms of civilization not our own, can pick and choose and assimilate and in short (aesthetically, etc.) claim our property wherever we find it.'

In observing this process of appropriation James was immediately and properly recognized by his contemporaries as the 'inventor' of the international novel and tale. It was his happy fate to begin his career at a moment when the social relationship between the new and old worlds was undergoing a rapid and radical change, and by temperament and upbringing he was uniquely qualified to record in fiction the impact of Europe upon his fellow-Americans. But in seeking to define the American relationship to Europe and, ultimately, the nature of the American identity, James was not working in an historical vacuum; he may have been the originator of the realistic international novel of manners but he too had his predecessors who in a variety of literary forms explored this same relationship. James's uniqueness, however, lies not merely in the skill with which he transmuted his predestined subject into art but also in the manner in which he was able to go beyond the limitations of a provincial, even, hemispheric, point of view, despite the fact that the origins of some of his works may be placed firmly in the nineteenth-century tradition of transatlantic social criticism.

The essential objectivity of James's moral vision is often ignored by partisan critics who fail, as did contemporary readers, to recognize the complexities in that vision and the manner in which it transcends the condition of the determining impulses. In the dialectic established in the novels and tales of the first twenty-five years of James's writing career, the rôles assigned to America and Europe are anything but simple; indeed, their ambiguity should preclude any facile judgments as to the moral superiority of the one over the other. F. R. Leavis was right to stress that in this period of James's career 'in the interplay between the diverse actualities of his experience, there is forming an imagined ideal positive that is not to be identified with any one of them'.[1]

## II

In a celebrated remark in 1872 James wrote, 'It's a complex fate, being an American, and one of the responsibilities it entails is fighting against a superstitious valuation of Europe.' In his early fiction and travel writing, collected respectively in 1875 as *A Passionate Pilgrim* and *Transatlantic Sketches*, he explored some of the effects of this superstitious valuation, principally in terms of the social and natural picturesque, so that the essays and tales complement and interact with one another to such an extent that at times the pages would appear interchangeable. Although James often strikes a recognizably Irvingesque note, he is distinguished from his competitors by the quality of the writing and the wit which together with the use of a discreet irony enables him to avoid both the extremes of a barbaric chauvinism or an undiscriminating enthusiasm.

One of the key tales of these years is that which gave James the title of his first collection and which, by extension, may be said to epitomize an entire range of response in a long sequence which culminates in the figure of Lambert Strether in *The Ambassadors*. *A Passionate Pilgrim* (1871) reflects something of James's own ecstatic discovery of English landscape in the widest sense, but at the same time it presents in dramatic fashion the substance of Henry James's Sr warning to his son of the perils resulting from too great an absorption in the 'artificial picturesque'.[2] Although the narrator pays his willing tribute to landscape he is only too well aware of the

---

[1] *The Great Tradition* (London, 1948), p. 146.

[2] This letter, written in response to Henry's enthusiastic description of Rome, is included in Ralph Barton Perry, *The Thought and Character of William James* (Boston, 1935), I, 134.

social and economic injustices which it obscures, of 'the pent-up moaning and groaning soul of the race' in the words of James's father. There is, it seems, a danger inherent in the American need for and tendency to create an artificial picturesque. When Searle, the infatuated pilgrim of the title, refers to the 'dead white wall' of his upbringing and education, it becomes like Melville's whale a solipsistic symbol in which the imagination may discern everything or nothing. The result is that the demands of the artificial picturesque often tend to exceed the possibilities of the European natural picturesque, and in the conflict between these two modes the passionate pilgrim is irretrievably caught.

One of the simplistic assertions which has impaired much Jamesian criticism is the equation of the celebrated and highly complex international subject with such appealing antitheses as American innocence versus European corruption. Inevitably, of course, there is some truth in this opposition, and it might be argued that the first classic confrontation of these qualities takes place in 'Madame de Mauves' (1874), a companion piece to 'A Passionate Pilgrim', where an American girl becomes the victim of a French baron. The events are somewhat stark and melodramatic, and the attitude to France and things French is a long way from that of *The Ambassadors*; but the complications in even this early tale make one realize that James, however tentatively, is here using the international theme as a means of suggesting and defining a moral reality which is neither American nor European and which is frequently obscured by the appearances of manners. The ambiguity of 'Madame de Mauves' derives not only from its abruptly melodramatic conclusion but also from Longmore's rôle as the revelatory centre of the action; for, with the exception of the important interlocutory second chapter, his is the point of view which prevails throughout the story. And to confuse his viewpoint with omniscient narration is totally to misinterpret the tale.

The situation is basically that which later provided the germ of *The American*: the idea of some 'insidiously beguiled and betrayed, some cruelly wronged, compatriot' who suffers at the hands of persons 'pretending to represent the highest possible civilization and to be of an order in every way superior to his own'. Euphemia Cleve's youthful 'superstitious valuation' of Europe is nourished by an idea of the social rather than the natural picturesque. The marriage relationship is used here for the first time to illustrate the conflict between European actualities and American illusions. But this clash of values functions as something more than the stereotyped contrast – treated exhaustively and exhaustingly in American periodicals after mid-century – between the American Protestant and the French Catholic ethic: it is the means by which James obliquely analyses the nature of the moral life. Landscape, for instance, functions as something more than an exotic backcloth. In the crucial seventh chapter in which figure the forest lovers and their message of life it becomes an analogue for Longmore's own state of mind: 'grasp forcibly at experience, lest you miss it altogether'. Madame de Mauves and (to a lesser extent) Longmore have engaged, however, in a conspiracy of conscience to pervert reality. The conclusion may give the victory to the American Puritan since the French pagan, awed by the massive moral authority exerted by his wife, chooses the same dramatic form of death as his brother-in-law. Yet in the course of this tale this simple equation of American innocence and European corruption has achieved a more profound meaning; as in 'A Passionate Pilgrim', James while presenting a traditional American image of Europe has treated it in such a manner as to deny unqualified sympathy to either of the dialectical partners.

Similar qualifications may be advanced in respect of two of the most famous of James's portraits, Christopher Newman in *The American* (1877) and Isabel Archer in *The Portrait of a Lady* (1881). As a consequence of the subtlety with which the international theme is handled, they too are more complex creatures than some readings of the novels would have us believe.

If *Roderick Hudson* (1875) possessed a factitious internationalism, one born of the elementary contrasts between New England and Rome, no such reservation can be applied to *The American* whose protagonist may be described as James's first full-blown, perhaps excessively inflated, international hero. This was the first of his works to be produced in direct response to an example of European 'blankness' in relation to the American character – in this case, as has been demonstrated, by the play *L'Etrangère* by Dumas *fils*.[1] The well-known account of the origin of the central idea of *The American* in James's later preface does not, of course, conflict with the suggestion that the novel was also a direct retaliation to the fabrications of the play; Dumas's drama strongly influenced the direction of the book, allowing James to continue to exploit the basic idea and at the same time providing him with an opportunity to refute European impressions of the American character.

[1] See Oscar Cargill, *The Novels of Henry James* (New York, 1961), pp 41–7.

Although not explicitly stated as such, behind James's account of the genesis of *The American* there looms the idea of nature's nobleman. Newman represents a combination of ideal qualities which had already been much in evidence in literature that sought to analyse the nature of the America–Europe relationship; he is James's only full version of the natural aristocrat who so engaged the attention of Adams and Jefferson and who was soon to be replaced by another dominant image – that of the American girl. In *The American*, for the first time, James dramatizes this traditional and stereotyped contrast between natural and artificial aristocracy in predominantly realistic terms and with an awareness of the high comedy involved. The spirit which animates some of the brilliant exchanges between Newman and Valentin is very different from that in David Humphreys' play *The Yankey in England* (1815) in which the principal character had stepped on to the European stage and announced at once simply and belligerently: 'My name is Newman. I am an American.'

If Newman exhibits many of the best characteristics of his race and nationality, he is also a not untypical product of the Gilded Age. His social innocence is but one aspect of his moral naïveté as a representative American in Paris. In his relations with the Bellegardes he is shown by their standards to be at best socially gauche and at worst positively ill-mannered. The deficiencies in his education – and *The American* is certainly a novel of an education – are exposed by a traditionally depraved Paris in which the sheen of fine manners conceals corrupt morals. Newman is in fact a more ambiguous figure than has been suggested by the comments of some American critics who chauvinistically tend to see him as the supreme embodiment of American energy and as the 'whole man'.

Yet his rôle as an idealized American inevitably implies that he be presented as essentially a noble man; if James had expanded the various suggestions concerning Newman's crassness and complacency then he would have been left without his true subject-matter which rested upon an equal stylization of the natural goodness of Newman and the innate badness of the Bellegardes. It might then have been a better novel but it would not have been the book James envisaged. The 'essence' of James's subject was that Newman should be 'ill-used' and, as he admits in the preface, he paid too little attention to the manner in which this injury should be brought about, with the result that the reneging of the Bellegardes becomes an arbitrary act which is associated more often with romantic than with realistic fiction.

The novel has to stand or fall by Newman's 'more or less convincing image' and therein lies the problem. In the same way that the plot of *Roderick Hudson* interferes with the real centres of dramatic interest, so too in *The American* the necessity for Newman to be opposed and defeated by representatives of a corrupt and ancient Europe prevents certain nuances of his character from being fully explained and developed. If one chooses to see in his behaviour, angular and simple as it is, that capacity for the magnanimous moral gesture which causes him to burn the implicatory paper, then James may be said to have succeeded in his original intention. On the other hand, the suggestion that Newman suffers from a characteristically American form of pride – the belief that money can buy anything, a wife as well as a housekeeper – causes his failure to win Madame de Cintré to be a just comment on this particular flaw. In general his defects of character are transformed into virtues by James's lively and ironic treatment, but the uneasy suspicion remains that if Newman, for all his engaging simplicity and charm, is not quite the ideal expression of his society, then it is that society of which he embodies the worst and the best that is also on trial.

Newman's demands upon life remain unsatisfied as, on a different level, do those of Isabel Archer in *The Portrait of a Lady*, which is often considered James's finest work. It is a rich novel which has been accorded superlatives and undergone a variety of interpretations. The thematic interests are many, and if the book does not possess the vigorous and explicit contrasts of *The American* or *The Europeans* these concerns still allow James to continue his examination and analysis of the moral life, but on this occasion finding his salvation in the figure of the Europeanized American in order to avoid the romantic elements which in *The American* he had to substitute for the real.

The claims Isabel makes upon life are associated with the strain of American idealism in her character. And she is by no means unique in her presumptuousness. Mrs Touchett is able to identify and 'place' Isabel's eagerness for life together with her inability to deal with it as a general quality often to be found in girls of her type. Her mistake is meant to be a characteristically American mistake made by a girl who embodies specifically American values in a pluralistic society where they are betrayed. In contrast to European women, Isabel consciously affronts her destiny in a manner which, it is suggested, is exclusively American.

As a result of her assumption that Osmond shares in the 'classic grace and harmony' of his surroundings – a sequence which demanded all James's novelistic skills – Isabel's transcendental imagination fails to distinguish between the centre of the composition and the frame surrounding it. There is, too, an element in Osmond's character which makes a strong appeal to Isabel; they both share in what T. S. Eliot termed *bovarysme*, the adoption of an aesthetic rather than a moral attitude towards experience. In both the novel and in the preface to its revised version, however, James's attitude is one of warm sympathy and indulgence. Her romantic idealism, her intellectual arrogance and her moral self- reliance are all seen as the faults of youth; we learn that 'she would be an easy victim of scientific criticism, if she were not intended to awake on the reader's part an impulse more tender and more purely expectant'. Yet, as commentaries upon James's work have shown, Isabel is anything but an easy victim. As with *The American*, if we choose to ignore the *general* narrative tone, Isabel's charm is seriously impaired by the negative aspects of her idealist heritage. Among her weaknesses, in addition to pardonable vanity, is that excess of imagination which links her with earlier pilgrims; she wants, according to Ralph, to see but not to feel. The final encounter between Isabel and Henrietta hints at more severe limitations. It is Henrietta who has changed, for on hearing that her friend is to marry the quintessentially English Bantling, Isabel's reaction is a strange one:

It was rather a disappointment to find that she had personal susceptibilities, that she was subject to common passions, and that her intimacy with Mr Bantling had not been completely original. There was a want of originality in her marrying him – there was even a kind of stupidity . . .

Isabel has, in effect, learned nothing; her typically American belief in the primacy of the intellect remains supreme for, in the face of what is likely to be the only happy marriage in the entire novel, she still retains a measure of arrogance. This evidence of Henrietta's simple femininity disappoints her; even after her own disastrous choice, she seems unable to conceive of marriage as anything other than a grand moral design or an abstract configuration of values. Despite the comedy implicit in Henrietta's reversal of her opinions, never has Isabel seemed so far from ordinary human affections as she does at this moment.

Inevitably such an interpretation emphasizes the less attractive aspects of Isabel's character when the whole tone of the novel is orientated in favour of her confronting and affronting her destiny in a manner to arouse a more sympathetic reaction. Her weaknesses

are also her greatest strengths in her betrayal by Madame Merle
and Gilbert Osmond. The rôle of this Europeanized pair is, of
course, crucial in the provision of yet another moral identity for an
'innocent' American, but the other characters also contribute. All
the Touchetts are splendidly observed, and each member of the
family possesses a distinctive and discriminating attitude to life. Part
of the sense of plenitude in the first third of the novel derives from
the way in which these characters are fully realized in description
and dialogue; they offer a series of antitheses in order that Isabel,
with the aid of Ralph's detached commentary, may allow her imagination to explore the possibilities afforded by European life.

In the first half of *Portrait of a Lady* Isabel pursues her illusion of
freedom and her quest for knowledge; in the second she is forced to
recognize that complete freedom and total knowledge are incompatible. The focus has altered from the presentation of external
events to the conflict within the mind of a central intelligence,
limited but endearing. Ignorant of good and evil, Isabel finally
discovers that outside her characteristically American system of
moral absolutes these qualities are not to be perceived in any such
direct and unambiguous relation. The sum of her tragic experience
is her knowledge of good-and-evil.

*The Portrait of a Lady* had been preceded by a short novel which
superbly exemplifies James's skill as a cultural equilibrist. Within its
self-imposed limits *The Europeans* (1878), pronounced thin and
empty by William James, is a perfect work. Originally serialized in
the *Atlantic Monthly*, the scheme for the novel as outlined by James
in a letter to Howells implies an intensely romantic structure which
suggests nothing so much as that *The Europeans* is a version of
pastoral – used here in the sense of a literary device through which
the nature of a particular social and moral reality is explored.
Although the pastoral mode involves a contrast between pastoral life
and a more sophisticated type of society, its purpose is not to extol
the virtues of the one at the expense of the other but to hold the
characteristic values of both in a state of equilibrium. In this sense,
*The Europeans*, if we choose with F. R. Leavis to regard it as a
dramatic poem, is a poetic dialogue between two modes of life and
two types of and attitudes towards experience which, at the same
time, because of James's introduction of the international theme,
becomes also a dialogue between America and Europe.

The Wentworth home is in the outskirts of Boston but the
atmosphere is entirely rural: the fields, meadows and the lake which
surround the house are repeatedly emphasized. But the basic con-

trast is not between Boston and the Wentworth acres, for even Boston itself comes to share in the Arcadian role which James attributes to the New England of the 1830s. The lack of urban sophistication displayed by Mr Broderip and other representatives of the city makes it quite clear that the dominant trope is not between the values of town and country but between the values represented by Europe (in the persons of Felix and Eugenia) and America (in the Wentworths). In James's development of the international subject the dramatic possibilities offered by the West–East migration were, of course, infinitely greater than those afforded by the reverse movement; but here, as in George Sand's romance *La Daniella,* for which James had a high regard, sophisticated products of a supposedly superior society are introduced into a predominantly rural world.

Eugenia and Felix enter an atmosphere of simplicity and trust, symbolized by the manner in which the 'front door of the big, unguarded home stood open, with the trustfulness of the golden age; or, what is more to the purpose, with that of New England's silvery prime'. Describing the Wentworth home to his sister, Felix claims for it 'the *ton* of the golden age'. Nature gives him a sense of 'luxurious serenity'; even the food is redolent of 'the mythological era, when they spread their tables upon the grass, replenished them from cornucopias, and had no particular need of kitchen stoves'. The basis upon which this simple ordered life rests is not derived from the traditional flocks but nevertheless it is not obtrusively in evidence; it is 'wealth without symptoms' which emphasizes a natural and un-ostentatious manner of life.

But in this Arcady – or at least in this New England version of it – there is a blight over the land in that its inhabitants seem to be suffering from some ancestral sin or aboriginal calamity. Their quiet but stunted lives are best exemplified by the presiding patriarch, Mr Wentworth. Boston in the fourth decade of the nineteenth century could hardly be described as theocratic, yet in *The Europeans* the social and intellectual landscape is as elaborately stylized as the moral one. (One of the few concessions to the Zeitgeist is the attribution of Emerson's essays as reading matter to Mrs Acton.) Mr Wentworth, Charlotte and Mr Brand are all presented as victims of a residual Puritanism which deeply affects their lives and characters, and it is specifically the function of Felix, the Europeanized intruder into this settled world of categorical imperatives, to restore to these individuals a sense of gaiety and freedom in order that they may conceive of life as 'opportunity' and not as 'discipline'.

The virtues of the Wentworths are not idealized; they may be innocent but they possess none of that freedom which James often regards as a corollary of innocence. An active dread of experience provides the opportunity for Felix to compare them to 'a large sheet of clean, fine-grained drawing-paper, all ready to be washed over with effective splashes of water-colour'; the simile is Felix's own and merely one of a number by which he expresses his ideal of moral and intellectual freedom. The only person who *seems* to be free from these morally restricting bonds is Robert Acton, but in one sense he turns out to be more rigidly committed to an abstract ideal of conduct than any of the Wentworths or Mr Brand.

The one person who is struggling to escape from the 'stony pastures' which surround the Wentworth house is Gertrude, James's 'free spirit', who eventually rejects the Puritan–pastoral ethic represented by her tutor Mr Brand in favour of the education Felix offers her. And the message of life to be enjoyed which he brings is essentially the same as that which Rowland in *Roderick Hudson* had offered Mary Garland before St Peter's. When she tries to be 'natural' she points up the nature of the paradox in the Europe–America antithesis: it is the representatives of court rather than those of the country who are seen to be truly natural in that they do not deny the life of the senses or the imagination. In effect, Gertrude rejects the imperatives of her pastoral environment for the concretes of experience outside that world.

But Gertrude is not alone in awakening from the moral coma with which the American characters are afflicted. Under the assumed cloak of frivolity Felix has been quietly changing and reordering the lives of these stricken people, the negative aspects of whose innocence have prevented them from a realization of their potentialities. Felix has been dismissed too easily. He is certainly comparable to a court jester whose clash with rural values leads to some splendidly comic scenes which serve also to expose the deficiencies in the Wentworth world. But he is also an imaginative painter who attempts to educate the aesthetic sense of his cousins, a moral physician who seeks to heal the injured psyches of these pastoral characters, and a Cupid-figure who brings about two marriages, including his own. He even succeeds in modifying the Calvinist lugubriousness of Mr Wentworth himself, a change which is most apparent in the remarkable last chapter of *The Europeans*.

Throughout the course of the novel its intensely dramatic qualities have been much in evidence: the limited settings, the sparse descriptions which almost amount to stage directions, the tightly-knit group of characters, the economy of the dialogue and the delicacy of the wit have all contributed to the dramatic effect. In the last chapter the various characters are gathered together in hymeneal rites and a new spirit of harmony and reconciliation is apparent. In tone it is inevitably reminiscent of the last scenes of Shakespearian romance. One by one, Felix, Gertrude, Charlotte and Mr Brand, each presses Mr Wentworth to give his consent to the marriage which a revitalized Mr Brand has agreed to perform. Mr Wentworth is still the serious patriarchal figure, but under the influence of the combined forces of youth and love, he consents to the union. When his own son informs him that he is to marry Lizzie Acton, the transformation begins: Mr Wentworth's attitude becomes one of 'jocosity'. And when his daughter and son-in-law have appropriately left for 'Bohemia' in the 'vaporous rosy cloud' to which James referred in his letter, it seems that the blight has finally been removed, for Mr Wentworth 'at last found himself listening' for the 'echo of a gaiety' which Felix and Gertrude now share. It is an eminently proper conclusion and one that completely justifies the tone of James's outline.

The rôle of Eugenia is much more complex than that of her brother and few seem to agree on the manner in which she is presented. At one point James's authorial voice is quite explicit as to her motives: 'she had come four thousand miles to seek her fortune, and it is not to be supposed that after this great effort she could neglect any apparent aid to advancement'. In this same passage both Robert Acton and Clifford Wentworth are equally explicitly postulated as the primary and the secondary means of that desirable advancement. But it is Eugenia's fate to be defeated by the positive aspects of that pastoral innocence which so appeals to her brother. Like him she is enchanted by the simplicity and charm of her cousins; at the same time there is something highly self-conscious in the quality of her reaction which sharply differentiates it from the enthusiastic spontaneity of his response. Her self-consciousness extends even to the picturesque. Whereas Felix accepts the natural landscape and paints it uninhibitedly, the Baroness wishes to improve upon it, as if to compensate for the lack of the social picturesque. She insists, for example, on acquiring an 'old negress in a yellow turban' whom she will be able to see 'sitting there on the grass, against the background of those crooked, dusky little apple trees, pulling the husks off a lapful of Indian corn'. She mystifies her cousins by a similar transformation of the little white house she has been given. The natural picturesque is insufficient for a woman of her taste and character. In terms of pastoral, she attempts to bring the court with her into the country; in terms of the international theme, she tries to establish a European enclave in an American setting, for it is from such accumulations that the Baroness derives her social being. Artifice is the keynote of her character.

It is one of the major ironies in this novel of ambiguities that Eugenia's rejection should ultimately derive from what she assumes to be an advantage: the lack of a standard of comparison for her 'remarkable self . . . gave her a feeling of almost illimitable power'. Yet this sense of power proves illusory, for the absence of any standard of comparison causes her richness and complexity of character to degenerate into mere flamboyant theatricality in the pastoral air. Her remark to Felix at the conclusion of the novel as she sits packing is not without its point: '*Bonté divine*, what rubbish! I feel like a strolling actress; these are my "properties".' For her, the play is over; the rustic audience has been awed by the display but no tangible offer of advantageous marriage has resulted. Ultimately, one feels, there is some truth in her self-deprecatory description of herself as 'a poor, wicked foreign woman, with irritable nerves and a sophisticated mind'.

Yet this is not to say that Eugenia is a Madame Merle in miniature. The same critical air of detachment encompasses her as it does the other characters; the ironic style of this 'Sketch', as James significantly sub-titled the novel, holds all the characters in a state of suspended judgment. The essential duality or the pastoral mode, its constant contrast of rural and urban values whether they take the form of an antithesis between nature and art or the opposition of America and Europe, involves a recognition of the typical virtues and vices of both ways of life. Even within the two conflicting groups there are individual differences and, in reading *The Europeans*, to insist on the superiority of one set of values over another is to ignore the implications of a sometimes gay, sometimes mordant irony which qualifies equally both European and American.

James's continuing rôle as cultural commentator is illustrated in another fashion by two typical and representative short stories of the late 1870s: 'Daisy Miller' (1878) and 'An International Episode' (1879). The ferocity of the response to these tales on both sides of the Atlantic was indicative of the dangers inherent in the part in which James had cast himself. The insistent actualities of the present made for a less inhibited reaction than the depiction of a New England dead and gone.

During his first adult visits to Europe James must have encountered examples of what Howells later termed the 'innocently adventuring, unconsciously periculant' American girl. The origin of the story is ascribed to an anecdote heard in Rome in 1877, but 'Daisy Miller' also presents in fictional form James's comment on a social phenomenon which had already been discussed at length in American periodicals. The considerable social, if not critical, uproar generated in the United States by the basically sympathetic portrait of Daisy tended to obscure the real meaning of the *nouvelle*. Daisy may have been the first of James's heroines to embody the spirit of her country, but the primary interest of the tale is not her guilt or innocence but the meaning and quality of her relationship with Winterbourne. The nature of his ethical dilemma is stressed by the manner in which his conflicting opinions of Daisy's conduct are balanced alternately against those held by society and against Daisy's provocative mixture of audacity and innocence. One of the ironies of the tale is that the expatriate American society, which is condemned by Daisy in Vevey and ignored by her in Rome, is ultimately right in its judgments. To insist on visiting the Coliseum at night as Daisy did constitutes not only defiance of social taboos but also defiance of common sense.

The figure of the American girl in Europe had been present in varying degrees in the pre-1875 tales: Charlotte Evans in 'Travelling Companions', Martha in 'The Last of the Valerii', Adina Waddington in 'Adina'. None of these heroines, however, has either the directness or the force of Daisy Miller, and only in the first of these stories had James used the American girl to express his interest in the conflict of manners. In Europe Daisy herself comes into the 'very pretty heritage of prohibitions' against which Nora Lambert had been warned in *Watch and Ward* (1871). Innocence, an admirable but in certain circumstances a dangerous, quality, is of course, as James maintained, the 'keynote' of her character. Another irony is that the only person to recognize this fact is not an American but an Italian, which suggests that the basic conflict in the tale is not so much between American and European manners as between the different sets of values represented by examples of 'conscious' and 'unconscious' Americans abroad. But if these representatives of the American social order are subjected to satirical treatment, so too is the Miller family, the typically American components of which James had scathingly noted in his 1870 essays on Newport and Saratoga.

The revenge of poor fated Daisy was, if anything, posthumous and confined to Winterbourne; Bessie Alden in 'An International

Episode' may be described as the first of the Jamesian heroines who takes, on behalf of her nation, the revenge to which many years of European social and cultural domination have entitled her. Her rejection of the wealth and position that Lord Lambeth has to offer is in itself a symbolic act. If *The American* indirectly reflects a natural enough indignation at the misrepresentations of Dumas's play, a similar reaction appears to have provided the stimulus for the writing of 'An International Episode'. Once more James hurried to defend – with his usual qualifications – his countrymen and women from misinterpretation and prejudice; once again he showed his concern for a true and accurate representation of America and a fair and proper analysis of American behaviour. On this occasion the formal critical protest was contained in a short note in the *Nation* for 30 May 1878; 'An International Episode', the indirect fictional refutation, appeared seven months later. The subject of James's note was a long story by Laurence Oliphant entitled 'The Tender Recollections of Irene Macgillicuddy', the contemporary success of which is something of a mystery. There seems little doubt, however, that James was strongly influenced in the writing of 'An International Episode' by Oliphant's story. At one point in 'Tender Recollections' Irene comments: 'No wonder we have to fall back upon English dukes, or any distinguished stranger we can find, when our own countrymen will not qualify themselves properly to be the husbands of intelligent and well-educated girls.' In effect what James does is to re-write her story in the light of this statement.

Basically the tale of an American girl who refuses to marry a peer simply because he is a peer, 'An International Episode' is also a refutation of what Oliphant conceives to be the attitudes of Americans towards the English aristocracy. For his own purposes of ironic contrast James preserves the same central device of introducing two Englishmen into a strange and alien environment; but in the writing of his tale he may be said to have inverted the values which are present in 'Tender Recollections'. Whereas Irene's recollections are set largely in New York, James's story divides with mathematical precision into neat sections: the first recording the American scene through English eyes, and the second describing England from an American standpoint. On this occasion, as on others, James deployed his satire from a mid-Atlantic point of view.

Critical obtuseness and patriotic misinterpretation may generally be said to have characterized the reception of these two stories. And to the history of the latter there must be added a postscript which, in the light of his 1878 essay 'Americans Abroad' with its plea for a greater understanding of Americans by Europeans, is highly ironic. Instead of James's tale being accepted or rejected on its literary merits alone, it brought about another incident in the long and frequently bitter war of social criticism. As James realized, it was 'an entirely new sensation for them (the people here) to be (at all delicately) *ironized* or satirized, from the American point of view, and they don't at all relish it'. He now found himself in the uncomfortable position of having written two stories which together pleased neither audience. The popular reaction in the United States to 'Daisy Miller' is well known; in England, as James mentions in the above quoted letter to his mother, the story was 'a really quite extraordinary hit'. One suspects that had Daisy been English rather than American the tale would have been a good deal less successful in England; she acted perhaps in the manner in which the majority of the English reading public expected her to act. (In her retaliatory *An English 'Daisy Miller'* of 1882 Virginia Wales Johnson, an American novelist who chose to live in Italy for most of her life, traced the scandalous life and pathetic death of a convention-defying *English* girl on the Continent.) It was therefore hardly surprising that the satire directed at the English nobility should be received with so ill a grace. James's portrait of the Duchess of Bayswater, while more tactful than Hawthorne's description of the English dowager in *Our Old Home*, did not escape censure and reproach. His chagrin at the fate of his tale is understandable. The prejudice and misinterpretation on which he had commented and to correct which his story may be said to have been partly written were to continue in the reception of 'An International Episode'.

A similar failure in the United States to understand 'The Point of View' (1882), a product of James's return visit in 1881 and 1882, to some extent justified his conjecture that the tale would 'probably call down execration' on his head, for the element of social criticism, particularly in Miss Sturdy's letter, is pronounced. Of the minor disturbance generated, John Hay was to remark that 'the worst thing in our time about American taste is the way it treats James' who, as a result of his expatriation, had become 'the prey of all the patriotisms'.[1] But it is not without significance that it is the stridently American Marcellus Cockerel who should have the last word in the debate: 'The Siege of London' (1883) effectively

[1] W. R. Thayer, *The Life and Letters of John Hay* (Boston and New York, 1915), I, 411.

dramatizes his definition of an aristocracy as bad manners organized. Other tales of this period which because of their concern with the observable contrast and conflict of European and American manners may be linked with 'The Point of View' are 'The Pension Beaurepas' (1879), 'A Bundle of Letters' (1879) and 'Pandora' (1884). In 'A Bundle of Letters' and 'The Point of View' this contrasting is so explicit – each tale consists of a series of letters juxtaposed for dramatic, comic or satiric effect – as to make one feel that they constitute a set of variations upon a theme: they are five-finger exercises in the technique of the international situation. Although in places they suggest an incipient dissatisfaction with the facile contrasts which were sometimes inevitable in James's subject, they offer amusing and perceptive insights into the differences between national psychologies, and once again the criticism is meted out impartially.

Even the solid veracities of *The Bostonians* (1886) and *The Princess Casamassima* (1886) did not strike contemporary readers as such. Although their merits may still be subject to debate, the two novels are very much complementary: reformist Boston with its faintly acrid tang is amply and finely achieved; revolutionary London springs to life in *The Princess Casamassima*, a novel which has sometimes received less than justice as a result of the ascription of authorial intentions that do not exist. But the reception of both was disappointing. When confronted with these portraits of two major cities, one American and the other English, the reaction of readers was typical of what James had experienced before. The reviewers of each nation, outraged by the depiction of what was familiar to them, responded more amiably to what they considered to be James's unfavourable presentation of another metropolis.

Unsuccessful though they were, these two substantial novels represented a new departure for James. Increased travel and improved communication had brought about a diminution of old international contrasts to such an extent that even such tangentially international tales as 'A New England Winter' (1884) and 'Georgina's Reasons' (1884) were set some forty years in the past; others such as 'Mrs Temperly' (1887) and 'Louisa Pallant' (1888) merely reflect the accelerating pace of social change and the constant mitigation of the conditions necessary for the international subject. And, as in the case of 'The Impressions of a Cousin' (1883), James was not above adding a consciously international flavour to an anecdote which, as the *Notebooks* demonstrate, originally possessed no such quality. The voyage in the donnée

which later became 'The Patagonia' (1888) was originally from
India to England and not from Boston to Liverpool; 'The Path of
Duty' (1884) somewhat gratuitously introduces an American
narrator to record what is unqualifiedly a tale of English social life.
But perhaps the best illustration of James's addiction to a usually
well-rewarded habit is offered by the development of *A London Life*
(1888) from the original anecdote. While Laura Wing is not
guiltless of a neurotic inverted chastity which causes her to interfere
in a way of life she does not understand but which James emphatically does not condone, the fact that she and her sister are
Americans creates a secondary, even an unnecessary, internationalism, for the actual situation depicted in no way requires
nationality to function as an index to character.

### III

In 'Lady Barberina' (1884), one of James's most brilliant tales of the
1880s, and one for which there was little corresponding social
reality in that the usual Anglo-American marriage presented the
union of the male Briton to the female American, Lady Barb
marries and goes to New York with Jackson Lemon, an Anglophile
and a doctor. But the central paradox of the story is that those
elements in her character which Lemon so admires are ultimately
seen to take their force and vitality from the English scene; when
taken out of its characteristic and habitual frame, her picture loses
its robust glow and wanes in the thin American air. Lemon himself
does not completely escape the charge of snobbery, and he is not
without that acquisitive strain which causes him to value his partner
as much as a possession as a wife. Since to some extent the
inevitable failure of his grand racial alliance is a just retribution for
his vanity, this *nouvelle* is more than an example of what one critic
terms 'anti-English stories of cultural comparison', for the irony is
directed equally at English ignorance of the United States and at
Lemon's social pretensions.

James's attitude towards the Anglo-American marriage seems to
be determined by a similar irony. Lady Marmaduke, we are told,
believed 'that an ultimate fusion was inevitable'; Lady Beauchemin,
too, maintains that 'English and American society ought to be but
one – I mean the best of each – a great whole'. Even Lord
Canterville seems to be affected by his eldest daughter's views that
some sort of selective international breeding would be an admirable
development. In 'Lady Barberina' the deflationary treatment is

perhaps primarily explained by the meddlesome qualities of the two principal exponents of the idea, but within five years James, if not specifically advocating a system of Anglo-American eugenic collaboration, was nevertheless close to this notion of an ultimate fusion of English and American into a common educated entity.

The same idea is presented in 'The Modern Warning' (originally published in 1888 as 'Two Countries'), another tale of an Anglo-American marriage. It presents an innocent woman caught between the claims of two countries which are symbolized in the persons of her husband and brother. In the same way as Sir Rufus's unconscious egotism parallels MacCarthy Grice's pathological Anglophobia, so too James attempts, somewhat unsuccessfully, to apportion the criticisms of each country equally; the political corruption of the United States is balanced by the 'misery and brutality' which Agatha sees outside her Liverpool hotel. Although the latter are insufficiently imagined, with neither the power nor the force of the similar episode in Melville's *Redburn*, Agatha's glimpse of an English world other than the one she has known is obviously included as a necessary element in the antithetical structure; but the terms in which it is presented seem to indicate lack of passion, indeed of interest, in the author, a reaction all the more surprising if one remembers the virulently anti-American original impetus to the story, Sir Lepel Griffin's *The Great Republic*. Sir Rufus's dislike of the United States is also made rather more convincing than the abstract detestation of England which James is forced to attribute to Grice's Irish blood. But James's concern here is not with the truth or falsity of the images with which the two men indict each other's nation; the primary centre of interest is meant to be the wife and sister who is sacrificed, admittedly in somewhat unlikely fashion, to the selfishness of two men and to history. The moral, if one may be said to exist, is that it is foolish and dangerous to set up differences where none really exist, to create divisions where none should be, to sacrifice happiness to ancient animosities which are artificially preserved in a world of shrinking boundaries. The implication, of course, is that in a society in which old contrasts have disappeared and traditional enmities forsworn there is no scope and little justification for the international subject. And indeed, in James's own case, except for the mellow and witty comedy of *The Reverberator* (1888), his typical subject dropped away for a decade before it re-emerged in a new guise in the three novels *The Ambassadors*, *The Wings of the Dove* and *The Golden Bowl*.

In a well-known letter of 1888 to his brother, James stated his new position unequivocally. Confessing his weariness with the 'international' state of mind, he wrote that he couldn't 'look at the English–American world, or feel about them, any more, save as a big Anglo-Saxon total, destined to such an amount of melting together that an insistence on their differences becomes more and more idle and pedantic'. For James the life of the two countries had become 'simply different chapters of the same general subject', and 'I have not the least hesitation in saying that I aspire to write in such a way that it would be impossible to an outsider to say whether I am at a given moment an American writing about England or an Englishman writing about America (dealing as I do with both countries), and so far from being ashamed of such an ambiguity I should be exceedingly proud of it, for it would be highly civilized'.

It became increasingly obvious to him that the longer he stayed in England the greater were the demands that country made upon his fiction. He had told Charles Eliot Norton that he wanted to become its 'moral portrait painter', and in 1890 he wrote to Howells: 'One thing only is clear, that henceforth I must do, or half do, England in fiction – as the place I see most today, and, in a sort of way, know best.' And, after his failure to write successfully for the theatre, this intention he carried out in novels such as *The Spoils of Poynton* (1897), *What Maisie Knew* (1897). *The Awkward Age* (1899) and *The Sacred Fount* (1901) where an increasingly serious social and moral criticism is presented in progressively intricate and mannered prose. Although his notebook entries of the 1890s offer evidence of a sporadic interest in the international subject, the quasi-allegorical 'Collaboration' (published in *The Private Life*, 1893) carried the debate a stage further. Here the claim that art knows no frontiers is effectively dramatized in the collaboration of a French writer and a German composer in the teeth of national disapproval. While the theme is certainly linked to those tales of the 1890s – 'The Middle Years' (1893), 'The Death of the Lion' (1894), 'The Next Time' (1895) – which concern themselves with the isolation of the artist, in this instance larger reverberations are heard. Yet the symbolic Franco-Prussian alliance is also a private one. Vendemer, we are told, was really in love but for this passion he would not sacrifice 'the truth he had the opportunity of proclaiming' and which finally he and his collaborator together assert on the Italian Riviera. The 'unnatural alliance' which provides the basis for this story demonstrates again that so personally cherished a theme as this is not entirely free from a sympathetic scepticism.

The civilized ideal which James expressed to his brother and which may be glimpsed behind the melodrama of 'The Modern Warning' is put forward on a number of other occasions at this time. The essential ideas of the 1888 letter, for example, are dramatized and expanded in James's dialogue 'An Animated Conversation', which was later included in *Essays in London and Elsewhere* (1893). In this conversation-piece it is maintained that 'an acuteness of national sentiment' between America and Britain is 'more and more an artificial thing . . .' The perception of this artificiality is what constitutes an 'education of the intelligence, of the temper, of the manners'; it provides an opportunity for two 'great peoples to accept, or rather to cultivate with talent, a common destiny, to tackle the world together, to unite in the arts of peace – by which I mean of course in the arts of life'. Here it seems is the germinal idea of that vast 'sublime consensus of the educated' which James later tried to record in his last novels. The coming together of the two nations which in the past was 'academic and official' is now 'practical' and 'social'. The result of improvement in all media of communication has been to make the world a 'Grand Hotel of the Nations', and out of the mingling of peoples and manners there emerges a characteristically Jamesian vision:

We fly to and fro, in our complicated, predestinated activity, and it matters very little where we are at a particular moment. We are all of us here, there, and everywhere, wherever the threads are crossed. And the tissue grows and grows, and we weave into it all our light and our darkness, all our quarrels and reconciliations, all our stupidities and our strivings, all the friction of our intercourse and all the elements of our fate. The tangle may seem great at times, but it is all an immeasurable pattern, a spreading, many-coloured figure. And the figure, when it is finished, will be a magnificent harmony.

In his attitude towards the idea of an organic Anglo-American community James may have been influenced by the later career of his friend James Russell Lowell, who proved to be an extremely popular Minister in London and who, according to James, produced 'a relation between England and the US which is really a gain to civilization'. It was, too, this aspect of his career which James recalled in his obituary article on Lowell where, in examining Lowell's position as a mediator between two countries, James seems very much to have in mind the function of the writer as a sort of international Orpheus, pacifying 'the great stupid beast of international prejudice' among nations which together constituted a single community of language and manners. It was, indeed, the rôle in which more and more he saw himself.

Although the political and racial aspects of the theory of 'Anglo-Saxonism' did not make an appeal to James, he could hardly have avoided Joseph Chamberlain's 'A Dream of Anglo-Saxondom' which was printed contiguously with James's essay 'The Suburbs of London' in *The Galaxy* of December 1877. This sense of a new relationship, which reached a climax at the turn of the century, postulated a society in which sharply differentiated national characteristics could no longer exist, a fact recognized by James in 1908 when he wrote that 'the *great* international cases, those that bristle with fifty sorts of social reference and overflow' were now 'equally taken for granted on all sides of the sea, have simply become incidents and examples of the mixture of manners . . . and the thicker fusion'. But if the old international contrasts were neither observable nor recordable they were replaced by the idea of 'a common intelligence and a social fusion tending to abridge old rigours of separation', that 'sublime consensus of the educated' which for James had been glimpsed behind 'all the small comedies and tragedies of the international'. Without this strong sense of a social and intellectual union, the possibilities of which had been sufficiently prefigured in *The Europeans* and *The Portrait of a Lady*, it is probable that *The Wings of the Dove* (1902), *The Golden Bowl* (1904) and even *The Ambassadors* (1903) would have emerged with radically different emphases.

While these novels employ elements, albeit transformed and transmuted, of the international subject, all in varying degrees reflect the achieved social fusion symbolically enacted in *The Golden Bowl* in which James presents a new humanism based on the resolution of conflicting moral sensibilities. In the increasingly rare and redemptive air of these works he escapes from the pressing sublunary concerns of his earlier fiction into a region where the representatives of two continents enter into a stylized dance. The characters, as James maintained, are certainly agents or victims; but the fact that they are also English, American, Roman, provides a rich emblematic dimension whose fabulous qualities have often been noticed and in terms of the 'magnificent harmony' established amply discussed.[1] In James's writings the splendour of this vision transcends the conditions upon which it was dependent and survives the equally sublime failure of the educated in 1914. His fiction together with the intelligence it reflects is without equal in a literature which R. W. B. Lewis has described in the preface to his *Trials of the Word* as 'the most international, the most cosmopolitan, the most *Western* of all the literatures of the Western world'.

[1] See, for example, Christof Wegelin's account in *The Image of Europe in Henry James*.

# 12

## MARK TWAIN'S GODS AND TORMENTORS: THE TREASURE, THE RIVER, THE NIGGER AND THE TWIN BROTHER

### Bernard Poli

Mark Twain is one of those authors – George Sand and George Eliot are other examples – whose pseudonyms have eclipsed their real names. He came into the world in 1835 as Samuel Langhorne Clemens, in the small Mississippi-river town of Hannibal, Missouri. His parents, of Virginia stock, had moved there from Kentucky. Sam grew up by the great river highway, in a region that was both Western and Southern (Missouri was a slave state). His restless impulses took him eastward as a journeyman printer, up and down the Mississippi as a steamboat pilot, and then farther west into the gold and silver settlements of Nevada. Here and in California he began as a newspaper columnist, and as a deadpan lecturer. He discarded an early pen name, 'Thomas Jefferson Snodgrass' (borrowed in part from *Pickwick Papers*), in favour of 'Mark Twain' (borrowed from steamboat days – a helmsman's call signifying that the boat was in two fathoms of water, enough to avoid running aground).

Twain's full literary career began to blossom in 1869 with a travel book, *The Innocents Abroad*, an account of American tourists in Europe and the Holy Land which poked fun at the conventionally gushing travelogues of the period. Success in domesticity accompanied success as a writer. In 1870 he married Olivia (Livy) Langdon, and was soon comfortably installed at Nook Farm, a sort of literary suburb of Hartford, Connecticut, where neighbouring authors included Charles Dudley Warner and Harriet Beecher Stowe. New England was to be his favourite corner of the United States. Apart from sojourns in Europe and New York City, he based himself in Connecticut until his death in 1910. But his best books – *Roughing It* (1871), *The Adventures of Tom Sawyer* (1876), *Life on the Mississippi* (1883), *The Adventures of Huckleberry Finn* (1885) – draw upon the scenes and emotions of his boyhood and youth. Life dealt him blows that staggered him. His son and two of his daughters died in heartbreaking circumstances. The publishing house in which he was a partner collapsed. He had invested his money and all his ebullient optimism in an elaborate typesetting machine, with disastrous results. For whatever reasons, the high spirits of his copious if erratic work coexisted with a caustic and increasingly bleak view of human nature. The transition can be traced from the basically indulgent social satire of *The Gilded Age* (1873; written in collaboration with C. D. Warner), through the perhaps unwittingly grim *comédie noire* of *A Connecticut Yankee in King Arthur's Court* (1889) and *The Tragedy of Pudd'nhead Wilson* (1894), to the bitter story of 'The Man Who Corrupted Hadleyburg' (1900) and the final fatalism of *The Mysterious Stranger* (posthumously published in 1916). Few of his many readers in Europe or America seem to have noticed the change. Loving the man and his books, they were content to regard him as a handsome, picturesque old celebrity, whose white hair and famous white suit clothed the white soul of an innocently mischievous little boy.

Among American writers Mark Twain should stand out as one of the least mysterious of great men. No secret document has revealed an unknown side of his personality, either in his adventurous youth or in his sedate married life. His eventful biography is clearly reflected in his major works which deal, directly or indirectly, with his own past; autobiographical pieces provide additional information (or additional fiction). Jane Clemens, Tom Blankenship, Joe Goodman or Horace Bixby have long been integrated into the Twain–Clemens Saga, and even little Satan, though he looks like a character trying to act his part in the wrong film, is now known to have played some of his tricks in Hannibal, Missouri. Man and legend remain inseparable.

And yet we cannot help being fascinated by a man who keeps something hidden from us. We look for a secret face of Mark Twain, as if he were the author of potentially greater books he could never write. The blame for his artistic under-development has been put on his wife or on the society of his time, but the conflict certainly lay on a deeper level, and an honest view of this prominent citizen of Eseldorf, USA, should start with portraits of Tom Sawyer and Little Satan as 'extraordinary twins'.

The key to Mark Twain's secret may very well be this double vision of the world seen through the eyes of the god-like child and the inseparable devilish tormentor. Samuel Clemens believed himself the victim of some 'mysterious stranger' and also the killer of his own ghost-like William Wilson. From the beginning his paradise was lost, and even before the images of despair became the core of his fiction in later years, his major works already contained an ambivalent picture of the world that was both heaven and hell to him.

Though he only by accident jumped on the band-wagon of the forty-niners, Mark Twain always set his course straight towards 'treasure-island'. After his bankruptcy he had no pangs of conscience when he closed his eyes to the evils of capitalism and clung to the coat-tails of Standard Oil tycoon H. H. Rogers. Sam Clemens's rise from Missouri rags to Hartford riches could have served Horatio Alger's purposes if some tragic episodes had been eliminated. If only the Paige typesetting machine had worked; if the biography of the Pope, which as its publisher he hoped every good Catholic would buy, had sold better, Mark Twain would have been a wealthy businessman. Unfortunately, as a financier, he only *almost* made a fortune, and, in his mining days, he only *almost* 'struck it rich'. There was a time when he exclaimed that everything he touched turned into gold; but in the same breath, he added that he was frightened at his own prosperity. Rightly so, because it did not last. This anguish about a found and lost treasure is an aspect of Mark Twain's fundamental ambivalence, a source of wild enthusiasm and torment which greatly influenced his writing. He served on the staff of the *Golden Era*, but was meant to become an unfortunate hero of the 'Gilded Age'.

The dream in its pure, archetypal form, is found in *Tom Sawyer*. Tom, though no fool in business matters, at first took pride in owning any number of worthless treasures: a tooth, a door knob, a dead cat, the core of an apple, and even Sunday school tickets or a Bible, futile rewards for hard work and pious learning which could, ironically, be traded in for worldly goods. Tom became a big boy when he developed an interest in real treasures and eventually discovered money buried deep in a mysterious cave. With it came other rewards for the young hero: Becky's kiss at the most pathetic point in the story, the unanimous applause of the community when he celebrated his success, and even the financial blessing of a prospective father-in-law who invested the money for him.

When he used his personal experience, Mark Twain expressed more ambivalent feelings about treasures. In his mining days, according to the story in *Roughing It*, Sam Clemens and his friend

Higbie once discovered a 'blind lead' which would have made them millionaires if they had done the required amount of work within ten days to become legal owners. But unpredictable circumstances forced the partners to go on various urgent errands. Without consulting one another, they left . . . and came back too late. Meanwhile the millionaire-to-be, in his wild plans for the future, had substituted this new treasure for a childhood dream, the 'Tennessee land', a large tract of territory he had inherited from his father and which should have made the family rich. To him a treasure is a miracle, a dream come true.

Another episode in the book reveals more about the way miracles happen. When miners see a calico dress hanging out of a wagon, they immediately rush to the man standing by and ask him to 'fetch her out'. The man pleads that his wife is sick, but the miners refuse to be persuaded, and, when eventually the woman appears, they literally worship her and reward her husband with the gift of twenty-five hundred dollars in gold. Treasure, dream, and a woman, a recurrent combination in Mark Twain's works, is the formula of success. Not without good reasons, since Mark Twain started writing *Roughing It* immediately after marrying the dreamlike Livy and becoming the proud owner of a beautiful house and an editorial chair in Buffalo, his father-in-law's wedding gifts.

Mark Twain was perhaps indulging in symbolic recollections of that period in 1893 when he wrote 'The £1,000,000 Banknote'. Referring to the miraculous 'million-pounder', which gave the hero a chance to meet and marry Portia, he said: 'It never made but one purchase in its life and *then* got the article for about a tenth part of its value.' In a less optimistic mood, he wrote 'The Esquimau Maiden Romance' the same year. In this tale a young man, just about to marry the daughter of the richest man of the tribe, also the owner of a beautiful house and of an incomparable collection of fish-hooks, finds himself accused of theft and is sent drifting away on an iceberg to pay for an uncommitted crime. Mark Twain had not quite made up his mind about Livy and the formidable Mr Langdon! A quarter of a century later he still felt divided between the 'million-pounder' of love and the twenty-one fish-hooks of despair.

If some details in *Roughing It* can be read as an almost transparent allegory of Mark Twain's financial and conjugal bliss, we must also return to our first example for a more complete picture of his state of mind. A treasure was found indeed but soon irrevocably lost. Mark Twain gives an odd and unconvincing reason for not doing the necessary improvements on his property, saying that he had to spend nine days nursing a friend, an 'old gentleman', who needed a third person to take care of him while he was suffering from an attack of 'spasmodic rheumatism'! It is hardly a coincidence that Jervis Langdon, Livy's father, happened to be very ill and died in August 1870, soon after Mark Twain married Livy, and precisely when he was struggling with the composition of *Roughing It*. This death must have been felt as the unfortunate loss of a bonanza, as well as a distracting circumstance which kept the young author from writing his book, but Mark Twain was also deeply impressed by the fatal curse that accompanied his unbelievable good fortune. This hypothesis is further supported by a remarkable 'coincidence': the name of the friend who needed so much care in the sick room is Captain John Nye. A friend of Livy's came to stay with the Clemenses after Mr Langdon's death; she, too, died after a painful illness, one month after Mr Langdon – her name was Emma Nye.

Pure treasures exist only in dreams. They are the millions Colonel Sellers hopes to make out of his inventions, in *The Gilded Age*. Meanwhile this character goes on feasting on turnips and pure water. Speculation, with more tangible dollars at stake, is corrupt. The Tennessee land symbolized the great expectations of the Hawkins family: a fortune would some day materialize because Mr Hawkins (Judge Clemens, of course) made a wise investment. We are still in Tom Sawyer's dream world. But the time to cash in on the bonanza has now come: the property with its buried treasures must be sold to the government, and this requires some clever bargaining and political manoeuvring. Immediately the Hawkins family split up: the adopted children (Clay and Laura) actively pursue a more or less legitimate reward, whereas the son and daughter, Washington and Emily, remain passive and ready to let the dream evaporate. Laura's ambition, her activities as a lobbyist, with all the sexual aspects implied in her outrageous flirting with Senators, her pseudo-marriage to Colonel Selby, her resumed liaison with him later, and the cold-blooded murder she perpetrates, make her an irretrievably lost girl. But, in spite of all her efforts the Tennessee land is not sold. The hopes of the family are ruined. The dream has become a curse. A lost girl and a lost treasure!

All fortune hunters in this book, however, are not necessarily immoral and bedevilled by ill-fated treasures or the intrigues of scarlet ladies. Look at the completely symmetrical picture of the 'good treasure' (a coal mine), earned by hard work, with the willing cooperation of honest workmen! An additional reward for so many virtues is the hand of a most accomplished and deserving young lady. The hero is Philip, the good, noble boy. Thanks to Warner's contribution, Horatio Alger was allowed to cast his long shadow on this picture of the Gilded Age.

Good treasures as well as evil ones are miracles; they come from the bowels of the earth or are buried deep in secret caves; they magically conjure up the presence of some feminine figure.

It seemed very unlikely that the turbulent waters of the Mississippi would suggest any fanciful episode of this kind. And yet, during his trip down the river, Mark Twain tells his companions a story entitled 'A Dying Man's Confession', which ends with the revelation of a treasure to be dug out of a house in Napoleon, Arkansas. The word bonanza, reminiscent of *Roughing It*, is even used in the title of a chapter. Like the 'blind lead' or the Tennessee land, however, the treasure has also vanished – the city of Napoleon was washed away by a flood many years before and the treasure is gone.

A long murder, revenge, and horror story introduces an unusual number of corpses into the narrative: a man finds his wife and child killed: he thinks he has identified the murderer but kills the wrong man, and we later witness the agony of the real killer in a German morgue – a death, by the way, quite comparable to that of Injun Joe in the cave. Two victims, two villains, four dead bodies and a bonanza. Great is the disappointment of Mark Twain's two companions, now cast in the roles of comedy rascals, who were eager to lay their hands on the 'loot'. The bonanza was both a dream and a curse. Related themes of love and disaster are also briefly sketched at the end of the story when Mark Twain indulges in personal recollections about Napoleon, 'town where I used to know the prettiest girl, and the most accomplished in the whole Mississippi Valley; town where we were handed the first printed news of the *Pennsylvania's* mournful disaster'. As in *Tom Sawyer* and *Roughing It*, the treasure immediately calls up contrasted memories of love and death.

*Huckleberry Finn*, in many ways, is a story about lost and found treasures. It starts with Huck renouncing his share in Tom's money, too late however to avoid the catastrophic return of Pap. It contains the episode of the *Walter Scott* to which Huck wants to give a 'rummaging' and where he finds a gang of murderers who will probably die as prisoners of the wreck. The house that floats down the river also contains treasures of odds and ends: eight dollars, a wooden leg, and . . . the body of a dead man who turns out be Pap. Jim's adventures can be summarized as the loss of the only capital he ever had to his name, forty dollars that vanished in a crazy investment (the poor man's Tennessee land) and that were made up to him at the end of the book as a reward for the faithful care he gave Tom after his wound. Jim himself becomes Huck's treasure, his 'nigger', whom he 'stole' from Miss Watson and who is in turn stolen away from him by the Duke and the King, another pair of rascals. Eventually Jim's freedom will come as a present from Miss Watson in her will, thus reintroducing the related theme of death.

The pattern is found in its complete and most elaborate form in the Wilks episode. A treasure is stolen by the Duke and Dauphin, then stolen again by Huck who hides it in a coffin, next to a dead man. It will have to be dug up later in the graveyard. Huck's plot to have the money restored to its rightful owner briefly turns the young hero into a romantic swain, full of chivalrous love for Mary Jane, a pure and beautiful young lady. But, as a true ancestor of the 'lone ranger', Huck banishes sentimental attachments from his heart. . . . Another perfect instance of the treasure, death and the dreamlike girl. In the wake of money, heavenly bliss and the torments of death are inseparable partners.

Mark Twain's nostalgia for the river and piloting has perhaps been taken too literally. No doubt the Mississippi period stands out as one of the happiest in his life. Images of Huck and Jim leisurely drifting down the river where 'life is mighty free and easy', or of a steamboat gliding into the night, are celebrated anthology pieces. But we have to reconcile this paradise on the Mississippi with the grief and despair felt by Sam Clemens when his young brother Henry died in a steamboat accident. The guilt complex which persecuted him all his life is a tormented aspect of his personality which has its counterpart in the images he gave of less happy forms of navigation. The twin pictures of the raft of leisure and the steamboat of destruction stand out as contrasted images in Mark Twain's fiction.

The first version of the trip on the river, given in *The Gilded Age*, suggests an exciting experience for the children, but steamboats are also associated with fright and destruction. The similarities between the explosion that made Laura an orphan and that of the *Pennsylvania*, which took Henry's life, are too obvious to be stressed here. More interesting is the sudden appearance of two steamboats taken to be the Almighty by Uncle Daniel, the kind and faithful slave. The steamboats so badly scare the old Negro, who was peacefully sitting on a log with a group of children, that the children all run into the woods, a situation not unlike that of Jim and Huck when a steamboat goes over their raft. The contrast is clearly between an island of peace and the thundering forces of destruction.

Steamboating, as described in *Life on the Mississippi*, is associated with the flush times of youth, and yet connected in a deeper and more private way with death. Henry's story, between the cub-pilot chapters and those devoted to the river revisited, is the real core of the book. But Mark Twain felt that he could not write a volume about his youth without introducing a child on a raft. The excerpt borrowed from *Huckleberry Finn* and so awkwardly interpolated at the beginning of the book, fulfils this need, psychologically counterbalancing the explosion scene. And though Mark Twain's intentions were obviously humorous when he retold the story of the two Indian lovers, in the last chapter of the book, it is nevertheless significant that the volume should end on a note of peace and serenity found on a happy island.

When it comes to heavenly places, none can surpass Jackson's Island as a paradise. It takes no symbolic interpretation to see that this island is the raft of happy youth. But then where in *Tom Sawyer* is the tormenting image of the steamboat? The answer is not that scenes of violence were purposely avoided in this book for children, since the death of Injun Joe or the graveyard episode are just as hair-raising as a steamboat explosion. Of course, Ben Rogers personifies a steamboat at the beginning of the book, and this may be interpreted as a way of exorcising evil memories. One may also describe Jackson's Island as a sort of mock-*Inferno* in which the children reside while they are believed to be dead. Can we go as far as picturing Tom crossing the Acheron at night in a canoe? The real explanation for the missing destructive steamboat in this book is that this episode is emotionally related to the death of Sam's brother, Henry, a brother who is very much alive in *Tom Sawyer* and personified as Sid.

When, in *Huckleberry Finn*, the world of childhood is left behind and real, meaningful adventures take their place, the raft and the steamboat become the two inseparable and opposed faces of the same reality. The book starts with the story of an orphan on a raft, Moses, and the most significant section of the volume begins when Huck and Jim, after meeting on an island, decide to drift down the Mississippi on a raft. It ends, before the grand *finale* and the winding up of the plot, when Tom, Huck, and Jim strike out in a canoe, 'easy and comfortable', for the island where Huck's raft was hidden. But, in the middle of the book and during the leisurely sailing of the two fugitives, the angriest-looking steamboat practically chews up the raft and does not even leave the two Ishmaels with a coffin to hang on to.

The idyllic and the tormented aspects of life on the river are two facets of the same reality. On one occasion they find themselves completely reconciled in a beautiful but dark vision: 'I rose up and there was Jackson's Island, about two miles and a half down stream, heavy-timbered and standing up out of the middle of the river, big and dark and solid, like a steamboat without any lights.' In the dark recesses of Mark Twain's mind, the river, like the treasure is an ambiguous god and tormentor.

Even when his adventures take the author through Nevada deserts, in *Roughing It*, the reader already familiar with Mark Twain's rhythms realizes that the stagecoach expedition has all the qualities of a delightful trip down the river. The driver, for instance, enjoys the mighty privileges of a pilot, including that of telling tall-tales, and the passengers quickly rearrange the mail bags in such a way that they seem to lie at ease on the logs of a raft or the bottom of a boat. This image of sleepy repose will be taken up later when Sam Clemens sails on the smooth surface of Lake Tahoe, letting 'the boat drift by the hour whither it would', giving himself up to 'the dreams the luxurious rest and indolence brought'.

As a contrast to these floating islands of bliss, we find a description of Mono Lake, a greyish-white sheet of water in the middle of a desert, and of two islands, covered with ashes, which Sam Clemens and his friend Higbie decide to explore in spite of their forbidding aspect. One of them is described as made up almost entirely of ashes and scorched or blasted rocks, whereas the 'furnaces' of the volcano underneath shoot out occasional 'jets of steam'. This steamboat-like island of silence and desolation clearly suggests death and destruction. The impression made on the reader when he discovers this Eliotian waste land is even reinforced by a description of a tempest on the lake whose alkali water severely burns the skin of the unfortunate travellers, and immediately after, by the story of a stove which explodes and nearly kills the narrator. Further proof of the identification of these ghastly pictures with recollections of Henry's death can be seen in the contrast between the horror they convey and the description of a single graceful tree, very much alive in the middle of the steam, but already part of the dead, 'like a cheerful spirit in a mourning household'. The two themes of fear and bliss, youth and death, life and destruction are inseparably welded in the superimposed images of the steamboat and the happy island, for seldom can the machine and the garden be reconciled in one picture of beauty.

When a steamboat kills a boy's father and his younger brother, according to the story Huck made up for the benefit of the Duke and the Dauphin, it is a tragedy; when it 'kills a nigger', in another imaginary version of Huck's adventures, it is immaterial, almost reassuring. The indictment of Southern society implied in this transcription of a child's ruthless racial prejudices clearly betrays Mark Twain's feelings of guilt and shame about the coloured man. His recollections of a milder form of slavery in Missouri, his numerous statements about the moral superiority of the black race and the very perfection of Jim in *Huckleberry Finn* have given Mark Twain the right to be called a liberal. But his Negroes are too consistently good to be true to the author's feelings; too many faithful servants, too many 'uncles' tell stories by the fireside to make Mark Twain's stand entirely believable. His Indians, on the other hand, are always traitors, villains and murderers. Of course, a personal literary hatred for Cooper's noble savages partly justifies his debunking of the red man. But, Joel Chandler Harris's Uncle Remus is also unbearable as a 'noble black man' and we often wish Mark Twain had created at least a few Negro villains, too.

Black men are all thoroughly good, Indians thoroughly bad. The black mate in the Ned Blakely episode in *Roughing It*, the young slave in *Tom Sawyer*, Uncle Daniel in *The Gilded Age*, and, of course, Jim, all stand on one side, the cruel Indians in Nevada and Injun Joe on the other. Mark Twain found himself so ill at ease when he had to deal with the two races simultaneously that, in 'Tom Sawyer Among the Indians', he did not know what to do with Jim (on the war path with his white friends!) and had to send him home quickly.

In *Huckleberry Finn* Mark Twain acknowledged the shocking inequality between races which prevailed in the South and, in *Pudd'nhead Wilson*, he confessed even more openly the resentment that existed between Negroes and Whites as a consequence of slavery. In autobiographical pieces he admitted that he had seen slaves beaten, and he also told the story of children who suddenly saw the body of a dead Negro rise out of the water in such a threatening manner that they ran for dear life. All this clearly reveals that his conscience as a white Southerner was tormented by fear and remorse. Under the superficial level of benevolence and liberalism lies a deeper layer of unsolved conflicts and racist reactions.

Beyond the barrier of silence or of old clichés, we find only a few significant hints. Apparently Mark Twain used the stereotype of the 'bad Indian' (a counterpart to that of the 'noble savage') in order to channel, sometimes in a humorous manner, his adverse reactions to coloured people, whereas the Chinese and the Negro became paragons of mild virtues practised by 'inferior' races. He never dared confront the problem squarely, and it is not the smallest paradox in his work that he should have written half a volume about the South revisited after the Civil War without making significant references to Negroes, except perhaps to say that Uncle Remus was white! In the second half of *Life on the Mississippi* he, however, betrayed his inner conflicts in a revealing episode.

In a chapter entitled 'Southern Sports', after a discussion on Northern and Southern moonlight and about 'artificial methods of dispelling darkness', Mark Twain tells the story of a visit to a cockpit in New Orleans. Two men are in the ring, a Negro and a white man, and though Mark Twain never says who is the owner of each bird, he goes on to explain that a 'big black cock' and a 'little grey one' were confronted. The author refuses to see the end of the battle (a refusal to take sides openly?), but if the sight was so pitiful, why did he take the trouble to find out how it ended, and to report that 'the black cock died in the ring, fighting to the last'?

Mark Twain perhaps honestly tried to come to terms with the Negro problem, but it was all too easy for one who lived in Hartford, Connecticut, to give himself a good conscience by writing 'A True Story'. The past and ambivalent feelings about the South survived. The changelings in *Pudd'nhead Wilson* make the black and white children into pseudo-twins and offer a pseudo-solution whereby the two races are defeated.

Of the American Negro, a dearly loved and deeply hated servant, Mark Twain made up two contradictory images, that of the 'good nigger' (a sentimental way of dealing with the problem of slavery) and that of the 'black Injun' (a secret outlet for his shame and resentment).

The further we go into themes that lay close to Mark Twain's heart, the clearer it becomes that his inner world is an ambiguous gallery of gods and tormentors: the treasure and the beautiful girl, the happy island and the 'good nigger' make up his private mythical heaven; whereas death, the destructive steamboat and the 'black Injun' haunt his secret Inferno. A recurrent binary pattern characterizes his way of acquiring experience and of rendering it. The various conflicts we have analysed seem to be mere dramatizations of a deeper psychological ambivalence. These contrasted inseparable images reveal an obsession with a reality that is one and yet double, and, on this more abstract level, they probably find an adequate expresssion in the theme of the twins, which epitomizes this tormenting paradox.

There are twins galore in Mark Twain's works, in detective stories, for instance, such as *Simon Wheeler Amateur Detective* or 'Tom Sawyer Detective'. There are also innumerable variations on the theme: pseudo-twins, disguises and the endlessly repeated symmetries, which range from the pointlessly abstract presentation of 'Gentleman A' and 'Gentleman B' in the '£1,000,000 Banknote' to the contrasted good little boys/bad little boys or to the polar opposition between the witchcraft of the Boss and the witchcraft of Merlin, the last two examples pointing to the complex and paradoxical symmetries of good and evil.

*Pudd'nhead Wilson*, though not a story about twins, deals with what may be called symmetrical children. The twin symmetries of the black child brought up as a white and of the white child brought up as a black lead to a complete deadlock and a total loss of identity for the two characters.

The theme had acquired such obsessional value with Mark Twain that he even wrote a whole story about Siamese twins. 'Those Extraordinary Twins' may be considered as mere extravaganza, but the circumstances in which this piece was written show that these circus freaks made into Italian gentlemen bear a direct relation to the world of Tom and Huck and that of Pudd'nhead Wilson. It is a grotesque but significant caricature of an inner tension between the author's two selves. It epitomizes Mark Twain's permanent and fruitless quest for identity.

Of this tension the last and perhaps the most revealing illustration is the well-known 'Encounter with an Interviewer'. In this pseudo-autobiographical piece Mark Twain explains that he had a twin-brother, that one of the twins was drowned in a bathtub when they were babies, and that he (Mark Twain) is the one that was lost. Such broad comedy does not deserve elaborate literary comment, but it brings the last touch, perhaps the most revealing, to our picture of the inseparable and symmetrical brother in Mark Twain's writings, and must be taken as a symptom of a deep-seated obsession with his double.

That this 'double' in the shape of a green dwarf, which symbolizes the conscience of the hero, was murdered by the hero himself in 'Some Facts Concerning the Recent Carnival of Crime in Connecticut' even gives an unusual and oddly Poe-esque flavour to this inner conflict. In a tormented mood of self-accusation and self-inflicted punishment, Mark Twain wrote: 'I tore him to shreds and fragments. I rent the fragments to bits. I cast the bleeding rubbish into the fire, and drew into my nostrils the grateful incense of my burnt offering.'

The discovery of this pattern will now make us aware of innumerable binary systems on which Mark Twain bases his variations when he spins out the thread of his stories: characters presented in pairs who reveal two sides of the author's personality such as Sid/Tom, Tom/Huck, Huck/Jim; dramatized narrators, as in *Roughing It* and *Life on the Mississippi*, who are identical to and yet different from the author himself; landscapes described in contrasted terms: mountain/water – river/shore – island/cave; and details of literary composition in which the author unwittingly betrays his method and perhaps also the secret topography of his psyche: the two steamboats, taken to be the Almighty by Uncle Daniel in *The Gilded Age*, the two Providences in *Huckleberry Finn*, one for Miss Watson and one for the Widow. When circumstances require several characters on the stage, they are again organized in pairs: Huck/Jim – Duke/Dauphin, or the two sets of children in *The Gilded Age*. These characters have interesting dividing lines: two out of four were adopted; two out of four are boys; Clay and Laura, the two adopted children, show a remarkable spirit of enterprise, whereas Emily and Washington are passive dreamers. In the same book one could also contrast the rôles played by the two colonels, Colonel Sellers and Colonel Selby.

All these examples, however, illustrate the use of a literary device on a conscious or almost conscious level and are not apparently loaded with deep emotional connotations. Several significant episodes in his western books reveal Mark Twain's difficulties with his other self. In order to escape from Pap's cabin, where he is kept prisoner, Huck kills a pig so that the villagers will believe he was murdered. This killing of another self parallels the violent death of a boy, almost the same age as Huck, who, for a while, becomes his inseparable brother, and is called, not by mere coincidence, Buck. A little later, when Huck has to make up a story for the Duke and the Dauphin to explain why he is travelling with Jim, he says that his Pap and his brother Ike died in a steamboat and raft accident; since there was indeed a raft and steamboat accident that involved Jim and Huck, the most significant invention here is that of a new dead brother, with again a very similar first name, Ike.

The Ned Blakely episode in *Roughing It* appears at first as one of those stories, almost irrelevant to the main narrative, that Mark Twain used in the traditional manner of the platform lecturer to vary his effects. Captain Blakely had a fight with Bill Noakes, the mate of another ship, and beat him; Bill Noakes took his revenge by killing the coloured mate of Captain Blakely (the Negro mate was described as his 'pet'). The latter wanted to execute the murderer immediately but was finally persuaded to assemble a court and jury. The case was clear and quick justice rendered. If we analyse the story, we find that the good Negro is confronted with two white men, a good one, Captain Blakely, and a bad one, Bill Noakes. This is a clear case of the 'nigger killer' and the 'nigger lover' in Mark Twain, a conflict that once more ends with the death of one of the twins. In fact, there is a striking symmetry between the two men, the name of Ned Blakely being almost an anagram of Bill Noakes, and we also notice an interesting black and white contrast in the very name of the islands where the story took place – Chincha Islands – for the chinch or chinch bug is a *white* winged *black* bug, an excellent emblem for the ambivalent feelings of the author.

In 'Frescoes from the Past' at the beginning of *Life on the Mississippi*, Huck, who has climbed aboard a raft, is eavesdropping on the conversation of a group of sailors. They are listening to a story told by one of the men. A raft was followed on the river by a strange barrel that seemed to bring a curse on the crew. In order to clarify the mystery, the captain decided to fish it out of the water and open it; the barrel contained a dead child. One of the sailors immediately confessed his crime – he had murdered his son and the body now followed him and haunted him on the river. The name of the baby was Charles William Allbright. When, a few minutes later, Huck is discovered and asked to give his name, he timidly blurts out: Charles William Allbright! This lie or Freudian slip betrays Huck's immediate identification with the dead child who, like himself, was the victim of his father's brutality. This is Huck's third dead 'brother', a striking similarity with the fate of Mark Twain's 'twin'.

The twin brother theme meant more to Mark Twain than a mere farcical device; it brought together, on a more abstract level, two obsessive and complementary patterns: a need for symmetry and a deeper need to destroy that symmetry, the old paradox of men with split personalities who know themselves as one and yet as two, and who dramatize themselves as two with the secret hope of reunifying their ego. This is no doubt the key to Mark Twain's central problem, the conflict between his dream and his despair, an interpretation that another look at his biography will probably bear out.

Fundamentally Mark Twain was a divided man, with allegiances to the North and to New England as well as to the South; he made his home in the East, but his roots were those of a Westerner. He had faith in himself, a sense of efficiency, but he was also besieged by doubts and often depressed. He believed in good causes and yet proved that he had preserved intact a Puritan faith in the corruption and depravation of man. As an American who lived through the days of the Civil War, he felt the conflict between the States as a sharp break, not only between North and South, but also between past and present, between the American dream and American alienation.

In his personal life, in spite of all his jokes on the 'turning point' of his career, Mark Twain knew very well when he became a different man. This happened around 1870, when, after publishing his first famous book, *The Innocents Abroad*, he started using his past as literary material, thus making the first thirty years of his life into a 'tank'. He then drew the line between the 'usable past' and the respectable present.

In 1870 he had married the daughter of a rich New England coal merchant, after falling in love with her portrait during his Holy Land 'excursion' on the *Quaker City* and winning her heart as well as her father's approval during a romantic courtship. Under the warm influence of 'Livy', and perhaps a little before under the tutelage of Mrs Fairbanks on the *Quaker City*, Mark Twain gained a sense of self-confidence. He thoroughly enjoyed the tender atmosphere of Victorian family life at home; he was grateful to his wife who 'civilized' and polished him; he liked being pampered and called 'youth'. Real life and the dream became one. The various ways in which he was tested by Mrs Fairbanks, by Livy's father, by the 'stern Puritans' of New England, and the literary trial of having a book published on the East coast made up a series of *rites de passage* out of which Mark Twain emerged the well-off and respected husband of a beautiful heiress.

During the heyday of success and matrimony, Mark Twain tried to bridge the gap between his two selves, and he symbolically discarded his other self – his lower self. When he revised his Holy

Land articles in order to publish them in book form, Mark Twain took out the slang and the vulgar jokes, but he also eliminated one character altogether, Mr Brown the crude Bœotian. Having to create 'Mark Twain' as a single and unified *persona* involved more than a process of revision. For an author who so completely identified with his narrator such a creation had deep significance. He now had to stand up alone, speak for himself, and drop some of the ambiguities which a dialogue between two stereotyped characters made possible. Knowing perfectly that there were two journalists in him, one for the East coast and one for the West coast, he set himself the task of reconciling them into one author.

Soon after the publication of *The Innocents Abroad*, Mark Twain started writing *Roughing It*, and the structure of the book is again a symptom of a deep crisis. Whereas the first person narrative and the absence of any permanent travelling companion reveals a continued attempt at unification, the old division reappears with a different structural function. Instead of embodying the two poles of his divided self in two characters juxtaposed in space, he interiorized the conflict in one character, the narrator himself divided between his past self, the tenderfoot, and his present self, the man of experience. In this manner the pattern of the inseparable companion, which had been used so far to express his aspirations, dreams and frustrations, became a way to measure the distance between past and present, East and West, innocence and sophistication.

The revised version of the Sandwich Islands articles which make up the last chapters of *Roughing It* contains a revealing image of this haunting other self who plagued Mark Twain all his life. He is described as a 'curious character . . . boring through and through me with his intense eye'. The mysterious man makes the author uncomfortable every time he unexpectedly makes his appearance. He even became so hateful to him that, says Mark Twain, 'for a week or two I stayed mostly within doors not to meet him'. The last time they were confronted, the narrator could barely control his rage when he heard himself accused of being 'ignorant as the unborn babe! Ignorant as unborn *twins*!'

The fundamental split in Mark Twain's personality was not healed by success, fortune, and marriage. Only for a short while were Sam Clemens and Mark Twain, Mark Twain and Mr Brown, reconciled in one character, that of a humorist proudly looking back on his own pilgrim's progress. Mark Twain's life and career remained a permanent dialogue between his two selves.

For Samuel Clemens, 'inseparable companions' were not mere literary creations but projections of his double self, in real life as well as in fiction. With his elder brother Orion, in early ventures in Nevada, or with Henry on Mississippi steamboats, he formed strong partnerships during his youth. In Western mining camps or editorial rooms he developed intimate friendships, nostalgically described in his reminiscences. After 1869 several attempts were made to renew old ties. Among these Western cronies, Dan De-Quille and Joe Goodman came to Hartford to talk about the old days; Bret Harte wrote a play, *Ah Sin*, in collaboration with Mark Twain. But these contacts were re-established out of their context, and they were failures mostly because new 'inseparable brothers' had taken the place of the old ones. The first and most prominent of them all is William Dean Howells, Twain's friend and literary adviser throughout most of his career. Seldom have two writers appeared so complementary as friends and so radically different as artists. With other men Mark Twain formed deep links of friendship, which can often be characterized as partnerships. With Charles Dudley Warner, his neighbour at Nook Farm, he wrote *The Gilded Age*; in Jo Twichell, a minister and another Nook Farm neighbour, he found a companion for his religious and metaphysical moods, but their friendship did not merely serve a spiritual purpose; in 1877 Mark Twain persuaded Twichell to take a trip to Bermuda in his company in order to carry on a dialogue that became material for articles later published in the *Atlantic Monthly* and as a volume called *Some Rambling Notes of an Idle Excursion*. This mode of travelling made into a technical aid for writing clearly shows that the Mark Twain/Mr Brown pattern used in early articles was not a mere literary device borrowed from other humorists, but a privileged way for Mark Twain to acquire experience and to establish a relationship with the world.

When the 'Old Times on the Mississippi' series in the *Atlantic Monthly* was completed, Mark Twain realized that not enough material had been gathered to make a book out of it. As a solution he immediately planned a trip to New Orleans with his friend Howells in order to introduce the theme of the river revisited. This project did not materialize in 1875, but was taken up seven years later. Osgood, his friend and publisher, was the new partner in this venture. Though he is metamorphosed into a poet in *Life on the Mississippi* and left with a very minor part to play, the reappearance of the old pattern is worth noticing.

Among major events of the same kind, the lecture tour organized by the 'twins of genius', Mark Twain and George Washington Cable, in 1884–5, can be given here as a final example of this 'inseparable brother' relationship.

Needless to say, the eagerness with which Sam Clemens adopted pen-names from the beginning of his career is a sign much more than a cause of a fundamental problem with his other self. As 'Thomas Jefferson Snodgrass' or as 'Mark Twain' he played the part of the humorist, but he also wanted to be the reporter, the city editor, the man on the spot with the accurate facts. While serving on the *Territorial Enterprise* in Nevada, he learned from Joe Goodman that 'unassailable certainty is the thing that gives a newspaper the firmest and most valuable reputation'. As an author his ambition was also to tell the truth. But, like Scotty Briggs, Buck Fanshaw's friend, who taught Sunday School in Virginia City, he could also 'tell the beautiful story of Joseph and his brethren to his class, "without looking at the book"'.

Every aspect of his life was 'double-barrelled'. The question he always implicitly or explicitly asked, 'Was it heaven or hell?', admits of no simple answer because heaven and hell were inseparable. How else could we account for his strange behaviour after the death of his father, for instance? It came as such a shock to young Sam that for a while he often walked in his sleep, but the odd consequence of this family tragedy was that he refused to return to school. In this Tom Sawyerish universe, being an orphan and playing truant are two faces of the same coin. The complete lack of reliable information on the childhood of Sam Clemens leaves us to guess the causes of his psychological conflicts, but it seems quite clear that the two strands of tragedy and the dream were closely interwoven from the beginning.

Under a whole range of sociological, historical, and personal factors that made up his two opposite selves – the upstart, the post Civil War candidate for gentility, the radiant and sometimes uncomfortable citizen of Hartford, Connecticut, or the father of prim and proper Suzy Clemens – lies a deeper conflict between Mark Twain's private gods and tormentors as illustrated in the contrasted and complementary metaphors of the bonanza and the cursed treasure, the floating island of happiness and the steamboat of sudden death, the friendly Negro and the hated Indian.

Looking back on his past towards the end of his life, Mark Twain wrote one of those innumerable unfinished stories into which he poured his nightmarish fantasies. He pictured himself living in Indiantown, at the confluence of the Indian River and the Mississippi. One of the most prominent citizens was called Godkin (explicitly interpreted as meaning little God), he was ghastly pale and dressed all in black so that people described him as 'the Corpse'. And the hero, David Gridley, had two faces, the public one, mere sham and humbug, the creation of his wife, and the private one, the real David, a low character, but full of vitality, a Vesuvius whom his wife kept under control 'by providing the rebel's boiler with a safety valve': he was allowed to blow off steam at home.

But who is David Gridley the artist? Is he the frustrated henpecked husband or the 'dusted off' author of *The Prince and the Pauper*? Both were sham-writers, and only the telescoped vision of his torments and dreams brought out the best in Mark Twain.

The most significant image he gave of himself is perhaps that of twin-authors, Huck Finn and Mr Mark Twain, whose worlds so ironically contrasted that they succeeded in telling the truth – mainly.

# 13

# 'YEARS OF THE MODERN':
# THE RISE OF REALISM AND NATURALISM

## Malcolm Bradbury

'Years of the modern! years of the unperform'd!'

Walt Whitman

'I don't intend to wear out my life drudging on this old place', said Wesley Fancher with a bitter oath.

Hamlin Garland, A Son of the Middle Border

'Basil! Basil!' cried his wife, 'This is fatalism!'

William Dean Howells, A Hazard of New Fortunes

I

The subject of this essay is the radical shift that occurred in American fiction in the final decades of the nineteenth century – a shift that was to have the most enormous consequences, for as a result a good many of the directions of twentieth-century American writing were laid down. I have argued elsewhere[1] that it was in the ferments of late realism and naturalism, which so affected American writing during the 1880s and 1890s, that the characters of American Modernism was forged; a Modernism that became apparent in American poetry during the First World War, and transformed American fiction during the 1920s. From the end of the Civil War – when a new generation of writers whose major figures were Henry James, Mark Twain and William Dean Howells brought a new spirit of realism into a form up to then dominated by the great American genre of romance – through to the turn of the century – when a second generation of writers who had imbibed the European news of naturalism, impressionism and decadence came to dominate – American fiction was shaken by the great processes of

---

[1] See Malcolm Bradbury, *The Modern American Novel* (London/New York, Oxford University Press, 1983).

change that were transforming the entire condition of American life. Not only American: in all the countries of the west, as the end of the century approached, people were facing that sharp and necessary encounter with the modern that Nietzsche announced man would have to make, altering all ideas of human nature, society, and the individual's place in history. The intellectual change came from an encounter with change itself, change as a basic continuous and accelerating process, of technologization, urbanization, secularization, modernization. The process was international, and shook all the major convictions and explanations crucial to nineteenth-century thought. But it was to function with an especial force in the United States, the nation most committed to the future, to modernization, to a place of leadership and dominance in the twentieth-century world. And since the novel is neither purely an aesthetic form nor simply a report on life and experience, but a narrative form constructed from our imaginative capacity to explore, explain and interpret the life of consciousness in the world, this transformation process was inevitably to affect the character of American fiction.

The scale of change in American life in the fifty years between the end of the Civil War and the outbreak of the First World War was vast. This was the period of a fundamental redirection in the nature and ideology of American society. If, as Richard Hofstadter suggests, America was born in the country and moved to the city, this was when that difficult journey was made. The Jeffersonian image of America as the land of Enlightenment pastoral, the nation of the self-sufficient farmer, pushing ever west, his spirit of freedom shaped by the character of the frontier itself, changed as the direction of motion altered, and Americans moved from homestead and small town into the frontier of modernity, the city. The American shock-city whose skyscrapers began to thrust upward in a technological miracle was also a place of population explosion and immigrant ghettoes; the rush of new immigration from Europe changed the demographic mix and introduced a new proletariat into the politics of American life. The technology that made the skyscrapers was one of the American wonders, part of an industrial takeoff which was to make the United States the world's dominant industrial nation by the century's turn. The new technologies linked the nation, by railroad and ever more complex industrial and communications systems, in a process that Alan Trachtenberg nicely calls in a book of this title (1982) 'the incorporation of America', transforming even rural and wilderness space into functions of the dominant business system. The system had its new impresarios, the great industrialists and Robber Barons who were now replacing and misplacing the old patriciates of American life. With their changed expenditure of capital came a new pattern of culture, scrutinized by novelists from Mark Twain (*The Gilded Age*, 1873, with Charles Dudley Warner) to Edith Wharton (*The House of Mirth*, 1905), the culture of an age of wealth hungry both for European treasures and the practical rewards of American technology. The very cultural centres of America moved, leaving the East Coast and the classic cultural capital of Boston, speading westward. Between materialist production and conspicuous consumption American culture divided, producing that split of materiality and idealism that became such a strong matter for speculation in American philosophical thought, above all in the tendency of Pragmatism. In general ideology, the world split between the old teleological–religious world-view and the new secular–scientific one – moving, said the great thinker-historian of American transformation, Henry Adams, from the virgin to the dynamo. The dynamos on display at the great American technological exhibitions, like the World's Columbian Exposition held in the shock-city of Chicago in 1893, pointed to a process of exponential growth which was, Adams said, changing the world, from a universe to a multiverse – and displacing all old educations, such as his own.

As the turn of the century came, with its special American promises ('The twentieth century will be American . . .', declared Senator Beveridge, 'The regeneration of the world, physical as well as moral, has begun . . .'), chiliastic feeling intensified, and in cultural and intellectual life the sense of transition seemed to reach its peak – so that (as Larzer Ziff shows in *The American 1890s*) the decade, with its strong generational feel, now appears a borderland between one artistic and intellectual universe and the next. That transformational feeling it shared with the spirit of intellectual and artistic life in other countries in the West; everywhere, says H. Stuart Hughes in *Consciousness and Society* (1958), one senses 'in one form or other a profound psychological change' as a Victorian world-view, a past synthesis, begins to splinter and a new sense of modern awareness enters general thought. The modes of thought that had served the nineteenth century – which had been, said Gertrude Stein, one of the new generation, 'so sure of evolution and prayers' – were being generally dislodged. 'The more we examine the mechanism of thought, the more we shall see that the automatic, unconscious action of the mind enters largely into all its processes', Oliver Wendell Holmes said in 1870, expressing a view that shaped the psychological preoccupation of his novels (*Elsie Venner*, 1861, *A Mortal Antipathy*, 1885). Causal, determining systems functioned not simply in the ever more complex and mechanical operations of society, they also apparently functioned in consciousness itself. William James observed this in *Principles of Psychology* (1890), though for consciousness he preferred not a mechanical but a fluid metaphor: 'A "river" or a "stream" are the metaphors by which it is most naturally described.' The changing processes of systems, the accelerating rhythms of inevitabilities of history, deeply affected the operations of mind – and, for that matter, the aesthetic apprehensions of art, if art could be allowed aesthetic apprehensions as it confronted so much overwhelming sociological material, filling the streets of the cities with struggle and contrast, old forms of culture and new. 'For all these new and evolutionary facts, meanings, purposes, new poetic messages, new forms and expressions, are inevitable', wrote Walt Whitman in 'A Backward Glance O'er Travel'd Roads' (1888). And what was true of poetry was equally true of fiction. As Whitman says, his *Leaves of Grass* over the thirty years from the 1850s to the 1880s recorded a new multitudinousness and had to create a new style of the modern. If no single novelist encompassed late nineteenth-century America as Whitman did in verse, we can nonetheless find the same radical evolution, from a 'romantic' to a 'modernist' universe.

II

*Versions of Realism*

In American fiction, as in other Western literatures, that path from Romanticism to Modernism was taken through Realism, the movement or tendency that from the 1850s onward dominated the spirit of fiction. The movement was international and had its theoretical roots in post-1848 Paris. To the tradition of American fiction it seemed particularly foreign, for in general American novels had taken the path away from society and history, towards myth and the encounter with nature and the wilderness. Yet from the 1850s onwards the signs were evident; the work of Melville and Hawthorne is already filled with the sense of a rushing American history driving toward a vastly more technological and mechanical future, and shows powerful new intuitions about the implications of an age that was devoting itself to utilitarianism, mechanism, secularism and urbanism. Leo Marx points out that in their work the machine has entered the garden of American writing, amending the timeless world of American romance, for the changing spirit of American society called for a new materiality in fiction, that 'very minute fidelity' of which Hawthorne speaks and to which his work is drawn. After the Civil War, realism seemed in America to take on a special meaning and flourish as nowhere else. It became an essential literary means for coming to terms with the new American history – the hard facts and dark lessons of the Civil War, the new social and industrial processes, the exploration of the spreading mass of American society and American geography as the nation enlarged, the rising conflicts of an age of massive urbanization and immigration, the new democratic scepticism. Its geographical locus became the places of change, the economically stressed homestead, the city, the battlefield. It offered writers a way of approaching new social facts and pressures, gave a new secular and scientific discourse for exploring an age of pragmatism and Social Darwinism, permitted both the progressive voice of social criticism and the pessimistic vision of an age overwhelmed by process and science. It became the natural voice of a generation of writers who had not grown up under Boston tutelage, but came from the farmlands and the cities and wrote in a familiar vernacular.

Realism was in no way a new word, or a new aesthetic; indeed almost every literary movement, however mannered, has in some fashion claimed realism as its aim. This is one of the most troubling of all the critical terms; reality – any relativist must assert – is a matter of interpretation, and not the expression of the nature of a thing, as America's most complex realist, Henry James, was to recognize. One age's realism is another's fiction or falsehood; this might encourage us to say (this is Northrop Frye's argument in discussing the five basic modes of art in *Anatomy of Criticism*) that literature has always moved ever more toward realism, reducing over the historical span the status of its heroes (from gods to kings to equals to inferiors), its dependence on myth in favour of contingency, the level of its telling (from high modes to low ones to ironic ones). Realism, then, is more than plain reportage of fact, but a structure of fiction which has a sceptical or demythologizing aspect. It has been particularly intimate with the novel as a discursive prose form, capable of assimilating the empirical and the contingent. It is a form masked as innocence, a structure of discourse that often seems a direct window to familiarity. But the manners and methods of realism take many different paths, from the strong empirical aspect of fidelistic realism to the concern with

large and impersonal forces and processes that we find in that
onward development of realism which is called 'Naturalism'. There
were many realisms in the America of the late nineteenth century:
the realism of social and moral analysis, and the realism of political
indignation, the realism of local colour and the realism of the mean
streets and the ghetto, the realism of fact-laden document, the
realism of self-conscious technique. What is clear is that realism
was the growing mode, a move away from the bias toward romance
and self-creating fictions that had marked the work of Cooper and
Poe, and even Hawthorne and Melville.

So realism came as local colour, that extension of geographical
but also empirical curiosity that we find in regional works like
Edward Eggleston's vernacular *A Hoosier Schoolmaster* (1871),
Edgar Watson Howe's *Story of a Country Town* (1883), or Sarah
Orne Jewett's fine stories of life in Maine, *The Country of the Pointed
Firs* (1896), where the influence of Flaubert is evident. It came as
anti-romantic war fiction displaying the pain and price of the Civil
War, like John William DeForest's *Miss Ravenel's Conversion from
Secession to Loyalty* (1867), or Albion Tourgee's Reconstruction
novel *A Fool's Errand* (1879). It was apparent in the rising field of
vernacular, often Southern or South-Western, folk humour, the
tradition that fed the fiction of Mark Twain; but equally in the
fiction of social process and political corruption that exposed the
moral flaws of the Gilded Age, like Henry Adams's *Democracy*
(1880), John Hay's *The Breadwinners* (1884) or Hamlin Garland's *A
Spoil of Office* (1892). It was a broad new temper, concerned
whether critically or affirmatively with exploring the new American
fact. But over the period from 1865 to the 1890s we can see a
marked change in its fundamental assumptions. The three great
figures of the epoch, Twain, Howells, and James, began writing in
the first, post-Civil War generation, and carried on into the second,
the era of the 1890s, and beyond. They were realists in different
senses – indeed Twain and James have often been seen as representing the polar extremes of American literary culture, redskin and
paleface, populist and cosmopolitan – but shared a general concept
of fidelistic realism of much the kind Howells was to fight for in his
journalism and express in *Criticism and Fiction* (1891): 'I confess I
do not care to judge any work of the imagination without first
applying this test to it. We must ask ourselves before anything else,
Is it true? – true to the motives, the impulses, the principles that
shape the life of actual men and women?' Howells spoke for the
spirit of Flaubert, George Eliot or Tolstoy, under American condi-

tions; realism's task was to take commonplace subjects and individual experience seriously, and treat them faithfully, making fiction not a source of symbolic or transcendental truths but of its own specific truth. Yet in all three writers, if in different fashions, we can see, over the period of the Gilded Age, this sympathetic fidelity grow ironized, the distance between writer and subject become less sympathetic, essentially more remote. By the 1890s, in consonance with a general mood, all three were in the grip of a profound pessimism, expressed in growing techniques of distance and added acts of artistic suspicion. And in this angularity and bitterness they display, what Northrop Frye calls the 'ironic' mode of writing, whose suspicion of fidelity and sense of aesthetic displacement leads toward Modernism.

This, for both social and intellectual reasons, was the broad direction of realism's evolution. A similarly ironic view emerged in the work of the new generation that was to come suddenly and strongly to notice in the 1890s – the writers of populist and progressive realist-naturalism like Stephen Crane, Hamlin Garland, Frank Norris, Ambrose Bierce, Theodore Dreiser and Jack London. Most of them took Howells as their guide and forerunner, but they dislocated his emphasis on realism as the humanization of the commonplace. For them, realism meant the recognition of an inhuman reality, a process of determinants allowing men little opportunity to define the basis of their own existence. Realism was indeed, as for Howells, not just a telling of the 'truth' about people but a matter of directing attention to people not enfranchised before in fiction – people like Howells' Silas Lapham, Norris's McTeague, Crane's Maggie Johnson, Dreiser's Jennie Gerhardt, the inelegant new businessmen and salesmen, the rural and urban proletariat. But behind them was a changing palpable world, of new experience in shock-cities, tenements, warehouses, sweatshops, skyscrapers, trusts. And that meant a new approach, to the forces of technology, science and materialism; an approach that did not idealize or humanize. Their world is not a world of culture and morals, or of individual hopes and satisfactions. It is a world of iron forces that 'really' determine existence: the biological constituents of man, the impersonal, machine-like operations of society, engaged in a climactic warfare seen at an analytic distance. For it was as if the mechanisms of science that were creating the new world might also solve them; so the novel must forget its humanism and become scientific. The traditional sequence of fictional plot, in which human beings fulfil their individual lives within the perspective of social reality, begins to fail for these writers; man's place in the universe and in the fictive plot becomes problematic. The writer, like Frank Norris's poet Presley in *The Octopus* (1901) might seek for the romance of human life but 'in the end, [he] found grain rates and unjust freight tariffs'.

As for 'reality' itself, that over two generations had changed too. Take, for example, Mark Twain's late bleak novel *Pudd'nhead Wilson* (1894). Twain starts it in the world of 'Howellsian' reality, evoking the dense society of Dawson's Landing, a slave-holding town on the Mississippi before the Civil War, snug, simple, but with clear social and moral virtues. He ends it in another 'reality', critical, distanced, derived in part from the scientific spirit of the outsider Pudd'nhead, who solves the problems of the town – they come when a black and white baby have been changed in the cradle – by the amoral science of finger printing, so turning to the one imprinted physical identity left in a world become one of disguises and shams, conscious and unconscious. Society and morals are historical variables; genetic inheritance is absolute. Though the moral life has its claims, though the community may be important, other forces make us what we are – and what we are is very little. The novel is devastatingly ironic; there are no real moral motives in this world, and few free choices. Twain's views are not just a 'personal' pessimism, as we are sometimes told. They draw on the main themes of the period – the sense of moral despair or detachment deriving from environmentalist or determinist views of man or society; the fascination with scientism, especially that having to do with biological, social or psychological evolution; the sense of social division, between past values and new brute forces with their claims. In two literary generations, American writers had turned their emphasis from the imaginative and creative aspects of works of fiction to the special capacity of fiction to particularize and authenticate a shared, known world. But now that familiar world was one, not simply of familiar experience, but of brute, obstructive, menacing reality – a complex of confinements and determinants.

Not all the writers of the 1890s went so far; but the conviction thrives then with especial force, as if American writing had found a native theme and mode. In the themes and forms of naturalism we can find a dominant stylistic temper for the decade. If, as Roland Barthes claims, one power of the novel is to give 'to the imaginary the formal guarantee of the real', then it is from such clusters of half-hopeful pessimism, such 'objective' yet half-doubted visions, that the communal conspiracy that we call 'reality' was made at this time. It was not just American life that had changed in a half-century; so had the entire idea of 'reality' as it expressed itself in fiction, in its view of what was basic to human experience and what structures and orders might embody it.

## Aspects of Naturalism

In 1891 – the year when Herman Melville, the only one of the 'classic' American novelists to live on into the new industrializing and corporealizing new America, died obscurely with his reputation almost gone, and at the start of a decade which saw a remarkable new texture enter the spirit of American fiction – the French novelist and disciple of Zola, Paul Alexis, produced what is now perhaps his most famous work, a five word telegram, sent in response to an enquiry by a Parisian literary journalist, Jules Huret, which read: 'Naturalism not dead. Letter follows.' Huret was investigating the place in modern letters of a broad congerie of neo-positivistic and progressive tendencies in fiction and drama that had been acquiring momentum as the European 'modern' movement from about the 1870s onward – the tendency that Georg Brandes had called the 'modern breakthrough' and that we particularly associate with Ibsen, Zola and, less precisely, Tolstoy. Indeed, as Huret sensed, by the 1890s naturalism in Europe was well past its heyday. Its intellectual framework was dissolving, its major proponents disappearing, and it was under pressure from two opposite sources – the opinion of the 'rearguard' (it was being prosecuted in public opinion and in England in the courts for its 'foulness') and the opinion of the avant garde, which questioned its status to be *the* modern movement. For in its emphasis on science and the denotative function of the word, it was giving way to a new stylistic phase of much more symbolist, post-impressionist bias, as the whole notion of a single, securable reality evaporated in the minds of other thinkers and artists. However, Alexis, in the letter that did indeed follow, and was printed by Huret in his *Enquête sur l'évolution littéraire* (1891), resisted the claims of the other movements – the decadents, the neo-symbolists, the psychological writers – to be the onward movements of literature; in this, he resisted some of the strongest currents of modernism. His argument was that naturalism did not simply represent a stylistic phase that would pass, as styles do; naturalism, with its dedication to science and truth, would be an essential part of the main social and intellectual currents of the twentieth century. Of Europe, on the whole, this claim was inexact

– except of countries like Russia, where Alexis's implication that realism or naturalism was part of that historical 'process' where false consciousness yields to true, where the dialectic of history takes the world closer to an ultimate reality, survived as dogma. But if we want a western example of a literary culture that has perpetuated naturalism, then it is to the United States we must turn, where the tendency has persisted with a special force into subsequent writing – not only as a fascination with poverty, violence and deprivation, as in the work of writers like Dreiser, James T. Farrell or Nelson Algren, but as a belief about the need for an immersion into the historically expanding pressures on human consciousness, as in Fitzgerald, Hemingway and Mailer.

Naturalism then, Alexis might have said, was alive and well and living in the United States, partly as a result of the natural momentum of a local colour tradition that, in an era when the intellectual felt dispossessed, assimilated the 'mugwump' passions of reform and began to take the gilding off the gilded age; partly as a facet of the journalism that was, in a heterodox democratic society, an essential medium of politics and social interaction; partly as a conscious aesthetic campaign referring to and cosmopolitanly invigorated by European influences. As European intellectuals were turning from Ibsen or Zola to Strindberg, and from positivism to intuitionalism, from Marx to Freud, American intellectuals were, with a *provincial* cosmopolitanism, turning to Zola. At about the time of Alexis's statement, Frank Norris – who like George Moore, the earlier, Anglo-Irish disciple of naturalism, had spent his aesthetic apprenticeship in London and Paris as an art-student – returned to study at the University of California at Berkeley, decided to be a writer, and was seen around campus with a 'yellow paper-covered novel of Zola in his hand'. Stephen Crane too, though not an avid reader of other men's books, was busy with Zola. At about the same date Hamlin Garland, in the process of his strenuous self-education, was wrestling with Zola's *Le roman expérimental*. Norris called himself a 'naturalist', Garland was a 'veritist', and Crane's own tendency was, as he ill-defined it, 'towards the goal partially described by that misunderstood and abused word, realism'. If one added to their works books like Harold Frederic's *The Damnation of Theron Ware* (1896), Henry Blake Fuller's *The Cliff-Dwellers* (1893), the early novels Henry Harland wrote as 'Sidney Luska' before he became editor of the English decadent *Yellow Book*, the novels of Jack London and Theodore Dreiser's *Sister Carrie* (1900), then one had something like a movement, an essential – though as we shall see, not the only – temper of the generation of the 1890s.

But to writers in an America now yielding its old ideals to vast upheavals, new ethnic and social mixes, a new heterogeneity of values and mores, the attraction of naturalism was more than the attraction of a theory. In *On Native Grounds* (1942), Alfred Kazin argues that American realism and naturalism did not, as in Europe, grow out of systematic ideas and literary doctrines, but emerged on native grounds 'out of the bewilderment, and thrived on the simple grimness, of a generation suddenly brought face to face with the pervasive materialism of industrial capitalism'. It was a primitive movement coming from awareness of the changes occurring in American life as the frontier closed, immigration increased, the problems of cities grew, and the progressive spirit intensified; it 'poured sullenly out of agrarian bitterness, the class hatreds of the eighties and nineties, the bleakness of small-town life, the mockery of the nouveaux riches, and the bitterness in the great new pro-letarian cities', and had 'no centre, no unifying principle, no philosophy, no joy in its coming, no climate of experiment'. It was indeed a remarkably pervasive and in many ways a notably local movement, and though it was a cosmopolitan tendency it set many American writers free of international literary influences as never before, turning them toward the detail of their own environment; 'Write of what you know! Write of your very own!' cried Edward Eggleston. As Garland said, it was democratic and very American, though also given to celebration of the superman and the great leader, in Jack London's work, for instance. It contained Utopian passions, though also bleak dystopian despair about the future, foreseeing worlds redeemed or else lost by new science and tech-nology (Edward Bellamy's *Looking Backward*, Howells's *A Traveller from Altruria* and Ignatius Donnelly's *Caesar's Column*). It could produce the pessimism of Ambrose Bierce's deeply macabre tales, or the boyish adventurous optimism of Jack London's; be a bitter literature of protest, a cry from the ghetto like Abraham Cahan's *Yekl* (1896), or from black life, like Paul Laurence Dunbar's novel *The Uncalled* (1898); or a work of muckraking socialist optimism, like Upton Sinclair's Chicago stockyard novel *The Jungle* (1906).

But if it regularly emphasized the fact and the knockabout of life, it did also have doctrines and literary theories. Yet again, when they are stated they disagree: realism differed from veritism differed from naturalism. 'In advocating veritism' wrote Garland 'I am not to be understood as apologizing for the so-called realists of the day. In fact they are not realists from Howells's point of view. They are indeed imitators of the French who seem to us sex-mad . . .' In turn Norris dismissed realism as a stultifying world of tea-cup tragedies, and demanded a naturalism that was a drama of the people encompassing 'the vast, the monstrous, the tragic', and looking to the unconscious parts of life, 'the unplumbed depths of the human heart, and the mystery of sex'. The sexual unconscious and the battle for women's freedom was one crucial theme, at its finest in Kate Chopin's *The Awakening* (1899), a novel about the erotic and emotional self-discovery of a New Orleans woman which ends, as many 1890s stories do, in self-abnegation and defeat. The unexpressed everywhere called for expression in a great revolt against the moral view and the Genteel Tradition – though the call for greater sexual candour was not really to become an issue until Theodore Dreiser tried to publish *Sister Carrie*, his story of an amoral sexual opportunist who is also a life-force, in 1900, a notable book which shocked its publisher (as even today complicated 'puritan' abhorrences underlie the American obsession with sexual frankness). Theories, literary and political, played their part in the general campaign to speak the unspoken, enfranchize the disenfranchized, muckrake, demythologize, and expose.

So realism partly came because of what America now was – a society in the forefront of modernizing change and shifting values. What particularly stirred American realist-naturalism was the coming of the modern, the consciousness of new cultural frontiers which freed individuals from old dependencies but submitted them to new ones. There was the city, drawing people in and changing the map of their consciousness and experience; the machine, changing the look of the street and the place of work, transfiguring communications; there was process, the feeling that change was a series of systems the human mind could not hope to master or control. The process, modernization, came out of the logic of American conditions and the facilities of the American mind, what Thorstein Veblen called its 'peculiarly matter-of-fact quality' which made it see process as cultural growth. If change was everywhere, then to stand and observe it was in effect to be a realist. One assumption behind realism was of the epical and seamless nature of experience, and hence the endless open extension of art. The writer amid the open scenario took his life-slice out of the many, finding his prototype in the journalist, at school to life, able to collect and personalize the facts with the authenticity of art while claiming for the art the authenticity of fact. Stephen Crane gives us a fable of this view of things in *The Red Badge of Courage*, as his hero yields ideals, individualism and personal imagination to an 'unselfish' immersion in which the mind becomes a machine: 'His accumulated thought upon such subjects was used to form scenes', notes Crane, and the passive mind taking in impressions becomes his hero's redemption, a synchronicity of thought and thing, a merging with the laws of life and history. Form, morals, imagination are therefore not enough; Henry Fleming must 'have blaze, blood, and danger, even as a chemist requires this, that and the other'. The result *can* be a kind of non-art – H. G. Wells once spoke of Crane as coming 'stark' into writing – but even journalism is never *really* an invisible language: it is a language of experience and a language of scepticism. The novel of experience easily becomes the novel of problems, mixing the authentic voice of one who has seen with the linguistic postures of social science. Hence by taking the rawer, often the sensational and violent, places of experience, by asserting authorial authenticity and immersion, a new disposition of the forces of fiction comes through. Realism is *not* simply a mode of getting down the brute fact and accumulated detail of life; it is, inevitably, an attitude towards, a theory of, literature. 'We are forming', said Hamlin Garland, 'a literature from direct contact with life, and such a literature can be estimated only by unbiased minds and by comparison with nature and the life we live.' But, however much the artist tried to think of himself as an initiate in experience rather than an initiate in art, however much he tried to desubstantiate the self-existence of language, to prove his truth by his wounds, realism was still an aesthetic proceeding. It had no new-given power to define reality. Rather it sought to redefine reality in literature, in the assumption that 'reality' – the familiar experience of the world, the ways men saw, knew, and felt it, the conditions determining their lives – had changed and that the modes of analysis were also in change.

When Zola, in 1880, made his famous statement on naturalism he called it *Le roman expérimental*. The analogy of experiment was scientific; the experimental novelist is 'he who accepts proved facts, who shows in man and society the mechanism of the phenomena which science has mastered, and who lets his personal sentiments enter in only concerning those phenomena whose determinism is not yet fixed, while he tries to control this personal sentiment, this *a priori* idea, as well as he can by observation and fact'. But Zola also meant something more like what we would mean by the 'experimental' novel. For the realistic word is the word that unveils and strips away; it brings about the modern; science and scepticism replace temporary truth with permanent realities. Zola's sensibility is transitional and apocalyptic; the new science of man is the wisdom of those who experimentally transcend the present. The characteristic fables of late nineteenth-century realism are tragedies of hope – fables of confinement and freedom, the confinement of a world that seems to work by logics and processes beyond the control of any individual destiny, the freedom of a world that seems open-ended to the future. They are works of cultural change, complex mixtures of joy and despair. While it is tempting to take them as forms of the ultimate statement of the literality of fiction, the literature of encounter with actuality, they are, rather, structures of changing knowledge facing and trying to fix a changing social experience. And that change in experience was, in post-Civil War America, deeply etched and ambiguously felt, through oscillating conflicts of emotion and intellect, hope and dismay – the inevitable ambivalences of a world whose conventional 'reality' was being disjointed.

The American realist writers of these decades are not the greatest figures in the world tally of realist genius. But there is an appropriate purity of distillation in their writing, as pressure appropriate to the tensions of a wildly booming society, which makes them crucial. At times this realism is little more than journalism. At others it is basically a sensibility, of the sort defined under 'MUGWUMP' in Ambrose Bierce's *Devil's Dictionary* (1906):

MUGWUMP, n. In politics one afflicted with self-respect and addicted to the vice of independence. A term of contempt.

That is to say, it is a literature of those who feel denied access, those for whom the real is contingent but might be necessary, those for whom the word is a substitute for the possibility of a moral or political act. Stylistically, the sense of individual powerlessness draws together the prose of patrician and populist, as represented in figures as seemingly opposite as Henry Adams and Hamlin Garland. But in certain writers it is also a literature of complex aesthetic passion. Consciously experimental, it expressed itself in numerous manifestoes; no previous American literary movement had stimulated so much public and private argumentation. Its texts lie in the essays and prefaces of Henry James, various discussions by Howells, culminating in *Criticism and Fiction* (1891), Garland's *Crumbling Idols* (1894), and Norris's *The Responsibilities of the Novelist* (1903); and though only James's writings rigorously consider how art creates 'the air of reality', to the point of constituting a great blueprint for modern creation, the other works display that the issues of realism and naturalism were now a matter of profound aesthetic concern. But while one face of realism is its apparently raw or critical address to subjects hitherto unexplored in American literature, another was the growth and refinement of artistic theory. And indeed, as time passed, the movement refined itself from one movement into another, evolving toward an ironic, impressionistic, pre-Modernist mode, its spirit of scepticism applied not only to life but the literary artefact itself. The change thus led the way into the aesthetic complexity of the modern arts, which is why the achievement of its key figures is so important.

III

*William Dean Howells* (1837–1920)

Like Mark Twain, who has been discussed elsewhere in this book, William Dean Howells was to function at the centre of American culture for the entire length of the Gilded Age, to experience its hopes, respond to its changes, and watch the flavour of American literature change around him. Twain and Howells were close literary contemporaries, starting their literary careers in the period of Civil War; both grew up in the West and came east to what was still the cultural and commercial hub of the nation, gathering up a wealth of national experience in doing so; both were essentially bred in journalism, and always had a sense of a substantial national audience they knew, provoked and satisfied. Both had a strong sense of the American past that was disappearing under the pressure of a world far more nakedly commercial, dominated by money-sense and moral crudity; both looked back to that old world but predominantly wrote about the new one. Both were literary moralists, if of different brands; where Twain's moral unease with the age that also buoyed him up often took him below social and moral constraints into the world of play and the pleasure-principle, Howells searched through commonplace social life to find the ways in which it might be morally invigorated, and this took him into a steadfast exploration of both the local detail and the general principles of American democratic-commercial society. Howells was born just two years after Twain, in 1837, in Martin's Ferry, Ohio, and (like Twain) he grew up in an atmosphere of journalism and the printshop, setting type for his Welsh printer-father and educating himself in newspaper work. When a campaign biography of Abraham Lincoln provided funds for a trip to Boston, he found an almost dreamlike welcome at the hands of Hawthorne, Lowell and Holmes, who greeted the representative literary Westerner with, said Holmes, an apostolic 'laying-on of hands'. The symbolism was apt; after political patronage won for him the post of American consul in Venice, Howells came back to settle in Cambridge on the *Atlantic Monthly*, that influential literary organ; and in 1871 he became its editor, a powerful cultural arbiter – and above all the main promoter of the new movement of realism, that movement of democratic compassion that was now shaping the work of the Europeans he admired, and seemed singularly appropriate to American experience.

Now Howells – the 'Dean of American Letters' – in some ways became Boston. He aided the young, adminstered critical reputations; he spoke for literature and the voice of taste. His novels brilliantly evoked the city in late nineteenth-century detail, especially the admirable *A Modern Instance* (1882) and *The Rise of Silas Lapham* (1885). He was always to see Boston somewhat from outside, and regard journalism in much the spirit of the provincial aspirant; and he never quite ceased, to be a journalist, writing always under high pressure. He felt the need to balance the 'idealizing' tendency of his adoptive New England with the 'realizing' tendency of New York. Indeed in 1889 he made what he calls in the preface to *A Hazard of New Fortunes* (1890) – a title, and a book, clearly very significant to him – a 'transition to the commercial metropolis'; though the move to New York was also a transition to a more radical intellectual ferment. It went along with other transitions: 'after fifty years of optimistic content with "civilization" and its ability to come out all right in the end', he told Henry James, in the fellowship of exile, 'I now abhor it, and feel that it is coming out all wrong in the end, unless it bases itself anew on a real equality'. He had turned to Socialism; he now sought to write in the Tolstoyan manner; he took to Henry George, Edward Bellamy and the political and literary conventions of the new generation of realists. Earlier he had assumed that an American realism would demonstrate a joy in the democratic commonplace, and that American novelists should concern themselves with 'the more smiling aspects of life, which are the more American, and seek the universal in the individual rather than in the social interests'. That view changed as well. It was all, he said in this preface, a 'moment of great psychological import' – one which, characteristically, he identified not only with his own emotions but with the nation's, which, too, were turning to 'nobler and larger' issues. In some sense, he rescinded his earlier work, but never quite achieved the task he set himself in the later; and in his last years his reputation began to lapse.

It has never fully recovered; Howells remained the most under-valued of the great American novelists. Certainly his work is un-even; from his first novel, *Their Wedding Journey* (1872), onward, he was producing something like a novel a year, most of them delight-ful but slight, touched with an attractive but provincial simplicity that suggests an undeveloped Henry James. But at best they are remarkably fine, for reasons that go beyond the fulfilment of a theory. For if the socio-moral novel, the novel which links the world of society with the world of value, has any firm footing in America, then it is in the work of Howells. James, in a sense, took the vein further, but America never provided a full field for his exploration; what strikes one about his 'American' novels is an absence of a properly testing experience, an absence that becomes devastating irony in a book like *Washington Square*. But Howells, unlike James, welcomed provinciality as a kind of cultural virtue, and he made it into a supreme literary material. His books come closer than those of any other American writer to a certain form of European realism; they demand to be read with that sort of exact tonal responsiveness, an acceptance of delicate moral signals, that we require in reading Jane Austen. But they are still insistently American; Howells is the great delineator of the moral pains and pleasures of the socially mobile and growingly material world of the post-Civil War decades. His characteristic theme is that of much nineteenth-century European fiction: how to relate a material to a moral economy, how to move in a mobile society. His characteristic issues belong to the same line of fiction: to whom does the nation belong, where does the moral inheritance lie, does money free or enslave? His charac-teristic heroes are those in upward momentum, the raw and the uncertain, the provincial spirits seeking success. Around the fringes of several of his novels lies an older patriciate to whom the opportunity to link moral and material satisfaction has been granted; they are cultural guardians, these Hallecks and Coreys, and Howells sees partly from their viewpoint. But his imaginative involvement is with the new men, the modern instances, for whom social movement contains the risk of moral unbalance. His world is a world of classes – but those tenuously stated, delicately stratified *American* classes whose manners fascinate him, but which are never quite permanent enough to subsist as a total lifestyle or culture. The difficulty of vivifying the moral centre of this not quite solid social world is Howells's sharpest concern, and the arena of his characters' most testing exposure.

In fact, that testing is usually plumbed in a particular context – the world of personal relations, above all the relations of the free, informal American family. In the weight attached to family life he reminds us, again, of English or of Russian novelists, and perhaps especially of Turgenev, whom he praised and who praised him. Here the male realm of work and money is alleviated, but also brought under scrutiny. It is the place where early love – 'romance' – modulates into affectionate ordinariness. It is the place where our moral and emotional lives are most exactly and unsparingly revealed. As his fiction develops he reaches out for larger and larger scoops of American life – the immigrant poor and labouring groups of *Annie Kilburn* (1888), or the social complexities of a New York both reactionary and radical in *A Hazard of New Fortunes* (1890) – but he continues to set these large public considerations against the small yet fundamental scale of domesticity. If at times this seems limiting, it is also the basis of his fullest successes. For if marriage and the family are, as he suggests (a little too schematically) in *A Modern Instance* (1882), peculiarly American forms of self-transcendence, they serve a vital function in upholding humaneness in a world whose old cultural and religious sanctions are weakened. *A Modern Instance*, which is about the waning marriage of Marcia and Bartley Hubbard and its final collapse in the Indiana divorce-courts, we are caught up in the electric play of their love affair, their marriage, the stages through which it deteriorates, their almost undeliberated separation. An equivalence is implied between the national economy and a personal economy; private lives become subtly 'illustrative'. So, in subjecting to imaginative analysis the daily dealings of a couple who are, as he insists, 'spiritually poverty-stricken', Howells perceives more than those day-to-day exchanges. Nonetheless it is in them that life is tested. 'Don't despise the day of small things!' says the lawyer Atherton in the novel, for it is in these that life is made or marred.

In that book Bartley Hubbard fails where it is granted to him to succeed – in the emotional life. But in Howells's best novel, *The Rise of Silas Lapham* (1885), the theme is reversed to create a more complex fable of moral and material achievement. Again the action is set among the 'middle' class of the Gilded Age, between established, cultured society (or Society) and the unconscious poor. Silas

Lapham has discovered a new source of paint and gone into business in the 'Poor Richard' way, making money through his own devices. The Civil War interrupts, and he comes back from soldiering into a new era of business. 'The day of small things was past', he says of this transformed commercial atmosphere. The phrase Howells had once put into Atherton's mouth now carries a different injunction; Lapham must go and extend, in fact, beyond his moral means. His paint business thrives. Moving economically upward, he becomes one of the solid Men of Boston, with a potential entrée into Society – in which he is however comically inept. The novel begins at the height of his success but with Lapham lost in a world too big for him. It is of course not only his social clumsiness that puts him at risk; rather it is that the climate in which the individualistic virtues can be held to be sanctified by wealth is over. The test is not only whether Lapham can enter Society, but – more important – whether he can relate his precepts to his social place. He is morally adrift; and the true rise of Silas Lapham comes at the end of the book, with his financial fall, when he refuses a corrupt deal that might save his fortune and reverts to a simple family life. This triumph in a way represents a reversion to his older, simpler, more provincial American virtues; but Lapham is left with the paradox that virtue does not bring its social rewards, nor sin its economic penalties. In acting as he does, he has somehow acquired a new moral economy, a fresh confirmation that virtue resides in the everyday workings of engrained good instinct.

We often call Howells's novels 'photographic' – the metaphor starts perhaps with Henry Adams's warm review of Howells's first novel – and their illustrative quality, their way of proceeding as much by vignette as plot ('The last thing for which I care', said Howells once, a little inaccurately, going on to claim that his effort lay in character and dramatic incident), their luminous vigour of the commonplace, is essential to their realism. Certainly Howells has in abundance the novelist's intrinsic gift for selecting precisely those elements in a situation that substantiate veracity (as in the tiny scene in *A Modern Instance* when the newly-married Hubbards dine at a cheap Boston restaurant and Howells notes the plates laid 'with a coarse red doily in a cocked hat on each', later adding that they do not betray use 'like the indiscreet paper napkin'). That sort of fully vested attention, that 'photographic' detailing of the amassed stuff and material of contemporary life, is a major feature of his talent. He is a superb recorder of his world in its liveliest places, a world that he saw with clarity because he was always contrasting it with

Europe, a world that he knew as a world of industrial capitalism. But his is not a realism of the contingent crowd; and his passion, which turned later to a radical passion, is to restore to the crowd the awareness of community, of moral brotherhood. His novels create a feeling, not only of familiarity, but of the *virtues* of the familiar – for the ordinary can betray us, as it betrays Bartley Hubbard, or, seen morally, it can save us, as it saves Silas Lapham. So if one part of Howells's realism is a realism of presentation, a fidelistic response to America's proliferating material universe, another part is a moral realism, a realism of assessment, a scepticism which nonetheless urges on that universe the test of an ordinary virtue. Hence Howells patently 'intervenes' in his novels, as the omniscient narrator, the rhetorical persuader, the maker of moral plots. But his notion of character, his way of structuring his tales according to the moral growth of a single life, his sense of the opportunity for the individual to determine the basis of his being, his sense of the rational and conscious powers of the human mind to overcome instinct, make him a very different sort of realist from some, at least, in the generation that succeeded him, though he was always to exercise a signficant influence over them.

## Hamlin Garland (1860–1940)

Some 25 years after Howells's pilgrimage to Boston and literature, a writer of that younger generation, Hamlin Garland, made a similar journey. Born on a Wisconsin farm, raised on the Iowa prairie, he had gone to the local seminary, imbibing the new spirit of Populism. By 1884, when he went to Boston to study in the Public Library, he had taken in the theories of Darwin, Spencer, Taine and Henry George, was a devout evolutionist, and yearned for a radical literature of 'stern facts'. Literature was, he felt, the manifestation of social forces at work, and he read avidly in contemporary writers, European and American, who confirmed his faith that a new age was coming to birth; 'The trouble is,' he said in a lecture, 'we have no novelist who can feel the great mental revolutions now going on around us.' By 1888 he was engaged in three novels and a play, and during the 1890s, helped by Howells, he published prolifically in the mode of what, in *Crumbling Idols*, he announced as 'veritism'. In 1893 he turned back west, to attend the World's Columbian Exposition held in Chicago, where Jane Addams worked in Hull House, and at the University a new urban sociology was under way; Chicago was the classic model for rapid, melting-pot urbanization, a scenario for those symptoms of amorphous growth and cultural relativism, for an agglomerating and accelerating environment bigger than the compass of any individual or traditional culture, that Georg Simmel had described in his 'The Metropolis and Mental Life'. At the Exposition, Harriet Monroe – self-appointed laureate to the event, later founder of *Poetry (Chicago)* – declaimed the dedication ode; and Garland (though disquieted by the sexuality of some of the new French painters on exhibition) delivered a paper on 'Local Colour in Fiction' and cried: 'Here flames the spirit of youth. Here throbs the heart of America . . .' In the same year he wrote a piece on the 'Literary Emancipation of the West', and in later days he recalled the mood of the city's aesthetic awakening: 'From being a huge, muddy windy market-place [Chicago] seemed about to take its place among the literary capitals of the world.' In that year, too, Henry Blake Fuller published *The Cliff-Dwellers*, about the Chicago business skyscraper and the crude materialism of the city, its ambiguous heroes being the financiers, its mood being that of ironically surveying the one great city in which 'all its citizens have come for the one common, avowed object of making money'. Dreiser was later to claim that it was Fuller who pioneered the way to a real expression of American life. But that was Garland's aim too. And he, like Fuller and later Norris and Dreiser, saw Chicago as the point of transition between the old world and the new. Especially in 1893: 1893 was indeed a good year for the transitional sensibility – the year of several important realist works, like Stephen Crane's *Maggie*, it was also the year when Henry Adams, at the same Chicago Exposition, first saw the dynamos on display and felt that they gave to history 'a whole new phase'. For the period of the 1890s, Garland functioned at the centre of this sort of sensibility; the age of the old was over, the age of the modern at hand; new thought and new consciousness in new places were being born; the evolutionary wheel was turning. The literature of the past, the literary shrines of the past, offered no guide; even earlier realism missed the *new* reality. 'We are about to enter the dark', he wrote in *Crumbling Idols*. 'We need a light. This flaming thought from Whitman will do for the searchlight of the profound deeps. All that the past was not, the future will be.' But by the turn of the century Garland had deserted Chicago and realism.

His best work falls in a small span of years, and is found in the stories in *Main-Travelled Roads* (1891: extended edition, 1893); *Jason Edwards* (1892), a novel which explores through the misfortunes of its unlucky hero the worlds of urban squalor, in tenement Boston, and rural squalor in the Middle West; *A Member of the Third House* and *A Spoil of Office*, both versions of the political novel, written with a Populist basis; a second, rather weaker, collection of stories, *Prairie Folks* (1893); and the novel *Rose of Dutcher's Coolly* (1895), about the growing up of a western girl and her emancipation in Chicago. There was always something raw about Garland's intellectual gifts, and he never achieved the single-handed power to *be* the novelist for whom he was seeking; still, there is a vivid centre to his best work, and it comes from a double vision, of an actual world in which man is adrift, and a rich alternative life in which man is attuned to his natural environment. Garland's best work is mainly that about the rural west from which he came, and which he sees with a complex series of contrasts. It was not his way of taking the glow off the individualistic life of the prairie farmers, of seeing them as economically exposed to the market as the city-man, that was new; the recognition that they were the victims of economic forces, and that rural squalor was as common as urban squalor, was already well-achieved in local colour fiction, in the work of Joseph Kirkland, for instance. What is fresh about Garland's best writing is the way in which he suffuses his sociological, political or journalistic report on conditions with a deep lyrical-tragic feeling, for which the short story is the natural form. That feeling comes out of a complex map of emotions which we are familiar with in his stylistic contemporaries like Hardy or Zola: on the one hand, a sense of a conditioned world, in which man is the victim of circumstances, and in which his human hopes constantly fail, and on the other hand that individual capacity to endure, to hope, to feel attuned to family and nature, and organically to grow.

In his memoir *A Son of the Middle Border* (1917), Garland recognized that what lay behind his vision of the 'hard and bitter realities' of his hometown people was the triple perspective of 'a former resident, a man from the city, and a reformer'. To this extent, the bitterness his characters feel is not without an element of self-justification; it justifies, that is, Garland's own going away. He describes his small-towners as longing for the world of which Garland tells them, a world of 'the great cities I have seen, of wonderful buildings, of theatres, of the music of the sea'. Beside such a romantic catalogue, subsistence farming seems sheer drudgery, and his Wesley Fanchers not surprisingly tire of the 'old place'. Garland both urbanizes and sentimentalizes these, his essential characters, and his is a somewhat equivocal posture. For though the city has taught him to see the objective causes and hence the tragedies, the shrivelling disenchantments of rural life, he also projects on to them a vision of the city and of emancipation that is itself romantic. Likewise his own pose of emancipation is a form of alienation from himself; he is never able to give the dream of urban freedom that basis in solid, proven worth that he is inclined to attribute to country life. The contradiction, the transitional sensibility, is one he shares with several later writers, including Sherwood Anderson and Sinclair Lewis. One of Garland's recurrent themes is the revenant, the man who, on a return visit from the city to his rural origins, discovers that the price of his own escape was the entrapment of others. 'A Branch Road', and 'Up the Coulé', two stories in the collection *Main-Travelled Roads*, are excellent versions of this experience. In the first Will, the hero, having through awkwardness and bad luck lost the girl he wanted to wed, goes away to the city. Prosperous and unencumbered, he returns – only to find her married into poverty and domestic slavery. He rescues her from resigned acceptance of 'a whole life of agony', and they flee together in the direction of Europe. In the second story Howard McLane, successful in New York, comes back home to find that his brother, whom he has neglected, has passed beyond Howard's belated willingness to help; he is a 'dead failure' that money can't rescue. Both stories turn on a view of rural life as a lost life, broken by hardship and punitive economics; and of education and the city as the sources of emancipation. Nonetheless Garland invests the broken farmsteads and surrounding countryside with a mixture of harshness and lyricism, just as he invests its people with a stubborn individualism as well as, at times, a brutish animalism. Their passion for emancipation is therefore the humanizing feature of their *present* situation, part of the psychology of hope rather than an achievable thing. But on this delicate psychological fulcrum Garland builds his stories, the result being a kind of sceptical poetry, in which the metaphors of condition and determinant, of circumstantial and economic forces, of the alienating powers of the world outside and the will within, merge with organic metaphors of nature meaningful and illuminated and a humanity capable of internal moral growth. Life, Garland says of one character, 'had stifled all the slender flowers of his nature; yet there was warm soil somewhere hid in his heart'. It is the same 'organic' spirit that 'saves' Rose from her stirring sexuality in *Rose of Dutcher's Coolly*: 'She was saved by forces within, not by laws without.'

For Garland men are subject to genetic, historical and economic formation, but they are also part of a universe conceived more personally and morally. He saw his 'veritism' as distinct from Howells's realism on the one side and scientific naturalism like Norris's on the other. He later suggested that the difference lay in his 'impressionism' – by which he meant 'a form based on the moment of experience, acutely felt and immediately expressed'. In such instantaneousness he does indeed hold his dualistic, transitional, view of man in suspension, creating thereby a mood of sorrow and lyricism that marks his best work. There was always a tendency to literary cliché in Garland, as in most of the realists; he had made the old forms and popular literary manners new by introducing, in his best writing, an element of moral scepticism. But when the pressure of attention and feeling is off, it is to the familiar forms that he reverts – as in his later writing, romantic Western novels that lay 'outside the controversial belt', as he said. In fact, this mixture of scepticism applied to one aspect of a popular convention, while other elements of the convention persist, is a common aspect of realist-naturalism, part of its bias towards a form almost of literary parody. We meet the same thing in Norris, whose novels oscillate between virtuous romances and unvirtuous ones packed with 'experience' and 'frankness'; and in Crane, as a kind of internal uncertainty. But in these two writers the environmentalist aspects are much more strongly drawn and the world of 'forces' is both without and within.

## Frank Norris (1870–1902)

Ten years later still, Frank Norris, born in Chicago, the city he was to capture so well in *The Pit*, was also to move East to Boston, and Lewis Gates's creative writing class at Harvard, to pursue his interest in literary naturalism. His parents had moved to San Francisco when he was fifteen; a little later when he decided to study painting they accompanied him to London and Paris. Norris was to make much of his concern with the struggles of real life, but he had a full artistic education. In Paris his tastes were for the medieval; only when he returned to California, to study at Berkeley en route for his father's business, did he assimilate Zola and the contemporary genetic science that turned him to fiction and to naturalism. The books he wrote at Harvard – *McTeague* (written in 1895 but not published until 1899) and *Vandover and the Brute* (never polished for publication, but printed posthumously in 1914) – were clear examples of Naturalist method, and the first is a notable novel. But Norris now felt the Naturalist's need for 'experience' and (following the model of Richard Harding Davis, the shadowy literary influence whose style reached through to Hemingway and Thomas Wolfe), he went to the battlefield as a journalist, initially to some early skirmishes of the Boer War and then to the Spanish–American war. It was a very literary battlefield, like World War I via the ambulance service, and Stephen Crane was there too. For war was the harsh reality of things hidden behind the patriotic myths, the image of competitive society, the place of muted modern heroism, and the absolute experience, all in one. Back in New York journalism and publishing, Norris discovered Theodore Dreiser for Doubleday and, after other novels, began his Epic of the Wheat in three volumes. Two – *The Octopus* (1901) and *The Pit* (1903) – appeared and then, as he was about to go to Europe to collect material for the third, Norris died suddenly of appendicitis at the age of thirty-two.

In his devotion to naturalism, Norris meant two things that showed up as a split in his sensibility. On the one hand, he meant life above literaure – 'the honest, rough-and-tumble, Anglo-Saxon knockabout that for us means life'. But he also meant a form of evolutionary science that put the weight on genetic inheritance and operative social processes; he meant a Zola-like objectivity of analysis which, for him, took the form of an interest in atavism and the war of the 'higher' and 'lower' parts of man's nature – whether in the form of an internal psychological struggle, or a struggle of the classes, or a struggle of the various races of the world. Norris's instincts were those of patriot and moralist, yet he projected an underworld of powers and instincts which he came more and more to regard as the true world, and not until Dreiser does any American novelist reach quite so far in suggesting man's 'victimization' by instinctual processes and universal energies – which may suggest that a life-force is at work in the world but which, in any given instance, suggests that the individual man is a machine or a reflex. In *McTeague* and *Vandover and the Brute* Norris looks at this in the individual, and it is the sexual energy that operates as the power; in *The Octopus* it is a 'social' force, that of the wheat, which functions both as an energy principle and the base of a capitalist ecnomy; in *The Pit* both the sexual and the broader forces furnish the theme. But in all of these, his best novels, Norris as storyteller objectively and scientifically creates a victimizing world.

In *McTeague* and *Vandover*, Norris in effect attempts two pathological case-studies. Both, in the absence of a Freudian rhetoric, exploit a contemporary convention, the theme of the double man divided between high and low instincts; it is the theme of *Dr Jekyll and Mr Hyde* and *The Picture of Dorian Gray*. Both are novels of degeneration; but Norris mutes his moral judgments, and operates creatively beyond them. McTeague is an ox-like Sweeney Agonistes, an unlicensed San Francisco dentist whose sexual instincts are brutishly awakened by Trina. Norris tells and develops his story melodramatically; McTeague finally kills Trina after the degeneration of their marriage, and he ends in the desert, handcuffed to the corpse of the man who has come to hunt him and whom he has killed. Vandover, the middle-class artist who becomes 'degenerate', is much more self-aware in his struggle with and final defeat by the 'weaker' element in himself. But in both books Norris, in presuming that both the moral and the sensual aspects of man are in some sense instincts, is compelled into a form of psychological rendering that recognizes the presence of unconscious forces whose energies, at best, he taps in the telling. At the articulate level of presentation, he is less than consistent, hardly sure whether ethics and morals are simply rationalizations or whether they are our claim to civilization and humanity. And in his gestures to larger forces he is as vague as Thomas Hardy – so the famous passage where he says of McTeague and Trina: 'Their undoing was already begun. Yet neither of them was to blame . . . Chance had brought them face to face, and mysterious instincts as ungovernable as the winds of heaven were at work knitting their lives together . . . [They] were allowed no choice in the matter.' This is classic naturalistic lore, of course, though naturalism tends to be unsure of its implications: we can take *McTeague* as a tragedy about those victimized by cosmic forces, or as a fable about atavistic brutalism. The important point, though, is that Norris's books are about the politics of competing forces (just like Brooks Adams's histories); and in these two books he is able to pursue seriously the life of the pliable consciousness – if, necessarily, in those who, by their degeneration, are more open than most to psychological and external determinants. In these novels, Norris explores the 'black, unsearched penetralia of the mind', and this leads him towards totally new treatments of human consciousness.

By the time Norris began the Epic of the Wheat trilogy, his emphasis had, however, changed. Now he was concerned with larger economies of force, larger laws of supply and demand; and his naturalism shifts from a psychological to a social mode. Given Norris's appetite for experience and his view of it, his belief in immersion and assimilation, this is not surprising, but it represents a marked change of manner. 'A big epic trilogy', Norris called it in his letters; and he said that it 'will be straight naturalism with all the guts I can get into it'. The guts were to include an element of mysticism, not something Norris was good at, and a 'whirling and galloping and tearing along' of the action. It was, in short, to be a romance of experience illuminated by a sense of the operative forces of existence. In the two books, and particularly in *The Octopus*, the result is a curious and fascinating bifurcation of the realistic and the naturalistic impulse, an elaborate divergence in authorial sensibility. *The Octopus* begins by evoking the harshnesses of life in the wheat-growing San Joaquin Valley of California, where the ranchers are subjected to the exploitation of the railroad octopus, which by controlling the freight-rates controls the regional economy. Norris proceeds as Garland might, showing instances of suffering, and – through the development of his central character, the poet Presley – indicating how the romance of California is undercut by the bitter actualities. Presley forgets the romance he wants to write and turns to experience and then to action, finally throwing a bomb on behalf of the ranchers who have leagued against the railroad. But the battles fail, moral right and wrong grow vague, dissolving into corrupt politics; and as they do so Norris extends the chains of causality, showing both ranchers and railroad in the grip of yet larger forces – indeed, part of a vast, cosmic law of force of which the wheat itself is the centre, actual and metaphoric: '. . . the WHEAT remained. Untouched, unassailable, undefiled, that mighty world-force, that nourisher of nations, wrapped in Nirvanic calm, indifferent to the human swarms, moved onward in its ap- pointed grooves.' The novel ends in a swirl of abstractions – force, indifference, relentlessness, and an image of some oblique but ultimate good in humanity's advancement: 'the individual suffers, the race goes on'. Critics have properly pointed out that this in- volves a literary inconsistency: the suffering has been imaginatively established, while the 'good' that will prevail in the end has not and remains a romantic abstraction. The result is a romance much more independent of immediate human affairs than anything Presley in his initial and, Norris suggests, his *immoral* aestheticism and disreg- ard of humanity and experience, had conceived. Norris in fact seeks romantically to maintain a sense of moral and ethical responsibility through which experience might lead to action, while creating a world of forces in which particular moral, or immoral, acts have no meaning.

It is tempting to read *The Octopus* as a realistic muckraking novel about the exploitation of farmers by the railroads, the capitalist system. It is likewise tempting to read *The Pit*, perhaps the better book, which deals with the wheat-trading pit at the Chicago Board of Trade, as a novel about the sterilities of commercialism: Larzer Ziff sees it as 'the first profound business novel because it rightly examines the psychic consequences of the commercialization of American life'. Certainly a large part of the research and the imaginative effort of both books turn them in that direction. Yet in both we cannot miss the extent to which Norris is concerned with dwarfing and ironizing his human plot: in the welter of world experience, its collision and process, man becomes infinitesimal. He becomes so not, as in Zola, as an implicit contribution to the historical process; Norris, unlike Zola, takes a static point in history and he is epical in space rather than time. One may suspect that the diminishing ethical unvierse implied in an epic of global causations worried Norris, but he carried his logic through. In so doing, he ran into the problem that E. M. Forster, in *A Passage to India* twenty years later, was to confront: the problem of unifying aesthetically and morally a fiction based on totally eclectic and therefore contingent experience. But Norris was no aesthete, and no modernist. In the modernists, such dilemmas are characteristically resolved by turning attention towards the symbolistic aspects of the novel, the unity of the harmonious aesthetic construct which transcends the contingencies of history. But, though his history is simply a welter of experience, Norris believes in experience, not art: in the reality of life in its ceaseless extension, in truth as more and more life, in the epical, enormous, ungovernable systems of a proliferating universe. He becomes a dualist, presenting man half as a creature morally able to control environment and act imperialistically on force, half as victim of cosmic exchanges in which any individual is momentary and infinitesimal. He becomes, too, a writer of unworked divisions which, had aesthetic obligations counted more with him, he might well have felt the pressure to resolve: though it is in the irresolution that some of the best fiction of the 1890s was made.

## *Stephen Crane* (1871–1900)

This is apparent in the sadly short career of Stephen Crane, the finest writer of the American 1890s, and the author of the best book by a young author in the decade, *The Red Badge of Courage* (1895), a novel of the American Civil War in which a good deal of modern

American writing originates. Yet there were to be two *Red Badges*, and two Stephen Cranes, one in America, where he was hailed as a great reporter and naturalist, and one in Britain, where he was hailed as a great experimentalist, author of 'a new thing, in a new school', as H. G. Wells put it in an appreciation, and, said Edward Garnett, 'the chief impressionist of his day'. The contradictions in fact filled his life. Born in Newark, NJ, son of a Methodist clergyman, he reacted against home, was a weak and unsatisfactory college student, and, when he turned to journalism and went to live in the Tenderloin district of New York City, a decidedly raffish and bohemian figure, wildly consuming experience, and renouncing in his writing 'the clever school in literature', seeking, he said, a new literary credo of 'nature and truth'. 'Later I discovered: my creed was identical with the one of Garland and Howells', he remarked; both these helped him greatly through his struggles up to 1895, when suddenly *The Red Badge* brought him his international reputation and contradictory fame. Like his contemporaries, Crane was conscious of two versions of art and its relation to reality – one that it derived from and copied experience, 'the real thing', and the other that it was a process of stylized formal making, the contrasted views of Naturalism and Impressionism. *The Red Badge* enhanced the contradiction; he had not been in a battle, and explained: 'I got my sense of the rage of conflict on the football field, or else fighting is an hereditary instinct, and I wrote it intuitively . . .' But thereafter he became a war correspondent, reporting battles and engaging in dangerous ventures like a filibustering expedition to Cuba, which led to his shipwreck and his story about it, 'The Open Boat'. In 1897, less for artistic reasons than unpopularity through his liaison with the former brothel-keeper Cora Taylor, he moved to England, to Brede Place, Sussex, and found himself an author among authors, befriended by figures like Conrad, James, Wells, Ford Madox Ford and Edward Garnett. This, one critic has said, should dispel any impression he was less than a conscious artist; but reading his letters suggests that this was not necessarily the atmosphere of his residence. Crane was an increasingly sick man whose best work was already done. In 1898 he tried to enlist in the Spanish–American war; found unfit, he became, like Norris, a correspondent in the field, returning to Brede and dying two years later, at only 28, of tuberculosis.

Crane's reputation still remains one split between that of the writer of realism and the novelist of a new Impressionism; and he was always a writer of the double claim. On the one hand there was always the pull beyond literature to life, which culminated in the moment at San Juan Hill when, he said, expression was thrown to the winds and he could be satisfied 'to wholly feel'. On the other there was a clear and evident desire to shape the impact of experience, the multiplicity of impression, into artistic form, finding the underlying and shapely artistic logic. The uncertainty haunts all his comments on writing. 'The one thing that deeply pleases me in my literary life . . .', he wrote, 'is the fact that men of sense believe me to be sincere . . . Personally I am aware that my work does not amount to a string of dried beans.' This was probably less humility than real doubt about whether he reported life or created it, was reality's medium, or its maker. 'I go ahead, for I understand that a man is born into the world with his own pair of eyes, and he is not at all responsible for his visions – he is merely responsible for the quality of personal honesty . . . I, however, do not say that I am honest. I merely say that I am as nearly honest as a weak mental machinery will allow.' These same equivocations inhabit the work itself. Was what he saw and felt a vision; or was it how things are? Was art consonant with life, or did it recreate, even obstruct, its 'meanings'? Wasn't the centre of any experience literally the experience per se, so that the real truth was that there was nothing whatsoever to 'say' about it? And wasn't the artist himself simply a product of his environment, not responsible for his vision, just a good, or a bad, camera? Crane never acquired a convinced aesthetic creed or a sure social philosophy, but he was never quite fully committed to the method of 'instantaneousness' either. The outcome was an ambiguous symbolism – a rejection of explicit meanings drawn from the action, but also an uncertainty about the epiphanic nature of the luminous moment. Eric Solomon nicely points out that large elements of pastiche and parody of conventional literary forms abound in Crane's fiction, as in 'The Bride Comes to Yellow Sky' – where the old myth of the west is infused, ironically, with 'newer', domesticated reality. But once again Crane holds the 'old' and the 'new' in suspension, in typically realist way; the modern vision is intruded into the old ways of seeing, yet the old ways provide the essential form. The result is a fiction of ironic juxtapositions, so unresolved as to suggest confusions rather than aesthetic sophistications – complex oscillations between a realistic sympathy, and a profound distaste for the ordinary; and so on. All this makes Crane the most interesting and elaborate of the realist-naturalists, the most self-aware and yet perhaps the least self-controlled. The effect of Crane's remarkably oblique fiction is to draw our attention away from that central thrust into experience which is his obsession, and towards the technical means he acquired for presenting it.

So we are aware, throughout Crane's stories and novels – works like 'The Open Boat' and 'The Blue Hotel', the short novel *Maggie: A Girl of the Streets* (1893) and the later companion-piece *George's Mother* (1896), and above all the best known book *The Red Badge of Courage* (1895) – of a distinctive mannerism, a prose injected with momentary attitudes, deriving from the characters and the author himself. To see what becomes of the realistic mode at Crane's hands, it is perhaps most instructive to look at *Maggie* and *The Red Badge of Courage*, both of which take classic realist themes – *Maggie* the honest poor girl's lapse into vice, and *The Red Badge* war seen from the battlefield by an ordinary soldier. Of course, both are classic *romance* themes as well; and Crane plays off the two versions against each other. In both stories he obviously demythologizes the old version, introducing moral objectivity and scepticism, yet he never thoroughly espouses the deterministic position on whose rhetoric he draws. *Maggie*, for instance, is a version of the city novel and the determinist novel, and in a note in his presentation copies Crane claimed explicitly environmentalist purposes:

... it tries to show that environment is a tremendous thing in the world and frequently shapes lives regardless. If one proves that theory one makes room in Heaven for all sorts of souls (notably an occasional street girl) who are not confidently expected to be there by many excellent people.

In fact, if one proves that theory one makes room in Heaven for everybody, which abolishes Heaven; but *Maggie* is not a novel of proofs. It abounds in the language of determinism – of tenement society as a war or a jungle; of social organization as a Darwinian struggle; of the powers of instinct pulling at and toppling the moral conventions; of the claims of raw 'life': 'Jimmy's occupation for a long time was to stand at street corners and watch the world going by, dreaming blood-red dreams at the passing of pretty women. He menaced mankind at the intersections of streets. At the corners he was in life and of life. The world was going on and he was there to perceive it.' Characters like Jimmy not only live in the world of Darwinian struggle but are created by it and have their appropriate victories, like Jimmy on his waggon triumphing over the struggles of the traffic. But Maggie herself – 'None of the dirt of Rum Alley seemed to be in her veins' – is a creature of dreams, hopes, and moral virtues *not* derived from the environment, even if her misfortunes are. Since the ideals represented by Maggie have to be explored, as well as the attitudes of the other characters, this produces an overall ironic detachment; indeed the language is an ambiguous mock-heroic tone, in which the 'little champions of Rum Alley' are at once aggrandized and diminished by the higher heroics with which they are persistently compared. And what is true of the tone is true of the remarkably oblique structure. Maggie is the centre of the action, yet is presented almost entirely through the other characters, in a sequence of vignettes. The sequence goes on beyond Maggie's death, itself only given by hint: two scenes follow, one showing the Darwinian triumph of the 'woman of brilliance and audacity' who has been throughout Maggie's opposite, the other showing Maggie's mother's inadequate moralizing. These two conclusions – one showing Maggie's failure to understand the world, the other the world's failure to understand her – leave an oddly inconclusive impression. Through this irony of artistic distance piled on artistic distance, instead of being brought close to the realities of life, we have been technically removed far away from it.

This is even more true of *The Red Badge of Courage*, a fable about the pursuit of experience that in fact places the question of what constitutes experience in extreme doubt. The action is seen through one consciousness, that of the 'youth', Henry Fleming, who seeks an heroic initiation into 'life' on the battlefields of the Civil War. By the end of the novel he has acquired his 'moral vindication', his red badge, his necessary wound; and though it is almost an accident it is also, like the other great wounds of American literature, a testament of authenticity. He discovers that 'the world was a world for him, though many discovered it to be made of oaths and walking sticks'. And nature, whose signals he has been striving to interpret, concurs: 'Over the river a golden ray of sun came through the hosts of leaden rain clouds.' It is not however a romantic consonance with nature Henry has discovered; but with the mass, machine-like, amoral impulse of the army. He has found that he is 'a very wee thing' and reconciled himself to what Crane, in a passage later deleted, calls 'the machinery of the universe'. He had indeed cancelled his individualistic imagination, met experience as experience, and transcended, by immersion, the contingency of the natural world and the individualism of the moral one. For part of his experience has been a demythologization of gallantry; war is an impersonal machine remote from right or wrong, and heroism an instinctual reaction scarcely to be distinguished from cowardice, save that one runs forward instead of backward. Henry becomes compelled to forgo his 'laws of life' and take the total experience as an impression, while seeking from nature and the universal machine some signal of meaning. The result *is* romanticism, curious, obverse; Henry's impressions of nature grow clearer, but in a stark and existential way: 'It seemed to the youth that he saw everything. Each blade of green grass was bold and clear . . . His mind took a mechanical but firm impression, so that afterward everything was pictured and explained to him, save why he himself was there.' But Henry's wise passiveness is also a kind of self-extinction, and the marriage of the world within us and without us is, unromantically, the merging of two machines. Yet the old metaphors of a neo-Wordsworthian romanticism persist – creating, again, an ironic ambiguity. Though the scenes are set in a sequence suggesting growth, they remain as scenes, images, impressions. Even such famous symbols as 'the red sun . . . pasted in the sky life a wafer' are not so much resonant symbols as painterly instances.

*The Red Badge of Courage* is thus a fable of immersion in experience which rejects the old laws and orders. It is also a drama of consciousness, of events interacting with the mind of an agent who – unlike Maggie – is at the centre of the action, and in an experimental relation with the universe. There is no literal level of the social action; again, as in *Maggie*, the world of actuality is curiously dematerialized – a world of instantaneous moments that also aspires to be a world of metaphors. For Crane seeks to convey not only experience but also wisdom. He is indeed a writer who, seeking the 'thing itself', hesitates between two ways of giving meaning to existence – one romantic and numinous, the other scientific and objective. It is also impressionism, a brilliant scenicality that never becomes a plot. Crane is complex in proportion as he is uncertain and vague. Nonetheless his books are strikingly fresh, above all in the way they ironize the familiar linear structures of fiction, and the humanistic anatomy of traditional plots. More than any other realist, except James, Crane reveals the technical complications behind the effort to grasp and interpret the new. But the outcome, far from being a more 'objective' or truthful report on American life, is rather a new world of styles – new structures, new relations between characters and their environment. In Crane this amounts less to a stating of reality than to a struggle with it; and in that he was, however crudely, right on the edge of what Ford, Conrad and James were doing – which is to say creating the new novel of experimentalism or modernism.

IV

*Looking Backward, Looking Forward*

When the twentieth century came, the first two great waves of realism and naturalism in America were more or less over. Of the older generation, Howells and Twain were past their best work; only Henry James was still a radical figure, just entering his great late phase – a phase that left realism behind, and entered on the great adventure of Modernism. Of the younger, early death undid many: Stephen Crane, Frank Norris, Kate Chopin, Harold Frederic (author of *The Damnation of Theron Ware*), in some cases at least of an excess of the experience they believed in. Garland abandoned veritism for Western romances, Henry Harland his ghetto realism for European romances – set, James commented, 'in the heavy, many-voiced air of the old Roman streets and the high Roman salons where cardinals are part of the furniture'. The chief realist-naturalist novel of the new century, Theodore Dreiser's *Sister Carrie*, came out in 1900, was virtually suppressed, and acquired its real meaning and influence only later. The writers who now dominated were the muckrakers and the literary adventurers, like Jack London and Upton Sinclair – though Naturalism also left its imprint on the Southern tragedies of Ellen Glasgow, the society fiction of Edith Wharton, and many another, to become thereafter, a primary influence on authors like John Steinbeck, James T. Farrell, Erskine Caldwell, Nelson Algren and even Saul Bellow. In Hemingway, Fitzgerald and Dos Passos we can trace its imprint – though by the time of their startling achievement, in the aftermath of another major modern war which disoriented cultural values and exposed mankind anew to brute facts and hard realities, the impact of what appeared to be the counter-movement of Modernism had grown strong. For some writers, notably Gertrude Stein, who also greatly influenced them, had read the lesson of the 1890s differently. Stein was a child of the Nineties, educated in psychology by William James, in her apprehension of fiction by his brother Henry, and what she had read in the decade was a radical and experimental view of the relationship between consciousness and experience, forcing consciousness back onto an attempt to understand itself. She took her thoughts to Paris, where they coincided with the rise of Cubism; and it was here, she suggested, as she wrote there under a Cézanne portrait, creating the post-Impressionist novel, that the twentieth century really began.

The Naturalistic vision, claimed Zola, Alexis and Norris, was to have a significant and central role in twentieth-century American writing, confining literature to the realm of fact, the life of experience, the biological desire for evolution, the positivist hope. But, Philip Rahv has observed, it was the last irony of Naturalism that it came along to make its inventory of a material and process-driven world at just the point when that world was beginning to dissolve under the challenge from the new sciences, and particularly psychology, and the arts were increasingly driven inward into exploring experience from the standpoint of the subjective and aesthetic. It could be said that if one of the most important statements of 1900 was Theodore Dreiser's work of social and chemical, or 'chemist', determinism, *Sister Carrie*, another was Freud's *The Interpretation of Dreams*. The solvents that began to challenge and dismantle innocent realism were there already in the 1890s, in Crane's ironized consciousness, Garland's instinct towards Impressionism, Norris's sense of a driving unconscious. The effort to define experience through the places of new experience, which were not just city and machine, but the new kingdoms of force they had constructed and the psychologies and fleeting modern awarenesses they compelled, had demanded new aesthetic modes. 'We don't want literature, we want life', Norris held in *The Responsibilities of the Novelist*; but life in its flux of reality proved elusive, an aesthetic snare. We want, said Norris, a fiction that 'proves something, draws conclusions from a whole congeries of forces, social tendencies, race, impulses', a fiction like a science; but science itself was growing ever more certain of its uncertainty, ever more conscious of the ambiguity of hypothesis and the hypothesis of ambiguity, ever more perceptive in challenging the accuracy of the perceiver. Naturalism, which ironized realism's innocent view of the familiar, and systematized its theories of man, morals and society, encouraged the generalizing and universalizing powers of art; but in devising new codes of reality to correspond to new maps of individual and social behaviour, it put the idea of commonsense reality into question.

Realism in America, Howells suggested, 'just came', an innocent reflection of new American hopes and dreams of social advance and improvement, an expression of life's authentic feel. But it did not 'just come', as Howells, who brought quite a lot of it across the Atlantic, must well have known. Writing is not innocent, not a safe language of fact. It is, of course, an interpretation, constructing a fictional system in which the real acts as metaphor for the status of modern fact and the condition of the modern individual. It is a language of change conscious at best of its own change, for it is not only the material world, the world of Veblen's 'matter-of-fact', that alters, but the picture of the human mind. In the work of Crane, the best of all the 1890s American writers, and the one who offered most to his successors in a century that would be overwhelmed, as Adams said, by its own plots and processes, we can see social reality fade, the individual's world now appearing as a complex pattern of vignettes and sensations, buried memories and psychic needs. Realism is not a description, but an enquiry, which reminds us that fiction cannot be neatly divided between those writers held firmly to the rule of the literal and experimentalists who pursue form or immaterial realities. The realist writers did not know they anticipated Modernism, though in the end many of them – from Flaubert to James to Crane and Joyce – found it. The work of American writers of fiction between 1865 and 1900 seemed at the time a large act of contemporary documentation in an age of expansion where the word chased the world, and not to do with art. In fact this is a founding period of art, and, when American writing discovered a full historical confidence in the 1920s, it also discovered there were significant antecedents, who had created not just a world of harboured American fact but an art of modern forms.

# BIBLIOGRAPHY

The titles that follow this introductory note are arranged so as to refer to the chapter-order of the book. Students of American literature are now far better catered for than was the case thirty or forty years ago. However, the paperback revolution of the 1950s and 1960s has come and gone; many titles available in that era have disappeared., Readers are advised to check on availability from *Books in Print*. Many American texts and monographs are also published in Europe, especially in London. In general, we have listed merely the primary *American* source of publication.

*Reference*. The most useful single volume of bibliography is probably Clarence Gohdes and Sanford E. Marovitz, *Bibliographical Guide to the Study of the Literature of the USA*, Durham, N.C.; 5th revised edn, 1984, though see also the bibliographical volume of Robert E. Spiller, *et al.*, *Literary History of the United States*, New York; 4th edn, 1974. James D. Hart, *Oxford Companion to American Literature*, New York; 5th edn, 1983, is a reliable general guide. Among more substantial compendia, see the *Dictionary of American Literary Biography*, Detroit, 1978– , which by 1985 numbered over 30 volumes, and *American Writers Before 1800: A Biographical and Critical Dictionary*, 3 vols, Westport, Conn., 1983, ed. James A. Levernier and Douglas R. Wilmes. There are valuable bibliographical lists and supplements, together with reviews of new work, in such periodicals as *American Literary Realism*, *American Literature*, *American Quarterly*, *American Studies International*, *Early American Literature*, *Journal of American Studies*, *New England Quarterly*, *Nineteenth-Century Fiction* and *PMLA* (*Publications of the Modern Language Association of America*).

*General Works*. Spiller *et al.*, *Literary History of the US*, still has value, though it may be superseded by the new *Cambridge History of American Literature*. There are some quite comprehensive anthologies of American literature, such as that in two volumes by Norton, though in the nature of such compilations they are better on short stories and short poems than on extended fiction and other forms of literature. Penguin and other firms have unabridged editions of major works, especially of fiction.

There is also the splendid *Library of America* series, 1982– , which is reissuing the 'classic' canon of American literature. Each volume contains 1200–1400 pages. There are, for example, to be 10 volumes of Henry James, 6 of Twain, 5 of Cooper, and 4 each of Melville, Washington Irving and W.D. Howells. Poe and Parkman are assembled in 2 volumes apiece. There are selections of Jefferson and Franklin in one-volume editions.

*Broad Interpretations*. A number of these are incorporated in the chapter bibliographies. Among further titles of importance are:

Bell, Michael D., *The Development of American Romance: The Sacrifice of Relation*, Chicago, 1980.

Ferguson, Robert A., *Law and Letters in American Culture*, Cambridge, Mass., 1984.

Gilmore, Michael T., *The Middle Way: Puritanism and Ideology in American Romantic Fiction*, New Brunswick, N.J., 1977.

Kazin, Alfred, *An American Procession*, New York, 1984.

Mills, Nicolaus, *American and English Fiction in the Nineteenth Century: An Antigenre Critique and Comparison*, Bloomington, Indiana, 1973.

Smith, Henry Nash, *Democracy and the Novel: Popular Resistance to Classic American Writers*, New York, 1978.

Some of the best writing on literature in the United States occurs within an American Studies context. Social and cultural aspects are explored in many books and articles that are not explicitly 'literary'. Developments in new modes of criticism, in feminist and ethnic analyses have also enriched discussion. This abundance can be confusing: it is, though, exhilarating.

## 1. *The Conditions of an American Literature*

Barnes, James, J., *Authors, Publishers and Politicians: The Quest for an Anglo-American Copyright Agreement, 1815–1854*, Columbus, Ohio, 1974.

Baym, Nina, *Women's Fiction: A Guide to Novels By and About Women in America, 1820–1870*, Ithaca, N.Y., 1978.

Bercovitch, Sacvan, ed., *The American Puritan Imagination*, Cambridge, Mass., 1974.

Bruccoli, Matthew, J., ed., *The Profession of Authorship in America, 1800–1870: The Papers of William Charvat*, Columbus, Ohio, 1968.

Chase, Richard, *The American Novel and its Tradition*, New York, 1957; London, 1958.

Commager, Henry S. and Giordanetti, Elmo, *Was America A Mistake? An Eighteenth-Century Controversy*, New York and London, 1967.

Cunliffe, Marcus, *The Literature of the United States*, Harmondsworth, 1954; 4th edn., 1986.

Douglas, Ann Scott, *The Feminization of America*, New York, 1977.

Feidelson, Charles S., Jr, *Symbolism and American Literature*, Chicago and London, 1953.

Fiedler, Leslie, *Love and Death in the American Novel*, New York, 1960; London, 1961; revised edn, 1966.

Fisher, Philip, *Hard Facts: Setting and Form in the American Novel*, New York, 1985.

Hoffman, Daniel G., *Form and Fable in American Fiction*, New York and London, 1961.

Hubbell, Jay B., *The South in American Literature, 1607–1900*, Durham, N.C., 1954.

Jones, Howard Mumford, *The Theory of American Literature*, Ithaca, N.Y., and London, 1948; 2nd edn, 1965.

——*O Strange New World*, New York, 1964.

Levin, Harry, *The Power of Blackness: Hawthorne, Poe, Melville*, New York, 1958.

Lewis, R. W. B., *The American Adam: Innocence, Tragedy and Tradition in the Nineteenth Century*, Chicago and London, 1955.

Lindberg, Gary, *The Confidence Man in American Literature*, New York, 1982.

Lynn, Kenneth S., *The Comic Tradition in America*, Boston, 1957; London, 1958.

Marx, Leo, *The Machine in the Garden: Technology and the Pastoral Idea in America*, New York and London, 1964.

Philbrick, Thomas, *St John de Crévecoeur*, New York, 1968.

Poirier, Richard, *A World Elsewhere: The Place of Style in American Literature*, New York, 1966; London, 1967.

Rahv, Philip, *Image and Idea*, Norfolk, Conn., 1948.

Slotkin, Richard, *Regeneration Through Violence: The Mythology of the American Frontier, 1800–1860*, Middletown, Conn., 1973.

Smith, Henry Nash, *Virgin Land: The American West as Symbol and Myth*, Cambridge, Mass., 1950; London, 1951.

Spencer, Benjamin T., *The Quest for Nationality: An American Literary Campaign*, Syracuse, 1957.

Spiller, Robert E., *et al*, eds, *The Literary History of the United States*, New York, 1949; 4th edn, 2 vols, 1974.

Stewart, George R., *Bret Harte, Argonaut and Exile*, Boston, 1931.

Sundquist, Eric, *Home as Found: Authority and Genealogy in Nineteenth Century American Literature*, Baltimore, 1979.

Tanner, Tony, *The Reign of Wonder: Naïvety and Reality in American Literature*, Cambridge, 1965.

Taylor, George, R., ed., *The Turner Thesis*, Boston, 1956.

Tompkins, Jane, *Sensational Designs: The Cultural Work of American Fiction, 1790–1860*, New York, 1985.

Turner, Arlin, *George W. Cable: A Biography*, Durham, N.C., 1949

Woodward, C. Vann., *The Burden of Southern History*, Baton Rouge, La., 1960.

Ziff, Larzer, *Literary Democracy: The Declaration of Cultural Independence in America*, New York, 1981.

## 2. Literary Culture in Colonial America

*Primary Texts*

*Early eye-witnesses*

The chief texts are to be found in the following collections:

Hakluyt, Richard, *The Principal Navigations, Voyages Traffiques and Discoveries of the English Nation*, London, 1927.

Purchas, Samuel, *Hakluytus Posthumus* or *Purchas His Pilgrimes*, Glasgow, 1906.

*Travels and Works of Captain John Smith*, ed. Edward Arber, Birmingham, 1884.

Wright, Louis B., *The Elizabethan's America: A Collection of Early Reports by Englishmen on the New World*, Cambridge, Mass., 1965.

*Puritan writings*

Most of these writings must be sought out in their original editions. Exceptions are:

Bradford, William, *Of Plymouth Plantation*, ed. Samuel Eliot Morison, New York, 1966.

Bradstreet, Anne, *Works*, ed. John Harvard Ellis, Gloucester, 1962.

*John Cotton on the Churches of New England*, ed. Larzer Ziff, Cambridge, Mass., 1968.

Mather, Cotton, *Magnalia Christi Americana*, 2 vols, Hartford, 1853.

Johnson, Edward, *Wonder-Working Providence*, ed. J. Franklin Jameson, New York, 1910.

Wigglesworth, Michael, *The Day of Doom*, ed. Kenneth B. Murdock, New York, 1929.

Williams, Roger, *The Writings*, 6 vols, Providence, 1866–74.

Winthrop, John, *History of New England 1630–1649*, ed. James K. Hosmer, 2 vols, New York, 1908.

An excellent representative anthology is *The Puritans*, ed. Perry Miller and Thomas H. Johnson, New York, 1938. Collections of Puritan verse are:

Jantz, Harold S., *The First Century of New England Verse*, Worcester, 1944.

Murdock, Kenneth B., *Handkerchiefs from Paul*, Cambridge, Mass., 1927.

## A diversity of cultures

Byrd, William, *The Secret Diary... 1709–1712*, ed. Louis B. Wright and Marion Tinling, Richmond, 1941.
——*Another Secret Diary 1739–1741*, ed. Marion Tingling, Richmond, 1942.
Sewall, Samuel, *Diary*, 3 vols, *Coll. Mass. Hist. Soc.*, 5th ser., V–VII, 1878–82.
Woolman, John, *The Journal and Essays*, ed. Amelia M. Gummere, New York, 1922.

## Towards revolution

The writings of John Adams, Thomas Jefferson and other leaders are available in a number of selected editions. Crèvecoeur's *Letters From an American Farmer* was reprinted London, 1913; the best paperback edition, also including the less famous *Sketches*, is New York, 1963. *Common Sense* is available in a number of modern editions.

## Edwards and Franklin

Definitive editions of the writings of Jonathan Edwards and the papers of Benjamin Franklin are being issued serially by the Yale University Press. Any works by these authors not yet available in the Yale edition are best consulted in *The Works of President Edwards*, ed. Edward Williams and Edward Parsons, 8 vols, Leeds, 1806–11, and since reprinted, 1817 and 1847; and *The Writings of Benjamin Franklin*, ed. Albert H. Smyth, 10 vols, New York, 1905–7.

## Secondary Works

### Early eye-witnesses

Barbour, Philip L., *The Three Worlds of Captain John Smith*, Boston, 1964.
Chatterton, Edward Keble, *English Seamen and the Colonization of America*, London, 1930.
Franklin, Wayne, *Discoverers, Explorers, Settlers*, Chicago, 1979.
O'Gorman, Edmundo, *The Invention of America*, Bloomington, Ind., 1961.

## Puritan writings

Bercovich, Sacvan, *The Puritan Origins of the American Self*, New Haven, 1975.
Grabo, Norman, *Edward Taylor*, New York, 1962.
Miller, Perry, *The New England Mind: The Seventeenth Century*, New York, 1939.
——*The New England Mind: From Colony to Province*, Cambridge, Mass., 1953.
Morison, Samuel Eliot, *Builders of the Bay Colony*, Boston, 1964.
Morgan, Edmund S., *The Puritan Dilemma: The Story of John Winthrop*, Boston, 1958.
——*Roger Williams: The Church and the State*, New York, 1967.
Murdock, Kenneth B., *Literature and Theology in Colonial New England*, New York, 1956.
Smith, Bradford, *Bradford of Plymouth*, Philadelphia, 1951.
Wendell, Barrett, *Cotton Mather: The Puritan Priest*, New York, 1891.
Ziff, Larzer, *The Career of John Cotton*, Princeton, 1962.
——*Puritanism in America*, New York, 1973.

## A diversity of cultures

Beatty, Richard Croom, *William Byrd of Westover*, Boston, 1932.
Cady, Edwin H., *John Woolman*, New York, 1965.
Smith, Henry Nash, *Virgin Land*, Cambridge, Mass., 1950.
Whitney, Janet, *John Woolman, American Quaker*, Boston, 1942.
Winslow, Ola Elizabeth, *Samuel Sewall of Boston*, New York, 1964.
Wright, Louis B., *The First Gentlemen of Virginia*, San Marino, 1940.

## Towards revolution

Aldridge, Alfred O., *Man of Reason: The Life of Thomas Paine*, Philadelphia, 1959.
Leary, Lewis, *That Rascal Freneau: A Study in Literary Failure*, New Brunswick, 1941.
Mitchell, Julia P., *St Jean de Crèvecoeur*, New York, 1916.
Schachner, Nathan, *Thomas Jefferson: A Biography*, 2 vols, New York, 1921.
Smith, Page, *John Adams*, 2 vols, Garden City, 1962.

## Edwards and Franklin

Aldridge, Alfred O., *Benjamin Franklin: Philosopher and Man*, Philadelphia, 1965.

Davidson, Edward H., *Jonathan Edwards: The Narrative of a Puritan Mind*, Boston, 1966.

Granger, Bruce I., *Benjamin Franklin: An American Man of Letters*, Ithaca, 1964.

Van Doren, Carl, *Benjamin Franklin*, New York. 1938.

Winslow, Ola Elizabeth, *Jonathan Edwards, 1703–1758: A Biography*, New York, 1940.

## General

The standard literary histories of this period are still those of Moses Coit Tyler: *A History of American Literature During the Colonial Period*, New York, 1878, and *The Literary History of the American Revolution*, 2 vols, New York, 1897.

Useful essays on nine early authors from William Bradford to C. B. Brown are collected in Everett Emerson, ed., *Major Writers of Early American Literature*, Madison, Wisc., 1972.

### 3. *The God that Neglected to Come:*
### *American Literature 1780–1820*

*Texts*

A new edition of Washington Irving's works is being published by Twayne, of Boston. A convenient edition of Crèvecoeur, which contains both *Letters from an American Farmer* and the less familiar, supplementary, *Sketches of 18th Century America*, came out in New York in 1963, edited by Albert E. Stone, Jr (repr. in Penguin American Library, 1981): and see an abridged edn of these two works, *The Divided Loyalist: Crèvecoeur's America*, ed. Marcus Cunliffe, London, 1978. For the Connecticut of Hartford Wits, see the anthology edited by V. L. Parrington, *The Connecticut Wits*, New York, 1926; repr. 1969. Brackenridge's *Modern Chivalry* has been edited by Claude M. Newlin, New York, 1927, and by Lewis Leary, New York, 1965. Charles Brockden Brown's *Ormond, Edgar Huntly, Jane Talbot*, and *Clara Howard* have been reprinted, Port Washington, N.Y., 1963.

*Critical works*

Axelrod, Alan, *Charles Brockden Brown, an American Tale*, Austin, Texas, 1983.

Brooks, Van Wyck, *The World of Washington Irving*, New York, 1944; London, 1945.

Cowie, Alexander, *John Trumbull, Connecticut Wits*, Chapel Hill, N.C., 1936.

Cuningham, Charles E., *Timothy Dwight*, New York, 1942.

Ellis, Joseph J., *After the Revolution: Profiles of Early American Culture*, New York, 1979.

Emerson, Everett H., ed., *American Literature, 1764–1789*, Madison, 1977.

Ford, Arthur L., *Joel Barlow*, Boston, 1971.

Hedges, William L., *Washington Irving: An American Study, 1802–1832*, Baltimore, 1965.

Howard, Leon, *The Connecticut Wits*, Chicago, 1943.

Kirker, H. and J., *Bulfinch's Boston, 1787–1817*, New York, 1964.

Kolodny, Annette, *The Land Before Her*, Raleigh, N.C., 1984; *The Lay of the Land*, Raleigh, N.C., 1975.

Leary, Lewis, *Soundings: Some Early American Writers*, Athens, Ga., 1975.

Mott, F. L., *A History of American Magazines*, vol. I, Cambridge, Mass., 1939.

Newlin, Claude M., *Life and Writings of Hugh Henry Brackenridge*, Princeton, 1932.

Nye, Russel B., *The Cultural Life of the New Nation, 1776–1830*, New York and London, 1960.

Pochmann, Henry A., *German Culture in America*, Madison, 1957.

Silverman, Kenneth, *A Cultural History of the American Revolution, . . . 1763–1789*, New York, 1976.

Spiller, Robert E., ed., *The American Literary Revolution, 1783–1837*, Garden City, N.Y., 1967.

Vitzthum, Richard C., *Land and Sea: The Lyric Poetry of Philip Freneau*, Minneapolis, 1978.

Williams, Stanley T., *The Life of Washington Irving*, 2 vols, New York, 1935.

Woodress, James L., *A Yankee's Odyssey: The Life of Joel Barlow*, Philadelphia, 1958.

## 4. James Fenimore Cooper:
### Cultural Prophet and Literary Pathfinder

Cooper, J. Fenimore, *Cooper's Novels* (32 vols), New York, 1859–61. (Published by Townsend and illustrated by F. O. C. Darley, this edition is the best complete edition, but is being replaced by the SUNY press edition cited below.)

——*The Writings of James Fenimore Cooper* (Albany, The State University of New York Press, 1980–

——*The Letters and Journals of James Fenimore Cooper*, ed. James F. Beard, 6 vols, Cambridge, Mass., 1960–8. The editor is also writing what should be the definitive biography of Cooper.

*Selected bibliography of literary criticism of Cooper*

Bewley, Marius, *The Eccentric Design: Form in the Classic American Novel*, London, 1955.

Chase, Richard, *The American Novel and Its Tradition*, New York, 1957.

Clavel, Marcel, *Fenimore Cooper and His Critics*, Aix-en-Provence, 1938.

——*Fenimore Cooper: Sa vie et son oeuvre: La jeunesse 1789–1826*, Aix-en-Provence, 1938.

Cunningham, Mary, ed., *James Fenimore Cooper: A Re-Appraisal*, Cooperstown, 1954.

Dekker, George, *James Fenimore Cooper: The American Scott*, London, New York, 1967.

Grossman, James, *James Fenimore Cooper*, New York, 1949: repr. Stanford, 1967.

House, Kay Seymour, *Cooper's Americans*, Columbus, Ohio, 1966.

Lawrence, D. H., *Studies in Classic American Literature*, Garden City, N.Y., 1953; first published in 1924.

Nevius, Blake, *Cooper's Landscapes*, Berkeley, 1976.

Peck, H. Daniel, *A World by Itself: The Pastoral Moment in Cooper's Fiction*, New Haven, 1977.

Philbrick, Thomas, *James Fenimore Cooper and the Development of American Sea Fiction*, Cambridge, Mass., 1961.

Ringe, Donald A., *The Pictorial Mode: Space and Time in the Art of Bryant, Irving and Cooper*, Lexington, 1972.

Spiller, Robert E., *Fenimore Cooper: Critic of His Times*, New York, 1931.

Walker, Warren S., *Plots and Characters in the Fiction of James Fenimore Cooper*, Hamden, Conn., 1978.

Winters, Yvor, *In Defense of Reason*, Denver, Col., 1947.

## 5. *Edgar Allan Poe*

### *Editions and texts*

The most complete edition of Poe is still James A. Harrison, ed., *The Complete Works of Edgar Allan Poe*, 17 vols,New York, 1902. Thomas O. Mabbott ed. 3 vols of the projected scholarly edition of Poe: *Poems* and *Tales and Sketches*, 2 vols, Cambridge, Mass., 1969, 1978, and his work has been continued by Burton R. Pollin who has ed. *The Imaginary Voyages*, Boston, 1981, and *The Brevities*, New York, 1985. Another excellent edition of the poems is Floyd Stovall, ed., *The Poems of Edgar Allan Poe*, Charlottesville, 1965. The letters have been ed. by John Ward Ostrom, *The Letters of Edgar Allan Poe*, 2 vols, New York, 1966. Readily available selections of Poe's work are: Edward H. Davidson, ed., *Poe, Selected Writings*, Riverside Edition, Boston, 1956; Stuart and Susan Levine, eds, *The Short Fiction of Edgar Allan Poe*, Indianapolis, 1976; David Galloway, ed., *Selected Writings of Edgar Allan Poe*, Penguin Books, Harmondsworth, 1967; Harold Beaver, ed., *The Narrative of Arthur Gordon Pym*, Penguin Books, Harmondsworth, 1975 and *The Science Fiction of Edgar Allan Poe*, Penguin Books, Harmondsworth, 1976.

### *Biography and criticism*

Allen, Michael, *Poe and The British Magazine Tradition*, New York, 1969.

Alterton, Margaret, and Craig, Hardin, *Allan Poe, Representative Selections*, New York, 1935; revised edition, 1962. Contains a scholarly introduction and notes, and a useful bibliography.

Campbell, Killis, *The Mind of Poe and Other Studies*, Cambridge, Mass., 1933.

Carlson, Eric W., ed., *The Recognition of Edgar Allan Poe*, Ann Arbor, 1966.

Davidson, Edward H., *Poe, A Critical Study*, Cambridge, Mass., 1957.

Fagin, N. Bryllion, *The Histrionic Mr Poe*, Baltimore, 1949.

Fisher, Benjamin Franklin, ed., *Poe at Work*, Baltimore, 1978.

Jacobs, Robert D., *Poe: Journalist and Critic*, Baton Rouge, La., 1969.

Ketterer, David, *The Rationale of Deception in Poe*, Baton Rouge, 1979.

Miller, Perry, *The Raven and the Whale: The War of Words and Wits in the Era of Poe and Melville*, New York, 1956.

Moss, Sidney P., *Poe's Literary Battles*, Durham, N.C., 1963.

Parks, Edd W., *Edgar Allan Poe as Literary Critic*, Athens, Ga., 1964

Pollin, Burton R., *Discoveries in Poe*, Notre Dame, 1970.

Quinn, Arthur Hobson, *Edgar Allan Poe: A Critical Biography*, New York, 1941.

Quinn, Patrick F., *The French Face of Edgar Poe*, Carbondale, 1957.

Rans, Geoffrey, *Edgar Allan Poe*, Edinburgh, 1965. Probably the best introduction to Poe available.

Regan, Robert, ed., *Poe: A Collection of Critical Essays*, Englewood Cliffs, N.J., 1967.

Stovall, Floyd, *Edgar Poe the Poet*, Charlottesville, 1969.

Stuart, Levine, *Edgar Poe: Seer and Craftsman*, Deland, Fla., 1972.

Thompson, G. R., *Poe's Fiction: Romantic Irony in the Gothic Tales*, Madison, 1973.

Wagenknecht, Edward, *Edgar Allan Poe: The Man Behind the Legend*, New York, 1963.

Walker, I. M., ed., *Edgar Allan Poe: The Critical Heritage*, London, 1986.

Wilbur, Richard, ed., 'Introduction' to *Poe: Complete Poems*, New York, 1959.

## 6. New England Transcendentalism

### Works by and about individual Transcendentalist authors

### Ralph Waldo Emerson

*The Complete Works of Ralph Waldo Emerson* (Centenary Edition), ed. E. W. Emerson, 12 vols, 1903–4. A new edition of the *Collected Works*, of which the first three volumes have appeared, 1971– , is being published by the Harvard University Press.

*The Journals and Miscellaneous Notebooks of Ralph Waldo Emerson*, eds W. H. Gilman *et al*, 16 vols, 1960–82.

*The Early Lectures of Ralph Waldo Emerson*, ed. S. E. Whicher, R. E. Spiller, and W. E. Williams, 3 vols, 1959, 1964, 1971.

*The Letters of Ralph Waldo Emerson*, ed. R. L. Rusk, 6 vols, 1939.

Allen, Gay Wilson, *Waldo Emerson: A Biography*, 1981.

Bishop, Jonathan, *Emerson on the Soul*, 1964.

Chapman, John J., *Emerson and Other Essays*, 1898.

Duncan, Jeffrey L., *The Power and Form of Emerson's Thought*, 1973.

Ellison, Julie K., *Emerson's Romantic Style*, 1984.

Hopkins, Vivian C., *Spires of Form: A Study of Emerson's Aesthetic Theory*, 1951.

Levin, David, ed., *Emerson: Prophecy, Metamorphosis and Influence*, 1975.

McAleer, John J., *Ralph Waldo Emerson: Days of Encounter*, 1984.

Nicoloff, Philip L., *Emerson on Race and History*, 1961.

Packer, B. L., *Emerson's Fall*, 1982.

Paul, Sherman, *Emerson's Angle of Vision*, 1952.

Porte, Joel, *Emerson and Thoreau*, 1965.

——ed., *Emerson, Prospect and Retrospect*, 1982.

Porter, David T., *Emerson and Literary Change*, 1978.

Rusk, Ralph L., *The Life of Ralph Waldo Emerson*, 1949.

Waggoner, Hyatt H., *Emerson as Poet*, 1974.

Whicher, Stephen E., *Freedom and Fate*, 1953.

### Henry David Thoreau

*The Writings of Henry David Thoreau* (Walden Edition), 20 vols, 1906. A new edition of *The Writings of Thoreau*, of which five volumes have appeared 1971– , is being published by Princeton University Press.

*The Journal*, a new edition of which the first two volumes have appeared, 1971– , is being published by Princeton University Press.

*Collected Poems of Henry David Thoreau*, ed. C. Bode, 1964.

*The Correspondence of Henry David Thoreau*, ed. C. Bode and W. Harding, 1958.

Anderson, Charles R., *The Magic Circle of Walden*, 1968.

Bridgman, Richard, *Dark Thoreau*, 1982.

Canby, Henry S., *Thoreau*, 1939.

Cavell, Stanley, *The Senses of Walden. Expanded Edition*, 1981.

Cook, Reginald L., *Passage to Walden*, 1949.

Garber, Frederick, *Thoreau's Redemptive Imagination*, 1977.

Harding, Walter, *A Thoreau Handbook*, 1959.

——*The Days of Henry David Thoreau*, 1965.

Lebeaux, Richard, *Young Man Thoreau*, 1977.

——*Thoreau's Seasons*, 1984.

McIntosh, James, *Thoreau as Romantic Naturalist*, 1974.

Metzger, Charles R., *Thoreau and Whitman*, 1961.

Moller, Mary E., *Thoreau in the Human Community*, 1980.

Paul, Sherman, *The Shores of America: Thoreau's Inward Exploration*, 1958.

Seybold, Ethel, *Thoreau: The Quest and the Classics*, 1951.

Shanley, J. Lyndon, *The Making of Walden*, 1957.

Stoller, Leo, *After Walden: Thoreau's Changing View on Economic Man*, 1957.


*Amos Bronson Alcott*

*Essays on Education 1830–62*, 1960.

*The Journals of Bronson Alcott*, ed. O. Shepard, 1938.

Bedell, Madelon, *The Alcotts: Biography of a Family*, 1980.

Dahlstrand, Frederick C., *Amos Bronson Alcott: An Intellectual Biography*, 1982.

Sanborn, Frank B., and William T. Harris, *A. Bronson Alcott: His Life and Philosophy*, 1893.

Shepard, Odell, *Pedlar's Progress*, 1937.


*Orestes A. Brownson*

*The Works of Orestes A. Brownson*, ed. H. F. Brownson, 20 vols, 1882–1902.

Brownson, H.F., *Orestes A. Brownson's Early Life, Middle Life, Later Life*, 3 vols, 1898–1900.

Gilhooley, Leonard, *Contradiction and Dilemma: Orestes Brownson and the American Idea*, 1972.
——*No Divided Allegiance: Essays in Brownson's Thought*, 1980.
Schlesinger, Arthur M., Jr, *Orestes A. Brownson*, 1939.

## Margaret Fuller

*Memoirs of Margaret Fuller*, ed. R. W. Emerson, W. H. Channing and J. F. Clarke, 2 vols, 1852.
*Margaret Fuller: An American Romantic*, ed. P. Miller, 1963.
*The Letters of Margaret Fuller*, ed. R. N. Hudspeth, vols 1–3, 1983.
Allen, Margaret V., *The Achievement of Margaret Fuller*, 1979.
Blanchard, Paula, *Margaret Fuller: From Transcendentalism to Revolution*, 1978.
Chevigny, Bell G., *The Woman and the Myth: Margaret Fuller's Life and Writings*, 1976.
Deiss, Joseph J., *The Roman Years of Margaret Fuller*, 1969.
Wade, Mason, *Margaret Fuller: Whetstone of Genius*, 1940.

## Theodore Parker

*The Works of Theodore Parker* (Centenary Edition), 15 vols, 1907–13.
Commager, Henry S., *Theodore Parker*, 1936.
Dirks, John E., *The Critical Theology of Theodore Parker*, 1970.
Frothingham, Octavius B., *Theodore Parker*, 1874.
Weiss, John, *Life and Correspondence of Theodore Parker*, 2 vols, 1864.

## Elizabeth Palmer Peabody

*Letters of Elizabeth Palmer Peabody*, ed. B. A. Ronda, 1984.
*Record of a School*, 1835, 1836.
Brooks, Gladys, *Three Wise Virgins*, 1957.

## George Ripley

Crowe, Charles R., *George Ripley*, 1967.
Frothingham, Octavius B., *George Ripley*, 1882.

## Anthologies of Transcendentalist writing

*Selected Writings of the American Transcendentalists*, ed. G. Hochfield, 1967.
*The Transcendentalists*, ed. P. Miller, 1950.
*The American Transcendentalists*, ed. P. Miller, 1957.

*Critical works wholly or partially concerned with Transcendentalism*

Albanese, Catherine L., *Corresponding Motion: Transcendental Religion and the New America*, 1977.

Aselineau, Roger, *The Transcendentalist Constant in American Literature*, 1980.

Brooks, Van Wyck, *The Flowering of New England, 1815–1865*, 1941.

Buell, Lawrence, *Literary Transcendentalism*, 1973.

Feidelson, Charles S., *Symbolism and American Literature*, 1953.

Frothingham, Octavius B., *Transcendentalism in New England*, 1876.

Goddard, Harold C., *Studies in New England Transcendentalism*, 1908.

Haraszti, Zoltan, *The Idyll of Brook Farm*, 1937.

Hutchison, William R., *The Transcendentalist Ministers*, 1959.

Lewis, R. W. B., *The American Adam*, 1955.

Marx, Leo, *The Machine in the Garden*, 1964.

Matthiessen, F. O., *American Renaissance*, 1941.

Miller, Perry, *Nature's Nation*, 1967.

Mumford, Lewis, *The Golden Day*, 1926.

Myerson, Joel, *The New England Transcendentalists and the Dial*, 1980.

Rose, Anne C., *Transcendentalism as a Social Movement*, 1981.

Simon, Myron and T. H. Parsons, eds, *Transcendentalism and Its Legacy*, 1966.

Tanner, Tony, *The Reign of Wonder*, 1965.

Vogel, Stanley M., *German Literary Influences on the American Trancendentalists*, 1955.

Wellek, René, *Confrontations*, 1965.

Winters, Yvor, *Maule's Curse*, 1938.

## 7. *Nathaniel Hawthorne*

*Texts*

*The Complete Works of Nathaniel Hawthorne*, with introductory notes by George Parsons Lathrop, Riverside Edition, Boston, 1883, was for a long time regarded as the standard text. It has now been almost completely replaced by the Centenary Edition (Columbus, Ohio), under the general editorship of William Charvat, Roy Harvey Pearce and Fredson Bowers. By 1985 the Centenary Edition had reached vol. 16. Vols 14–16 furnished annotated editions of the *French and Italian Notebooks* and of Hawthorne's *Correspondence*. Note also *The Completed Novels*, ed. Millicent Bell, and *Tales and Sketches*, ed. Roy H. Pearce — two impeccable volumes in the *Library of America* series, New York, 1984.

*The American Notebooks of Nathaniel Hawthorne*, ed. Randall Stewart, New York, 1932.

*The English Notebooks by Nathaniel Hawthorne*, ed. Randall Stewart, New York, 1941.

*Biography and criticism*

Arvin, Newton, *Hawthorne*, Boston, 1929.

Baym, Nina, *The Shape of Hawthorne's Career*, Ithaca, N.Y., 1976.

Bell, Michael D., *Hawthorne and the Historical Romance of New England*, Princeton, N. J., 1971.

Bewley, Marius, *The Complex Fate*, London, 1952.

——*The Eccentric Design: Form in the Classic American Novel*, New York and London, 1959.

Brodhead, Richard H., *Hawthorne, Melville, and the Novel*, Chicago, 1976.

Colacurcio, Michael J., *The Province of Piety: Moral History in Hawthorne's Early Tales*, Cambridge, Mass., 1984.

Crews, Frederick C., *The Sins of the Fathers: Hawthorne's Psychological Themes*, New York, 1966.

Dauber, Kenneth, *Rediscovering Hawthorne*, Princeton, N.J., 1977.

Davidson, E. H., *Hawthorne's Last Phase*, New Haven, 1949.

Donohue A., ed., *A Casebook on the Hawthorne Question*, New York, 1962.

Doren, Mark Van, *Nathaniel Hawthorne: A Critical Biography*, New York, 1949.

Erlich, Gloria C., *Family Themes and Hawthorne's Fiction*, New Brunswick, N.J., 1984.

Feidelson, Charles, Jr, *Symbolism and American Literature*, Chicago, 1953.

Fiedler, Leslie, *Love and Death in the American Novel*, New York, 1960; London, 1961.

Fogle, R. H., *Hawthorne's Fiction: The Light and the Dark*, Norman, Okla., 1952.

Folson, J. K., *Man's Accidents and God's Purposes: Multiplicity in Hawthorne's Fiction*, New Haven, 1963.

Gollin, Rita K., *Nathaniel Hawthorne and the Truth of Dreams*, Baton Rouge, La., 1979.

Gross, S. L. ed., *A 'Scarlet Letter' Handbook*, San Francisco, 1960.

Hawthorne, Julian, *Nathaniel Hawthorne and His Wife*, 2 vols, Cambridge, Mass., 1884.

——*Hawthorne and His Circle*, New York, 1903.

Hoeltje, H.H., *Inward Sky: The Mind and Heart of Nathaniel Hawthorne*, Durham N.C., 1962.

Hoffman, Daniel G., *Form and Fable in American Fiction*, New York, 1961.

Hull, Raymond E., *Nathaniel Hawthorne, the English Experience, 1853–1874*, Pittsburgh, Pa., 1980.

James, Henry, *Hawthorne*, London, 1879.

Lee, A. Robert, ed., *Nathaniel Hawthorne: New Critical Essays*, Totowa, N.J., 1982.

Levin, Harry, *The Power of Blackness, Hawthorne, Poe, Melville*, New York, 1958.

Lewis, R. W. B., *The American Adam: Innocence, Tragedy and Tradition in the Nineteenth Century*, Chicago, 1955.

Lombardo, Agostino, 'I racconti di Hawthorne' in *Il simbolismo nella letteratura nord-americana*, Florence, 1965.

——*Un rapporto col mondo: Saggi sui racconti di Nathaniel Hawthorne*, Rome, 1976.

McWilliams, John P., *Hawthorne, Melville, and the American Character*, New York, 1984.

Male, R. R., *Hawthorne's Tragic Vision*, Austin, Texas, 1957.

Matthiessen, F. O., *American Renaissance*, New York, 1941.

Mellow, James R., *Nathaniel Hawthorne in His Times*, Boston, 1980.

*Nathaniel Hawthorne Journal*, 1971– .

Pearce, Roy Harvey, ed., *Hawthorne Centenary Essays*, Columbus, Ohio, 1964.

Stein, W. B., *Hawthorne's Faust: A Study of the Devil Archetype*, Gainesville, Fla., 1953.

Stewart, Randall, *Nathaniel Hawthorne: A Biography*, New Haven, 1948.

*Studi Americani*, No 1, Rome, 1955; partially devoted to Hawthorne.

Turner, Arlin, *Nathaniel Hawthorne: An Introduction and Interpretation*, New York. 1961.

——*Nathaniel Hawthorne: A Biography*, New York, 1980.

Waggoner, H. H. *Hawthorne: A Critical Study*, Cambridge, Mass., 1955.

——*The Presence of Hawthorne*, Baton Rouge, La., 1979.

Wagenknecht, Edward, *Nathaniel Hawthorne: Man and Writer*, New York, 1961.

Winters, Yvor, *Maule's Curse*, Norfolk, Conn., 1938.

Wilson, Edmund, ed., *The Shock of Recognition*, New York, 1943; contains criticism by Melville, Poe, Henry James, D. H. Lawrence and T. S. Eliot.

Young, Philip, *Hawthorne's Secret: An Un-Told Tale*, Boston, 1984.

## 8. Herman Melville

### Editions

The works of Melville, are being reissued in the Library of America. Older editions, popular or scholarly, are incomplete, or hard to come by, or unsatisfactory in other ways.

### Biography

Howard, Leon, Herman, Melville, Berkeley and Los Angeles, 1951; London, 1952.
Miller, E. H., *Melville*, New York, 1975.

### Letters

Davis, Merrill R., and William H. Gilman, eds, *The Letters of Herman Melville*, New Haven, 1960.

### Criticism

Arvin, Newton, *Herman Melville*, New York and London, 1950.
Branch, W. G., *Melville, the Critical Heritage*, London, 1974.
Cameron, Sharon, *The Corporeal Self: Allegories of the Body in Hawthorne and Melville*, Baltimore, 1981.
Herbert, T. Walter, *Marquesan Encounters: Melville and the Meaning of Civilization*, Cambridge, Mass., 1980.
—— *Moby Dick and Calvinism: A World Dismantled*, Newark, N.J., 1977.
Higgins, Brian, *Herman Melville, an Annotated Bibliography*, Boston, 1979.
Lawrence, D. H., *Studies in Classic American Literature*, New York, 1923.
Matthiessen, F. O., *American Renaissance*, New York and London, 1941.
Miller, James E., Jr., *A Reader's Guide to Herman Melville*, New York, 1962.
Miller, Perry, *The Raven and the Whale*, New York, 1956.
Mumford, Lewis, *Herman Melville*, New York, 1929; revised edn, New York and London, 1963.
Olson, Charles, *Call Me Ishmael*, New York, 1947; London, 1967.
Rogin, Michael Paul, *Subversive Genealogy: The Politics and Art of Herman Melville*, New York, 1983.

Rosenberry, Edward H., *Melville and the Comic Spirit*, Cambridge, Mass., and London, 1955.
Warren, Robert Penn 'Melville the Poet', *Selected Essays*, New York, 1958; London, 1964.

## 9.  *Walt Whitman*

*Works by Walt Whitman*

*Leaves of Grass*, Brooklyn, 1855.
*Leaves of Grass*, Brooklyn, 1856.
*Leaves of Grass*, Boston, 1860.
*Drum-Taps*, New York, 1865.
*Leaves of Grass*, New York, 1867.
*Democratic Vistas*, Washington, D.C., 1871.
*Leaves of Grass*, Boston, 1882.
*Specimen Days and Collect*, Philadelphia, 1882.
*Leaves of Grass*, Philadelphia, 1891.
*Calamus*, ed. R. M. Bucke, Boston, 1897.
*The Wound Dresser*, ed. R.M. Bucke, Boston, 1898.
*An American Primer*, ed. Horace Traubel, Boston, 1904.
*The Gathering of the Forces*, ed. Cleveland Rodgers and John Black, New York, 1920.
*Leaves of Grass: Facsimile Edition of the 1860 Text*, ed. Roy Harvey Pearce, Ithaca, N.Y., 1961.

*Selected and collected editions*

*Complete Poetry and Selected Prose and Letters*, ed. Emory Holloway, New York, 1938.
*The Complete Poetry and Prose of Walt Whitman*, Introduction Malcolm Cowley, New York, 1948.
*The Poetry and Prose of Walt Whitman*, ed. Louis Untermeyer, New York, 1949.
*Walt Whitman: Complete Poetry and Selected Prose and Letters*, ed. Emory Holloway, London, 1967.
*Walt Whitman: Complete Poetry and Collected Prose*, with notes by Justin Kaplan, New York, Library of America, 1982.

*Critical, textual and biographical studies*

Allen, Gay Wilson, *Walt Whitman Handbook*, Chicago, 1946.
——*The Solitary Singer*, New York, 1955.
Asselineau, Roger, *L'Evolution de Walt Whitman après la première édition des Feuilles d'Herbes*, Paris, 1954; translated as *The Evolution of Walt Whitman*, 1960.
Bowers, Fredson, *Whitman's Manuscripts: Leaves of Grass*, 1860, Chicago, 1955.

Chase, Richard, *Walt Whitman Reconsidered*, New York, 1955.

de Selincourt, Basil, *Walt Whitman: A Critical Study*, New York, 1914.

Donoghue, Denis, *Connoisseurs of Chaos*, New York and London, 1966.

Fausset, Hugh I'Anson, *Walt Whitman: Poet of Democracy*, New Haven, 1942.

Feidelson, Charles, Jr, *Symbolism and American Literature*, Chicago and London, 1953.

Hindus, Milton, ed., *Walt Whitman: The Critical Heritage*, London, 1971.

Jarrell, Randall, *Poetry and the Age*, London, 1953.

Kaplan, Justin, *Walt Whitman: A Life*, New York, 1980.

Lawrence, D. H., *Studies in Classic American Literature*, New York, 1923.

Matthiessen, F. O., *American Renaissance: Art and Expression in the Age of Emerson and Whitman*, New York, 1941.

Miller, Edwin, H., *Walt Whitman's Poetry*, New York, 1968.

Miller, James E., Jr, *A Critical Guide to Leaves of Grass*, Chicago, 1957.

Pearce, Roy Harvey, Introduction to *Leaves of Grass: Facsimile Edition of the 1860 Text*, Ithaca, 1961.

——*The Continuity of American Poetry*, Princeton, 1961.

Santayana, George, *Interpretations of Poetry and Religion*, London, 1900.

Spitzer, Leo, *Essays on English and American Literature*, ed. Anna Hatcher, Princeton, 1967.

Zweig, Paul, *Walt Whitman: The Making of the Poet*, New York, 1984.

## 10. *New England: The Universal Yankee Nation*

Editions of authors mentioned in this chapter exist in a fairly satisfactory variety, often in paperback. The most complicated canon is that of Emily Dickinson: Thomas H. Johnson and others have laboured to produce an authentic sequence. Old editions of the works of the established New England authors are usually quite easy to locate, and usually acceptable. Reprint editions of some of these, e.g. for Longfellow and Lowell (AMS), have recently been produced.,

Adams, Henry, *Letters of Henry Adams, 1858–1918*, 2 vols, Boston, 1930, 1938.

Allen, Margaret V., *The Achievement of Margaret Fuller*, University Park, Penna, 1979.

Arvin, Newton, *Longfellow: His Life and Work*, Boston, 1963.

Brooks, Van Wyck, *The Flowering of New England, 1815–1865*, New York and London, 1936.

——*New England: Indian Summer, 1865–1915*, New York, 1940; London, 1941.

Doughty, Howard N., *Francis Parkman*, New York, 1962.

Duberman, Martin, *James Russell Lowell*, Boston, 1966.

Dusinberre, William, *Henry Adams: The Myth of Failure*, Charlottesville, Va., 1980.

Fredrickson, George M., *The Inner Civil War: Northern Intellectuals and the Crisis of the Union*, New York, 1965.

Gelpi, Albert J., *Emily Dickinson: the Mind of the Poet*, Cambridge, Mass., 1965.

Higgins, David J., *Portrait of Emily Dickinson: the Poet and her Prose*, New Brunswick, N.J., 1967.

Howe, Mark A. De Wolfe, *Holmes of the Breakfast Table*, New York, 1939.

Levenson, J. C., *The Mind and Art of Henry Adams*, Boston, 1957.

Levin, David, *History as Romantic Art: Bancroft, Prescott, Motley, Parkman*, Stanford, Cal., 1959.

Lodge, Henry Cabot, *Early Memories*, Boston, 1913.

More, Paul Elmer, *Shelburne Essays on American Literature*, selected and edited by Daniel Aaron, New York, 1963.

Pearce, Roy Harvey, *The Continuity of American Poetry*, Princeton and London, 1961.

Pollard, John A., *John Greenleaf Whittier, Friend of Man*, Boston, 1949.

St Armand, Barton L., *Emily Dickinson and Her Culture: The Soul's Society*, Cambridge, Mass., 1984.

Samuels, Ernest, *The Young Henry Adams*, Cambridge, Mass., 1948.

——*Henry Adams: The Middle Years*, 1958.

——*Henry Adams: The Major Phase*, 1964.

Sewall, Richard B., *The Life of Emily Dickinson*, 2 vols, New York, 1974.

Solomon, Barbara M., *Ancestors and Immigrants: A Changing New England Tradition*, Cambridge, Mass., 1956.

Story, Ronald, *The Forging of an Aristocracy: Harvard and the Boston Upper Class, 1800–1870*, Middletown, Conn., 1980.

Taylor, William R., 'Francis Parkman', in M. Cunliffe and R. Winks, eds, *Pastmasters: Some Essays on American Historians*, New York, 1969; rev. edn, 1987.

11. *Henry James: The Prey of all the Patriotisms*

*The Novels and Tales of Henry James* ['New York Edition'], 24 vols, New York, 1907–9; repr. 1961.

*The Novels and Stories of Henry James*, ed. Percy Lubbock, 35 vols, London, 1921–3.

*Complete Tales of Henry James*, ed. Leon Edel, 12 vols, London, 1962–4; Philadelphia, 1962–4.

*The Letters of Henry James*, ed. Leon Edel, 4 vols; Cambridge, Mass., 1974–84.

*The Tales of Henry James*, ed. M. Aziz, Oxford, 1973– .

Edel, Leon and Laurence, Dan H., *A Bibliography of Henry James*, 3rd rev. edn, Oxford, 1981.

Edel, Leon, *The Life of Henry James*, 2 vols, Harmondsworth, 1977.

Matthiessen, F. O., *The James Family*, New York, 1947.

Anderson, Charles R., *Person, Place and Thing in Henry Jame's Novels*, Durham, N.C., 1977.

Beach, Joseph Warren, *The Method of Henry James*, New Haven, 1918; enlarged edn, Philadelphia, 1954.

Bradbury, Nicola, *Henry James: The Later Novels*, Oxford, 1979.

Cargill, Oscar, *The Novels of Henry James*, New York, 1961.

Dupee, F. W., *Henry James*, New York, 1951; London, 1951.

——ed., *The Question of Henry James*, New York, 1945.

Edel, Leon, ed., *Henry James: A Collection of Critical Essays* (Twentieth Century Views), Englewood Cliffs, 1963.

Gard, Roger, ed., *Henry James: The Critical Heritage*, London, 1968.

Graham, Kenneth, *Henry James: The Drama of Fulfilment*, Oxford, 1975.

Holland, Laurence B., *The Expense of Vision*, Princeton, 1964.

Kappeler, Susanne, *Writing and Reading in Henry James*, London, 1980.

Krook, Dorothea, *The Ordeal of Consciousness in Henry James*, Cambridge, 1962.

Leavis, F. R., *The Great Tradition*, London, 1948.

Margolis, Anne T., *Henry James and the Problem of Audience*, Ann Arbor, 1985.

Matthiessen, F. O., *Henry James: The Major Phase*, London and New York, 1946.

Poirier, Richard, *The Comic Sense of Henry James*, London, 1960;
    New York, 1960.
Putt, S. Gorley, *A Reader's Guide to Henry James*, London, 1966;
    Ithaca, 1966.
Tanner, Tony, ed., *Henry James: Modern Judgements*, London, 1968.
Wegelin, Christof, *The Image of Europe in Henry James*, Dallas, 1958.

### 12. Mark Twain's Gods and Tormentors: the Treasure, the River, the Nigger and the Twin Brother.

In addition to the thirty-seven volumes of the 'Definitive Edition' of *The Writings of Mark Twain*, New York, 1932, the following books contain important literary material. Some will be published in the comprehensive edition under way at Berkeley, under the imprint of the University of California Press. They will include shorter uncollected pieces.

*Mark Twain's Notebook*, ed. A. B. Paine, New York, 1935.

*Mark Twain in Eruption*, ed. Bernard DeVoto, New York, 1940.

*Mark Twain of the Enterprise*, ed. H. N. Smith and F. Anderson, Berkeley, 1957.

*The Autobiography of Mark Twain*, ed. Charles Neider, New York, 1959.

*Mark Twain-Howells Letters*, ed. H. N. Smith and W. M. Gibson, Cambridge, Mass., 1960.

*Letters from the Earth*, ed. Bernard DeVoto, with a Preface by H.N. Smith, New York, 1962.

*Mark Twain's Satires and Burlesques*, ed. F. R. Rogers, Berkeley, 1967.

*Which Was the Dream?*, ed. J. S. Tuckey, Berkeley, 1967.

*Mark Twain's Hannibal, Huck and Tom*, ed. W. Blair, Berkeley, 1969.

### Major critical works

Andrews, Kenneth R., *Nook Farm, Mark Twain's Hartford Circle*, Cambridge, 1950.

Bellamy, Carmen G., *Mark Twain as a Literary Artist*, Norman, 1950.

Brooks, Van Wyck, *The Ordeal of Mark Twain*, New York, 1920.

Budd, Louis J., *Mark Twain: Social Philosophy*, Bloomington, Indiana, 1962.

Covici, Pascal, *Mark Twain's Humor*, Dallas, 1962.

Cox, James M., *Mark Twain, the Fate of the Humorist*, Princeton, 1966.

DeVoto, Bernard, *Mark Twain's America*, Boston, 1933.

Emerson, Everett, *The Authentic Mark Twain: A Literary Biography of Samuel L. Clemens*, Philadelphia, 1984.

Ferguson, John DeLancey, *Mark Twain, Man and Legend*, New York, 1943.

Hill, Hamlin, *Mark Twain: God's Fool*, New York, 1973.

Kaplan, Justin, *Mark Twain and Mr Clemens*, New York, 1966.

Ketterer, David, ed., *The Science Fiction of Mark Twain*, Hamden, Conn., 1984.

Lynn, Kenneth S., *Mark Twain and Southwestern Humor*, Boston, 1959.

Poli, Bernard J., *Mark Twain Ecrivain de l'Ouest*, Paris, 1965.

Rogers, Franklin R., *Mark Twain's Burlesque Patterns*, Dallas, 1960.

Sattelmeyer, Robert and Crowley, J. Donald, eds, *One Hundred Years of 'Huckleberry Finn'*, Columbia, Missouri, 1985.

Smith, Henry N., *Mark Twain: The Development of a Writer*, Cambridge, Mass., 1962.

Stone, Albert E., *The Innocent Eye*, New Haven, 1961.

Weeter, Dixon, *Sam Clemens of Hannibal*, Boston, 1952.

Welland, Dennis, *Mark Twain in England*, Atlantic Highlands, N.J., 1978.

## 13. 'Years of the Modern':
### The Rise of Realism and Naturalism

## General Studies

### General studies of Realism

Auerbach, Erich, *Mimesis: The Representation of Reality in Western Literature*, trans. Willard R. Trask, Princeton, N.J., 1953.

Barthes, Roland, *Writing Degree Zero*, London, 1967.

Becker, George J., *Documents of Modern Literary Realism*, Princeton, N.J., 1963 (anthology with good introduction).

Block, Haskell M., *Naturalistic Triptych: The Fictive and the Real in Zola, Mann and Dreiser*, New York, 1970.

Grant, Damian, *Realism*, London, 1970.

Levin, Harry, *The Gates of Horn: A Study of Five French Realists*, New York and London, 1963.

Stern, J. P., *On Realism*, London, 1972.

### Studies of American Realism and Naturalism

Ahnebrik, Lars, *The Beginnings of Naturalism in American Fiction, 1891–1903*, Uppsala, Sweden, 1950; New York, 1961.

Berthoff, Warner, *The Ferment of Realism: 1884–1919*, New York, 1965.

Bradbury, Malcolm, *The Modern American Novel*, London and New York, 1983 (opening chapters).

Brooks, Van Wyck, *The Confident Years: 1885–1915*, New York and London, 1952.

Cady, Edwin H., *The Light of Common Day: Realism in American Fiction*, Bloomington, 1971.

Cowley, Malcolm, 'Naturalism in American Literature', in *Evolutionary Thought in America*, ed. Stow Persons, New Haven, Conn., 1950.

Fiedler, Leslie, *Love and Death in the American Novel*, New York and London, 1960.

Pizer, Donald, *Realism and Naturalism in Nineteenth Century American Literature*, Carbondale, Ill., 1966.

Rahv, Philip, 'Notes on the Decline of Naturalism', in Becker, cited above.

Schneider, Robert W., *Five Novelists of the Progressive Era*, New York and London, 1965.

Taylor, Gordon, *The Passages of Thought*, New York and London, 1969.

Walcutt, Charles C., *American Literary Naturalism: A Divided Stream*, Minneapolis, 1956.

## More general studies of the period

Harris, Neil, ed., *The Land of Contrasts, 1880–1901*, New York, 1970.

Jones, Howard Mumford, *The Age of Energy: Varieties of American Experience, 1865–1915*, New York, 1971.

Kazin, Alfred, *On Native Grounds: An Intrepretation of Modern American Prose Literature*, New York, 1942; rev. edn New York, 1966.

Martin, Jay, *Harvests of Change: American Literature, 1865–1914*, Englewood Cliffs, N.J., 1967.

Trachtenberg, Alan, *The Incorporations of America: Culture and Society in the Gilded Age*, New York, 1982.

Ziff, Larzer, *The American 1890: The Life and Times of a Lost Generation*, London, 1967.

## Individual Authors

### Stephen Crane

#### Texts

A new collected edition is under way, supervised by Fredson Bowers (Charlottesville, Va.).

Follett, Wilson, ed., *The Work of Stephen Crane*, 12 vols, New York, 1925–7.

Stallman, R. W., ed., *Stephen Crane: An Omnibus*, New York, 1966. Various reprints including:

*The Red Badge of Courage*, Modern Library, N.Y., 1951.

Oxford World's Classics, London, 1960 (plus stories); Norton Critical Editions, New York, 1962 (annotated text, backgrounds and sources, selected criticism).

*Stephen Crane: Stories and Tales*, Vintage Books, New York, 1955.

*Maggie and Other Stories*, Modern Library, 1933.

#### Critical-biographical

Bassan, Maurice, ed., *Stephen Crane: A Collection of Critical Essays*, New Jersey, 1967.

Berryman, John, *Stephen Crane*, New York, 1950.
Cady, Edwin H., *Stephen Crane*, New York, 1962.
Solomon, Eric, *Stephen Crane in England*, Columbus, Ohio, 1966.
——*Stephen Crane: From Parody to Realism*, Cambridge, Mass., 1967.

## Hamlin Garland

### Texts

No collected edition. Various reprints, including:
*Main-Travelled Roads*, Signet Books, N.Y., 1962, Rinehart Editions, N.Y., 1954.
*Rose of Dutcher's Coolly*, facsimile edn, AMS Press, New York, 1969.
*Crumbling Idols*, ed. Jane Johnson, Cambridge, Mass., 1960.

### Critical-biographical

Holloway, Jean, *Hamlin Garland: A Biography*, Texas, 1960.
Pizer, Donald, *Hamlin Garland's Early Work and Career*, Berkeley, 1960.
Schorer, Mark, 'Hamlin Garland' in *The World We Imagine: Selected Essays*, New York and London, 1969.

## William Dean Howells

### Texts

Collected edition now appearing from Indiana University Press, 1968 onwards. Henry Steele Commager, ed., *Selected Writings of William Dean Howells*, New York, 1950. Various reprints of major works, including:
*A Modern Instance*, Riverside Editions, Cambridge, Mass., 1957.
*The Rise of Silas Lapham*, Riverside Editions, Cambridge, Mass., 1957; Oxford World's Classic edn, London, 1948.
*A Hazard of New Fortunes*, Oxford University Press, London, 1965; Bantam Books, New York, 1960.
*Criticism and Fiction*, eds, C. M. Kirk and R. Kirk, New York, 1959.

### Critical-biographical

Bennett, G.N., *William Dean Howells: The Development of a Novelist*, Norman, Olka., 1959.

Cady, Edwin H., *The Road to Realism: The Early Years, 1837–1885, of William Dean Howells*, Syracuse, N.Y., 1956.
——*The Realist at War: The Mature Years, 1885–1920 of William Dean Howells*, Syracuse, 1958.
Carter, Everett, *Howells and the Age of Realism*, Philadelphia, 1954.
Able, Kenneth E., ed., *Howells: A Century of Criticism*, Dallas, Texas, 1962.
Lynn, Kenneth, *William Dean Howells: An American Life*, New York, 1971.
Millgate, Michael, *American Social Fiction: James to Cozzens*, Edinburgh, 1964.
McMurray, William, *The Literary Realism of W. D. Howells*, Carbondale, Ill./London, 1967.
Vanderbilt, Kermit, *The Achievement of William Dean Howells: A Reinterpretation*, Princeton, 1968.

## Frank Norris

### Texts

*The Complete Works of Frank Norris*, 10 vols, Garden City, N.Y., 1928.
*The Literary Criticism of Frank Norris*, ed. Donald Pizer, Austin, Texas, 1964.
Various reprints, including Evergreen and Bantam edns.

### Critical-biographical

French, Warren, *Frank Norris*, New York, 1962.
Marchand, Ernest, *Frank Norris: A Study*, Stanford, 1962.
Pizer, Donald, *The Novels of Frank Norris*, Bloomington, Ind., and London, 1966.
Walker, Franklin, *Frank Norris: A Biography*, New York, 1932.

### Other Authors

O'Donnell, Thomas F., and Cranchere, H.C., *Harold Frederic*, New York, 1961.
Griffin, Constance M., *Henry Blake Fuller : A Critical Biography*, Philadelphia, 1939.
O'Connor, Richard, *Ambrose Bierce: A Biography*, New York, 1967; London, 1968.

## TABLE OF DATES

1584  Founding of the 'lost colony' of Roanoke (North Carolina).

1607  Founding of Jamestown by the Virginia Company of London.

1619  Appearance of the first Negro slaves in North America, brought to Jamestown by a Dutch ship.

1620  Landing of the Pilgrim Fathers (*Mayflower*).

1636  Establishment of the Massachusetts Bay Colony; founding of Harvard College.

1664  Capture of New Amsterdam (New York) from the Dutch.

1681  Grant of Pennsylvania to William Penn.

1693  Founding of William and Mary College, Virginia.

1701  Founding of Yale College, Connecticut.

1702  Publication of *Magnalia Christi Americana* (Cotton Mather).

1741  Beginning of the religious revival known as the Great Awakening.

1754–60  French and Indian War (final defeat of the French in North America, leading to the cession of French Canada by the Treaty of Paris, 1763).

1775  Battle of Bunker's Hill.

1776  Declaration of Independence.

1775–83  Revolutionary War (commander-in-chief George Washington; independence of 'these United States' recognized by the Treaty of Paris, 1783).

1787  Philadelphia constitutional convention (new Constitution ratified 1788).

1789–97  Presidency of George Washington.

1801–9    Presidency of Thomas Jefferson.

1808    Further importation of slaves into the United States prohibited.

1812–4    War of 1812 against Britain.

1819–20    Publication of *The Sketch Book of Geoffrey Crayon, Gent.* (Washington Irving).

1820–1    Missouri compromises over slavery (attempt to fix a line separating free from slave states).

1823    Publication of *The Pioneers* (James Fenimore Cooper); (*Last of the Mohicans*, 1826).

1823    Monroe Doctrine (warning against further European colonization on the American continent).

1829–37    Presidency of Andrew Jackson.

1830    US population c. 13 million.

1839    *Hyperion* (Longfellow).

1843    *History of the Conquest of Mexico* (W. H. Prescott).

1845    Annexation of Texas.

1846–8    War with Mexico (acquisition of western territories including the present states of California, Arizona and New Mexico).

1848    *Tales of the Grotesque and Arabesque* (Edgar Allan Poe); discovery of gold in California.

1850    *Representative Men* (Emerson); *The Scarlet Letter* (Hawthorne).

1851    *Moby-Dick* (Melville); *Conspiracy of Pontiac* (Parkman).

1852    *Uncle Tom's Cabin* (H. B. Stowe); *The Blithedale Romance* (Hawthorne).

1854    *Walden* (Thoreau).

1855    *Leaves of Grass* (Whitman); *Hiawatha* (Longfellow).

1858    *The Autocrat of the Breakfast-Table* (O. W. Holmes).

1860    US population c. 32 million.

1861–5    Presidency of Abraham Lincoln (assassinated 1865); Civil War and eventual defeat of the Southern Confederacy by the forces of the Union.

1869    Completion of the first transcontinental railroad.

1869–77    Presidency of U. S. Grant.

1871    *Democratic Vistas* (Whitman).

1873    *The Gilded Age* (Mark Twain and C. D. Warner).

1875    *Science and Health* (Mary Baker Eddy).

1876    Founding of Johns Hopkins University (Baltimore); invention of the telephone (Bell).

1877     Invention of the phonograph (gramophone; Thomas A.
         Edison).
1879     *Daisy Miller* (Henry James); *Progress and Poverty* (Henry
         George)..
1880     *Democracy* (Henry Adams); US population c. 50 million.
1881     Assassination of President James A. Garfield; founding
         of the American Federation of Labor.
1883     Brooklyn Bridge completed (J. A. and W. A. Roebling).
1885     *The Adventures of Huckleberry Finn* (Twain); *The Portrait of
         a Lady* (James).
1885     *The Rise of Silas Lapham* (W. D. Howells).
1886     *The Bostonians* (James); *Little Lord Fauntleroy* (F. H.
         Burnett); *Triumphant Democracy* (Andrew Carnegie);
         Haymarket Massacre (Chicago); death of Emily
         Dickinson.
1888     *Looking Backward* (Edward Bellamy).
1889     Establishment of Hull (settlement) House, Chicago (Jane
         Addams).
1890     Sherman anti-trust act.
1891     Formation of the People's (Populist) Party.
1893     Chicago Columbian Exposition.
1894     *Wealth Against Commonwealth* (H. D. Lloyd).
1895     *The Red Badge of Courage* (Stephen Crane).
1896     Klondike gold rush; presidential election campaign –
         McKinley v. Bryan; Supreme Court (*Plessy v. Ferguson*)
         sanctions legal segregation of black Americans.
1898     War with Spain (invasion of Cuba; occupation of the
         Philippines).
1899     *McTeague* (Frank Norris); *Theory of the Leisure Class*
         (Thorstein Veblen).
1900     *Sister Carrie* (Theodore Dreiser); US population 76
         million.

# INDEX